A SHORT HISTORY OF
SWITZERLAND

A SHORT HISTORY OF
SWITZERLAND

BY

E. BONJOUR
Professor of Swiss History in the
University of Basel

H. S. OFFLER
Reader in Medieval History in the Durham Colleges
of the University of Durham

AND

G. R. POTTER
Professor of Modern History in the
University of Sheffield

OXFORD
AT THE CLARENDON PRESS

Oxford University Press, Ely House, London W. 1

GLASGOW   NEW YORK   TORONTO   MELBOURNE   WELLINGTON
CAPE TOWN   IBADAN   NAIROBI   DAR ES SALAAM   LUSAKA   ADDIS ABABA
DELHI   BOMBAY   CALCUTTA   MADRAS   KARACHI   LAHORE   DACCA
KUALA LUMPUR   SINGAPORE   HONG KONG   TOKYO

ISBN 0 19 821408 1

First published July 1952
Reprinted August 1952
Reprinted from corrected sheets of the second impression
1955, 1963, 1970, 1974

Printed in Great Britain
at the University Press, Oxford
by Vivian Ridler
Printer to the University

PREFACE

THE original suggestion which led to the writing of this book came from the Swiss organization *Pro Helvetia* soon after the end of the Second World War. Circumstances have prevented its completion as quickly as was originally hoped and the authors express their gratitude to *Pro Helvetia* and to its secretary, Dr. Naef, for much help and forbearance. Chapters I to V have been written by Mr. Offler, Chapters VI to VIII by Professor Potter, and Chapters IX to XII by Professor Dr. Bonjour. Mrs. Hottinger of Zürich translated Professor Bonjour's section at a time when she was busily engaged with other work. Our thanks are also due to Mr. G. R. Crone, Librarian of the Royal Geographical Society, who helped in securing material for the compilation of the maps, and to the Librarians of the University Library of Basle and of the Zentralbibliothek at Zürich.

E. B.

H. S. O.

G. R. P.

CONTENTS

LIST OF MAPS

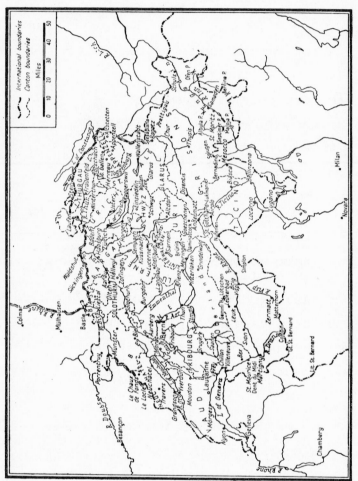

SWITZERLAND: POLITICAL

I

THE COUNTRY AND ITS PEOPLE

To the question 'What is Switzerland today?' an atlas and a book of reference can provide the beginnings of an answer. The map shows a small country lying between the territories of France, Germany, Italy, and Austria, in an area bounded—speaking very roughly indeed—by the Rhine, the Alps, and the Jura. This republic is a confederation of twenty-two cantons, three of which are subdivided into half-cantons; all retain a large measure of autonomy within the limits of the federal constitution. A population of some four and a quarter millions gives an average density of 268 inhabitants to the square mile,[1] and these mouths Switzerland can feed only by selling and buying abroad. Despite the stimulus given to home production of foodstuffs between 1939 and 1945 by the Wahlen plan, grain, meat, and even some dairy products have still to be imported; the considerable manufactures, the result of an industrialization which gained enormous impetus in the nineteenth century, are largely dependent on foreign raw materials. For though the pavements of Europe have been surfaced with the asphalt of the Val de Travers, the mineral resources and extractive industries of Switzerland are small: except for the anthracite of the Valais there are few coal deposits which can be worked economically, and this fact has hindered the exploitation of the native iron and manganese ores. Pastoralism and livestock farming and the treatment of their products, a varied textile industry, engineering construction ranging in scale from the watch manufactories of the Jura to the locomotive shops of Winterthur, a rapidly expanding chemical industry—all abundantly supplied with hydro-electric power: these, together with much skilled activity in international insurance and banking, and an incomparable technique for converting scenery into money, are the fundamentals of Swiss economy as the statistics give them.

Map and statistics combine to emphasize that Switzerland's prosperity is derived less from natural riches than from the ingenuity of her people and her position as a state dominating

[1] Population figures are those of the census of 1941.

communications through the western and central Alps. Since men have had a history they have sought Italy and the Mediterranean from north-west Europe: for purposes of secular administration under the Roman empire; for purposes of religion in the centuries when the pope ruled a united western church from Rome; for purposes of trade, when the basis of Europe's commerce remained the colportage of luxuries coming from the Levant; at all times for reasons of curiosity and recreation. He who wishes to reach Italy from the north by land must find some way of surmounting the barrier of the Alps. And if it is in Switzerland that this barrier reaches its most formidable heights, it is Switzerland which offers the greatest number of convenient passes: the Great St. Bernard, the Simplon, the St. Gotthard, the Lukmanier, the San Bernardino, the Splügen, the Septimer, the Maloja–Julier system.

It is the historian's business to give depth and solidity to such considerations of what Switzerland is by showing how she has become what she is. He has to face a serious initial difficulty. As a political unity Switzerland is a gradual growth, coming late to maturity. Nowhere is this better reflected than in the story of her name. In English we still use a form of the *Schwizerland* by which the Swiss themselves described their country till about the middle of the eighteenth century, when they discarded it for the shorter *Schweiz*. But Schwyz—the difference in spelling is a mere contrivance of convenience—is the name of one of the smaller cantons; of all twenty-two only seven are inferior to it in size and density of population. It is as if England were called Norfolk, or the U.S.A. Connecticut. To understand how the name of this small canton came to be given to the country as a whole it is necessary to look back to the thirteenth century, when four of the valley communities round lake Lucerne, roughly represented by the modern cantons of Schwyz, Uri, and Unterwalden, united in a perpetual alliance. Through the centuries this nucleus attracted to itself additional members until in the nineteenth century the number became complete and Switzerland reached its present limits. Already by the middle of the fourteenth century the publicists of the Habsburg dukes of Austria, the chief opponents of the nascent confederation, were applying to it the name of its most active and pugnacious member, Schwyz. In part their intention was abusive; they did not neglect the opportunity of playing on

2

the German sense of Schwyz as 'sweat' to suggest that the confederates, besides being legally and morally in the wrong, were also people of unpleasant habits. Consequently, the name long remained unpopular with the Swiss. They called themselves, and were called by those eager to obtain their favours, 'the Confederates', 'the Confederation', 'the League of High Germany'. Not until the eighteenth century did *Schweiz*, the original term of abuse, become a respectable title freely accepted by the Swiss; when towards the end of the century the Swiss historian Johannes von Müller gave currency to the style which was to become definitive, 'the Swiss Confederation', this pleonasm was at the end of a long historical evolution.

This gradual emergence of the name and fact of Switzerland presents awkward problems for the historian. When may he first properly speak of Switzerland? Perhaps from the date of the first alliances of Schwyz, Uri, and Unterwalden in the thirteenth century? But the early confederacy, even when strengthened by new adhesions and confirmed by military successes, hardly seemed assured of permanence before the end of the fourteenth century; its independence in international law was not recognized until the peace of Westphalia in 1648, and at the Congress of Vienna in 1815 Barthold Georg Niebuhr could still maintain that this recognition was a piece of bungling which should not have been permitted. The Switzerland of the modern map did not exist until the nineteenth century. But from the opening of the historic record, for centuries before Switzerland was a name or a fact, in the area which she was later to occupy events were occurring which made her emergence possible and shaped her development. In what framework are these happenings to be presented? Are we to speak of Celtic Switzerland, Roman Switzerland, Frankish Switzerland, though we know well enough that there was no Switzerland in Celtic, Roman, or Frankish times? To do so is to sacrifice accuracy for the sake of brevity of phrase. Yet the alternative is to relate the individual histories of the various regions today comprehended in Switzerland, up to the date at which each of them became part of the confederation. And that method, essential as it is for detailed inquiries, clearly is not well suited to the purpose of summary exposition.

Geographical coherence might perhaps be expected to provide compensation for the absence of early political unity in the Swiss

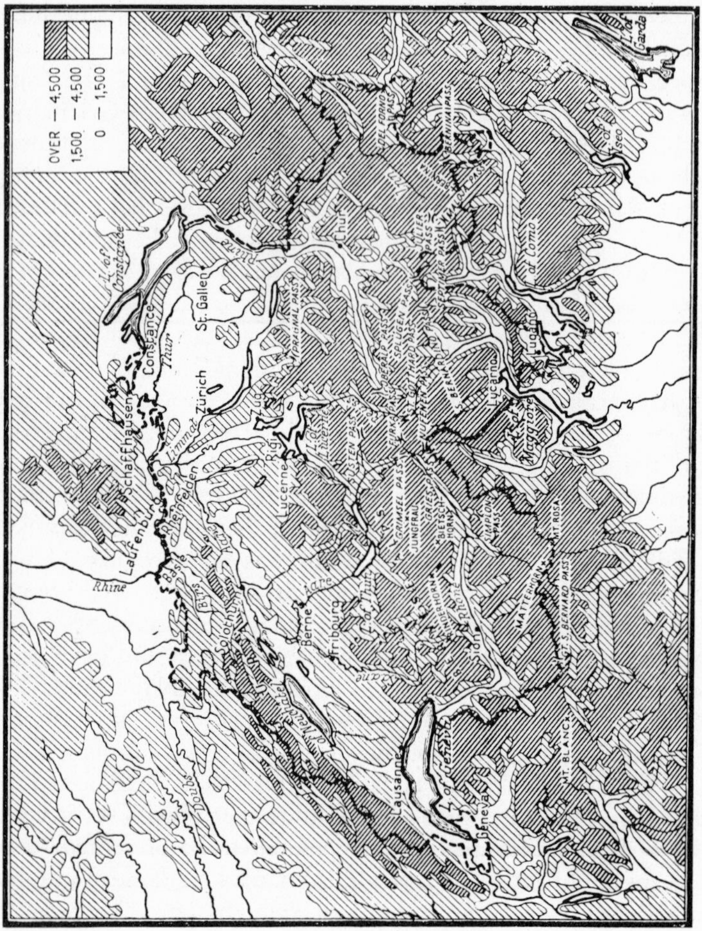
OVER — 4,500
1,500 — 4,500
0 — 1,500
Rhine
Basle
Laufenburg
Rheinfelden
Schaffhausen
Constance
L. of Constance
Thur
Limmat
Zürich
St. Gallen
Zug
Rigi
Lucerne
Aare
Birs
Solothurn
Berne
Fribourg
L. of Thun
Lausanne
L. of Geneva
Geneva
Doubs
Rhone
Sion
Chur
Lugano
Locarno
L. of Maggiore
L. of Como
L. of Iseo
L. of Garda
GRIMSEL PASS
JUNGFRAU
SIMPLON PASS
MT. ROSA
MATTERHORN
GT. S. BERNARD PASS
MT. BLANC
JULIER PASS
BERNINA PASS

SWITZERLAND: OROGRAPHICAL

area. But a closer examination of the map destroys the illusion that Switzerland is a geographical unity, handily contained within the 'natural' frontiers of the Rhine, the Jura, and the Alps, which it was always her 'destiny' to attain. On all sides these limits are exceeded: at Schaffhausen and at Basle the frontier projects beyond the Rhine; Basle is situated to the west of the Jura range, so that its geographic affinities are with Alsace rather than with Switzerland; a whole canton, Ticino, lies south of the Alps, while another, Grisons, stretches over the Alpine watershed southwards into the Val Mesocco and the Val Poschiavo; to the east there is no compelling 'natural' reason why the cantonal and national frontier with Austria should run where it does, for the tectonic break between the eastern and western Alps lies far back to the west, marked by the course of the northward-flowing Rhine. There is complementary evidence of another kind: the economic hinterlands of three of the most considerable industrial centres of Switzerland, Basle, Geneva, and St. Gallen, are largely outside the Swiss frontier. That frontier is not simply the result of some overriding geographic determinism; the chances of history have had an important part in its making. Switzerland is an historical and not merely a natural creation.

Nevertheless, to the continuous historical changes in the Swiss area natural conditions have provided a comparatively stable background. Nature, indeed, has not been wholly unchanging: the Gries pass from the Val Formazza into the Rhone valley is now glaciered, and there are indications that in Roman times it was not; the archaeologists investigating the prehistoric lake-dwellings of Switzerland bear witness to important changes in the water-level of the lakes; deforestation in the high valleys of the Alps seems to have been continuous from the middle ages onwards until it was checked by governmental action in the present century. Yet these are only matters of detail: broadly speaking the challenges issued by environment to the inhabitants of the Swiss area have been constant, and recurrently they have provoked the same response. Swiss mercenaries are not an invention of the fifteenth century, nor Swiss innkeepers of the nineteenth. Overpopulation was driving the Celtic inhabitants of the Alpine valleys to service in arms for pay in the third century before Christ; in the thirteenth and fourteenth centuries the leading political families in the Alpine cantons were drawing much of their prosperity from the organization of transport and accommodation for travellers over the passes.

The characteristic of the natural conditions of Switzerland is diversity. To mention Switzerland is, of course, to evoke the Alps, which, together with their pre-alpine dependencies, cover more than three-fifths of the area of the country. The *massif* of the Aare and the St. Gotthard is at once the orographical and the hydrographical centre of the Alps. Here all the great Swiss rivers have their source: the Rhone, thrusting south-westwards and splitting the heart of the Alps with its valley; the Rhine, whose upper course prolongs the line of the Rhone towards the north-east till near Chur it takes its northward bend to lake Constance; the Aare, flowing through the Bernese Oberland and Mittelland before turning north-eastwards to join the Rhine, and the Aare's tributary, the Reuss, flowing slightly west of north from the St. Gotthard—neither of them comparable in size with the great river with which at last they mingle, yet perhaps equally important in Swiss history; the Maggia and the Ticino, which reach lake Maggiore down the southern slopes of the Alps. It is the deeply cut valleys of these Alpine rivers, opening access to the passes, which have made Switzerland pre-eminently a transit land: that much is undeniable even if we refuse to go all the way with the geopoliticians and say that it is these accidents of structure which have created Switzerland. In the main it is in the Alps that have arisen two of Switzerland's most important industries, the entertainment of tourists and the manufacture of hydro-electric power. And it is these mountains which have served as stimulus to a rich, though unequal, effort of artistic and imaginative creation.

But despite their wide extent the Alps maintain only a fifth of the Swiss population, and the proportion decreases. The heart of modern Switzerland lies outside them, in the band of hill country —'plateau' perhaps hardly expresses its variety adequately—some 150 miles long and 30 miles wide, which stretches from lake Geneva north-eastwards to lake Constance. Here glacial action has almost everywhere left its mark on a terrain broken into hills and valleys, tilting down to the trough along which the Aare makes its way beneath the Jura to the Rhine. Despite asperities of climate this is the region of most intensive cultivation and settlement in Switzerland, comparable to Belgium in the closeness of its network of road and rail; here dwell six-tenths of the Swiss people, on an average of over 400 to the square mile. It is the classic area of Swiss urban development: Zürich, the one modest giant, with well over 300,000 inhabitants; Berne, the federal capital, less than half as large; and, far more typically, a host of smaller towns like Zofingen, Aarau, Olten, Langnau, or Burgdorf, which with populations barely exceeding 10,000 yet contrive to be the active centres of many kinds of industry. 'A garden sown with factories' is a French geographer's phrase. Aargau (the lower valley of the Aare) and Thurgau (the catchment area of the river Thur between lakes Zürich and Constance) have always been the corn-growing districts of Switzerland. Moreover, by its livestock farming the hill country has secured a predominance which we commonly and wrongly attribute to the pastoralism of the Alps; from this area Switzerland has drawn not only her bread but also most of her butter. Some three-fifths of the milk cattle of Switzerland are stall fed on the 'plateau'; from here, rather than from the Alpine pastures, the export market in dairy products is supplied. And it is conditions here which have determined the fact that Switzerland shows a higher density of agricultural labour on the land than any other country in western Europe—about 15 per 100 acres compared with 11 in France and 2 in England—so that in some districts the consequences of extreme subdivision of peasant holdings are acutely felt.

Hill country and Alps are both screened climatically from the north-west by the Jura mountains, a range neither as high nor as imposing as the Alps but appearing to the writers of the early middle ages a no less formidable obstacle by reason of its dense forests. In contrast to the high Alpine valleys, where men have built their dwellings of wood and trees are scarce, the houses here are of stone and trees remain in abundance; forests cover a third of the area of the Bernese Jura. But in the valley bottoms there is much meadow and arable land, and industry is to be found scattered throughout the range. In the high Jura of Neuchâtel there is a tradition of fine work; since the eighteenth century the native lacemakers have turned to the clock-making which now centres round La Chaux-de-Fonds, a town of 30,000 inhabitants strangely situated at a height of 3,200 feet. The Bernese Jura has paper-making and silkweaving as well as clock-making; at the northern end of the range economic life is dominated by Basle. For Basle's silk-ribbon industry, like the embroidery manufacture of St. Gallen, is not wholly concentrated in the town; the work-shops of the country-side supplement the urban factories. And many of these rural workshops, and the homes of many of the factory employees of Basle, in times of peace lay over the frontier in Germany. The same tendency for economic rationalism to over-ride political boundaries can be remarked on a smaller scale in the Ajoie of Porrentruy, a country district lying isolated on the north-west slopes of the Jura. The Ajoie has long sold its cattle and fruit in Alsace rather than in Switzerland.

The geographers proceed to break down these three broad natural divisions of Switzerland, the Alps, the 'plateau', and the Jura, into a dozen or more distinct sub-regions showing well-marked differences in natural conditions. One example, climate, may serve to illustrate these diversities. Spring comes to Bellinzona long before it reaches the valleys to the north of the Alps. Ticino is a land of heat and great moisture where maize and figs and almonds flourish and all the typical fruits of southern Europe except the olive. In the drier Valais tracts of vegetation are to be found—in the neighbourhood of Sion, for instance—which closely resemble the *garrigue* of the western Mediterranean. In contrast the climate of the 'plateau' is often harsh: Fribourg averages 124 days of rain in the year and 40 of mist. Height alone is no sure guide to severity of climate, for the rainfall in the pre-alpine districts is commonly heavier than in the high Alps. The most mountainous canton of Switzerland, Grisons, has become an habitual sanatorium for the consumptive because of its dry clear air; here rye and potatoes grow at 4,500 feet, and cattle can be grazed up to 4,000 feet higher. Among the mountains all depends on the situation and configuration of the individual valley. If it runs east and west, its northern and southern slopes will be two very different worlds, for the one will trap and the other be neg-lected by the sun. An intrusive influence, uncomfortable and dan-gerous but also beneficial, is exercised by the *Föhn*, the hot dry wind from the south, two days of which, according to the Swiss proverb, are worth a fortnight's sun, and to which in part are due the chestnuts, the orchards, and the vines of the valley of the Reuss and along the shores of lakes Lucerne and Zürich.

If we seek a single formula to express the richness of diversity in Swiss geography, it must run somewhat in these terms: the dominant facts are height and broken relief, and it is they which

8

have permanently influenced human occupation and organization. They have made for a general poverty in agriculture. This
is a point on which the vineyards of the Valais and of the shores
of the Swiss lakes, the cornfields of Aargau and Thurgau, must
not be allowed to deceive us, for they form but a small part of the
whole picture. Until the triumph of industrialization Switzerland
was essentially a pastoral country, and over much of it the cow was
too exclusively the basis of existence for that existence ever to be
abundant outside a few centres of industry and exchange, except
when it was enriched by the booty of foreign wars. Moreover, the
dominant geographical facts tended to keep Switzerland parochial
as well as poor. Difficulties of communication localized activity.
What mattered was the valleys in which men lived rather than the
mountains which they did not climb except to feed their cattle.
When circumstances forced it to look beyond its own boundaries
the valley community became an important element in the political growth of Switzerland. But the impulse was spasmodic, and
when it was not being felt the valley lived for itself. Because of the
awkward natural obstacles common in the lower reaches of Alpine
valleys, circulation tended to cross from one valley to the next over
some convenient pass rather than to descend towards the low-
lands. The St. Gotthard *massif* admirably illustrates the possibilities of this kind of intercommunication. From the upper valley
of the Aare (Haslital) the Grimsel pass gives access to the Val de
Conches, whence it is possible to reach the valley of Urseren by the
Furka; Urseren leads to the upper valley of the Reuss, which is
joined by the Oberalp pass to the valley of the Vorderrhein and by
the St. Gotthard to the Val di Bedretto, from which the Nufenen
pass gives access again to the Val de Conches. The circle is considerable, but it remains closed. Men could use it without finding
occasion to emerge from the high valleys; in their travels they
merely exchanged the localism of their own valley for that of the
next, which would be little different in kind because it was the
product of much the same conditions. Conservatism was the air
in which much of Swiss history evolved; limitations of experience
helped to engender it.

To allow due weight to localism is not to deny the capital influence exerted on the making of Switzerland by the long-distance
routes across the Alps. There is no paradox here: international

4990

9

B

roads are not necessarily destructive to the particularisms through which they pass, still less to those which they merely skirt; it cannot reasonably be alleged that the railway which created Crewe has endowed its inhabitants with a breadth of outlook superior to that of other communities. What are the transalpine routes? This inquiry leads far afield, for the use of the Alpine passes has always been governed by the means of access to them.

Approach to the Alps from north-west Europe is masked by the Jura mountains. The traveller of the pre-railway age might turn this preliminary barrier at its northern end through the gap formed by the course of the Rhine: mastery of this gap was the fortune of Basle. But Basle itself was still to the west of the Jura; the traveller thence was faced by a choice of routes. He could proceed up the Rhine valley by water or by land, though rapids made the first way difficult, and the confluence of the Aare and Rhine was an obstacle on the second; he could strike away from the river, climb the Bötzberg, make the easy crossing of the Aare at Brugg, and so gain Zürich or lake Constance; or, lastly, he could pass the outliers of the Jura over the upper or lower Hauenstein to Olten, to continue his journey south-westwards to Avenches and lake Geneva, or south-eastwards into central Switzerland through the Weggital and by lake Sempach to lake Lucerne. If he had come through Burgundy rather than Alsace, he would probably choose to pass the Jura from Besançon over the Col de Jougne, and so reach lake Geneva.

The Jura once surmounted, the most obvious ways into and across the Alps were offered by the valleys of the Rhone and the Rhine, which lead back to the central *massif* where both rivers have their source. For the traveller by the Rhone routes the starting place was the eastern end of lake Geneva; leaving the Rhone valley at Martigny he could climb the Great St. Bernard, and descend into Italy by the Val d'Aosta, or he could follow the river upstream to Brig before turning south to the Simplon pass, the Val d'Ossola, and Lombardy. The Rhine valley could be joined either at the eastern end of lake Constance, or from Zürich, by way of lake Zürich, the Linth valley, and the Walensee, in the neighbourhood of Maienfeld. Chur was the key point on the Rhine route to the north of the Alps, as Chiavenna was to the south; between them, there were many ways of passing the watershed. One led over the Lenzerheide and up the Oberhalbstein and then down into the Val Bregaglia either by the Julier–Maloja passes or by the Septimer; another followed the valley of the Hinterrhein, up the Domleschg, and by the *Via mala*, descending either to Chiavenna by the Splügen pass or into the Val Mesocco and so to Bellinzona at the head of lake Maggiore by the San Bernardino. Alternatively, Bellinzona could be reached from Chur along the valley of the Vorderrhein, over the Lukmanier pass, and down the Val Blenio.

Bellinzona also held the southern end of the one great pass system in Switzerland independent of the upper valleys of the Rhone and Rhine. Past Bellinzona the valley of the Ticino leads northwards to the St. Gotthard pass; thence the valley of the Reuss opens a way to lake Lucerne from which the traveller could proceed northward either by way of lake Sempach to Olten and across the Jura by the Hauenstein, or down the Reuss till it joined the Aare, and so at last to the Rhine, or by way of lake Zug and the Sihl valley to Zürich.

These details are tedious, but they are important. The transalpine routes, their courses determined by the passes, the river valleys, and the lakes, are a permanent factor in Swiss and in European history. Except the Septimer, all the passes have roads today; probably all, except the St. Gotthard and the Septimer, were already known and in use in Roman times. In the Alps nature has posed an eternal problem of communication; the answers which she has adumbrated have been no less stereotyped. But through the centuries many changes have occurred in the comparative popularity of the various routes. The most frequented pass in Roman times was undoubtedly the Great St. Bernard, whence ran the great military road along the sub-Jurassic trough to Windisch, and then across the Rhine at Zurzach to the sources of the Danube. This route continued to carry much traffic in the middle ages; the hospice on the pass for the comfort of travellers, of which we first have record in 1125, had been founded in the previous century by St. Bernard, archdeacon of Aosta. On the other hand, the Simplon counted for little before the thirteenth century, and while the Rhine passes south of Chur, especially the Lukmanier and the Septimer, were much used in the early middle ages, later they were overshadowed by the more direct route from Italy to the lower Rhine offered by the St. Gotthard.

That the St. Gotthard came late to prominence was due to a

natural obstacle in the approach to it from the north. The route here follows the valley of the Reuss, but between Andermatt and Goschenen the river breaks though a gorge, the Schöllenen, the sides of which are at one point impassable. No doubt at all times it was possible to avoid this difficulty by scaling the neighbouring heights, but the route could not become frequented until the gorge was bridged. The date at which the Reuss valley was converted from a *cul-de-sac* into an international highway by the building of the Devil's Bridge is thus a matter of considerable interest. Unfortunately it cannot be stated precisely. Though plausible arguments can be adduced for the first third of the twelfth century, the weight of evidence seems to favour the early years of the thirteenth; certainly by this later date man had so improved the route as to make it available for international traffic. So doing, he greatly influenced the growth of the Swiss confederation. The opening of the St. Gotthard brought the secluded valley communities of central Switzerland into the main stream of European affairs; it increased their prosperity and thus their self-assertion; perhaps it provided the channel by which a breath of the communal ideas then current in north Italy came over the Alps. Above all, the desire of powerful dynasties to control and exploit the new artery impelled the communities through which it ran to co-operate in defence of their independence.

Today, though great railway tunnels run beneath the St. Gotthard and the Simplon, the roads which these tunnels threatened to kill have been saved by the petrol-engine. And the traveller by road from northern Europe to Italy, however different his speed and his conveyance, is still tied to the same routes as his ancestors. At the top of the Great St. Bernard he is where Buonaparte's army marched on the way to Marengo; where John de Bremble, monk of Christ Church, Canterbury, shuddered in February 1188, yet did not neglect to consider literary effects; where Sigeric, archbishop of Canterbury, passed on his homeward journey from Rome in 990. On the St. Gotthard he can call to memory not only Suvaroff and his Russian army but also the countless pack-trains which from the thirteenth century onwards carried the riches of the Mediterranean towards the Rhine.

To the Swiss the Alpine passes have meant much more than an exercise in antiquarian sentiment. The passes have shaped Swiss policy; indeed, that there is a Switzerland to have a policy is due in some part to them. For if the territorial growth of the confederation was the result of aggregation about a nucleus, the process was not simply fortuitous; a conscious effort of expansion was sometimes dictated by the necessities of 'pass policy'. Possession of the pass alone is never enough; if it is to be useful to the holder he must seek control also of the approaches to it, and that search may take him far. This was the impulse which led the central cantons to aggression on the southern slopes of the Alps, till with Val Ticino and Bellinzona they were masters of the approach to the St. Gotthard from Italy. The same motive can be seen working in Lucerne's thrust north-westwards towards Sempach, along the line continuing the St. Gotthard route to the Rhine, and in the determination with which Grisons till 1797 maintained possession of Chiavenna and the Valtelline, which controlled from the south not only the passes into the valley of the upper Rhine but also those over the Bernina into the Engadine and through Vintschgau to Meran and Bozen in Tyrol.

One aspect of Swiss communications remains to stress, since modern developments have obscured it: the great part played by waterways until the railways stole their traffic. Karl Meyer has remarked how the young confederation of Schwyz, Uri, Unterwalden, and Lucerne in the early fourteenth century was held together by the lake round which these cantons clustered, just as on a greater plan the Mediterranean had once given unity to the Roman empire. The long water stretches on the Alpine routes were particularly important when it was a question of moving bulky goods in ages when roads were bad. From Lombardy lakes Maggiore and Como provided convenient access to Bellinzona and Chiavenna; on the St. Gotthard route north of the Alps a water passage over lake Lucerne could not be avoided, for there was no road along the banks of the lake until the *Axenstrasse* was built between Brunnen and Flüelen in the nineteenth century; from the eastern Alpine passes and Chur to the lower Rhine it was customary either to follow the river to Bregenz and then to embark on lake Constance, or, more usually, to take boat over the Walensee, then down the Linth to lake Zürich, and so by the river Limmat to the Aare and the Rhine. The extent to which traffic was expedited by the water system of Switzerland deserves attention; it is useful to remember also that the prince of mountain generals, Lecombe, mounted an amphibious operation during his campaign of 1799 in central Switzerland, and that in the same year Suvaroff found himself in desperate straits for lack of shipping to convey his troops across lake Lucerne.

The contrast between the comparative stability of natural conditions and the changing varieties of men who have lived among them is obvious. But there is a third factor to be considered. For the most part Switzerland is mountainous, and man has been able to survive in the mountains only by reason of the animals which he has been able to keep. Especially in the Alps his pattern of existence has been created by the peculiarities of mountain pastoral economy, by the need of rearing sheep and goats and cows. It is a commonplace that the native of the high Swiss valleys has spared little interest for the peaks above him unless he is a guide by profession; often he has left it to the climber or the tourist to give them their names. His affection has been directed to the grassy slopes above the forest line on which stock can be fed when the sun has melted the snows. From the eighth century at the latest he has called these pastures alps; for their possession, valleys for centuries conducted litigation and armed strife with their neighbours; in the regulation necessary to prevent undue exploitation of the open alp by individuals the valleys found their education in economic co-operation, and perhaps, though less immediately, in political consciousness.

Once allowance has been made for wide possibilities of local variation, the essential traits of Alpine pastoral economy can be simply defined. It is the middle term between nomadism, in which the whole tribe migrates with its flocks, and the long range transhumance known, for instance, on the Spanish *Meseta*, in which the beasts wander far with the seasons under the care of a few herdsmen while the owners remain settled in permanent dwellings. In the Alps human habitation is fixed in the villages, and the seasonal migration of the herds is comparatively short in range. Every summer, in mid- or late July, the cattle are sent up to the grass of the alp above the forest line; there they remain grazing in charge of their keepers at successive stages of altitude until autumn drives them down to their villages, generally by the end of September. In autumn as in spring they may find grazing below the forest line, but for much of the year they must be stabled and stall fed. The difficulty of winter keep, the vital problem of all north European stock raising, is exaggerated in the Alps by the length and severity of the season; the number of animals which can be fed in the short summer is out of all proportion to that for which fodder can be provided during the other nine months of the year, and so it is normal for the communal regulations of the Alpine pastures to limit the total number of cattle which any one man may send on the village alp in summer to that which he can feed in winter. Hay mown on the alp—part of which may be enclosed for the purpose —and brought down to the village when snow has made sledding easy, forms a great part of the stock of winter feeding stuff.

The struggle to feed the cattle in winter has always made life in the Alps laborious, though of late the sowing of new grasses has considerably increased the yield of the mountain pastures. In the past restricted communication added to the burden by imposing the attempt at self-sufficiency in crops ill-suited to the climate. At Alpine altitudes conditions are harsh for cereals, and the useful-ness of the potato as a substitute had hardly been discovered before the second half of the eighteenth century. Autumn crops must be sown in summer and may take a full year to ripen; if the snow lies late, spring planting is not possible till May, and then the harvest is not ready before the autumn snows and must be cut green and hung to ripen on racks or in barns. Mid-August in a single Alpine village may find men broadcasting seed immediately behind the plough, while not far away others are reaping. This arable complement to the Alpine grazing economy is sometimes too readily forgotten. It is poor, so that the high valleys have often had to import grain from the 'plateau' or from Alsace, and have done this the more readily as communications have improved, but the intense labour which intermittently it involves frees pastoral life in the Alps from any hint of that idleness which sometimes attaches to it elsewhere.

Goats are not fastidious about where they conduct their dread-ful depredations; sheep, though they thrive best on the drier slopes —for instance, in the Valais—can reach heights inaccessible to larger beasts. But the basis of man's life in the Alps remains the cow; on it, alive or dead, he has fed; with it he has bought from outside what he has been unable to produce for himself. A surfeit of Alpine cheeses brought the Roman emperor Antoninus Pius to his end in A.D. 161, in distant Etruria; the classical agronome Columella tells of the cows sent down from the Alps to act as foster-mothers to the calves of the working cattle of Italy. And the importance of stockbreeding in Switzerland extends far beyond the Alps to the hill area where, indeed, the majority of Switzerland's cattle are now to be found, reared in circumstances other than those of the Alpine world and fed on cultivated forage crops and imported concentrates. What is known of the history of this animal population? A Roman bronze now at Martigny shows the head of a beast which might belong to the breed which flourishes in the Val d'Hérens today. Can this be taken to establish a real continuity? Are the cattle of Switzerland indigenous; have they had on the Swiss scene a permanency greater than that of *la bête humaine*?

That is probable of at least one common breed. In central and eastern Switzerland, to the south of a line drawn from lake Constance to Martigny in the lower Valais, a small brown or grey cow predominates which, there can be little doubt, descends directly from the shorthorn—*Bos brachyceros*—whose remains are to be found in the neolithic lake-dwellings and of whose continuing presence in Switzerland there is henceforward satisfactory evidence. The Romans, it seems probable, introduced a larger animal with a short head—*Bos brachycephalus*—which maintained itself as a pure breed as far north as lake Zürich till the end of the middle ages. The Val d'Hérens breed which flourishes today in the valleys branching southwards from the Valais may well be a persistent remnant of this Roman importation; to a cross between the Roman shorthead and the native shorthorn is perhaps due an unusually large type of brown cow still to be found in Schwyz, Zug, and Lucerne. But nearly three-fifths of the total of Swiss cattle are to be found in the hill country of western Switzerland, and this is the area of the mottled cow, the red and white cattle of Simmental, and the black and white of Fribourg. Uncertainty surrounds the origin of this mottled breed, but it is not likely that it has long been established in Switzerland, for no trace of a *Bos frontosus* has been found there in ancient or medieval remains, and it is possible that the breed is a late introduction, coming in from Burgundy or Alsace in the seventeenth and eighteenth centuries. Similarly, most of Switzerland's other livestock—her horses, sheep, and pigs—owe much to importation in modern times, though some representatives of very ancient native breeds survive in the remote valleys of Grisons and the Valais.

The Swiss area has never been monopolized by a single race of men. The archaeologists have been able to distinguish at least four very different cultures even in neolithic times, and they have inferred the probability of as many different peoples. The evidence of racial heterogeneity becomes patent when the Romans added the Swiss area to their empire. The Celts of the west were balanced in the east by the Raetians, who were probably a branch of the Veneti, an independent group of the Indo-germanic family of peoples; in the Ticino valley the dominant Lepontii were Celts, but they formed only a thin layer over an earlier Ligurian population by which their culture was strongly influenced. A final ethnological confusion was introduced when Roman rule broke down in the fifth and sixth centuries and Switzerland was occupied by the Germanic Alemannians and Burgundians. The process of that penetration must be considered later in detail; its result was to leave a permanent impression on the linguistic map of Switzerland which is now a country of four languages: German–Swiss, French, Italian, and Romansh.

Romansh can be disposed of summarily, for only one Swiss in a hundred speaks it. This debased Latin (in the Engadine it is still called Ladin) is the tongue of the descendants of the Romanized provincials who fled to the high valleys in face of the invading Germans. Slowly it has lost ground to German, till today it is heard only in a single canton, Grisons, in the valleys of the Vorder- and Hinterrhein, and in the Engadine. Italian, the first tongue of 6·2 per cent. of the Swiss population, is spoken by the inhabitants of the areas south of the Alps conquered by the confederates from the fifteenth century onwards. The primary linguistic boundary, between German- and French-speaking Switzerland, is far older, for it reflects tribal differences in the Germanic settlements. The Burgundians were first settled in the south-west, round lake Geneva, as a measure of imperial policy, and afterwards they thrust north-eastwards towards the Aare and the Reuss. Isolated from their Germanic homeland and the possibility of reinforcement, they were few in number among a strongly Romanized Celtic population. Thus they came to adopt the tongue of the Celtic provincials, as the Franks did in France, and from this provincial Latin issued the French which is the first tongue of a fifth of the Swiss people. The Alemannians in the north-east, on the other hand, were more numerous, and maintained direct contact with their homeland; they took possession of an area which was far larger and had been less effectively stamped, by Roman influence than that occupied by the Burgundians. So here the Germanic tongue prevailed; the modern linguistic frontier, which leaves the cantons of Geneva, Vaud, and Neuchâtel, much of Fribourg, a smaller part of Berne, and about half the Valais as French-speaking, roughly represents the line of division between Burgundian and Alemannian settlement. Thus the greater part of Switzerland is left to German-speakers, who are in an overwhelming absolute majority, forming 70·9 per cent. of the population of the country.

Despite their numerical inferiority the French and Italian languages enjoy complete equality with German–Swiss in official business; though Romansh is a recognized national language its use is not compulsory in public affairs. This liberal handling of the problem of minority tongues is a token of tolerance and political wisdom, and it has favoured the development of those polyglot capacities which have eased Switzerland's relations with the foreigner. Knowledge of languages has helped the Swiss man of business, the courier, and the waiter abroad; it has also bred a willingness to make the foreigner at home in Switzerland. The list of eminent political refugees for whom Switzerland has provided asylum runs from Arnold of Brescia in the twelfth century to Lenin in the twentieth, and is not yet closed. She has accepted, too, a mass immigration of foreign workers. As a result of this wave, coming mainly from Germany and Italy after the first quarter of the nineteenth century to meet the needs of the new industrialization, some 400,000 foreigners were domiciled in Switzerland in 1930; in 1920 27 per cent. of the inhabitants of Basle were foreigners. These are remarkable figures, even when it is remembered that the path to Swiss citizenship is not easy even for the alien who has long been resident on Swiss soil, since to become a Swiss national it is necessary to belong to a canton, and that in turn depends on membership of a commune within the canton.

The Swiss have shown considerable self-confidence in permitting this aggravation from outside of a native diversity already, it might seem, dangerously abundant. To existing differences in language the Reformation brought the additional complication of a confessional cleavage. Today, the majority of the population in twelve cantons is Protestant; in ten, Catholic; for the whole of Switzerland the proportion of the two confessions is 57·3 per cent. to 41 per cent. Relations between church and state are left to the decision of the individual cantons, under the overriding principle of the federal constitution that every man shall have freedom to exercise his own religion, or no religion, as long as he does nothing to endanger public order. While a canton may, and often does, support the churches of its confessional majority, free churches flourish alongside the cantonal establishment. Toleration has passed, it is sometimes boasted, into laicity: to a modern lawyer the confederation is 'a lay state, the laws and institutions of which have no confessional basis'.[2] This may be an accurate enough account of constitutional theory, but it hardly regards sufficiently the continuing stresses to which the often delicate balance between Catholic and Protestant has subjected the Swiss nation. The influence of confessional differences on the history of modern Switzerland can no more be safely neglected than, say, that of nonconformity on English politics in the nineteenth century.

The religious crisis of the sixteenth century was as desperate in Switzerland as anywhere in Europe. The successful effort to surmount it did not immediately produce perfect tolerance of freedom of conscience; even today the conscientious objector to military service is liable to sentence by court martial. But there was encouraged a most profitable hospitality towards comrades in confession who were being persecuted in other lands. Italian Protestants fleeing from the Counter-Reformation to Zürich in 1555 revived there the silk manufactures which had been moribund since the fourteenth century; it was from the Huguenots that Geneva learnt the art of clock-making; as a result of the Revocation of the Edict of Nantes in 1685 a further immigration of French Protestants brought technical improvements into the silk and cotton industries, and introduced about 1700 into the Jura of Neuchâtel the lace manufacture from which the inhabitants learnt the manual dexterity which within a century they were to turn to the making of watches. Perhaps nowhere has the reception of religious refugees produced more obvious economic advantages than in Switzerland; even without the backing of the moral argument these advantages would justify the addition

[2] G. Sauser-Hall, *The Political Institutions of Switzerland*, Zürich, 1946, p. 91.

caused by this reception to the existing complexities of national structure.

Is it possible, out of these varieties of habitat, occupation, race, language, and faith to produce a typical Swiss? Is he to be tall or short? Blond and Germanic or swarthy with the sun of the south? Catholic or Protestant? German-speaking or Romance? With the eye of a mountaineer or with a clerk's spectacles? With the hands to contrive a delicate piece of clockwork, or to wring a farmer's living from a high Alpine valley? Ruskin, with an assurance of which we have lost the secret, made the attempt at characterization in *Modern Painters*:

There has been much dispute respecting the character of the Swiss, arising out of the difficulty which other nations had to understand their simplicity. They were assumed to be either romantically virtuous, or basely mercenary, when in fact they were neither heroic nor base, but were true-hearted men, stubborn with more than any recorded stubbornness; not much regarding their lives, yet not casting them causelessly away; forming no high ideal of improvement, but never relaxing their grasp of a good they had once gained. . . . You will find among them, as I said, no subtle wit nor high enthusiasm, only an undeceivable common sense, and an obstinate rectitude. They cannot be persuaded into their duties, but they feel them; they use no phrases of friendship but they do not fail you at your need.[3]

The praise in these handsome words has been somewhat tarnished by fashion's changes. The virtues of the Swiss have been found wearisome; their limitations have been more advertised. As historian of the art of war in the middle ages Sir Charles Oman was, of course, much concerned with the Swiss: if he had to admit their technical proficiency and the intensity of their patriotism he could not forbear to sneer at their lack of magnanimity. This is the aspect on which modern attempts to describe the psychology of the Swiss nation commonly fasten: the Swiss, it is said, are a petty-minded, prosaic, and mercenary people.

The adjectives, which are disputable, are less important than the noun, which is not. Perhaps a fair measure of agreement may be found for a more positive statement of the qualities of the Swiss people. It would be pretty generally admitted that for centuries the Swiss have shown a strong determination to conduct their own

[3] *Modern Painters*, part vi, chap. ix, paras. 12 and 14: quoted by Arnold Lunn, *Switzerland and the English*, London, 1944, p. 113.

affairs; to preserve their freedom to do so they have accepted, as a matter of course rather than of controversy and lament, the obligation of compulsory military service. A strong conservative streak runs through their democracy: heraldry is a national passion, and women remain excluded from political rights. Their exposed situation as a small nation lying surrounded by major political units, with all of which they have linguistic and cultural as well as economic ties, has given the Swiss a vested interest in the maintenance of international order and bred a conviction of the rightness of neutrality which is something more than a merely prudential philosophy. But such generalizations are apt to be jejune, though they do assume a fact which is important—the reality of a united Swiss nation. How this unity has emerged from the diversities which nature seems to have imposed and events to have exasperated is the problem of a history of Switzerland.

Sir Max Beerbohm would deny that this problem has attraction. In an amusing, rather bilious little essay he once declared that everything worth knowing of Switzerland's history could be stated in a few lines of a guide-book: Switzerland has had but one hero, William Tell, and he is a myth. Perhaps Tell is less easily disposed of than Sir Max thought. But it is true that Swiss history can no longer be written simply in terms of the heroic and ultimately successful resistance of democratic peasants to the forces of royal and aristocratic tyranny. It was long written thus, and so well written that the currency of this version dies hard although its foundations have been shattered. Discussion of the changing attitudes of historians to the questions concerning the origin of the confederation may properly be reserved to a later chapter. What must be confessed at the outset is the deficiency of our knowledge, especially of the early centuries of Swiss history, since the sources are here so scanty that any account must be either tentative or dishonest. If the picture sometimes approximates to truth, this is mainly due to the work of Swiss scholars who, from the sixteenth century onwards, have been indefatigable in inquiry into their national history, and, on the whole, remarkably unprejudiced in the presentation of their results. Sometimes they may have misunderstood, but only rarely have their misunderstandings been perverse. And perhaps we in England, with the example of our own seventeenth century before us, should be the last to deny the utility of an occasional misunderstanding of national history.

II

CELTS AND ROMANS

THE years 60 and 59 B.C. were critical for the Roman republic. In Rome the three dynasts, Pompey, Crassus, and Julius Caesar, captured the constitutional machinery; republican liberties were at an end, and the prospect to dictatorship lay open. To perpetuate its power the triumvirate needed the support of armies in the provinces, and it contrived that to Caesar, consul in 59 B.C., should be assigned Cisalpine and Transalpine Gaul. Once master of these Celtic provinces already subject to Rome, Caesar directed his attention to the wider Celtic world which still kept its independence. It was a Celtic people settled in the Swiss area which paid the first price of Caesar's ambition: an ambition which harmonized well enough, in this instance, with Rome's interests and the tradition of her relations with her neighbours. By conquest Switzerland was brought into the main stream of western civilization, and, for the first time, into the light of written record.

The Greeks used the name 'Celts' in a very wide sense to describe all the fair-haired peoples dwelling north of the Alps. During the last millennium before Christ the Celts had wandered and settled over much of the area between the Atlantic and the Black Sea. They penetrated into France, the British Isles, and Spain; by the fifth century B.C. they had reached Italy; they drifted down the Danube valley and left settlements in Asia Minor; they held the area of modern Germany perhaps as far as the Elbe and also Bohemia. These peoples formed neither a political, nor, in any proper sense, a racial unity. But there was among them sufficient homogeneity for ancient authors to consider them as a whole, distinct, on the one hand, from the more highly civilized Greeks and Romans of the Mediterranean basin, and, on the other, from the less advanced Germanic tribes which lay to their north and east. It is Celts whom the opening historic record shows in possession of much of Switzerland, superimposed on the Ligurians, who themselves represented a later layer of settlement than the neolithic and bronze age men who had made their homes on platforms supported by piles rising out of the waters of the Swiss lakes.

And it is from a Swiss site, at the egress of the river Zihl from lake Neuchâtel, occupied, it would seem, by Celts from *c*. 250 to *c*. 100 B.C., that the culture of Celtic Europe during the later iron age has been given its name of the La Tène civilization.

Neither the Alps nor the lands immediately to the north of them were well known to the Greeks, and no description has survived earlier than that of the historian Polybius *c*. 130–120 B.C. From this time onwards recurrent conflict between Celts and Romans caused the latter to set down in writing what they could discover of the peoples who then inhabited the Swiss area. Though predominantly they were not exclusively Celtic: the upper valley of the Rhine from lake Constance to the high mountains of Grisons was occupied by the Raeti, a wild and barbarous segment of the Veneti of north-east Italy, who themselves formed a distinct group of peoples of the Indo–European family. Speaking roughly, the line of division between Celts and Raeti ran from lake Constance southwards to the valley of the Linth, and thence to the St. Gotthard. But the boundary was not rigid, and in the mountains it can hardly be drawn. We do not know whether Raeti or Celts held Uri; each in turn appears to have occupied Glarus; perhaps at this date Urseren was not settled at all. Moreover, the superior culture of the Celts seems to have exercised a pervasive influence well inside Raetian territory. Yet at least it is clear that when men first began to describe the inhabitants of Switzerland they distinguished between two dominant races; the composition of the layers beneath cannot be determined precisely.

Among the Celts a number of different peoples can be named and localized. The valleys of the Ticino and the Vorderrhein were occupied by the Lepontii, whose Celtic culture was strongly tinctured by that of the primitive Ligurian inhabitants. Four Celtic tribes held the Valais, and Geneva and the region to the south of its lake belonged to the Allobroges, who had been conquered by the Romans in 121 B.C. and incorporated into the province of *Gallia Narbonensis*. To the west of the Jura, between Rhine and Rhone, was the territory of the Sequani; it was perhaps not till the middle of the first century B.C. that the Raurici became established in the neighbourhood of Basle. Most extensive of all were the lands of the Helvetii. On the east they marched with those of the Raeti; to the west they were limited by the Jura; to the south by the Alps and lake Geneva. Northwards their boundary was indeterminate;

at one time it had extended to the river Main, and at the beginning of the first century B.C. there were still Helvetian settlements to the north of the Rhine. But here was being felt the increasing pressure of the Germanic tribesmen, who, driven by what impulses we cannot know, were moving relentlessly from their homes in north-eastern Europe towards the kindlier climates of the south.

It is unnecessary to suppose a primordial and permanent antagonism between Celts and Germans; indeed, so much Celtic influence did the latter absorb that it is sometimes difficult to be certain of their identity. Thus when in the last decade of the second century B.C. a branch of the Celtic Helvetii, the Tigurini, allied themselves with the Germanic Cimbri to raid the Roman provinces, it remains doubtful whether the third party to the plan, a tribe called the Teutoni, were Celts or celticized Germans.[1] However this may be, the movement seemed for a time to imperil the Roman republic. By 107 B.C. the Tigurini had defeated a Roman army and slain a Roman consul on the middle Garonne; two years later the united Celtic and Germanic hordes broke two consular armies on the lower Rhone in the neighbourhood of Orange. After ravaging Gaul and marching about in Spain they planned nothing less than a double attack on Italy. The Teutoni were to advance from Gaul along the coast; the Cimbri and the Tigurini were to cross the eastern Alps into Lombardy. The danger to Rome was averted by the military genius of Marius. In the autumn of 102 B.C. he crushed the western division of the invaders at Aix in Provence; in the following summer he annihilated the Cimbri near Vercelli. The Tigurini, who had remained in reserve in the Alps to the east of the Brenner pass, escaped the slaughter and returned to the north, perhaps at this time taking up their permanent settlement in south-west Switzerland about Avenches.

Commonly it is the activities of the Cimbri in these events which have attracted most attention, for they provide the first instance of conflict between the Romans and the Germans who were ultimately to overrun the Roman empire in the west. No less significant is the part played by the Celts, the Tigurini, and perhaps also the Teutoni. They appear as belligerent peoples, capable in this

---

[1] Some scholars suggest that the difficulty is artificial, because they suppose that the name 'Germani' was anciently applied to Celts originally dwelling to the east of the Rhine. On this supposition the Cimbri and the Teutoni were Celts, just as the Tigurini.

instance of co-operation with the Germans. But the alliance of
Celt and German was a matter of temporary convenience which
did not long check Germanic penetration into Celtic territory. A
generation after the expedition of the Cimbri the German advance
southwards had become more urgent, and it was favoured by
divisions among the Celts. When about 70 B.C. the German leader
Ariovist led his confederation of tribes across the Rhine near
Mainz, he was welcomed by the Sequani of Alsace as an ally
against their enemies, the Celtic Aedui of central Gaul. But the
ally soon showed that he intended to be master; by 61 B.C. Ariovist
had shattered the Aedui; then he turned to deprive the Sequani
of their lands. A wedge of German settlement threatened to separate the Celts of Switzerland from those of the west. At this the
Helvetii took fright, and planned a mass migration from the area
south of the Rhine where many of them, who had been forced
from their more northerly homes by the pressure of the Germans
during the last two generations, had hardly yet had time to become established settlers. Their goal was the Atlantic seaboard
of south-west Gaul, known to some of the elders by the expedition
of the Tigurini nearly half a century before.

This project, instigated by the nobleman Orgetorix and complicated by his personal ambitions of achieving kingship over the
Helvetii and of promoting a confederation of monarchies among
the peoples of Gaul, persisted beyond his death. By the spring of
58 B.C. the Helvetii were ready to start their journey; contingents
of other Celtic peoples had joined to swell the total to 368,000 men,
women, and children; the fighting men may be estimated at a
quarter of that figure.[2] The evacuation was to be complete and
final; the Helvetii had burnt their towns, their villages, their crops.
Their easiest route to the mouth of the Garonne was to cross the
Rhone at Geneva, and then, skirting the southern end of the Jura,
to pass through the Roman province of Transalpine Gaul. For
permission to do this they addressed themselves to the Roman
authority. That authority was Caesar, and permission was refused.

Caesar's refusal to tolerate the passage of a vagrant horde
through Roman territory may readily be understood. But how
are we to explain his continued hostility to the migration when

[2] These are Caesar's figures. Some modern scholars consider them impossibly
high and would put the total of the Celtic horde at no more than 150,000.

the Helvetii had chosen another route which, crossing the Jura further north and passing by arrangement through the lands of the Sequani, no longer touched Transalpine Gaul? Was it the calculation of a politician, determined to provoke a conflict for the sake of the prestige which victory would bring? The imputation is not wholly just: the interests of Rome were involved as well as the personal ambitions of Caesar, for the establishment in western Gaul of a new Helvetian state near the Roman frontier might well be thought to represent a menace to the Roman peace. Whatever may have been his motives, Caesar took the offensive; he pursued the Helvetii into Aeduan territory and defeated them, after stubborn battle, at Bibracte (Mont Beuvray, near Autun). The Helvetii who survived the battle he forced to return as dependent but privileged allies of Rome (*foederati*) to the Swiss lands which they had abandoned, lest the vacant area should attract further German advances.

Thus the history of Roman Switzerland may be said to have opened at Bibracte, which proved the prelude to Caesar's complete conquest of Gaul, a political achievement fundamental for western civilization. And Caesar knew how to defend the empire he was founding: in the year of Bibracte he defeated Ariovist in Alsace and drove the Germans back across the Rhine.

Yet at Caesar's death much was still provisional in the relations of Rome to the Swiss area. An attempt in 57 B.C. to establish Romans in the Valais, and so to secure the route from Italy to Gaul over the St. Bernard, broke down. But the Helvetii remained Roman allies, and two colonies of legionary veterans, at Nyon on lake Geneva (*Colonia Julia Equestris*) and at Augst near Basle (*Colonia Augusta Raurica*, founded after Caesar's death but apparently on his instructions) served as eastern outposts to defend Roman communications between the Rhone at Lyons and the new frontier on the Rhine. It was left to Augustus to complete Caesar's work and to bring the territory of the Helvetii into the provincial system of the empire. In the Augustan reorganization of Gaul the Helvetii were attributed to *Provincia Belgica*. The same reign saw their eastern and southern neighbours lose their independence. Between 16 and 13 B.C. Augustus's stepsons, Drusus and Tiberius, carried out completely successful converging attacks on the Raetians and the Vindelician Celts who lay south of the Danube in the neighbourhood of Augsburg. These new conquests were thrown together with the Valais, where the Celtic tribes had submitted to Roman rule some dozen years earlier, to form the province of *Raetia*. The whole area of modern Switzerland had thus been brought under Roman administration, though it was far from being consolidated into a single unit of government.

For its further history the question of the imperial frontier was vital. If that frontier continued to be the Rhine the territory of the Helvetii would retain the character of an advanced zone, continuously garrisoned and subject to attack. In A.D. 9 Augustus's plan to project Rome's frontier to the Elbe crashed when the Germans overwhelmed Varus's army in the Teutoburger Wald, and for the time being Rome was reduced to organizing her frontier on the Rhine. Of the four legions which composed the army of the upper Rhine, which had its headquarters at Mainz, one was stationed among the Helvetii at Windisch (Vindonissa), a strong position between the rivers Aare and Reuss dominating the route leading from lake Geneva to the Rhine and also the roads running east and west behind the frontier. But the Romans did not long remain satisfied with this arrangement. Under the emperor Claudius (A.D. 41–54) they pushed forward along the valley of the Wutach as far as the sources of the Danube; under the Flavians the systematic conquest of the lands between Rhine, Main, and Danube was undertaken, and before the end of the first century it had been completed by the drawing of a *limes*. As this advance proceeded Switzerland ceased to be an area of frontier provinces. By A.D. 101 no further need was felt for a garrison in Vindonissa, and the legion was withdrawn. For the next century and a half Celtic and Raetian Switzerland enjoyed under Roman rule an almost unbroken peace in which a civilization composed of native and Roman elements had opportunity to flourish.

Any account of the Roman occupation must draw its material almost exclusively from Celtic Switzerland; about Roman *Raetia* we are very ill-informed. Two elementary considerations are fundamental. First, the fact of Roman rule brought no great influx of strangers into Switzerland. The soldiers and administrators must always have been comparatively few, and they were drawn from every province of the empire: their origin might be Spanish, or African, or oriental; frequently, of course, it was Celtic. Of all the inscriptions which have been collected for the Roman period in Switzerland, not one must imperatively be referred to an inhabitant of the city of Rome. What united these soldiers and officials was not racial or national feeling but a common legal status as Roman citizens and the common enjoyment of a civilization which they were convinced was the only tolerable way of life. And, secondly, the Celts among whom they came were not barbarians, separated from them by an impassable abyss of cultural inferiority. The Helvetii prized wit as well as military prowess. In weapons and tactics and discipline the Celts in Switzerland, as elsewhere, were inferior to the Romans who defeated them. Their social organization seems to have been loose; the kings of earlier times had disappeared and an aristocracy of great landowners lorded it over masses of slaves and half-free men. But they had known permanent settlements; in preparation for the great migration of 58 B.C., Caesar tells us, they had twelve towns to burn and 400 villages. In agricultural technique they had much to teach their conquerors, and they were capable of fine decorative art, until native feeling was distorted by imitation of alien models. Nor were they wholly ignorant of the higher civilization of the Mediterranean world. From about 600 B.C. there existed at the mouth of the Rhone the Greek colony of Massilia (Marseilles), and though the importance of Massilia as a channel through which Greek influences made themselves felt on the Celts has perhaps been exaggerated, there is reason to believe that considerable communication took place by way of the Danube valley. The Celts of Switzerland, with gold washed from the Kleine and the Grosse Emme, had imitated the coins of Philip of Macedonia; in the absence of a native alphabet, Greek characters were borrowed to write Celtic words, and presumably the muster lists which, on Caesar's testimony, the Helvetii carried in 58 B.C. were drawn up in Greek letters in the Celtic tongue. We must not set the cultural level of the Swiss Celts in pre-Roman times too high: the imitations of Greek coins, originally excellent, soon degenerated, and literacy on any extensive scale awaited the introduction of Latin speech and script. But clearly the Helvetii had an appetite, an eager receptivity, for the new refinements and amenities which Rome could offer, and something indigenous to contribute, which would amalgamate with the importations from the Mediterranean to form a new regional civilization.

If we except the officials, who were normally transient, the garrison troops, and those individuals who had acquired the status as a personal right, for long the only full Roman citizens in Switzerland were the veterans settled in Caesar's colonies at Nyon and Augst, and in Avenches (Aventicum) which the emperor Vespasian raised to a colony after the unrest of A.D. 69. The legal position of the great mass of the inhabitants can be understood only by reference to the administrative divisions of the area. These were subject to pretty frequent change, and, indeed, the only principle which can readily be discovered is that at no time under Roman rule did Switzerland form a unit for administrative purposes. Nor did the administrative boundaries commonly coincide with those of tribal settlement. Under Augustus nearly all Switzerland fell either to *Provincia Belgica* or to *Raetia*. Either in the time of Claudius, or, less probably, about A.D. 171 under Marcus Aurelius, the Valais was separated from *Raetia* and joined to part of Savoy to form a new province, *Alpes Graiae et Poeninae*, governed by an imperial procurator; the Vallenses were specially privileged with the 'Latin Law', and before the end of the first century they had attained full Roman citizenship. Geneva and the surrounding region belonged to *Gallia Narbonensis*, under its senatorial proconsul; here the inhabitants became Roman citizens in A.D. 40. It is possible that about A.D. 90, in the reign of Domitian, the tribal organizations of the Helvetii and the Raurici were transferred from *Provincia Belgica* to *Germania superior*, ruled by an imperial legate from Mainz. An imperial procurator (after *c.* A.D. 165 an imperial legate) governed eastern Switzerland together with Tyrol and the Bavarian–Swabian plateau; this province continued to bear the name *Raetia*. Though many of their inhabitants held the status as an individual right, as a whole neither *Germania superior* nor *Raetia*, comprehending between them by far the greater part of Switzerland, enjoyed full Roman citizenship until A.D. 212 when Caracalla's edict extended this privilege to all free men of the empire.

There is no evidence that this disability was found onerous. Under the imperial administrators the population was organized into *civitates*: urban communities, such as the colonies Nyon and Augst; tribal communities, such as the *civitas Helvetiorum* and the *civitas Rauricorum*. These communities—of the organization of the Raeti we have little information—remained ethnologically

Celtic; that is probably true even of the colonies, for the veterans settled in them would mostly be Celts. They retained a wide freedom of self-government, which they exercised in forms imitated from the Roman world, with elected magistrates, an *ordo decurionum*, and the like, to bear responsibility for administration and the quota of taxes under the supervision of the somewhat remote imperial officials. A member of such a community, governed immediately by his own kind, even if he had to pay imperial taxes, enjoying the Roman peace, even though he might not in law be fully a Roman citizen, was little inclined to be disloyal to an empire in the benefits of which he participated and the civilization of which he sincerely admired. The peoples of Switzerland fought in Rome's armies: the Helvetii and the Raurici were employed as auxiliary troops, though less extensively than the warlike Raeti; a regiment of cavalry was maintained from the inhabitants of the Valais.

A single incident comes to disturb this picture of acquiescence to Roman rule. Its prominence is perhaps due less to its intrinsic importance than to the accident that the greatest of Roman historians wrote an account of it, while so much of the rest of our knowledge of Roman Switzerland has to be elicited from the arid and disjunct evidence of inscriptions and archaeological remains. This is the story which Tacitus tells. In A.D. 68 the emperor Nero killed himself in a suburban villa, and with him the first imperial dynasty, the Julian–Claudian, came to an end. The Rhine armies proclaimed Vitellius emperor, and the army of upper Germany under the legate Alienus Caecina planned to march to Italy to support the claims of Vitellius, firstly against Galba, the candidate of the praetorians, and then against Otho, who supplanted and murdered Galba in January A.D. 69. The route from the Rhine led through Switzerland, where Caecina intended to add to his forces the fourth legion of his command, the 21st *Rapax*, which had relieved the 13th at Vindonissa in the time of Claudius. The 21st legion, probably composed of Raetians, was already on ill terms with the Helvetii amongst whom it was stationed. And the Helvetii had shown that their sympathies were with Galba. Caecina therefore converted his march into a punitive expedition; he defeated the Helvetii in battle and then proposed to destroy their capital, Avenches. Only by direct appeal to Vitellius did the Helvetii save their city from Caecina, who passed on to

Italy, there to defeat Otho and afterwards to betray the cause of Vitellius to Vespasian. His feat of leading four legions, some 30,000 men, over the St. Bernard in either March or early April A.D. 69, when the snow conditions would be at their worst, was extraordinary: the nearest comparable undertaking, Buonaparte's crossing of the St. Bernard in 1800 before Marengo, took place in May. The competitor who emerged successful from the struggle for the empire, Vespasian, had perhaps some ties of sentiment with Avenches; this may be the reason why the results of the events of A.D. 68–9 were not unfavourable to the Helvetii. The 21st legion was replaced at Vindonissa by the 11th, *Claudia pia fidelis*, and Avenches was raised to the status of a colony and a city of Roman law, though this did not imply the grant of Roman citizenship to the Helvetii in general.

The incident is evidence of some friction between the natives and the garrison troops. But it did not show a calculated disloyalty born of some hypothetical resurgence of Helvetian national feeling. Celts and Raetians harboured no permanent hostility towards Rome's empire, nor any hope of throwing it off. For to belong to that empire was to have the opportunity to be a civilized man. The servants of the Roman government who came to Switzerland, few though they may have been, brought the example of a more elaborate way of life, and demanded standards of comfort unheard of before. And though it would be unwise to overrate their technical capacities, they showed how these material demands might be met by turning to problems of engineering their incomparable skill in the organization of labour. In Switzerland, as elsewhere, the Celt was versatile enough to adopt the new fashions. The veterans in the colonies, the legionaries at Vindonissa, naturally looked for the baths, the theatres, the circuses, to which they had been accustomed when serving in other parts of the empire; from them the provincials learnt similar desires. The remains of the public works of the period, the amphitheatres at Windisch (Vindonissa), Avenches, Martigny, and Augst, the theatres at Avenches and Augst, the great east door to the town walls of Avenches, the aqueducts which carried water to these cities, are abiding, if fragmentary, monuments of Rome's influence in Switzerland. That influence was not exercised in a void, but in a living world with a pre-existent culture of its own. What the Celts adopted from the Romans they coloured with their own peculiarities; the result was no mere transference to Swiss soil of triumphant foreign models but an individual Romano–Celtic civilization.

Even the most characteristic mark of Roman occupation, the system of admirable roads which joined Italy and Transalpine Gaul to lake Geneva, lake Geneva to the Rhine and Danube, Basle to Zürich and lake Constance and Bregenz, Bregenz to Chur and the eastern Alpine passes, was not wholly a Roman creation. The lines of the great routes had already been laid down in pre-Roman times; the Celts had probably bridged the Rhone at Geneva, and continued the great axis from Geneva beneath the Jura to the Rhine across that river by a bridge at Zurzach (Tenedo). For the movement of troops and the convenience of administrators the Romans improved and extended what they found, often with notable skill. Probably the march of Alienus Caecina over the St. Bernard in the spring of A.D. 69 would have been impossible but for the work effected on this road by the orders of the emperor Claudius. The northern continuation of this route, by which the garrison at Vindonissa maintained communication with the south, has preserved a remarkable example of Roman road-making skill: to the east of lake Biel (Bienne), between Fräschels and Studenberg, the carriage-way was built over a marshy stretch of moor on an embankment composed of millions of piles. About the construction of vehicles the Celts perhaps had something to teach, but the Romans, at least, made the roads fit for the use of wheels. Under Roman rule the surface of the roads was improved; they were better policed and organized with rest houses and customs barriers. But more important was the fact that they became longer. For all roads did lead to Rome, and thence again to the ends of the civilized world.

In planning and building towns, in providing them with plentiful water-supplies and places of public recreation, in giving the example of how they should be governed, the Romans undoubtedly introduced much that was novel. But they did not originate town life in Switzerland. The twelve *oppida* which the Helvetii destroyed before commencing the migration of 58 B.C. were permanently inhabited. Again and again the toponomy of Roman settlements betrays a Celtic origin. Noviodunum (Nyon), Dunum (Thun), Eburodunum (Yverdon), Minnodunum (Moudon), were all, the suffix *-dunum* indicates, and the archaeologist's spade has confirmed, Celtic fortified places before they were

Romanized. Geneva, Avenches, Vindonissa, Lausanne, are all Celtic names; there were sites of Celtic *oppida* before the Romans came at Tenedo (Zurzach) and near Berne. From this list it may be inferred that although Roman Switzerland had only three cities of full Roman law, Nyon, Avenches, and Augst, there were many other fairly considerable aggregations of population. To them must be added the villages, erected, ribbon-like, along the main roads, or using a road-crossing to extend in depth, and tending, as far as their modest resources allowed, to imitate civic institutions and ways of life.

On the country-side also, Rome left its imprint. The typical rural dwelling-place of the well-to-do provincial in Switzerland, and the centre of the normal unit of agricultural exploitation, became the villa, the country house on the Roman model. The ground plan of the Swiss villa might remain essentially Celtic, but it was transformed externally by the use of the Roman building material, stone, and by the addition of the Roman portico; internally it might be beautified by Roman mosaics and heated by Roman hypocausts. Variation in size and type of the villas is endless: one might come near the dimensions of a palace, with its own workshops, producing goods for sale as well as consumption, and with barracks to house the multitude of slaves who cultivated the owner's wide estates; another might house a modest family tilling unaided the land which it owned. It is probable that the great estate worked by servile or semi-servile labour continued to reflect in Roman times the pre-Roman social organization. Of villages of free peasant proprietors there is little trace in Roman Switzerland; if they existed, it was in backwaters of barbarity.

The villas were as potent a factor in Romanizing the Celt as the towns and townships. These islands of Romanity spread their influence about the surrounding country-side, bringing knowledge of new fruits and plants and vegetables from the south. The introduction of the vine, despite the attempts of Roman legislators to prevent wine being produced north of the Alps, is a classic example of the economic benefits which Switzerland derived from belonging to the international system of Rome. Nor was traffic wholly one-way: Roman Switzerland could still export corn; the cattle and cheeses of the Alps were appreciated in Italy; bronze containers made in the workshops of one Gemellianus, at Baden on the Limmat, have been found in many provinces of the empire.

33

On art the effects of the Roman connexion were not happy; perhaps the attempt to imitate Hellenistic–Roman naturalism ran too contrary to the native tradition. But in religion, synthesis of the Celtic and Roman strains proved easy enough. The eclecticism of the early centuries of the Roman empire tolerated the persistence of the old Celtic gods, though sometimes now disguised under Latin names and worshipped in Roman temples; in the towns the official worship of the emperor was attended to as a token of proper piety and political conformity and as an avenue to social advancement. Legionaries who had served on distant frontiers and the ubiquitous Levantine traders and quacksalvers spread the cults of more exciting deities from the east: Isis and Osiris, Cybele and Mithras. Only after the conversion to Christianity of the emperor Constantine did the empire gradually come to experience the predominance of a single religion which in its jealousy for men's souls could brook no rival. The first evidence of Christianity in the Swiss area is rather belated, but an inscription of A.D. 377 shows that a Roman prefect in the Valais was a Christian, and four years later a bishop from Martigny was present at a synod at Aquileia. By the end of the fourth century we may assume a thin network of Christian churches over western Switzerland with bishops at Nyon, Avenches, Basle, Martigny, and Geneva.

Not till A.D. 451 is there mention of a bishop in *Raetia*, at Chur. Perhaps the lateness of this date is not fortuitous, but hints how widely the degree of Romanization varied in different parts of Switzerland. Of *Raetia* during the most prosperous period of Roman rule so little evidence has survived as to suggest that here, aside from the main road running from the eastern passes to Bregenz—and the importance of this route was not great— Roman influence was never strong. It was earliest and most intensive in the Valais and about lake Geneva; thence it spread north-eastward, along the great military road Vevey–Vindonissa, and along the lateral routes from Basle to Zürich, lake Constance, and the Danube. In central Switzerland and the Alps Roman remains are much less frequent, though discoveries continue to enlarge the known area of Romanization. The villa penetrated into mid-Switzerland as far as lake Lucerne, presumably from the Valais over the Grimsel pass and down the Haslital; it has been suggested that Lucerne's name is Roman. Of the Reuss valley we are less certain, but even in this region the names Uri and Urseren seem Roman, and many of the commonest terms in the vocabulary of Alpine economy have a Latin origin. But, in general, a clear distinction can be drawn between the south-west and the rest of Switzerland. In the former area the inscriptions show how Roman influence affected every detail of ordinary life; elsewhere, from the neighbourhood of Solothurn northwards, the inscriptions are fewer and less beautiful, and are mostly concerned with purely administrative matters. This is a difference which will give individuality to Romance Switzerland.

Yet this distinction is of limited value. It tells how the intensity of Romanization varied comparatively between one area and another, but it does not solve the more difficult problem of the absolute intensity of Romanization in any one place. How far, even in the south-west, did the Celts put off the native and become Roman in speech, in habit, in mind? Was this a result achieved, if at all, only by the upper orders of Celtic society? These are questions which have not yet received wholly satisfactory answers. Some linguistic pointers are significant. Though Latin became the language of business and literacy there are indications that in the last centuries of Roman rule Celtic reasserted itself. In many of the later inscriptions the names preserved are purely Celtic; from A.D. 202 distances on the imperial roads began to be marked no longer in Roman miles but in Celtic *leugae*; where place-names in the two languages existed side by side the Latin form tended to be supplanted by the Celtic: Forum Claudii by Octodorus (Martigny), Julia Equestris by Noviodunum (Nyon). There is reason to suppose that Celtic was still being widely spoken even in the south-west at the time of the German invasions in the fifth and sixth centuries.

If peace be the criterion, Roman Switzerland enjoyed its golden age in the century and a half following A.D. 100. Building was elaborate and ambitious. To this period can be assigned the completion of the finely designed unity of theatre, temple, and forum at Avenches; the conversion of the circus at Augst into a theatre betokened a change of audience and new, less brutal tastes. This is not the place to discuss why the skies turned sombre over the Roman empire in the third century; what deep-lying technical, political, military, or other deficiencies caused the colossus to stumble, and at last, in the west, to fall. There was no simple catastrophe, no sudden violation of civilization by barbarian attack. We now better understand to what extent civilization had become barbarized, and the barbarians civilized, before Roman rule passed away. Yet the violences which accompanied the change cannot be disregarded. By the middle of the third century the economic condition of the empire was deplorable: the pressure of German tribesmen bore irresistibly on the northern frontier of the Roman world which they had learnt to know and covet. The defensive line, the *limes*, between Rhine and Danube buckled; in A.D. 259 a confederation of German tribes, the Alemannians, broke into Switzerland and destroyed Avenches, which was never to be fully restored. Their devastating inroads were frequently repeated. Vindonissa was again occupied by Roman troops, for once again Switzerland had become a collection of frontier provinces.

From the end of the third century a series of able and determined emperors exerted almost superhuman efforts to restore the situation. They riveted on the crumbling structure of empire an iron system of discipline, the tyranny of the corporative state, so that every resource might be turned to the prime purpose of defence. Communications to the rear of the Rhine frontier were protected by new castles: at Kaiseraugst, near Basle, Burg, near Stein am Rhein, Irgenhausen, on the Pfäffikersee, Oberwinterthur, and Schaan in modern Liechtenstein. Kaiseraugst could contain a legion, but for the rest these modest and utilitarian foundations reflect the stringencies of the time; whole towns with their houses and fortifications now cover an area less than that occupied by the great public places in Augst or Avenches two centuries before. The administrative framework of the empire was reshaped by diminishing the size of the individual province and separating the military from the civil command. In this reorganization the Helvetii and the Raurici were thrown together with the Sequani to form a new province, *Maxima Sequanorum*, ruled by a *praeses* from Besançon; *Raetia* was divided into two provinces with a common military commander; the Valais, Geneva, and the Ticino all fell to different provinces. No more under the late than under the early empire was Switzerland administered as a unity.

The superbly organized state of siege delayed for a century and a half the triumph of the Germans. Rome was still capable of defeating them in the field: with a victory over the Alemannians near Vindonissa in 298 Constantius, the father of Constantine the Great, secured fifty years of peace for the Helvetii; in 357 the Alemannians were again defeated, by the emperor Julian near Strasbourg; Valentinian I (364–75) fortified the line of the Rhine from lake Constance to the sea and perhaps completed the series of intercommunicating watch-towers along the river, the remains of more than fifty of which can be traced on the stretch between Stein am Rhein and Basle. But the strain of continuous military effort was enormous, and within the Roman armies the barbarian element became ever more prominent; barbarian generals in the imperial service made themselves the arbiters of the empire's fate. From the beginning of the fourth century it had become necessary to divide the defence of the empire, and when one emperor sat in Constantinople and another in Italy, each was inclined to solve his immediate problems at the expense of his co-ruler. In the last quarter of the century the Huns arrived in Europe from the Asiatic steppes, and their savage conquests gave a more urgent impetus to the Germanic 'Wandering of the Peoples' which for centuries had been feeling its way towards the Mediterranean. Constantinople, firmly fortified, and able to draw upon the resources of Asia Minor, managed to survive, but the wave which had broken on her washed over the empire in the west. By 401 the Visigoths under Alaric were threatening Italy; in an attempt to avert the danger Stilicho, *magister utriusque militiae* of the western empire, withdrew the garrisons from north of the Alps.

As in Britain, obscurity covers the end of Roman rule in Switzerland. It is probable that Roman control did not last long after the troops had departed, and that it had failed even before the deposition of the last emperor, Romulus Augustulus, had symbolized in 476 the complete collapse of the empire in the west. The connexion with Italy grew feeble; few Roman coins, and no Latin inscriptions dealing with imperial administration, have been discovered in Switzerland dated later than 400.

The lands of the more or less Romanized Celts of Switzerland were now occupied by two Germanic peoples, the Alemannians and the Burgundians. That this occupation produced profound ethnological and linguistic changes, the results of which persist, is obvious enough. But it is not easy to state precisely how and when and in what stages the occupation took place. The literary evidence for these disordered times is scanty and inconclusive, and though archaeology and place-name study supplement our knowledge most usefully, they do not wholly compensate for the absence of a clear literary tradition. The course of events can be traced with least hesitation in the south-west.

During the second quarter of the fifth century, while the emperors sat helpless in Italy, the imperial tradition was being kept alive in Gaul by Aetius, a provincial from Silistria on the Black Sea, who had extorted from the western emperor the title of *magister utriusque militiae* and the dignity of patrician. Half barbarian by education, his ambitions were those of many a barbarian leader from Alaric to Theodoric the Ostrogoth—to maintain the glory of the empire's civilization, and yet by service to become its master. He turned his unequalled knowledge of the Roman, Hun, and German worlds to the attempt to ensure Rome's survival, now by concluding alliances with, now by fostering enmities among, the barbarian peoples. From 413 the Burgundians, established on the middle Rhine, had represented a formidable threat to Gaul; in 436 Aetius destroyed their kingdom with the help of Hun mercenaries—it is the theme which medieval Germany was to embroider into the *Nibelungenlied*. In 443 he transferred what was left of the Burgundians to the area of modern Savoy, perhaps with the intention of using them to guard the approaches to Italy; Geneva became the residence of Burgundian kings. Originally the status of these new allies of the empire was not exorbitantly privileged; they were established peaceably and endowed with a determinate portion of the lands and labour resources of their provincial hosts. But after Aetius's murder in 454 and the breakdown of his schemes, the Burgundians pressed northward into western Switzerland, into the modern cantons of Vaud, the Valais, Fribourg, and Neuchâtel, and into the Bernese Jura. Before the end of the century they had certainly reached the line of the Aare, probably that of the Reuss, perhaps even that of the Limmat. How far this movement took place as a forcible seizure of lands and men left without government, how far as an officially recognized extension of settlement in a still Roman province, cannot easily be determined. Its results can be more readily described. The Burgundians were few in number, and the part of Switzerland which they occupied was that which had been most intensely influenced by Rome. Consequently, although they remained politically the masters, in other ways they were assimilated to the Romano-Celtic population whose speech they came to adopt (though perhaps less rapidly than has sometimes been supposed). Modern French-speaking Switzerland is approximately the territory settled by the Burgundians from the fifth century onwards; its tongue is essentially the transmuted Latin of the Celtic provincials.

The settlement of the Alemannians in northern and central Switzerland took a different course, and its process is more obscure. During the fifth century the Alemannians had probably seized Alsace and Basle, and undoubtedly they had made raids south of the Rhine. But did they at this time settle permanently in the territory of the Helvetii? Or did the frontier of the empire on the Rhine, from lake Constance to Basle, remain substantially intact until the beginning of the sixth century and serious penetration by the Alemannians into Switzerland begin only after 500? The answers are disputed. But whenever it may have begun, the large scale migration of the Alemannians to the south of the Rhine, lasting throughout the sixth and seventh centuries and beyond, differed greatly from the wild raids of the third century. The object now was settlement, not booty. The Alemannians were far more numerous than the Burgundians, and they were still in direct contact with those of their peoples who remained north of the river. The lands on which they fell were the least effectively Romanized in Switzerland. So here it is the German who absorbs, or expels, or annihilates the Celt, and imposes his language. Roughly speaking, we can equate Alemannic with German-speaking Switzerland.

There are indications that for a time in south-west Switzerland Burgundians and Alemannians lived intermingled. Between the two great linguistic divisions the line did not harden suddenly, but shifted for centuries, with the general tendency for Alemannian settlement to gain ground at the expense of the Burgundians. In the sixth century the Burgundian area extended as far east as the Reuss, if not beyond, but by the ninth it had receded to the line of the upper and middle Aare. Nor did the Alemannian advance halt here; whereas at the beginning of the tenth century Morat, Anet, and Bienne on the left bank of the Aare were still Romance in speech, by the thirteenth century German was spoken as far west as the river Sarine.

A similar gradual advance of Germanic influence occurred in those districts of central and eastern Switzerland which had been saved by their height and isolation from the early inroads of the Alemannians. The process here was slow, and never perfectly accomplished. It was not until the ninth century that Germans working up the Haslital crossed the Grimsel pass and colonized the upper valley of the Rhone. And farther to the east, in the Swiss part of Roman *Raetia*—the upper valley of the Rhine and the Grisons—the first effect of the invasions was to provoke a Romanization perhaps more intense than had been known while *Raetia* was still a province of the empire. This region, in which the epigraphic remains of Roman times are extremely scanty, became the refuge for the Celtic provincials fleeing from the lowlands before the Germans. They brought with them their Roman speech and customs, and it was thus that in *Raetia* peculiar survivals of debased Romanity in the terminology of administration and law persisted far into the middle ages, and the Latin tongue, Raeto-roman, put up a strong resistance to the advance of German in the upper valley of the Rhine. Bregenz and Arbon on lake Constance were still inhabited by 'Romani'—Latin-speaking provincials—at the beginning of the seventh century; much of the Rhine valley north of Chur remained Romance in speech till about 1000; not till the fifteenth century did the German tide submerge Chur itself, and in Prättigau and Montafon Raeto-roman held out for another 100 years. And today, in the valley of the Vorderrhein and in the Engadine, the speech of the Latin provincials persists as Romansh and Ladin. Yet even here in the Grisons, islands of German settlement, in the Rheinwald and the Safiental, about Davos and elsewhere, witness how Alemannians from the upper Valais entered *Raetia* in the thirteenth century, both directly over the Furka and Oberalp passes, and also from the south. Thus even the mountain penetralia of Romanity were not wholly safe from the advancing Germans.

On this note, consideration of Celt and Roman in Switzerland may close. In a strict sense there was no Roman Switzerland, for the Romans did not find a unity nor did it occur to them to create one. Yet the racial and linguistic patterns of modern Switzerland cannot well be understood without reference to the Roman occupation and to the way in which it was brought to an end by the wanderings of the German peoples. In the south-west, where

Rome's influence had gone deep, the provincials, though subjected by the Burgundians, in some ways took their captors captive; in the mountains of the Grisons natural obstacles checked the full extension of German power. But over most of the Swiss area Germanization went steadily forward from the sixth century until it reached its limits in the sixteenth. From the fall of the western empire until the independence of the confederation is complete, Swiss history will be part of German history.

III

GERMANIC SWITZERLAND

To the confusion attending the failure of Roman rule in western Europe a term was put by the rise to hegemony of one German people. Under the Merovingian Clovis and his successors the Franks who had conquered Roman Gaul gained supremacy over many of their German neighbours; Roman universalism was replaced in the west, at a lower level, by the universalism of a Frankish empire. Italy escaped the Franks: occupied by the Ostrogoths towards the end of the fifth century, in the sixth she experienced an attempt at reconquest by the Roman emperor at Constantinople; on the ruins left by the struggle between Goth and Roman, the Lombards established themselves in the north and centre of the peninsula where they maintained their independence for 200 years. Burgundians and Alemannians were less successful. The Burgundian kingdom was finally conquered and annexed by the Franks in 534, and its tribal identity vanished; when at the end of the sixth century there is once again mention of a kingdom of Burgundy the name is applied to a mere division of the Frankish realm, which comprised a far wider area and far more varied elements than the orginal Burgundian settlements. Clovis had already defeated the Alemannians before the end of the fifth century, and some at least of them had sought to evade the Frankish threat by seeking the protection of the great Ostrogothic ruler, Theodoric. But in 536 Witigis, king of the Ostrogoths, faced by the east Roman attack on Italy, bought Frankish neutrality by withdrawing his patronage from the Alemannians, whose territories both north and south of the Rhine now fell under Frankish overlordship. At about this time *Raetia* too became subject to the Merovingians.

Can we assume the effective incorporation of the Alemannians as well as the Burgundians into the Frankish state? Were their lands divided into the normal circumscriptions, the *pagi*, of the Frankish empire, under royal officers, the counts? Was the *praeses* of Chur in *Raetia*, for all his Roman title, no more than a Merovingian official? The evidence hardly allows the definitely affirmative answers which have sometimes been given to these questions.

It is significant that the Alemannians remained pretty obstinately heathen throughout the sixth century: which they would scarcely have been allowed to do if the overlordship of the Christian Frankish kings had been intensively exercised. But it is clear that tribal distinctions gave way to conveniences of state: thus the district of Basle, which was certainly an area of Alemannian settlement, was governed as an integral part of the Frankish kingdom in the sixth century, and in the seventh was joined to Strasbourg to form the duchy of Alsace. And in the reign of Dagobert (622–39) Frankish rule over the Alemannians was certainly more than nominal.

Yet the Frankish empire was essentially the creation of masterful kings, and strength of monarchy alone could guarantee its continuance. The later Merovingians failed to respond to this necessity. Germanic law provided for the division between heirs of the father's property, and this equitable principle prevented the emergence of a rule of primogeniture to settle succession to the state. The Frankish kingdom was regarded as a patrimony to be divided between the sons of a dead king; in the recurrent partitions, and the strife which they bred between the heirs, Clovis's realm was dismembered and the power of the monarchy dissipated. Moreover, physical and mental degeneration seems to have overtaken the Merovingian stock; the violent, energetic rulers of earlier times were succeeded by *rois fainéants* who, after the first third of the seventh century, became puppets in the hands of the Frankish nobles. By this time the Burgundians were too thoroughly a part of the Frankish kingdom to take advantage of the slackening of control at the centre, but a strong revival of tribal consciousness can be observed among the Alemannians. Unlike the Burgundians they had preserved their tribal unity, at least over a wide area to the east of the Rhine and the Aare, and here by the second half of the seventh century their independence had become almost complete. They maintained a national army under their own leaders, who were no mere officials of the Frankish king but true tribal chiefs, stem-dukes, showing little deference to the Frankish crown whose power hardly extended beyond the Rhine.

A rebirth of the Frankish monarchy prevented the emergence of an Alemannian state in south-west Germany. From the late seventh century members of the Carolingian family were vigorously using their position as Mayors of the Palace at the Merovingian courts to reconstitute the unity of Clovis's realm and to dominate his wretched successors. They checked the inroads of the Saracens into western Europe and reasserted Frankish mastery over the German peoples of the Continent. Their attack on the stem-dukes of Alemannia, begun by Pepin of Heristal, was brought to a successful conclusion by his grandson Carloman in 746. The stem-dukes disappeared, and the lands confiscated from them and their supporters gave the Carolingians an important footing in Alemannian territory. Alemannia was absorbed into the administrative organization of the Frankish empire. Its customary law remained—the *Lex Alamannorum* had been committed to writing early in the eighth century—but this law was administered under the supervision of officers of the Frankish king.

The breaking down of provincial isolation brought some compensation for the loss of provincial autonomy. By 751 the farce of the Merovingian puppet kings had been played out; the Carolingian mayor, Pepin the Short, disposed of the old dynasty and took the Frankish crown. On Christmas Day 800 the title of Roman emperor, in abeyance in the west since the deposition of Romulus Augustulus, was revived for Pepin's son Charlemagne. The new style added only dignity to Charlemagne's already preponderant position; by 774 he had conquered the kingdom of Lombardy, and in long wars against the Frisians and the Saxons he extended Frankish rule to the Elbe. With the revival of the Roman empire in the west—however grotesque the disparities between the antique model and the new—Alemannia recovered its natural importance as a transit area; under Charlemagne and his successors Zürich, once the site of a Roman customs station, begins again to appear in the records, and their new interests in Italy caused the Carolingians to turn their attention to *Raetia* which controlled important pass systems over the Alps.

Charlemagne's empire was wider, and, we may think, more effectively governed than that of Clovis. But despite all differences the Carolingian state had this in common with the Merovingian: in both the mainspring was the personality of the ruler. Too much depended on that accident; too little on institutions capable of carrying the burden of government. No more than the Merovingians was Charlemagne able to solve the question of succession: the state remained, not a unity at all costs to be preserved, but a legacy from which had to be satisfied the ambitions of all the sons of the ruler. There were also new problems: posed by economic retrogression, perhaps; certainly by the onslaughts from outside which became more serious as the ninth century grew older. The raids of the Norsemen, the Saracens, and the Magyars beat upon an empire imposing in size but primitive in structure. The result was its rapid disintegration; amid the fragments are dimly to be discerned the political divisions of modern Europe.

Less than thirty years lay between the death of Charlemagne and the treaty of Verdun (843) which ratified the partition of his empire between his three grandsons. To the eldest, Lothair, went the imperial title, Italy, and a kingdom called after him Lotharingia, which stretched from the North Sea to the Alps and was delimited, speaking very roughly indeed, by the rivers Meuse and Saone and Rhone on the west, and by the Rhine and Aare on the east. To one side of this middle kingdom lay that of the west Franks, ruled by Charles the Bald; to the other Lewis the German governed a congeries of German peoples, Franks, Saxons, Bavarians, Thuringians, Alemannians. Once again Switzerland was divided politically, for west of the Aare the area of Burgundian settlement fell to Lothair, while Alemannia north of the Rhine and a large, though disputed, part of it south of the river belonged to the east Frankish kingdom of Lewis.

This uneasy division outlasted the Carolingian dynasty. When the direct line of Lothair became extinct in 875 the attempt of Charles the Bald and Lewis the German to secure his possessions was denied complete success by the rise of two non-Carolingian dynasts who managed to usurp kingship over portions of the middle kingdom. In 879 the Frankish nobleman Boso had himself elected king of Provence; in 888 Rudolf, son of Conrad count of Auxerre, set up the kingdom of Transjurane Burgundy, comprising the northern part of Savoy and nearly all Switzerland between the Jura and the Reuss, on the basis of the duchy of the same name formerly held by his father. During the second quarter of the tenth century, as the result of a treaty of cession, the kings of Transjurane Burgundy gradually extended their power over Provence; henceforward the two kingdoms, including Burgundian Switzerland and extending from Basle to Nice, were held together until the dynasty died out in 1032.

Meanwhile Alemannia was sharing the fate of the east Frankish kingdom. Here the last Carolingian died in 911 without heirs, and necessity brought to the throne by some form of election the duke of Franconia, Conrad. The ambiguities of Conrad's title, the disorders of the last years of Carolingian rule, and, above all, the devastating raids of the Magyars, encouraged the recrudescence of particularism among the various German peoples whom the Franks had subjected. Their military leaders came into prominence by undertaking those functions of defence and administration of which the crown seemed incapable; after a long interval, in 911 there is once again mention of a duke of Alemannia, a certain Burkhard, also called count of Raetia. To foil the aspirations of the dukes to independence, which threatened to splinter Germany into tribal principalities, was the great achievement of the Saxon dynasty which followed Conrad on the German throne in 918. A succession of energetic rulers defended the prerogatives of the crown and the unity of the realm against the attempts of the dukes to exploit local differences in their own interests. By the beginning of the eleventh century the Saxon kings had been largely successful: the dukes had been denied an absolute hereditary right to their duchies, and they had been unable to establish control over the church and the counts within them; against their pretension to be regarded as tribal chiefs, stem-dukes, the crown had made good the principle that they were no more than royal officials.

Nor were the super-abundant energies of the Saxon kings wholly occupied in Germany. The vacuum of power left by the collapse of Carolingian rule on their western and southern frontiers attracted their intervention in the middle kingdom and beyond the Alps. In 962 the second king of the Saxon line, Otto I, made himself master of northern and central Italy, and resuscitated the title of emperor in the west which had been meaningless for three-quarters of a century. In the system of communications of Otto's empire the Swiss area had an important part to play, and it is perhaps justifiable to interpret Otto's substantial privileges for the bishop of Chur and the abbey of Einsiedeln as moves designed to secure the routes from Germany to Italy by way of the upper valley of the Rhine and its passes. The influence of the German king in Alemannia south of the Rhine was not established without effort. In the early decades of the tenth century Rudolf II, king of Transjurane Burgundy, had pushed his power eastwards into Aargau, and even into Thurgau. Zürich was claimed as a Burgundian town; its name appears on Rudolf's coins, and documents from Zürich were dated by Rudolf's regnal years. Not till Rudolf had been defeated near Winterthur by Duke Burkhard of Alemannia, c. 920, was Zürich secured for the German kingdom. Otto went over to the offensive against Burgundy and made its king his client. As a result of this dependence, when the Burgundian dynasty died out in 1032 the German crown inherited its possessions. In 1033 Conrad the Salian, already king of Germany and of Italy and Roman emperor in the west, became king of Burgundy also. The German king had achieved his triple crown; the full extent of modern Switzerland—the Burgundian lands east of the Jura, the duchy of Alemannia, the valleys to the south of the Alps —was again under a single ruler. Whatever his other titles, that ruler drew the bulk of his resources from Germany, and until the successful rejection of obedience in the fifteenth century the political history of the Swiss area is inseparable from that of the German kingdom in the middle ages.

The wider story can only be touched upon. In its constitutional aspect it shows a marked contrast to developments in the other great states of western Europe. In France, after the replacement of the Carolingian by the Capetian dynasty in 987, the crown from feeble beginnings gradually built up its power until by the thirteenth century the French king was not far from being complete master of his realm, and was certainly the most imposing ruler in Europe. England had experienced the growth of a strong monarchy even earlier, under the Norman and Angevin kings, by whom the foundations of national unity had been laid. To Germany, on the other hand, where in the tenth century the Saxon kings had created a monarchy incomparably more impressive than was to be found elsewhere in the west, the succeeding centuries brought a series of grave declensions in royal power. The tasks of government which the crown was unable to perform fell to other hands: in particular, to the noble dynasties which, within the sphere of their local influence, constructed territories over which in time they arrogated to themselves sovereign rights. And so Germany emerged from the middle ages as a loose confederation of numerous almost independent states over which the German king, the Holy Roman Emperor, exercised little more than nominal supremacy.

The reasons for this failure of the monarchy in medieval Germany defy simple definition and they are less to our purpose than the results. Although the beginnings of decline can be traced back to the eleventh century, the process was not continuous, but was interrupted by successive hopes and disappointments of revival; perhaps not until the first half of the fourteenth century did the crown lose to the princes its last chance of exercising effective control over Germany. There is no single factor which will explain all these vicissitudes. The acquisition of the Italian crown and the imperial title by Otto I can no longer be regarded as a sufficient key to the complex problem, for the later failures of the German kingship cannot be understood simply by reference to the weight of external preoccupations imposed by imperial policy. It is undoubted that the long struggle of the last two Salian emperors, Henry IV and Henry V, with the papacy for the control of the imperial church—the so-called Investiture Controversy, lasting from 1076 to 1122—greatly weakened the crown to the profit of the princes; undoubted, too, that the renewal of the papo-imperial struggle under Frederick Barbarossa, Henry VI, and Frederick II (1152–1250)—this time for the control of Italy—nullified whatever plans the masterful Hohenstaufen dynasty might have had for reorganizing the government of Germany. But it seems vain to impute to any single episode or to the weakness of any single personality decisive influence on the progress of a debility which, despite temporary improvements, grew cumulatively worse over three centuries. Catastrophes there were: the premature death of Henry VI in 1197, the contest for the throne between two rival candidates from 1198 to 1207, the Great Interregnum from 1254 to 1273, when Germany knew no effective king at all, the murder of Albert I in 1308, which fatally postponed the hope of a hereditary monarchy: yet the catastrophes did not cause, but merely accentuated, an idiosyncrasy of the German constitution which had already become inveterate. The crown weakened: the corollary was the growth of the power of the nobles and especially of that superior class among them to which, after Frederick Barbarossa's reorganization of the feudal order, the name of princes may properly be given.

In the Swiss area, as elsewhere, the absence of continuous effective royal control favoured particularism. To this there was no tribal basis. The duchy of Alemannia which came to life again at the beginning of the tenth century persisted (often under the alternative name of Swabia) for more than 350 years. But it was not the supreme organization of the whole Alemannian people; the duke was a royal officer rather than a tribal leader, and for long periods the office remained in the hands of members of the royal family. Moreover, by the end of the eleventh century Alemannia had begun to disintegrate politically, for its dukes lost their hold south of the Rhine. During his struggle with the papacy the emperor Henry IV was opposed in Germany by an anti-king, Rudolf of Rheinfelden, duke of Swabia, elected by the princes, who, after Rudolf's death,[1] supported the claims of Berthold II of Zähringen to the duchy, to which Henry had appointed Frederick of Hohenstaufen. By 1098 peace had been restored in Germany; while the Hohenstaufen retained the duchy of Swabia, as a gesture of reconciliation the Zähringer was allowed to keep the personal title of duke and was enfeoffed with the crown's rights in Zürich and its district. This juncture was critical for Switzerland. As heirs to Rudolf of Rheinfelden the Zähringers had obtained in 1090 considerable possessions to the west of the Aare; though their home was in Breisgau, where they owned much land, the settlement of 1098 had assured the highest title in Swabia to their rivals, the Hohenstaufen. Accordingly, after 1098 the attention of the Zähringers naturally turned to the south of the Rhine, to the attempt to bring their possessions in eastern and western Switzerland as closely as possible together, and as naturally their footing in Zürich tended in time to loosen the connexion between Swiss Alemannia and the rest of the duchy north of the Rhine.

With the Zähringers there appears on the Swiss scene the first and perhaps the most notable of the great families which, by their efforts to create a principality embracing both Alemannian and Burgundian territory, bridged the distinction between these two areas of settlement and so prepared the way for a united Switzerland. Princely attempts at territory building provide the material for much of the political history of Germany from the twelfth century to the fifteenth. Commonly, where one family failed, another succeeded. What gave Switzerland an identity and a history was that here the dynastic effort was defeated by a unique combination of rural and urban communities.

---

[1] In 1080.

What was the cultural and social background to the rise of the Swiss communities? To answer the first part of the question it is necessary to examine the fortunes in Switzerland of the only institution capable, for some centuries after the great invasions, of keeping a spark of the old civilization alive.

The Germanic invaders of the fifth and sixth centuries were neither all nor obdurately heathen; their leaders were often led by a *parvenu* admiration of Roman standards to adopt the new official religion of the empire. But the form of Christianity most comprehensible to them was often the Arian heresy, with its denial of Christ's perfect divinity. Perhaps it was their Arianism which did more to divide the Burgundians from the orthodox provincials among whom they settled than differences of race or language. The advance of heresy in the west was checked and the complications which must have accompanied religious strife between conqueror and conquered were averted by the conversion of the great Frankish war-lord, Clovis, to orthodox Christianity; in contrast to the Arian states in Italy and Spain the Frankish empire henceforward received the full support of the Christian hierarchy, which was almost the sole remaining repository of the administrative traditions of the ancient world. To the Merovingians and the Carolingians the alliance of church and state was fundamental; it provided the most effective means of governing and educating their heterogeneous empire. In the great missionary work which remained to be done, the church could therefore rely on active support and rich endowments from the Frankish rulers.

The bishoprics founded in Switzerland in Roman times had not survived without alteration the coming of the Arian Burgundians and the heathen Alemannians. Before 561, for instance, the bishop of Avenches had lost all of his diocese which lay east of the Aare to the new bishopric of Constance, and at the beginning of the next century he moved his seat to Lausanne. And the theoretical completeness of diocesan organization cannot disguise how limited was the hold of Christianity on Switzerland during the first centuries of the German occupation. The bishops, when they were not engaged on missionary journeys, sat within their cathedral cities —Geneva, Lausanne, Sion, Chur, and Constance; outside these centres there were few churches, and the same word, *paganus*, could be used to denote a countryman or a heathen. In Switzerland, as elsewhere, the main work of conversion fell to the monasteries. The earliest foundation, St. Maurice in the Valais, dates from 515, but it was a century later that the enthusiasm of the Irish monk missionaries, led by St. Columbanus, gave vital impulse to Swiss monasticism. Spreading from Luxeuil in Burgundy, the influence of Columbanus produced as its first fruit monasteries planted in the wilds of the Jura, at Romainmôtier, Ste. Ursanne, and Moutier-Grandval; from 610 he was active in Alemannian territory, preaching to the Germans and to what remained of the Romanized Celtic population about lakes Zürich and Constance. When he departed for Italy in 623 his favourite follower, Gallus, was too ill to travel and stayed behind. Gallus fixed his cell in the forest solitude east of Arbon, and about him soon congregated others attracted by the fame of his sanctity. This Celtic monastic settlement, with its incoherent constitution and perhaps excessively ascetic customs, achieved no great distinction for a century, till it was reorganized in 747–8 by the Alemannian Otmar as a Benedictine house. By this time it had attracted the attention of the Carolingians, for whom the cultivation of monasticism was in part a device to extend Frankish influence in Alemannia, and henceforth the abbey of St. Gallen flourished.

Alemannia was to know other great monasteries whose reputation was international and in whose prayers tenth-century English kings took steps to be remembered: Reichenau, founded in 724 by the Visigoth Pirminius—to whose influence was due also the foundation of Pfäfers (c. 731)—Rheinau, and, two centuries later, Einsiedeln. Yet St. Gallen may be taken as a master type of the civilizing work of monasticism. By the favour of kings and nobles it grew into a rich and powerful landlord, but also it grandly fulfilled its functions as a centre for the propagation of Christianity and the conservation of the remaining fragments of the culture of antiquity. To St. Gallen and similar foundations, rather than to the bishops, was due the network of parish churches which completed the conversion of eastern Switzerland; monastic example gave the lead to agricultural improvement and to colonization of the forests and the wastes. Above all, in the ninth and tenth centuries St. Gallen reached oecumenical importance as a home of learning. Irish monks, with a tradition of classical scholarship unravaged by Germanic invasion, had given St. Gallen its beginnings, and even after the abbey had shed its Celtic character accomplished Irish scholars and Irish manuscripts found there a refuge from the raiding Norsemen who, from the end of the eighth century, were destroying Ireland's own civilization. But by this time native forces were active at St. Gallen, busied not only in preserving the heritage of the past by copying manuscripts in the *scriptorium*, but also in seeking out new paths in literature. The monk Ekkehard IV, who in the eleventh century continued the abbey history, the *Casus Sancti Galli*, has left an abidingly attractive picture of the intellectual life sustained there in the late ninth century by the three friends Notker Balbulus, Ratpertus, and Tutilo, whose individualities he depicts remarkably. Notker, the accomplished Latin poet and the author of the lively collection of anecdotes concerning Charlemagne, the *Gesta Caroli Magni*, was besides, under French influence, the composer of the first sequences, the free verse forms intended as mnemonics for the modulations of the *Alleluia* in the mass. Tutilo the musician, a cunning carver of ivory, and an early master of those dialogue insertions into the liturgy which were of incalculable importance for the development of medieval drama, had about him, it has been well said, something of a Renaissance *uomo universale*. Ratpertus was a poet as well as an historian. And in the next century the abbey produced Ekkehard, no longer accepted as the author of the epic *Waltharius* but yet a notable religious poet, and his nephew Notker Labeo, perhaps the first writer to use German prose as a vehicle for original expression.

After the middle of the eleventh century the literary bloom passed from St. Gallen. Other institutions, ecclesiastical and lay, were beginning to supersede the monasteries as nurseries of culture in the west, and it is but a reflection of this general process that when the next traces of a Swiss literature appear, towards the end of the twelfth century, its home is now in the courts of the nobility. The great name is that of a layman, Hartmann von Aue, a member of the class of *ministeriales*—fighting men, unfree in legal status, yet hardly distinguishable from the nobility in manner of life and social consideration. Hartmann, from Eglisau in the modern canton of Zürich, with his rhymed Arthurian romances, masterpieces of form, breathes an air of art for art's sake into the twelfth century. To the same social class belonged another Swiss epic writer, Rudolf von Ems, near Chur. On the other hand, a third, Conrad, called from his birthplace von Würzburg, but long resident in Basle, was a member of the *bourgeoisie*, writing for the city patricians. In the other great literary art form of the time, the courtly love lyric, Switzerland produced no practitioner to rank with the giants; the most interesting of the Swiss *Minnesinger*, Johannes Hadlaub, who wrote at Zürich at the beginning of the fourteenth century, resembled Conrad von Würzburg in origin and audience. In literature as in other matters the well-to-do townsmen were by now imitating the ideals and the tastes of the nobility. It was not at a princely court but at Zürich, amid a society of *ministeriales* turned townsmen, that was put together in the early fourteenth century the most extensive of all the lyric anthologies of medieval Germany, the Manesse MS. now at Heidelberg.

Clerical, noble, *bourgeois*: these consecutive phases of Swiss writing reflect a social differentiation of long standing. To make the tale complete must be added the peasant, on whom all rested. He did not find his literature till there emerged in the late fourteenth century that characteristic form of the *Volkslied*, the historical ballad. The ballads recount his victories over the feudal nobility at Sempach and at Näfels. By what path had he come so far?

No longer may we speak of the German invaders of the Roman world as complete barbarians. Neither may we conceive of their settlements as those of egalitarian democracies of free men, replacing the slave exploitations of the empire by the community holdings of the clan. Among Alemannians and Burgundians there is early evidence of wide social and economic inequalities; the chiefs who led the migrations took a large part of the profits of conquest for themselves and for their close companions in arms; lesser free men did less well, and behind them came a train of the unfree, placed in the power of others by their birth, their crimes, or by the misfortunes of war. In the new order imposed on the Swiss area by the German occupation, lordship of man over man appeared as an elementary fact, as it had done in Celtic and Romano–Celtic times.

It remained a dominant note in social relationships throughout the middle ages and beyond, in Switzerland as over the greater part of western Europe. The common unit of rural economy became the manor, the lord's great holding, cultivated by the labour services of dependants to whom he granted some portion of his lands for their subsistence. In composition this labour force, comprising the mass of Europe's peasantry, was heterogeneous almost beyond comprehension. Some of its members were of servile origin, the mere chattels of the lord, to be sold and married at his discretion, yet found more prolific and more profitable workers if established on lands which they could till for themselves than if treated simply as household slaves. Others had been small free men whom economic stresses, the disorders of society, or the naked pressure of a powerful neighbour had forced to commend their free lands to some lord's protection; they had given up their lands to him and then received them back to hold as tenants by rents and services. Power attracted service, or could impel it, however much the arbitrary exercise of power might be restrained by the growth of customary guarantees for the dependant. Perhaps this much may safely be said of manorialism in general. For its particular aspects in Switzerland the sources are scanty until the fourteenth century, and arguments from analogy are obviously dangerous. In the absence of more convincing evidence the conventional account may serve, but only as a frame and not as a picture. Manorialism was widespread but not ubiquitous; it was less a system than an almost infinite series of local expedients whereby lordship was exercised in the economic sphere; its organization was not static but subject to the influence of changing economic conditions.

Other men who escaped the material tie to the lord and kept their lands free, yet fell under his judicial control, for lordship was as avid of jurisdiction as of land. At the height of its power the Frankish monarchy had been able to maintain a comprehensive system of public justice; under the early Carolingians, for instance, we can think of the empire as divided into circumscriptions (*pagi*: *Gaue*) in which the counts as royal officials not only exercised the king's authority over all free men, but also presided—in person, or represented by the hundredmen—over the popular courts in which these free men came together to judge their peers. But even in Carolingian times these popular courts of the hundred, under the supervision of the royal officials, had no monopoly of justice. Elements of seigneurial jurisdiction were already apparent. The lord had exclusive right of judgement over his serfs, for they were his chattels; he held his court, too, for disputes relating to the holdings of his tenants, free as well as unfree.

It was with these seigneurial courts that the future lay. The efficiency of the county organization and of the popular courts under the royal officials declined with the power of the German monarchy. The counts came to regard the performance of their functions less as an office held from the king than as a right, a source of profit and power, inherent in themselves and transmissible to their descendants. Meanwhile, the competence of the count's courts was being eaten away by royal grants of immunity. Great ecclesiastical and lay proprietors secured the exemption of their lands from the count's control. From the area over which immunity had been granted the royal officials were excluded; henceforward it was the lord who here exercised the jurisdiction of the count, and though in so doing he was in theory acting as a delegate of the king, in practice the right came to be looked upon as his personal pertinence. Immunity, which had perhaps originated as a device to strengthen royal supervision of justice, degenerated, as the monarchy weakened, into an abdication by the king of his prerogative to see justice done to all his free subjects; the lords added to their manorial and tenurial courts an almost uncontrolled franchisal jurisdiction.

The extent of the lords' judicial power did not end here; it spread even beyond their possessions and their immunities. Limitations in administrative technique reduced government in western Europe during the early middle ages to a series of personal relationships. There was not sufficient literacy to breed a bureaucracy, nor the regular revenues to pay one, and even had a bureaucracy come into existence, it is doubtful whether the state of communications would have allowed it to work. The great landowner could be brought into at least theoretic subordination to the crown by the institutions of feudalism, and through him the king could hope to exercise some authority over the sub-vassals. But what of the small free man who remained outside the feudal hierarchy, holding his land of no man, not as a fief but as allod? The county organization which was intended at once to control and to protect him in the name of the king broke down. It was the lord who filled the breach by offering his protection to, or imposing it on, those who were bound to him by no tenurial ties. The lord as protector (in Latin *advocatus*: in German *Vogt*) made himself responsible to higher authority for the conduct of his protégés, but to balance this responsibility he assumed over them those rights of jurisdiction which he had inherited or usurped from the collapse of the county organization. Frequently thereby the protected suffered a diminution of freedom; invariably there resulted an extension of seigneurial rights beyond the geographical limits of the lord's lands and immunities. Thus the protectorate became an essential part of his power. In these ways, in south-west Germany between the ninth century and the thirteenth the most important element of medieval government, jurisdiction, passed almost completely from the control of the royal officials into that of the great land-owners. In effect the county organization was replaced by a regime of protectorates and seigneurial rights.

This concentration of power in the hands of the lord bore heavily on the legal and economic independence of the free peasantry. An often-quoted passage in the annals of the abbey of Muri in Aargau throws light on the sort of thing which was happening in eleventh-century Switzerland. Some peasants of the village of Wolen, free men owning their own free land, sought the protection of a powerful lord called Guntramm. They surrendered their lands to him and received them back to hold for rents. But once they were his tenants Guntramm began to make additional demands from them: labour services on his demesne and pay-ments for the use of the forest. Protests, even an appeal to the king, proved useless; when the village of Wolen passed into the posses-sion of the abbey of Muri the services of the formerly free peasants had become customary and the abbey continued to exact them.

It is certain that this was no isolated incident; violence and fraud played their part in the extension of lordship, and lordship often found it profitable to force down the status of its dependants. But complete loss of liberty was not the uniform and general fate of the peasantry throughout the Swiss area; it may be assumed—though the fact has recently been much disputed—that in parts of Switzerland free cultivators persisted throughout the middle ages from the time of the Germanic settlements onwards.

Three factors helped to bring this about. In the first place natural conditions made pastoral agriculture the dominant mode in Switzerland. In arable districts, where the lord had a demesne, he was faced by the problem of finding labour to till it. Not until the thirteenth century does he seem to have resorted to wage labour; instead, he used the labour services of his tenants. It was, therefore, essential that these services should be abundant, and there was thus an incentive to bind the dependent cultivators as closely as possible to the manor, with evil effects on their personal freedom. But for the large part of Switzerland given over to pastoral life the demesne was far less important and the need for labour services, though still present, was less urgent. Thus a factor which elsewhere worked powerfully against peasant freedom here lost much of its cogency.

Secondly, the German settlements of Switzerland had not been intensive. The lowlands were occupied first, for they lay most conveniently in the path of the invaders who only slowly penetrated into the inner Alpine valleys. There thus remained ample room for colonization, and that possibility was commonly favourable to peasant independence. If the lord proved too exigent, his tenants might fairly readily find land elsewhere: that was a consideration which may well have limited his demands, and even when it did not, it may have provoked the peasantry to remove themselves from his power. Much colonization was, of course, the result of the enterprise and activity of the lords themselves, who sought to increase their revenues by opening up new lands. In this case, the lords would expect to maintain control over the settlements due to their initiative, but even so the peasant colonists could probably obtain advantageous terms. This was certainly true of the German-speaking settlers who were attracted into Grisons from the upper Valais in the thirteenth century and later. The feudatories of Grisons who promoted these migrations in order to increase their military resources, found it necessary to endow the new settlers with liberties far more extensive than those enjoyed by the native peasantry; for instance, the lower jurisdiction over the new communities was pretty generally exercised by an official (*Amman*) whom the 'free Valaisans' had themselves chosen.

Lastly, the pressure of lordship was in some sense relieved by the competition of another allegiance. Medieval agriculture demanded much communal decision and control. If arable farming were carried out on the open-field system, there had to be regulation of the times of ploughing, harvest, and grazing; it was equally important that the use of the forest and waste, which played so vital a part in medieval economy, should be managed in the general interest; the open mountain pastures, the alps, had to be protected from ruinous exploitation by the individual. Thus in any agricultural area common interests called for some form of communal organization comprising all the inhabitants, whether free or unfree, whether dependent or not on a manor. This agricultural community was not necessarily co-terminous with any single manor or lordship. The local lord might make his influence strongly felt within it; he might assert his ownership over the lands it occupied and make his manorial court the instance for enforcing the decisions of the communal assembly. But he could not dispense with it, nor could he destroy it, for its functions were essential. The community of associated agriculturalists retained its collective life; though its primary purpose was economic, in areas where lordship was weak or absent it came to show itself capable of assuming political responsibility.

The early history of the agricultural community in Switzerland is obscure. To call it a *Markgenossenschaft* would perhaps tie to it too strict a technical term, of which the sense is bedevilled by learned controversy. In the one area of Switzerland from which any considerable body of evidence for the agrarian conditions of the early middle ages has survived, the possessions of the abbey of St. Gallen, the *Markgenossenschaft* strictly defined makes its appearance comparatively late, and there are indications that this may be true also of the cantons round lake Lucerne. Yet there is certainly evidence of some form of communal organization, for which we may suppose an economic basis, in the central valleys of Switzerland as early as the tenth century.

Although by no means all the rights which the lords came to exercise were derived from the ownership of land, territorial possessions formed the hard core of lordship. They were often widely dispersed, a manor or group of manors here and there, as accidents of marriage or inheritance or purchase had determined. Convenience and efficiency, it might seem, demanded that the lords should consolidate their scattered holdings. In fact they do not appear to have been much concerned to do this. There were some purely economic advantages in maintaining estates strewn over a wide area, and in any case, from the twelfth century onwards, with the growing evidence of weakness in the central government of Germany, the lords' interests had become political rather than economic. They aimed at rising above mere landownership to the creation of a sphere of power; they sought possession of castles, strategic points on important routes, regalian rights of toll and criminal jurisdiction, protectorates over churches and monasteries, which would allow them to dominate a far wider area than they could hope to possess as landlords. Their manors provided the economic, and sometimes the strategic, foundation for these ambitions; manorial dependants were valuable only in so far as they enabled the lord's lands to be profitably cultivated.

This attitude was modified as a result of the large-scale changes in the economy of western Europe which began in the eleventh century. The new intensification of exchanges, the break-down of local self-sufficiencies in European life made money more desirable. By the middle of the thirteenth century the lords in south-west Germany had discovered that their dependants were patient of taxation, and that therefore it was wise to multiply their numbers. Thus impetus was given to the process of expanding lordship into sovereign territorial power over as wide an area as possible and of converting dependence in all its varieties into a uniform subjection to the *dominus terrae*. At the same time the lords took steps to increase the efficiency of their rule; castles became the centres of new administrative divisions; rights and revenues began to be more rigorously ascertained, recorded, and exacted. Admirable instruments for this new policy were found among the *ministeriales*,[1] the *Dienstadel*, who formed as close an approximation to a class of professional administrators as Germany had yet seen, and whom servile origin, despite their social rank, made the more obedient to the lords to whom they belonged. Government in Germany became more intensive in the twelfth and thirteenth centuries than it had ever been before. It was ceasing to be a mere matter of personal relationships between suzerain and vassal, lord and serf, and was coming to mean, however imperfectly as yet, supreme and exclusive control of a definite area by a ruling dynasty. But it must be emphasized, this was mainly a regional and particularist development in the German constitution. The chief authors and beneficiaries of the change were the lords and not the crown.

This was the result of the debility of the German monarchy. And while in some parts of Germany, in Bavaria, for instance, and in Austria, there was a single personage, the duke, able to use his exalted office to monopolize the advantages of the new tendency and to ensure that it was the duchy which should be the unit of

[1] See p. 52 above.

effective government, matters stood differently in Switzerland. Burgundian Switzerland had no duke, and the 'rectorate' which the German kings established there did not survive the extinction of the Zähringer dynasty in 1218; in Alemannia south of the Rhine the duchy of Swabia, in the hands of the Hohenstaufen, played no effective part from the end of the eleventh century until it expired in 1268. So in Switzerland the way was left open for less eminent lords to take upon themselves the task of building territories: members of such families as Lenzburg, Kiburg, Froburg, Habsburg, Toggenburg, and Savoy. Commonly they called themselves counts, but it is useless to seek continuity between their attributes and those of the counts of Carolingian times. The latter were royal officials, whose title implied definite functions exercised in the name of the crown; to the counts of the twelfth and thirteenth centuries the title itself, which in some cases was self-bestowed, meant little. In some instances they might find that the right of high justice was the decisive element in ensuring their sovereign control over an area; in others, it was comparatively unimportant. The territories which were being created in these centuries had no single root, no single principle of legitimacy. Terms of power, not terms of law, describe the process. It was in their character as lords and protectors over land and men in general that the dynasts found the resources to build their sovereignties.

It would be rash to apply the word 'state' to these constructions: perhaps even 'territory' is too definite a term. That is what some of them will indisputably have become by the fifteenth century. But in the thirteenth they were rather aspirations than achievements; they still lacked geographical homogeneity and stability, and they were at the mercy of dynastic accident. A well-contrived marriage might augment them; plurality of heirs might lead to partition and disintegration. And, of course, not all lords became territorial rulers: death and debts progressively thinned the ranks of the competitors. The causes of the genetic decay which overtook so many of the older noble families of south Germany in the twelfth and thirteenth centuries are more obscure than those of their economic embarrassment. The increasing exchanges, the 'buoyancy of the prices' of the time, were onerous to the less resourceful of the seigneurial families. For the sake of class prestige they were forced to maintain a higher standard of life than before, but their revenues came mainly from land, and were fixed by custom hard to change. If they failed to open up new sources of income from colonization and taxation, or to tap the profits of trade by erecting tolls and founding towns, they were apt to fall into debt from which they could free themselves only by pawning or selling the lands and jurisdictions on which their power was based. In these ways, from the twelfth century to the fourteenth, many a promising embryonic territory came to nothing. For the 'territory' was still no more than a complex of public and private possessions, rights, and jurisdictions, of most disparate origin and scattered location. Only the grip of the dynast held it together; if the grip relaxed there was always a neighbouring family ready to seize the opportunity.

Ecclesiastical corporations were immune from many of the accidents which befell lay dynasties. Yet on the whole the church in Switzerland failed to convert its great possessions in land and lordship into sovereignty. The failure can be explained by the extent to which the churchmen were forced to submit to lay protection. Just as the dynasts imposed their protectorate over the small free man, so they made themselves the protectors (*advocati*: *Vögte*) of the churches and monasteries. There were duties of lordship which ecclesiastics might well feel diffident about undertaking: the armed defence of their lands, the execution of judgements of blood, and so forth. Such matters would be referred to a lay *advocatus*, who, if he were to be useful, would have to be powerful, and who, though he might have obtained the office as a fief, would be tempted to regard it as an absolute possession. Thus within the ecclesiastical lordships there tended to develop a kind of dyarchy between the churchmen and their lay protectors. The bishop or monastery might, for instance, be found retaining the yields of the manors and the right of low justice, while the *advocatus* held the high justice and a general right of protection—for which he exacted a tax—over all the dependants of the lordship against the outside world. Such a division of competence would provide the *advocatus* with a valuable means of extending his dynastic power, but it gravely hampered attempts on the part of the churchmen to make territories out of their lordships. The abbey of St. Gallen succeeded, and likewise the bishops of Basle, Constance, Geneva, and Lausanne, yet these ecclesiastical territories could never rival in extent or in aggressive capacity those of the four lay dynasties which in turn took the lead in the struggle for power in Switzerland—Zähringen, Kiburg, Savoy, and Habsburg.

Dynastic history must be largely a matter of genealogical detail and the minute enumeration of the gain and loss of estates and jurisdictions. But the story of the Zähringers is redeemed from aridity by the surprising scale on which they worked. The homeland of the dynasty was in Breisgau and the Black Forest, where it demonstrated such remarkable capacity in the extension and consolidation of its possessions that historians have talked freely —and perhaps unwisely—of a Zähringer 'state' in the twelfth century. By displaying the same qualities in the acquisitions which they made at the end of the eleventh century to the south of the Rhine,[2] the Zähringers linked the fates of German and Romance Switzerland. In 1127 Conrad V of Zähringen obtained from the German king the title of 'rector' of the Burgundian kingdom, to which little attention had been paid since its union with the German crown in 1033. Conrad was unable to make his vice-regal title effective to the west of the Jura, and later in the century the emperor Frederick Barbarossa took that part of the Burgundian problem into his own hands. But in Transjurane Burgundy at least, the Zähringers found their rectorate a valuable *point d'appui*. Here the crown lands of the kings of Burgundy had fallen after 1033 to the German king; the rectorate helped the Zähringers to bring these lands under their control as imperial fiefs and so to augment the already considerable possessions which had come to them as allods from the inheritance of Rudolf of Rheinfelden. The mesh of Zähringer power was stretched over the Swiss plateau from the edge of the Bernese Oberland as far west as lake Neuchâtel, transcending the legal and linguistic boundary between Burgundian and Alemannian. To confirm strategic mastery and to increase their revenues the Zähringers founded towns and gave privileges to towns already *im Werden*: on their own lands, Fribourg, where an important trade route crossed the river Saane; Thun, at the head of its lake; Burgdorf, on the Emme: on their imperial fiefs, Berne, where the windings of the Aare formed an easily defensible peninsula. They fortified at Laupen and Gümmenen further keys to the crossings of the Saane and

[2] See p. 49 above.

also the advanced position of Morat; their activity extended to the Pays de Vaud, to Yverdon, and Moudon.

In the breadth and energy of their territory building, and especially in their promotion of towns, the Zähringers were leading the tendencies of the time. If the Germanic invasions greatly reduced they did not wholly destroy the rich town life of the Roman occupation. Problems of continuity are dark, but in the ninth century Geneva, Lausanne, Solothurn, Chur, and Zürich are to be found enjoying a limited prosperity, mostly as centres of ecclesiastical administration; episcopal business had given Basle and Sion more importance than they had known in Roman times; round the monasteries at St. Gallen and Lucerne and Schaffhausen wholly new settlements had arisen with some of the characteristics of towns. The great expansion of western Europe's trade in the late eleventh and the twelfth centuries gave impetus to the increase and complication of urban life. Merchants multiplied in number and importance, and their purposes demanded facilities for congregating at convenient places along the trade routes where·they might enjoy a greater security and a wider freedom than were to be found in a manorialized country-side. The lords were quick to see the advantages to be gained by founding on their lands new commercial settlements with town law, for merchants were a source of tolls and taxes and loans, and the permanent garrisons within the town fortifications had military value for the defence of the still loose territorial complexes. Therefore the Zähringers' example was widely followed; a raging fashion for the systematic foundation of towns, generally in connexion with an existing settlement or castle, seized the Swiss dynasts. At the beginning of the thirteenth century German Switzerland possessed some sixteen towns; by the end the number had reached eighty. The foundations of three families may serve as a sample to save the tedium of a complete enumeration. To the Kiburgers, Winterthur, Diessenhofen, Frauenfeld, Zug, Aarau, Baden, Lenzburg, Mellingen, and Sursee owed their town status; to the Habsburgs, Brugg, Laufenburg, and Bremgarten. In the first half of the thirteenth century the Froburgers gave town privileges to a series of settlements dominating the routes over the Jura by the upper and lower Hauenstein: to Zofingen, Olten, Liestal, Waldenburg, Friedau, Wiedlisbach, and Aarburg.

Fashion went too far. Many of these new foundations had

neither important industries nor an adequate local market area; they were condemned from the start to insignificance, and depended for their livelihood largely on agricultural activity. Dwarf towns with some 200–1,000 inhabitants enjoyed a legal status somewhat superior to that of the surrounding country-side, but were in no position to shake off the control of the lords who had founded them. But others, like Basle, Zürich, Schaffhausen, Solothurn, Lucerne, Fribourg, Berne, and St. Gallen—all in existence before the close of the twelfth century—did rise to more than local economic importance. And in them the number and prosperity of the citizens or some peculiarity of social structure within the town might lead to a demand for self-government through officials who were no longer the lord's nominees but the chosen representatives of the townspeople. For such communal independence a pattern lay near, in Lombardy, where the towns, having freed themselves from the rule of their lords by the first half of the twelfth century, in the second had successfully defended their freedom against the greatest of the Hohenstaufen emperors. In Switzerland progress was slower, but here from the beginning of the thirteenth century in some of the larger towns the elected organ of the citizens, the council, is to be found contending for superiority with the seigneurial officials. Towns whose lords were weak and distant—e.g. Lucerne, which belonged to the abbey of Murbach in Alsace—and especially towns such as Berne and Zürich, which depended directly from an empire now enfeebled, contested, or vacant, had gone far on the road to communal autonomy by the end of the thirteenth century.

The promises of unity and vigorous rule for the Swiss area inherent in the policy of the Zähringers were dashed by the extinction of the dynasty in 1218. To say that their exertions had prevented the creation of a territory in western Switzerland by either the Hohenstaufen or by the bishops of Basle is too negative an estimate; they left behind, if not a political testament, at least an indication how the Swiss plateau might be welded together politically. But that the basis of their power was personal is shown by the dispersion of their possessions after 1218; their imperial fiefs fell back to the emperor, and their allodial lands south of the Rhine went to increase the territories of their relatives by marriage, the Kiburgers.

This family had been settled in Thurgau since the eleventh century; by the last quarter of the twelfth the fortunes of marriage and inheritance had made it preponderant in northern Switzerland. The Kiburgers were counts and great lords in Thurgau; they held Baden and Aarau in Aargau, and Arth and Zug. Their power was extended by protectorates over the monasteries of Beromünster in Aargau and Schännis north of the Walensee; in west Switzerland the Zähringer inheritance brought them Fribourg, Thun, Burgdorf, and more. About 1250 these lordships were divided between uncle and nephew: Hartmann IV took the ancestral possessions in Thurgau and Zürichgau; Hartmann V, Zug and Arth and what lay west of the Reuss. With Zähringer lands the younger Hartmann had acquired some tinge of Zähringer traditions. Profiting by the collapse of the Hohenstaufen empire he was eager to lay hands on the imperial fiefs in Burgundy; in 1253 he seized Laupen and Grasburg, and designed to make Berne and Morat and the Haslital his own.

Again failure of the dynasty destroyed a budding territory. In 1263 Hartmann V died, leaving only an infant daughter, Anna; a year later Hartmann IV, to whom his wife Margaret of Savoy had given no children, died also. The double question of Anna's wardship, and what portion of Hartmann IV's possessions was to fall to his widow, held matter of conflict between Burgundian and Alemannian interests, and, indeed, between Burgundian and Alemannian law. It was fought out between Peter, count of Savoy, Margaret's brother, and Rudolf IV, count of Habsburg, nephew of Hartmann IV: both, as they showed on wider stages, politicians of consummate ability.

His contemporaries nicknamed Peter 'the little Charlemagne', but this very junior cadet of the house of Savoy had few of the initial advantages of the Frankish emperor. He had reached the age of sixty before he secured control of the county of Savoy in 1263, and until then he had only a younger son's portion and his own capacity with which to make his way. One great stroke of fortune helped: the marriage of his niece Eleanor of Provence to Henry III in 1236 opened to him a career of distinction and gain in England as adviser to the crown. From 1240 to 1263 he is to be found playing an important part in the constitutional debate and in shaping English foreign policy. Yet at the same time Peter was active nearer home, creating for himself a territory to the north of lake Geneva, where Savoy had first set foot at Moudon in 1207. By policy and force, from 1237 onwards, he mastered the numerous small feudatories of the Pays de Vaud, the heart of Romanized Switzerland, and the impetus of success carried his attention further northwards and eastwards. In order to escape the grasp of Hartmann V of Kiburg the imperial towns Berne and Morat put themselves under Peter's protection in 1255; he received the Haslital in fee from the German king William of Holland; in 1257 the election (albeit disputed) as German king of his relation and long associate in English affairs, Richard of Cornwall, gave hope of further favours, of which the token in earnest was the grant of the imperial strong-place Gümmenen in 1259. The plans of the Zähringers seemed on the point of realization, though now from the west under a Burgundian ruler. Thus the problem of the Kiburgers' inheritance was crucial for Peter; could he but acquire their possessions in western Switzerland the possibility of unifying the Swiss plateau lay open before him.

As brother of Hartmann IV's widow, Peter had some legal grounds for moving; he could probably rely on such support as the German monarchy, in Richard of Cornwall's hands, could give. Against his competitor—Rudolf IV of Habsburg—he held his own in the field during the hostilities which dragged out their course from 1265 to 1267. But in 1268 Peter died, and his death robbed Savoyard policy of its driving force. It was the Habsburgs who won the main part of the Kiburg inheritance, and so became the dominant family in Switzerland.

Between Lenzburg and Windisch a ridge of the Jura approaches the right bank of the lower Aare. On it stands the Habsburg— *Habichtsburg*: the castle of the hawk—built about 1020 by the Alsatian Bishop Werner of Strasbourg to protect lands held by his family since the tenth century. The site of the new fortification was admirably chosen. Within a few miles there met the rivers Aare, Reuss, and Limmat, offering access by their valleys to the plateau, to lake Lucerne and to Zürich. This 'water-gate of Switzerland' was dominated by the Habsburg, from which Werner's descendants took a name notable in Europe's history for six and a half centuries. The nucleus of their Swiss possessions lay about the castle, in a triangle of which the apex was formed by the confluence of the Aare and the Reuss and the base by the lands of the abbey of Muri, over which the Habsburgs exercised proprietorial rights as founders. Protectorate over another monastery brought Habsburg influence into central Switzerland; in 1135 Werner III of Habsburg, count of Alsace, appears as *advocatus* of the Alsatian abbey of Murbach, which owned manors scattered along the route from Basle to lake Lucerne. A further increase of Habsburg power in this area came in 1173, for with the extinction of the Lenzburg dynasty in that year the Habsburgs secured the reversion of some of its possessions: Sempach and Willisau, and the comital rights in Zürichgau, which carried with them powers of public jurisdiction over the valleys in Schwyz and Nidwalden.

Alsace, Aargau, central Switzerland: these were the regions where Habsburg influence was strongest, to judge by the provisions of the treaty regulating the succession to Count Rudolf II, who died in 1232. While this treaty maintained the principle, so dear to the Habsburgs, of an indivisible family holding of all the Habsburg possessions, it did distinguish spheres of administration for the two sons of Rudolf II. The elder, Albert IV, gained a predominant position in the county of Aargau, and was to hold Habsburg and Brugg, Bremgarten, Meienberg, and Säckingen on the Rhine; the younger, Rudolf III, took Laufenburg on the Rhine (from which his line came later to be called Habsburg-Laufenburg), while the main comital rights in Zürichgau gave him control over central Switzerland, including Schwyz and Nidwalden; the imperial fiefs held by the family in Alsace continued to be held in common. To repair the dilapidation of the dynasty's strength caused by this administrative division; to consolidate the three discrete areas of Habsburg influence into a single whole, and thus to obtain control over the whole length of the newly opened St. Gotthard route from the Alps to the Rhine; to subject this territory to a uniform and efficient administration: these were the aims with which Count Rudolf IV succeeded his father Albert IV as head of the senior line in 1239 or 1240.

They were worthy of the powers of perhaps the greatest Habsburg of all time. What distinguishes Rudolf IV is his extraordinary appetite for acquisition and the genius with which he satisfied it. From his father he inherited no more than seven lordships; within ten years of his death his heirs possessed fifty in south-west Germany alone. The first great increment came from his successful intervention in the question of the Kiburg inheritance. From

Hartmann IV's portion Diessenhofen, Winterthur, and Frauenfeld soon fell to Habsburg, but even after the death of Peter of Savoy the problem of Hartmann V's heiress, Rudolf's ward Anna, remained unsettled. In 1273 Rudolf at last found the solution: he married Anna to his cousin, Eberhard I of Habsburg-Laufenburg, while by way of beneficial purchase to indemnify himself for the expenses of guardianship he received from Anna all the Kiburg possessions east of the Aare—that is to say, the Kiburg towns in Aargau, and Sursee, Zug, and Arth—and from Eberhard I the rights of Habsburg-Laufenburg over Willisau and Sempach, Schwyz and Nidwalden. In Aargau, Thurgau, and central Switzerland Rudolf's position appeared inexpugnable; it remained to secure communications between his Swiss territory and the Habsburg possessions west of the Rhine. That demanded a forcible settlement with the bishop of Basle, whose lands protruded wedge-like to separate Aargau from Alsace. The bishop was being held besieged in his own city when the news was brought in September 1273 that the electoral princes were about to choose Rudolf as German king. 'Lord God, sit tight in heaven', exclaimed Bishop Henry, 'or this Rudolf will usurp your seat.'

IV

THE ORIGINS OF THE CONFEDERATION

IN choosing Rudolf of Habsburg as German king the electoral princes perhaps mistook their man; if so, the grounds of their error are not difficult to understand. Rudolf was not the penniless count which later legend delighted to make him; his possessions in south-west Germany were great and growing. Neither was he yet in the first class of territorial magnates; he was not even of princely rank. What the electors seem to have had in mind was to provide Germany with a king capable of rescuing the crown from nullity but not expected to interfere seriously in the process by which the princes were becoming sovereign within their own territories.

The circumstances of the first three-quarters of the thirteenth century had accelerated this tendency. A final most acute phase of the struggle between papacy and empire had been provoked by the Italian schemes of Frederick II (1212–50), and it was in Italy that the Hohenstaufen dynasty found its end in 1268. The German throne which the Hohenstaufen had deserted overtly in 1251— and in practice even before—was occupied uneasily by papal anti-kings or competed for by rival foreign princes. None of them secured much more than a local following in Germany, where effective central power had ceased to exist well before 1254, the date conventionally given for the beginning of the Great Interregnum. The magnates did not neglect these opportunities. What royal rights the king could not be persuaded to grant away to them they simply usurped; contested elections enhanced the position of the electoral princes and overshadowed the hereditary element in the making of the German monarch. When the Interregnum was brought to an end by Rudolf's election in 1273, to many his prospects must have seemed those of a respectable liquidator of a bankrupt institution.

Rudolf declined this modest part. He was determined to revive the monarchy, and he understood perfectly what was necessary to enable him to do this. The king must become stronger than the princes in terms of their strength: that is to say, he must acquire territorial preponderance in Germany. And hereditary succession to the throne must be established in order to put an end to those dismal alienations of royal authority to the princes which had become the normal accompaniment of every election. After a critical half-century the scheme of a Habsburg hereditary monarchy came to nothing, and with it faded the last chance of a unified Germany in the middle ages. But in the meantime the power of the house of Habsburg had been enormously extended by the unrelenting exercise of royal right. The most striking example came early in Rudolf's reign. Between 1276 and 1278 he turned all the resources of kingship to dispossess Ottokar king of Bohemia of the duchies of Austria, Styria, and Carinthia, and Carniola and the Wendish Mark; in 1282 he enfeoffed his sons with the most desirable of these forfeitures, Austria and Styria. Henceforward, Habsburg and Austria will be interchangeable terms; in the rich colonial lands of the east the dynasty had gained an immense addition to its real power which in turn might be put to the business of governing Germany.

These changes in the Habsburgs' fortunes had repercussions in the area where they had first come to prominence. Before 1273 Rudolf had been the most powerful and possessive dynast in south-west Germany, but one avenue of escape had remained open to those whose independence he threatened: to some extent they could rely on the support of the German crown. Now this resource was gone, for dynast and German king were one. Wider preoccupations as king had not caused Rudolf to lose his interest in Switzerland, where he continued to acquire whatever he could: thus in 1277 he bought the lordship over Fribourg from the house of Kiburg-Burgdorf, and in 1291 the town of Lucerne from the abbey of Murbach. After 1285 there are hints of more comprehensive intentions; while Austria and the eastern lands were to be the portion of Rudolf's eldest son Albert, for the second, Rudolf, an appanage in the west was to be created, a revival of the duchy of Swabia, or of the old kingdom of Burgundy. For this the way was prepared in the Swiss area by a confusion of royal and dynastic rights which was probably deliberate; administration of both was in the hands of the same Habsburg officials who were less intent on distinguishing the capacities in which they were acting— whether as instruments of the king or of the Habsburg family— than on creating a system of government which would please their master. Old freedoms were threatened by submersion beneath the uniformity of a Habsburg 'state'. In the reaction to this danger of various communities with traditions of independence are to be found the origins of the Swiss confederation.

The communities immediately concerned were those of the valleys about lake Lucerne in central Switzerland: Uri, Schwyz, and Unterwalden, which may be called by anticipation the forest cantons.[1] Though great landowners had their manors and their serfs in these valleys, Uri, Schwyz, and Unterwalden contained a considerable element of free peasantry. The origins and antiquity of this 'freedom'—which must be understood in the relative sense proper to the times—are still matters of dispute. The theory that the free peasants to be found in the central valleys in the thirteenth century descended from free communities established on crown lands in the forest wastes south of lake Zürich by the Merovingians, in order to act as frontier guards to the Frankish empire, is attractive but hardly sufficiently substantiated; recent attempts to show that many of the peasants of Uri owed their freedom to the fact that they were colonists, and that this may well have been true of the other valleys also, have not been wholly successful. Whatever the origin of this free element—which it is simpler, and perhaps safer, to regard as persisting from the time of the Germanic occupation—its importance, together with the necessity of the co-operation of all in the details of Alpine economy, had early promoted in the valleys the fusion of all the inhabitants into communities which in some sense overrode, though they did not abolish, the ordinary divisions of feudal lordship. The name of the valley ceased to be merely the expression of a geographical area or even of the totality of its inhabitants, some of whom might depend economically and legally on one lord, some on another, and many on no lord at all. Comprehending both these senses, it came to denote something more: an entity in its own right with a will and consciousness of its own, a *universitas*, as the thirteenth century would call it. As early as 955 the men of Uri felt that they had attained the legal personality of a community.

The emergence of a community of this kind did not, of course,

---

[1] *Waldstätte*—the forest place—as a collective title for Uri, Schwyz, and Unterwalden was first used officially in 1309. The term 'canton' to denote a member of the confederation was imported from France, hardly before the middle of the fifteenth century.

imply its political independence any more than the corporate nature of a medieval town necessarily excluded the dominance of a lord. The degree of freedom enjoyed by the valley community, the *Talschaft*, was determined by the extent to which it had to suffer within itself the exercise of political rights by external instances. At the beginning of the thirteenth century in Uri, Schwyz, and Unterwalden[2] the title to the most important of these rights—justice—was in the hands of the great dynasties of the neighbourhood. As *Reichsvögte* of Zürich the Zähringers had the oversight of justice in Uri; in succession to the Lenzburg dynasty the Habsburgs had become in 1173 counts in Zürichgau, and so possessed a general jurisdiction of public origin throughout the valleys of Schwyz and Nidwalden in addition to their normal rights of seigneurial justice over the dependants of the manors which they held there.

How far the dynasts' title to jurisdiction was put into practice is a question which admits no easy answer. They had the right to appoint the judges, but they were dealing with men predominantly free and geographically remote; moreover, it was a principle of the customary law of Swabia that the lord's choice of judges needed the approval of his subjects. Though the evidence is not conclusive it may perhaps be assumed that the men who dispensed the most common form of justice—the low justice, into which judgements of blood did not enter, in contrast to the high justice, into which they did—although they were appointed and invested with their powers by the *Reichsvogt* of Uri, or in Schwyz and Nidwalden by Habsburg as count of Zürichgau, were chosen among the natives of the valleys and were accepted by them. In the thirteenth century each valley has several of these *Ammänner* exercising the low justice over the free men and in some sense representing both the overlord and the community; to one among them some sort of superiority came to be attributed, and to him in time was given the title of *Landamman*. Under these conditions the extent to which the overlords interfered in the affairs of the valleys must have depended very largely on the power and inclinations of the individual dynast, to whom in any case the

[2] The use of the name Unterwalden at this period, though convenient, is not strictly accurate. It would seem that the two valleys Ob- and Nidwalden remained separate for most of the thirteenth century. They coalesced in 1291–2 and formed a unity till 1333 when each again in many respects went its own way.

right of high justice was reserved, for it was he who held the *Blutbann* from the king.

The more distant the overlord the greater would be the freedom enjoyed by the valley and the more certain that with the *Ammänner* the interests of the community rather than those of the overlord would predominate. In thirteenth-century Germany the most distant overlord possible to imagine was the highest of all, the German king. The opening of the St. Gotthard route to Lombardy had given the Hohenstaufen rulers, obsessed by their Italian schemes, a lively concern with the valleys through which the pass was approached from the north. Uri benefited from this circumstance in 1231. After the Zähringers had died out in 1218 the protectorate over the valley had fallen back to the crown, by which it was pawned at some unknown date to the Habsburgs. But in 1231 a royal privilege declared the pawn redeemed; Uri was, and should permanently remain, immediately subject to the empire. And though it is extremely probable that the initiative here had lain with the crown, as a measure to secure its communications with Italy, the progressive decay of the German kingship transformed the privilege of immediacy into a charter of independence. In title the king was overlord of Uri, and so it was his business to appoint the judges, but in fact, from the middle of the thirteenth century, the community must have provided for itself in this matter, for there was no one else in a position to do so.

The course of the struggle between the emperor Frederick II and the papacy brought about much the same state of affairs in Schwyz. In the administrative division of the Habsburg possessions which followed the death of Rudolf II[3] comital rights over Schwyz and Nidwalden had fallen to the younger line, Habsburg-Laufenburg, whose head Rudolf III adhered to the papalist party against the Hohenstaufen in 1240. Thereupon the emperor Frederick II issued a privilege which removed Schwyz from Rudolf's control by recognizing its immediate dependence on the empire. This privilege, issued when Frederick was already under the ban of the church, could be more easily impugned than the charter of 1231 for Uri; the Habsburgs had a colourable case when they denied its validity and maintained that their rights

[3] See p. 67 above.

over Schwyz persisted unimpaired. But in fact nowhere in the valleys, except perhaps in Obwalden, do the Habsburgs of the younger line seem to have been able to exert much influence. Whether they appointed the *Ammänner* in Schwyz and Nidwalden we do not know. It is highly probable that during the period when Germany was without a generally recognized ruler, from 1254 to 1273, the valleys made much progress towards creating for themselves the organs necessary to exercise those rights of public jurisdiction which dynasts had once held and continued in part to claim.

To this development of valley autonomy the year 1273 brought a double threat. The weak line of Habsburg-Laufenburg sold its claims over Schwyz and Unterwalden to the active and ambitious Rudolf IV of Habsburg;[4] later in the year Rudolf was elected German king. In this capacity, by virtue of the privilege of 1231 he was immediate lord of Uri; by family right he could claim comital rights in Schwyz and Unterwalden, to whom the subterfuge that they were direct dependencies of the crown was useless now that the crown itself was a Habsburg possession. From the Hauenstein to lake Lucerne the St. Gotthard route already lay within Rudolf's grasp; to complete his hold on this increasing source of revenue he needed to incorporate the valleys of central Switzerland in the Habsburg territory south of the Rhine. Rudolf began to take the necessary administrative action; after a generation or more of practical autonomy Uri, Schwyz, and Unterwalden once more experienced the active intervention of lordship.

The necessity of some arrangement for joint action between the valley communities became evident. There was no lack of example. During the decline of their power in the thirteenth century the German kings had encouraged the practice of voluntary confederation. To allow commerce to be carried on amid the clash of dynastic ambitions, to produce conditions of life at all tolerable amid the prevailing disorders, regional associations, *Landfriedensbünde*, had been formed for the preservation of the peace within determinate areas; their members undertook to accept arbitration of disputes among themselves, to observe a common penal code, and to take joint action against breakers of the peace. Such unions might be nation-wide, like the great *Landfrieden* pro-

See p. 68 above.

claimed at Mainz in 1235 by the emperor Frederick II, but they were not always as extensive, nor did they always depend on royal promotion. The party divisions resulting from the excommunication and deposition of Frederick II by the pope caused urban and rural communities in south-west Germany to seek mutual support. Between 1247 and 1251 Schwyz and Obwalden were in alliance with the imperialist cities Zürich and Berne (itself head of a Burgundian town league) against Lucerne, which held to the papalists. The third valley, Uri, seems at this time to have thrown in its lot with the papal party rather than with Schwyz and Obwalden. But the trend towards union was clear, and before the end of the century confederation between the three valley communities was an established fact.

But at what date, under what circumstances, and for what precise purposes Uri, Schwyz, and Unterwalden first reached the state of permanent alliance are among the most obscure questions of Swiss history. The first documentary evidence comes from a treaty dated August 1291. In consideration of the malice of the times the three valleys[5] pledge mutual assistance against all enemies; disagreements among the allies are to be settled peaceably by arbitration; regulations are laid down for the prevention and punishment of violent crime: within the area of the confederation the self-help of the feud is to give way to regular process of law. The alliance on these terms is to last for ever. This document, rediscovered in the archives of the canton of Schwyz in 1760, is commonly regarded as the foundation charter of the confederation, and it is from 1291 that Switzerland reckons her anniversaries as a state. Yet it is clear from the tenor of the treaty that what happened in 1291 was only the renewal, with some amplification, of an older union. To this original alliance no certain date can be assigned. Many suggestions have been offered: the period of acute struggle between the Hohenstaufen and the papacy in the forties of the thirteenth century; 1251–2; 1257–8; 1273; the spring of 1290. Perhaps it is for 1273 that the most plausible case can be made out. The threatening uncertainties of that year, when Rudolf of Habsburg bought the comital rights over Schwyz and Nidwalden and was elected German king, seem to provide the most likely background for the

---

[5] The parties to the treaty in August were Schwyz, Uri, and Nidwalden. Obwalden does not seem to have joined the alliance before December 1291, and so come together with Nidwalden to constitute Unterwalden.

first formal alliance of the forest cantons. But this is no more than conjecture.

The problem of interpretation is as difficult as that of chronology. What was the import of the alliance of 1291 and its precursor? Did they, or either of them, imply an act of rebellion aimed at throwing off a tyranny which Rudolf of Habsburg had succeeded in imposing on the valleys? To admit this is to endow the alliance of the three valley communities with a political intention at least as early as 1291 and to subscribe to the belief that by 1291 something which may be called the Swiss state existed. Or was the alliance in these thirteeth-century beginnings merely another *Landfriedensbund*, of the kind so common in Germany at that time, limited to preventing disturbances of the public peace and establishing by consent improved forms of judicial procedure among its members? In that case it would lack both ulterior political and specifically anti-Habsburg purpose. The terms of the oldest form of union are concerned exclusively with matters of justice and judicial procedure: with the effort to reduce as far as may be the use of the feud. It is not even certain that this earliest union was due solely to the initiative of the valley communities; the lord[6] with the right of high justice over them may well have had some part in bringing it about. Certainly it is not directed against him. And again in 1291 the times were threatening enough to make provision for preserving the peace intelligible. Rudolf of Habsburg died on 15 July, and there was every indication that his death would be followed by a rising in south-west Germany of all those who felt oppressed by the growing power of Habsburg. Was the alliance of August 1291 no more than an attempt on the part of the valleys to minimize in their own area the effects of these foreseeable disorders by renewing and strengthening their earlier union?

A single article, added in August 1291 to the original form of union, may have reference to a grievance against Habsburg administration. The confederates now declare that they will accept no judge who has bought his office or who is not a native of the valley. The claim that the *Ammänner* were to be natives acceptable to the communities was an old pretention, and one which Rudolf, after he came to power in 1273, had gone at least some way

---

[6] i.e., in the case of Schwyz and Unterwalden, if the earliest union is to be dated before 1273, the younger branch of Habsburg; if after 1273, the senior branch.

towards admitting. But normally the management of the dynasts' territorial complexes was entrusted to professional administrators from the lower nobility, the *ministeriales* who, despite their social rank, were of unfree origin. Considerations of ability rather than their geographic affiliations governed the appointment of these men and their transference from office to office. Rudolf's desire for the stricter organization of his possessions, and his own long absences in Austria and in Germany at large, brought these officials (*advocati*: *Vögte*) into especial prominence in the Habsburg lands in south-west Germany, for the younger son, Rudolf, who had been designed to rule there had predeceased his father. To the *Vögte* was delegated indifferently the exercise of family and of royal rights of every kind, including jurisdiction. That a *ministerialis* had been exercising jurisdiction in Schwyz on Rudolf's behalf may be inferred from a promise which he made in February 1291 that henceforth he would set no man of servile origin to judge the free men of Schwyz. In view of this withdrawal by Rudolf in February it is not easy to accept the proposition that a few months later, at the time of his death, Habsburg officials were exercising in his or in their own interests[7] so monstrous a tyranny that the forest cantons were impelled to throw it off by violent means. That the article concerning native judges in the alliance of August 1291 reflects a grievance about the past and a precaution for the future is certain. Low justice was henceforth to be exercised only by *Ammänner* originating from the valleys and acceptable to the inhabitants, as had been the practice in the past, probably till the mid-eighties, when Rudolf's ministerial *Vögte* had beome established. But neither this article, nor any other in the union of 1291, sufficiently supports the inference that by the time of Rudolf's death a potentially revolutionary situation had been brought about in the forest cantons by the excesses of Habsburg administrators.

To turn from text to context for an interpretation of the early unions is to be frustrated by the uncertainties of the historic tradition. In the thirteenth century the forest cantons produced no historian of their own whose work has survived, and they were

---

[7] The *Vögte* commonly aimed at converting their office into a lucrative personal possession, by farming it or holding it in pawn as security for unpaid wages.

too remote and unimportant for any other writer to concern himself about. Not until 1315, when by defeating the feudal host of Leopold of Austria at Morgarten they influenced a matter of European interest—the struggle for the German crown between Wittelsbach and Habsburg—did Schwyz, Uri, and Unterwalden impress themselves on the notice of the chroniclers. The earliest narrative account of the origin of the confederation, contained in the White Book of Sarnen (Obwalden), was not written down in its present form until about 1470. By that date the Swiss had been fighting the Austrians for a century and a half, and though the narrative in the White Book may derive from fourteenth-century sources which are now lost, it is probable that by the time that the primitive account of the origin of the confederation came to be written in the form we now possess, it had been coloured by the fact of the long struggle with Habsburg. In 1470 the antagonism between Swiss and Habsburg was a reality; the author or editor of the White Book narrative naturally supposed that the antagonism always had been a reality, and so found in it the reason why the confederation came into being.

Yet the account in the White Book, however dubious a source, has such high dramatic qualities that it continues to serve as the basis of popular belief about the origin of the confederation. This is the story it tells. Uri and Unterwalden were settled in Roman times by free colonists with the permission of the emperor; Schwyz by emigrants from Sweden who had been forced to find a new home by pressure of over-population. After a long period of freedom the three cantons submitted themselves to Rudolf of Habsburg, when he was king of Germany, on the condition that he would respect their liberties and that they were always to remain immediately dependent on the crown. Rudolf kept his word, but after his death his officials behaved tyrannically. Still worse occurred when the original line of Habsburg died out and the cantons had passed into the power of the counts of Tyrol.[8] Various ambitious feudatories of the neighbourhood persuaded the counts to enfeoff them with the office of *Vogt* over the valleys and then proceeded to abuse their position. Enraged by the excesses of these *Vögte*, who had seized their cattle, interfered

---

[8] This error was compounded from a misunderstanding of two facts: firstly, the division of the Habsburg possessions between the Albertine and Leopoldine lines in 1379; secondly, the Habsburg inheritance of Tyrol in 1363.

with their women, despised their liberties, and made humiliating demands upon them, representatives from the three cantons came together in the wood called the Rütli, to the west of lake Uri, and having there made a secret oath to drive out their oppressors, returned to their valleys to organize the conspiracy. Meanwhile Gessler, *Vogt* in Uri, had set up his symbol of jurisdiction—his hat on a staff—at Altdorf, and had ordered that all were to salute it. William Tell refused to obey; he was seized, and having been forced by Gessler to shoot an apple from his son's head he was led northwards as Gessler's prisoner. On the way by boat over lake Uri Tell escaped by leaping ashore at the *Tellenplatte*, and later he ambushed and killed Gessler in the Hohle Gasse as the *Vogt* was traversing the short tongue of land between lakes Lucerne and Zug. The news of Tell's deed precipitated the rising; the castles of the oppressors went up in flames, and the three cantons renewed the secret oath of confederation made by the first conspirators.

This chronicle tradition of the origin of the confederation, derived ultimately from the White Book, was given additional verisimilitude and literary form at the hands of Aegidius Tschudi, the Renaissance historian from Glarus who died in 1572, though his *Chronicon Helveticum* remained in manuscript till 1734–6. This story, popularized by Johannes von Müller's *History of the Swiss Confederation*, published in 1786, and dramatized for Europe by Schiller in *Wilhelm Tell* in 1804, had already received some critical glances in the eighteenth century. In the nineteenth it was drastically handled by Eutych Kopp (from 1835 onwards) and by other sceptical historians of the documentary school. They dismissed it as a concatenation of fables without historic worth; nothing could be found to substantiate it in the available documents; Tell and his apple and his arrows were demonstrably filched from Scandinavian mythology by way of the twelfth-century Danish chronicler, Saxo Grammaticus. Latterly, the pendulum has swung: popular fantasy, it has been argued, may embellish or distort, but is incapable of creating a legend from nothing; the account given in the White Book of Sarnen has a solid core of historicity, however much disguised by later accretions. What slight additional evidence has been brought to light in the last half century—it is almost all archaeological—gives some support to this reaction. For the chronicle tradition tells of castles in the forest cantons destroyed by an insurrection of the inhabitants, and the spade has confirmed that these castles existed and that they were destroyed.

Can we, neglecting manifest errors and absurdities, accept the main proposition of the White Book narrative: that the confederation was born in violence, in the expulsion from the valleys of foreign—that is to say, Habsburg—officials? The account is circumstantial as to places and persons, but our version dates from *c.* 1470 and by that time the errors and incomprehensions of generations of copyists had undoubtedly distorted many of the proper names of the primitive account. No longer, certainly, is it possible to reject the chronicle tradition out of hand as a simple fabrication. Elements of authenticity are there. It is, for instance, not wholly improbable that some inhabitant of Uri gained renown by a successful shot from behind a rock at an unpopular Habsburg *Vogt*. And though it is unlikely that his name was William Tell, it would be folly to underestimate the historical importance of his legend. Before the end of the fifteenth century belief in the myth was established; in Tell was personified the tradition of intrepid resistance to the foreign oppressor, and in his story the Swiss nation has found inspiration in times of jeopardy. That is indisputable, even if Tell's existence is not. The significance of the chronicle tradition as a creative factor in Swiss history is undoubted, and so the concern of Swiss scholars to show that the tradition is indeed reliable can really be understood. But great difficulties still lie in the way of exploiting it as an historical source, for it has yet to be reconciled passably with the statements and the silences of the documents.

And even if we are to assume that the events which the White Book relates happened within a short space of time, as a single dramatic incident, to what date is this incident to be ascribed? The White Book does not tell us, and learned opinion, so far as it accepts the White Book at all, is still divided between 1291 and 1315. The point is vital, for if the events we hear of in the chronicle tradition, or anything like them, took place in 1291, then the union of August 1291 must be interpreted in a highly political sense, and becomes the defiant organization of free men to resist the intolerable burden of Habsburg oppression.

That interpretation cannot easily be read out of the terms of the union alone, nor is it forced on us by what is yet known of the context of the union; before we can accept it we need firmer evidence both of the defiance and of the oppression than has yet been brought forward. So far as the union of 1291 and its precursor looked at all beyond the relations of the valleys with each other, their purpose seems to have been conservative rather than revolutionary, preventive rather than remedial. Yet even when regarded less as an offensive weapon against existing evils than as a shield against evils feared in the future, the thirteenth century unions of the forest cantons lose only immediate, not ultimate, political significance. The voluntary association of the three communities to do justice and to prevent violence among themselves, and to preserve their customary rights against attack from outside, had been struck for an indefinite period: it is in that sense that we must understand the 'perpetuity' of the alliance of August 1291. Yet in fact it became permanent, and within quarter of a century it proved to be an adequate preparation for political independence.

The forebodings which we may suppose to have led the forest cantons to renew their confederacy in August 1291 were only partly justified by events after Rudolf of Habsburg's death. There was, indeed, a general uprising in the south-west against his heir, Albert of Austria, led by the disgruntled junior line, Habsburg-Laufenburg, and supported extensively by those to whom the increase of Habsburg power had become onerous—by Zürich, Lucerne, Savoy, and the Burgundian towns. From October 1291 an alliance with Zürich brought Schwyz and Uri within the ambit of this anti-Habsburg league. But Albert mastered the outbreak without much difficulty; by August 1292 Zürich was willing to come to terms with him, and for a period in the autumn he seemed to be meditating a campaign against the forest cantons. He did not find it necessary to march, and gradually hostilities, if such there were, must have died away: there is no notice of a formal peace. This inactivity on the part of an energetic ruler is perhaps an additional reason for doubting that the confederation of 1291 had been accompanied by any violent demonstration against Habsburg in the forest cantons.

For them the benefit of time was working. Rudolf had been unable to impress on German opinion the necessity of hereditary monarchy: too many interests were concerned in maintaining the easy profits of the electoral system. Under Rudolf the German monarchy had once again become formidable; the answer of the

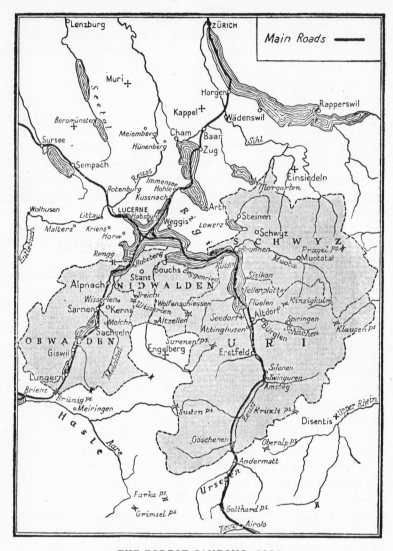

THE FOREST CANTONS, 1291

princes was to transfer it to families more pliant and less powerful than Habsburg. In May 1292 the electors chose as Rudolf's successor, not Albert of Habsburg, but the Rhenish Count Adolf of Nassau. At once the pressure of combined royal and dynastic power which had weighed so heavily on south-west Germany from 1273 to 1291 was relieved. Never again was it to be exerted quite as effectively. For though Adolf kept Albert from the German throne for only six years, Albert's kingship was denied full fruition; in 1308 he was murdered by a member of his own family at a moment when he seemed on the point of making the German crown a permanent Habsburg possession, and so perhaps restoring it to some dignity and force. Again the electors changed the dynasty; Henry count of Luxemburg was elected king. And when Henry died the Luxemburg party supported the duke of Bavaria, Lewis, against Albert's son Frederick the Fair in the disputed election of October 1314. The long contest for the kingship which followed turned at last in favour of Lewis the Bavarian; in 1322 Frederick was defeated and captured by his rival at Mühldorf; his brother, Leopold of Austria, abler and more vigorous than he, died four years later. These dates mark the end for more than a century of serious efforts by Habsburg to gain the German throne; with the triumph of the electoral principle the victory of localism in Germany was assured.

The crisis of the German constitution offered to the forest cantons repeated opportunities of playing off king against dynast. Since 1231 Uri's immediate dependence on the crown had been unchallenged; Rudolf had confirmed it in 1274, and no Habsburg legalist wasted his time disputing it. As long as a Habsburg was not German king Uri could depend on the protection of the crown against Habsburg. But initially the legal position of Schwyz and Unterwalden was less favourable. Habsburg could contest with some show of right the validity of Frederick II's privilege of 1240 for Schwyz; it is doubtful whether Unterwalden, in whole or in part, had received any imperial privilege at all in the thirteenth century. And in the absence of undisputed proof that they depended immediately from the crown, both Schwyz and Unterwalden were subject to the comital powers which Rudolf of Habsburg had acquired for his line from Habsburg–Laufenburg in 1273.[9]

[9] See pp. 67–68 above.

These deficiencies in legal status the valleys set about repairing with tact and persistency whenever the German king was at odds with the Habsburgs. Thus King Adolf of Nassau's quarrel with Albert of Austria in 1297 produced a royal confirmation of Schwyz's privilege of 1240; in 1309 Henry of Luxemburg, when still fresh in the saddle, was persuaded to confirm the documents in which Frederick II and Adolf had guaranteed the immediate dependence of Schwyz from the crown, and also those—which probably had never existed—which granted the same status to Unterwalden. In the open war for the throne which broke out in 1314 between Lewis the Bavarian and Frederick of Austria the forest cantons adhered to the former and reaped the desired harvest of privileges. By twenty-five years of opportunist policy Schwyz and Unterwalden thus built up their pretention to be on the same legal footing as Uri: to be communes owning no superior but the king. The corollary that the king was indeed their master had little practical effect. Both Henry of Luxemburg and Lewis the Bavarian appointed a single official to conserve royal rights over all three communities, but this *Reichsvogt* represented less a derogation from the real independence of the valleys than a recognition that they now formed an indissoluble whole. That is the implication of the collective term *Waldstätte*—forest place— used from 1309 to describe the unity made up of Schwyz, Uri, and Unterwalden.

There is remarkably little evidence of Habsburg opposition to these developments even during the period when it might be expected most—from 1298 to 1308 when Albert of Austria was German king. While no difficulty seems to have arisen over the Habsburgs' enjoyment of their manorial rights in Schwyz and Unterwalden, the question of their political power in these valleys, though kept alive, was not pressed to an issue. The ambiguity of the legal position helped the cantons to progress still farther on the road to self-government; the decisive factor in the making of the headman of the valley, the *Landamman*, was no longer nomination by the *Vogt* but election by the community. The *Landammänner* became communal officers in the fullest sense; their political and administrative activity grew in importance, and as the fourteenth century advanced they extended their competence beyond the low justice to judgements of blood. It was to these communal officers, and not to nominees of their own, that the Habsburgs wrote when they wished, for instance, to commend the interests of churches and monasteries to the inhabitants of the valleys. The advance towards autonomy is well illustrated in 1294 when the community of Schwyz is to be found composing its own code of law about questions of mortmain and inheritance.

The inference must be that there was no attempt at this time to impose direct Habsburg administration on the valleys. But Habsburg renounced neither its claims nor its ambitions. The valleys might obtain their parchments from distant German kings; the real power in south-west Germany was still Habsburg. In the first years of the century Albert had caused the immense family possessions there to be made the object of rigid scrutiny and written record. By now Habsburg held Glarus and Lucerne as well as Zug, and so had gained the approaches to the central Alps. The valley of the Reuss and the St. Gotthard pass itself were temptations which could not in the long run be resisted, and the way to them led over the growing independence of the forest cantons. In 1310 the inhabitants of Schwyz were fortifying the entrances to their valley; the action was symptomatic of the uncertainties of the times.

By 1315 opportunity, pretext, and will for a Habsburg assault on the forest cantons were all present. In the struggle for the German crown between Frederick of Austria and Lewis the Bavarian the sympathy of the cantons was, of course, with the latter; by March 1315 at the latest they were in communication with him. A minor matter precipitated conflict. For many years controversy about the boundaries of Alpine grazing rights had smouldered between the men of Schwyz and their neighbours to the north, the abbey of Einsiedeln. In January 1314 Schwyz attacked the abbey, did much damage there, and carried off some of its monks as hostages. This economic squabble set political undercurrents in motion, for since 1283 the Habsburgs had been protectors of Einsiedeln. Here they had a pretext for a sharp settlement with the troublesome confederates which would deprive Lewis the Bavarian of an ally and fill in an important corner of the incomplete mosaic of Habsburg territory. Frederick put the forest cantons under the ban of the empire, and warfare on a small scale had been waged against them by Habsburg's clients for some time before the most enterprising of Frederick's brothers, Leopold, planned with some strategic skill a formal campaign in central Switzerland. While one force was to hold Unterwalden engaged by an advance over the Brünig pass from the Entlibuch and naval forces from Lucerne were to operate across the lake against the exposed flank of Schwyz, Leopold himself was to direct a frontal attack. His shortest route, along the shore of lake Zug, seems to have been barred by confederate fortifications at Arth, so he preferred the road which ran along the right bank of lake Aegeri. On this road, at Morgarten on 15 November 1315, his feudal host was completely routed by the footmen of Schwyz and Uri, and the rest of his plan collapsed. The slaughter of notabilities made a European sensation comparable with that caused by the defeat of the French chivalry by the townsmen of Flanders at Courtrai in 1302. To contemporaries the overthrow of the mounted knight by a peasant militia fighting on foot was a monstrous and inexplicable reversal of the proper social order; we can see more clearly that the confederates' victory at Morgarten was due to wise choice of position and to tactical surprise.

Military success was followed by reinforcement of the alliance. The open war with Habsburg demanded a restatement of the terms of confederation and this was given in a new union dated 9 December 1315. This document, which remained the legal basis of the relations between the three cantons until 1798, repeats the articles of 1291 but now in German dress; the maintenance of internal peace is still an important consideration; the union has not lost its character of a *Landfriedensbund*. But the war has added new emphases. No member is to make peace or alliances without the consent of the others; for the duration of the war the Habsburgs are to lose their seigneurial rights within the area of the confederation. The ambiguities which befog the meaning of the earlier alliances have now disappeared. By 1315 political purpose has become paramount in the union of the three cantons. Their confederation is a perpetual alliance directed against Habsburg.

V

GROWTH AND CONSOLIDATION

THE war between the forest cantons and Austria which opened with Morgarten lasted for rather more than a century and a half. As in the great contemporary struggle between England and France, hostilities were spasmodic. Long periods of truce restored a semblance of peace: from 1318 to 1335, from 1336 to 1351, from 1355 to 1364, from 1368 to 1386, from 1394 to 1415. But these slackenings of tension brought no answer to the question of political mastery nor did any firm possibility appear of reconciling the conflicting legal contentions in which the controversy was expressed. To the claim of the forest cantons that they were free communes depending directly and exclusively from the German king, the Habsburgs continued to oppose the demand for recognition of their inherited rights of government in Schwyz and Unterwalden.

Even on the legal issue the cantons could not rely unreservedly on royal support. From 1308 to 1438 Luxemburgers and Wittelsbachers contrived to deny the German crown to Habsburg, but royal policy remained of necessity opportunist. There was no consistent tradition of hostility to the Habsburgs, who were opposed or wooed by the crown according to the changing exigencies of German politics, and at bottom there was perhaps always more sympathy between crown and dynast than between crown and commune. In its early years the confederacy had profited by the enmities between Habsburg and the German kings Henry of Luxemburg and Lewis the Bavarian, but it could not deceive itself about the reliability of the crown as an ally. Both Henry and Lewis had been willing to sacrifice the forest cantons out of hand when the interests of the crown demanded an understanding with Habsburg. In 1311 Henry conceded an inquiry into the validity of Habsburg's claims in the cantons, and promised that if the claims could be substantiated he would support them; in 1334 Lewis signalled his new friendship with Habsburg by allowing such an inquest to be held, though its findings in favour of Habsburg could not be enforced. Lewis's successor, Charles IV of Luxemburg, long remained on excellent terms with the dukes of Austria. Thus it was clear that for the sake of a political advantage the king was liable to agree that the pretentions of Schwyz and Unterwalden to immediacy should be subjected to an examination from which they could hardly expect to emerge favourably; no fourteenth-century ruler showed any disposition to support the cantons in the field. Useful as the assertion that they depended directly from the crown had been to the cantons in the past, alone it was not a sufficient guarantee for the future. And were the cantons to be thrown upon their own resources for resistance it was imperative that these should be strengthened by enlarging the area of the confederacy.

For though the valleys were fortresses irreducible by direct attack, they were ill-fitted to withstand a perpetual state of siege. An estimate of their population in the fourteenth century can be little better than a guess: perhaps it amounted to twenty or thirty thousand. Certainly it was too great for the poor natural resources of the valleys; that is indicated by the drift of the men of Uri and Schwyz into mercenary service, and by their long and bitter squabbles over grazing rights with the neighbouring abbeys of Einsiedeln and Engelberg. For much of their corn, for the salt for their cattle, for the steel of their weapons, the valleys depended on imports from or through the Swiss plateau, which were liable to interruption by a Habsburg blockade; as long as the route from Lucerne to the Rhine was under Habsburg control, the prosperity drawn by the innkeepers and muleteers of Uri from the St. Gotthard traffic was at Habsburg's mercy. Thus there was urgent need to widen the geographical basis of the confederacy. By the end of the fourteenth century this need had been met by the admission of five more members.

The expansion deeply affected the nature of the confederation. Glarus, a member from 1351 to 1355, and permanently from 1388, was a valley community of the same kind as the original confederates; Zug, whose permanent adhesion dates from 1365, although it comprised a small town as well as three rural communes had much the same social composition as Schwyz or Uri. But the other new members were towns, possessing—it is no tautology to add at this period when the name was often given to swollen villages—distinctly urban characteristics: Lucerne (1332), Zürich (1351), and Berne (1353). The co-operation on an equal footing of rural and urban communities was peculiar to Switzerland, and this fact has been used, perhaps with too great facility, to explain why the communal movement succeeded there when it failed over the rest of western Europe. Undoubtedly the towns introduced new capacities —financial, political, and strategic—which greatly strengthened the confederation. But at the same time the homogeneity of sentiment of the original league of Alpine valleys was lost, and new diversities of purpose strained the structure of the expanded union. On ultimate analysis the cement which held it together was still common hostility to Habsburg. But the immediate causes of the new adhesions were less obvious and they can only be understood in detail.

Nearest in place and motive to the first confederates stood Lucerne. Centre of the deanery which included the forest cantons, a frequented market and the port where the Reuss leaves the lake on its northward course to the Rhine, her ecclesiastical and economic connexions with Schwyz, Uri, and Unterwalden were old and close. Her espousal of the papalist cause against the Hohenstaufen had drawn Lucerne at some time between 1247 and 1251 into war with Schwyz and Obwalden, Zürich, and Berne. But in 1291 she had joined her former opponents in the great anti-Habsburg league, for her progress towards autonomy under the rule of her own council had been checked by Rudolf of Habsburg's purchase, in the year of his death, of lordship over the town from the abbey of Murbach. The gesture of 1291 was ineffectual, and henceforward the council of Lucerne had to contend, not with a weak and distant ecclesiastical suzerain, but with the Habsburg administration intent on reducing the town to a docile constituent of Habsburg territory. In the war of Morgarten Lucerne had thus been forced to support her overlord against the forest cantons. A hard problem faced the ruling class, the well-to-do merchants who formed the council of Lucerne. If they elected to submit permanently to Habsburg rule they had to fear a progressive diminution of the communal liberties which they had acquired during the previous century, and their trade would be interrupted by the blockades which Habsburg periodically attempted to enforce against the forest cantons. The alternative, a determined effort to curtail Habsburg's power over Lucerne, could be successful only with the help of Austria's enemies.

It was on this that the choice fell: on 7 November 1332 Lucerne struck a perpetual alliance with Schwyz, Uri, and Unterwalden.

The terms of this accession are interesting for the light which they throw on the way the public law of the confederation was to develop as its numbers grew. While using the union of 1315 as a model, the act of 1332 in no sense superseded it. The bond between Schwyz, Uri, and Unterwalden continued to be that of the earlier engagement; in 1332 the three cantons did no more than take Lucerne as an ally in perpetuity by way of addition to, rather than absorption in, the original union. Lucerne remained in enjoyment of her own town law; she was not admitted into that community of justice created over and above the three individual cantons by the pacts of 1291 and 1315. Moreover, care was taken to prevent Lucerne becoming the arbiter of the confederation by arrogating to herself the office of mediator if discords should break out between the valleys. And after 1332, as before, Lucerne was a Habsburg possession; a strong pro-Habsburg party persisted in the town for many years, and complete emancipation from Habsburg overlordship did not come for more than half a century. Yet these limitations cannot seriously detract from the importance of the first enlargement of the confederation. The confederates had secured lake Lucerne, and thereby communication with each other and with the Swiss plateau; in their aggressive hostility towards Habsburg they had not shrunk from taking as an ally an Austrian subject town and comforting it in rebellion. To this defiance Habsburg made no effective reply.

Lucerne, like Schwyz and Unterwalden, was a commune fleeing its lord's control. Zürich cannot be brought under the same formula. For Zürich was an imperial city where nearly all trace of the former lordship of the convent of Fraumünster had disappeared by the beginning of the fourteenth century and where the German king contented himself with a yearly tax. Like the other communities of south-west Germany she had felt the menace of the tentacular growth of Habsburg power; she had participated, with mediocre success, in the rising which followed Rudolf's death in 1291; in 1330-1 she had had to spend much money in buying herself free from the Habsburgs to whom Lewis the Bavarian had pawned her. But while Zürich was not prepared to budge on the article of independence, she could not afford too open a display of antagonism towards Habsburg. Her silk manufactures made her the only considerable industrial town of the Swiss area in the early fourteenth century, and the trade which brought the raw material and disposed of the products of her industry used routes which Habsburg could control; the town nobility, sprung for the most part from former *ministeriales* of the religious houses in Zürich, often found careers in Habsburg service. Such considerations prevented the growth in Zürich of the intransigent hostility to Habsburg which had marked both the history of the forest cantons since 1315 and the adhesion of Lucerne. Zürich's permanent entry into the union in 1351—there had been previous temporary alliances with the confederacy—was not so much an expression of enmity towards Habsburg as an expedient sought by a dictatorial burgomaster to perpetuate his subversion of the urban constitution.

The organ of communal self-government in Zürich, the council as it had developed in the thirteenth century, was composed of the more prosperous merchants and the town nobility. The latter element declined in importance, and as the industrial classes had as yet no share in political power, the government of Zürich tended to become a commercial oligarchy. It was a pattern common enough in the German towns of the time, and in Zürich as elsewhere it became unbearable to the unenfranchised industrial workers, now organized into craft-gilds, who were expected to bear every burden of civic responsibility except that of participation in town government. A wave of disturbance in the Rhineland towns in the thirties of the fourteenth century resulted in the gilds winning a greater influence on the town councils at the expense of the merchant interest. Zürich's revolution in 1336 had this peculiarity: a member of the old town nobility, Rudolf Brun, put himself at the head of the popular movement and brought about a constitutional settlement in which power was so nicely divided between the gilds on the one hand and the joint representatives of the nobility and the merchants on the other, that he himself, elected burgomaster for life, was the effective dictator of Zürich. He had perhaps consciously imitated the tactics, he had certainly reached the position, of the contemporary Italian tyrants. The parallel with Italy went farther. At Brun's instigation the defeated party was proscribed, and in exile it nursed its hatreds and plotted, with outside help, to overthrow the existing order. It was much like the world which Dante knew too well.

The *émigrés* from Zürich found refuge on the north shore of the lake at Rapperswil, in the territory and under the patronage of the count of Laufenburg-Rapperswil, which was the name now borne by the junior branch of Habsburg. Thence in February 1350 they attempted to seize Zürich, but the *coup* failed, and Brun retaliated by occupying Rapperswil. Gradually, and, it would seem, against Brun's wishes, Zürich's difference with Laufenburg-Rapperswil, originating in a question of internal politics, widened into a conflict with the senior line of Habsburg, the security of whose territories in the March, south of lake Zürich, was closely bound up with the fortunes of the younger line. By September 1350 Habsburg and Zürich were at war; on 1 May 1351 Zürich entered into a perpetual pact with the forest cantons and Lucerne.

In form and intention this alliance did not differ from the engagements for mutual assistance into which Zürich had often entered with other powers in the past. The terms of 1351 closely resembled those of a treaty arranged between Zürich and Habsburg as recently as August 1350. Expediency alone had led Zürich, involved in unwelcome controversy with Habsburg, to seek alliance with Habsburg's most consistent opponents. The pact of 1351 left the contractants in the position of equal and independent partners, and Zürich at least, despite the clause of perpetuity in the treaty, seems to have envisaged only immediate advantages. Indeed, the solidarity of interest which brought Zürich and the forest cantons together in 1351 was frequently to be severely tested in the future; hardly before the second half of the fifteenth century had it been transformed into a permanent solidarity of sentiment. For the moment the alliance served its purpose. In the three sieges to which Habsburg subjected Zürich between September 1351 and July 1355—once, for a short period, with the assistance of the German king Charles IV and all the apparatus of an imperial war—the town was aided in its successful resistance by the forces of the forest cantons. They were rewarded by two concessions in the peace terms negotiated at Regensburg in 1355: Austria recognized the existence of the confederation, and for the time being passed over in silence its claims to political power in Schwyz and Unterwalden. For his part, Brun had assured the continuance of his regime in Zürich: little more had been at issue, and that secure, he saw no reason to prolong a conflict which had been disastrous for Zürich's commerce. In the peace of Regensburg Zürich consented to mediate between Habsburg and the forest cantons, and even agreed, in certain eventualities, to assist Habsburg against the valleys with which four years before she had made a perpetual union. Within a year of the peace Brun had brought about an alliance between Zürich and Austria; he died in 1360 a Habsburg pensioner. He had well enough understood both his own interests and those of the town he ruled; it would be futile to accuse him of infidelity towards Swiss national aspirations which did not yet exist.

On a short view the alliance with Zürich seemed of doubtful value to the confederacy. But the war of 1351–5 had shown the way to gains which after an interval were permanently to increase its size and strength. Until well into the thirteenth century the valley community of Glarus had remained under the mild lordship of the abbess of Säckingen and her officials. Between 1264 and 1288 Rudolf of Habsburg acquired from the abbess her rights over Glarus, which in time became restive under the weight of Habsburg administration. Already in 1323 the valley had allied with Schwyz against Duke Leopold of Austria; the outbreak of the war for Zürich in 1351 offered the forest cantons the opportunity of freeing their neighbours, and at the same time of denying Habsburg a dangerous avenue of flank approach to central Switzerland. In the autumn the confederates occupied Glarus. Liberation was not unconditional; the perpetual pact made by Schwyz, Uri, Unterwalden, and Zürich with Glarus on 4 June 1352 left the external relations of Glarus under the supervision of the other confederates. Less than a month later the Habsburg township and region of Zug entered the confederation on the same terms as Zürich and thus assured what had before been doubtful, the communications between Zürich and Schwyz. In 1355 the peace of Regensburg returned Zug and Glarus to Austria's overlordship, but the habit of subjection had been broken. In pursuit of an independent policy of expansion northwards, Schwyz broke the peace and seized Zug in 1364–5. The war with Habsburg which followed was closed by the armistice of Thorberg in 1368, which despite its ambiguities left Zug within the confederation. Though Habsburg reserved some financial rights and its claim to lordship, in fact from this time onwards Zug was a protectorate of Schwyz. In 1388 Glarus also recovered its membership of the confederation.

The third town member, Berne, with some five or six thousand inhabitants, was much the same size as Zürich, and perhaps twice as large as Lucerne. Like Zürich, Berne was an imperial city owning no lord but the German king and paying little enough attention to that remote and feeble suzerain. This position she had contrived to establish during the thirteenth century; in contrast to her neighbour, the other Zähringer foundation, Fribourg, which in 1277 had fallen under the lordship of Rudolf of Habsburg, Berne had escaped the clutches of the dynasts, though for a passing period she had been forced to accept the protection of Savoy. The extinction of the original line of Kiburg in 1264 and the passing of the rump of its possessions in western Switzerland to the far weaker dynasty of Kiburg-Burgdorf,[1] favoured Berne's independence, which she promoted by an active policy of alliances with the other powers of Burgundian Switzerland. Standing rather aside from the great trade routes and lacking important industry, Berne had been essentially a centre of government from the time of her foundation by Berchtold IV of Zähringen in 1191. This tradition, embodied in a ruling class in part descended from the former Zähringer administrative nobility—the most illustrious example is the family von Bubenberg, members of which are to be found in control of Berne's fortunes at practically every crisis from 1235 to 1393—shaped the course taken by Berne as an independent commune. She became an aggressive city state, with policy and war as her trade, by which she extended her power beyond the town walls over the surrounding country-side into the Oberland, the Mittelland, and the Seeland. The decaying feudatories of this area were forced to sell or pawn their lordships to her for the money which her credit always allowed her to raise in Basle; alternatively their subjects were seduced by the grant of Bernese citizenship to be held outside the walls: by the middle of the fourteenth century Berne had some 3,000 of these *Ausbürger*, who provided ready pretexts for Berne to interfere in other men's lordships. Desire to promote these territorial interests, rather than antagonism to Habsburg, brought Berne into the confederation in 1353.

In the past considerations of policy had frequently led to temporary alliances between Berne and the forest cantons. With Schwyz and Obwalden and Zürich she had taken part in the imperialist siege of Lucerne in 1247–51; she had joined the anti-Habsburg coalition in 1291; in 1323 concern to prevent Habsburg

---

[1] This was the line founded by the marriage of Eberhard I of Habsburg-Laufenburg with Anna of Kiburg in 1273. See p. 68 above.

from acquiring the possessions of Kiburg-Burgdorf in western Switzerland had led her to a pact of mutual assistance with the forest cantons, at that time still in a state of uneasy truce with Austria after the battle of Morgarten (treaty of Lungern, August 1323). The friendship then initiated served Berne well in 1339, when Fribourg and the feudatories of the Jura and the middle valley of the Aare combined in an effort to check the alarming increase of Berne's territorial influence. Fribourg and her allies had the moral support of Fribourg's overlord, Habsburg, and also of Lewis the Bavarian, whom Berne, because he was at odds with the pope, had refused to recognize as German king. Berne had the help of Solothurn and the forest cantons, and contingents from the valleys played a most distinguished part in Berne's victory at Laupen on 21 June 1339 over Fribourg and the feudal coalition. But she did not adopt from her allies their inveterate hostility towards Habsburg, with whom, indeed, her designs of territorial expansion over the Swiss plateau and in the Oberland made agreement advisable. The treaty of alliance arrived at between Berne and Habsburg in 1342, and renewed in 1358, 1363, and 1370, gave Berne for forty years a free hand in western Switzerland.

How did Berne come to make a perpetual alliance with the forest cantons on 6 March 1353 despite this pledged friendship with Habsburg? The explanation lies in the necessities of her policy in the Oberland. In 1334 Bernese citizenship had been imposed on the lords of Weissenburg, who were forced to grant to Berne the protectorate over the Haslital which they held from the empire; at the same time Berne had strengthened her hold over the monastery of Interlaken and its possessions, which included the valleys of the Lütschine. Haslital and the Lütschine valleys could show examples of valley communities very similar to those of the forest cantons, and their aspirations to independence aroused sympathies in Unterwalden, which had easy access to them over the Brünig pass. When the peasants of the Lütschine valleys and the Bödeli rose against the monastery of Interlaken in 1349, they were supported by Unterwalden, and Berne was forced to intervene to restore the monastery's authority. It was to neutralize this dangerous democratic influence in territory which she was making her own that Berne entered into the perpetual pact of 1353; Schwyz and Uri, it was hoped, would restrain Unterwalden from inciting Bernese subjects to rebellion. Thus a minor question of territorial interest determined Berne's entry into the confederation at a care-fully chosen moment when there seemed some prospect of peace between Habsburg and the forest cantons. When that prospect failed Berne had to give preference to her older engagement, in accordance with which she had—albeit half-heartedly—taken the part of Habsburg in the first and second sieges of Zürich in 1351 and 1352. It is likely that within eighteen months of her alliance with the forest cantons Berne joined Habsburg in the third siege of Zürich against her new allies. In such opportunism there seemed little promise that Berne would ever regard the pact with the confederates as of first importance. Her interests were still primarily Burgundian, and it was not till 1415, when the profits of the joint attack on the Habsburg possessions in Aargau were to be shared, that membership of the confederation became a guiding motive of her policy.

In the half century after Morgarten the confederation emerged from the Alpine valleys; by 1368 it extended over the Swiss plateau as far as lake Zürich to the north and the borders of Romance Switzerland to the west. Over the many other leagues of the time it had the advantage of geographic unity: the nucleus of the four cantons grouped round lake Lucerne communicated with Zürich through Zug and with Berne through the Bernese subject posses-sions in the Oberland. But suggestions of temporary expediency surrounded the adhesions of Zürich and Berne. Against their with-drawal in the future the clauses of perpetual validity common to all the acts of alliance did not offer a complete guarantee; this promise, which perhaps in any case implied indefinite duration rather than permanency, was not peculiar to the confederation: it had been made and broken in other German leagues. After the peace of Regensburg Glarus had fallen back under Habsburg over-lordship; Habsburg influence in Zug had not yet been finally destroyed. To the members of the expanded but looser confedera-tion of the last third of the fourteenth century the impulse to sub-ordinate their particular interests to a common purpose came from a renewed appreciation of Habsburg strength.

The Habsburgs had taken no effective revenge for Morgarten; Lucerne, the richest of their towns in Switzerland, had been allowed to escape their control and join hands with their enemies; they had been unable to bring help to Fribourg during the war of Laupen; the war with Zürich from 1351 to 1355 had ended in a peace which passed over in silence Habsburg claims in Schwyz and Unterwalden. Yet it would be unsafe to infer from these facts a decay of Habsburg power in the fourteenth century. The main interests of the house had shifted since the time of Rudolf of Habsburg, and the possessions in south-west Germany, the *Vorlande*, had lost importance in comparison with Austria and the other lands in the east. It is not easy to keep matters in focus from a solely Swiss viewpoint. For to the Swiss the struggle with Habsburg must be almost the sum of their history in the fourteenth century, while to the Habsburgs of the time the Swiss represented but a single problem in the business of an empire stretching from Alsace to the Adriatic and the borders of Hungary. Even so, Habsburg did not neglect the *Vorlande*. Considerable gains in Alsace and Breisgau were brought into closer connexion with the possessions of the house in Switzerland by the acquisition of Villingen in 1326 and of Rheinfelden and Schaffhausen in 1330. Both the success of Austrian policy after the peace of Regensburg in frustrating the efforts of Zürich and Schwyz to make themselves masters of the shores of lake Zürich, and the brilliant feudal assembly at Zofingen in 1361 at which Duke Rudolf IV of Austria received the fealty of his vassals from Alsace, Swabia, Sundgau, Aargau, and Thurgau provide evidence that Habsburg power in south-west Germany was not yet in irremediable decline.

Undoubtedly the organism was vast and ponderous, ill-fitted for quick decision or immediate action. When the French noble Enguerrand de Coucy, to support his claim to a heritage from Habsburg, in 1375-6 led hordes of unemployed mercenaries from the Anglo-French war plundering and ravaging into Aargau and western Switzerland, it was not Habsburg but the local authorities, particularly Berne, which took effective steps to get rid of this nuisance. But Habsburg had not lost its instinct for profitable acquisition; in 1363 at last it added Tyrol to Styria and Carinthia; its influence mounted in the Rhine valley between lake Constance and Chur and in what is now called Vorarlberg; a consolidated Alpine state, which would absorb the communities of central Switzerland, seemed within the range of Habsburg ambition. In 1379 a new efficiency was introduced into the direction of Habsburg affairs. Until then the scattered possessions of the house had been held and governed in common by the descendants of Rudolf of Habsburg, but in that year the surviving members of the family, the brothers Albert III and Leopold III, agreed to a division of their inheritance: to Albert went Austria, to Leopold Carinthia, Carniola, Styria, Tyrol, and the lands in south-west Germany. A new concentration of effort was possible, which made Leopold III potentially as dangerous a menace to the independence of the Swiss communities as Rudolf had been a century before.

One important process had accelerated since Rudolf's time. In Switzerland, as elsewhere, during the fourteenth century the collapse of the lesser nobility progressed notably. By excessive partition of inheritances and by the working of economic forces which have been described rather than explained, many feudal families were reduced to a destitution which seems at last to have affected their capacity to breed. Throughout Germany this fact left the way clear for the territorial princes to complete the construction of their states. It favoured the Habsburg projects in the Rhine valley and in Vorarlberg. But in western Switzerland there was a competitor for the profits to be made from the ruin of the feudal world. Berne had long been showing that a commune was as well able as any dynast to create a territory. By multiplying the number of her external citizens (*Ausbürger*) and by financial and military pressure she had been successful in imposing her rule over much of the area between the Alps and the lower Aare. Kiburg-Burgdorf was the only considerable dynasty which remained in this region, and the fate of its lands between the Aare and the Grosse Emme was thus of the first importance to the directors of Berne's territorial policy. Made desperate by his declining fortunes, in 1382 Rudolf II of Kiburg-Burgdorf attacked Berne's ally Solothurn. In a war which lasted for two years and in which, for the first time since 1353, she called for and received the help of all the confederates, Berne shattered the dynasty. Kiburg was forced to cede Thun and Burgdorf, and thus Berne, which already held Laupen, reconstituted for herself the strategic triangle from which the Zähringers had once dominated the plateau; the family of Kiburg-Burgdorf, until its miserable extinction in 1417, remained in clientage to the city state.

During this war no help came to Kiburg-Burgdorf from its kinsman Leopold III of Habsburg, and Leopold's neutrality had heavy consequences for the future of the Habsburg possessions south of the Rhine. For with the disappearance of the buffer state of Kiburg-Burgdorf Berne came into immediate contact with Habsburg territory, and in view of Berne's aggressive policy the possibility of conflict drew near. The alliance between Berne and Habsburg which had persisted since 1342 had lost its meaning, and this was at a critical conjuncture in German history.

In the seventies and eighties of the fourteenth century a wave of political and social unrest swept over western Europe. England, France, Flanders, Florence, and Germany were all the scenes of violent attacks on constituted authority. In Germany the issue can be stated in simpler terms than elsewhere: the feudal and the communal worlds came into collision. In a gesture of self-defence against the encroachments of the princely territory-builders, and of defiance against the lesser nobility which in its disorderly deliquescence was a pestilential hindrance to commerce and communication, the German towns made a supreme effort at co-operation. The league of imperial towns in Swabia, founded in 1376 and numbering some 100 members, united in 1381 with the league of Rhenish towns. In February 1385 Zürich, Berne, Solothurn, and Zug came into this great alliance. But the forest cantons refused to join, and Lucerne, bound by the pact of 1332 to enter into no new commitments without the consent of her allies, was able to promise only indirect support to the league. Nevertheless, Lucerne judged conditions favourable for an attempt to throw off the remnants of Habsburg overlordship and to carve out for herself at Habsburg's expense a territory such as Berne and Zürich already possessed. In December 1385 war was precipitated by Lucerne's seizure of the Habsburg administrative centre Rothenburg; the Habsburg township Sempach and the Habsburg valley Entlebuch found citizenship of Lucerne imposed upon them. With the notable exception of Berne, the confederates joined in the attack on Habsburg.

Duke Leopold accepted the challenge the more willingly as the Swabian and Rhenish towns showed no stomach to fight on behalf of the confederation. In June 1386 he planned the first formal campaign against central Switzerland since the time of Morgarten. On its advance against Lucerne his feudal army was routed near Sempach on 9 July by the forces of Lucerne and the forest cantons. Leopold was killed in the battle and his son was still under age; the dismay among the leaderless Austrians allowed the Swabian towns to negotiate a truce lasting till February 1388. At its expiry

Albert III of Austria thought to avenge his brother and restore the tottering prestige of his house by reconquering Glarus, which at the outbreak of the war had expelled the Austrians and revived its membership of the confederation, dormant since 1355. Again a mounted Austrian expedition was committed to warfare in a valley; in April 1388 the peasants of Glarus, almost unaided, destroyed the Austrian forces at Näfels. Meanwhile Berne had at last stirred, not, indeed, to appear in the main theatre of war, but to lay hands on the Habsburg lordships of Büren and Nidau, and so to strengthen her hold on the lower Aare and in the neighbourhood of lake Biel (Bienne). Zürich's attempt to add Rapperswil to her territory was less successful.

By 1389 the war had petered out. The anxious mediation of the Swabian league brought about a truce for eight years, which was prolonged for another twenty in 1394, and in fact lasted until 1415. The war of 1385–9 was decisive for the establishment of the confederacy. Lucerne, Zug, and Glarus made good their claims to independence, for though Zug and Glarus agreed to continue certain payments to Habsburg, it was only on the condition that the Habsburg administration was withdrawn. Lucerne kept Rothenburg, Wohlhusen, Sempach, and the Entlebuch; besides Büren and Nidau, Berne kept Unterseen in the Oberland and the upper valley of the Simme, which had been taken from Fribourg during the war; by securing the protectorate over the subjects of the abbey of Einsiedeln, Schwyz extended its influence to the southern shore of lake Zürich. To Habsburg the loss of these territories amounted to expulsion from the western Alps and pre-Alps; the moral results of the confederacy's victories at Sempach and Näfels were even more weighty. The Austrian attack had foundered in military disasters too awful to invite repetition; Habsburg lost its nerve for the offensive. After 1394 the question no longer was whether Habsburg could reassert its rights over Lucerne and Schwyz and Unterwalden, but whether it could protect its remaining possessions south of the Rhine, in Aargau and Thurgau, against confederate aggression.

Within the Swiss area between the beginning and the end of the fourteenth century the disposition of power had shifted remarkably. The agent of change was a peculiar creation, hardly definable in the usual terms of public law. For if it is convenient to speak of a Swiss confederation in the fourteenth century, the phrase must not be strictly pressed. There was nothing in the nature of a single federal pact to which all the members had successively adhered. What existed in 1394 was really a bundle of confederations; no less than six distinct instruments had been found necessary to bind the eight members (the VIII *Orte*). Within this series there were separate groupings of three, four, five, and six cantons, and these groupings were held together only by certain common elements: Schwyz, Uri, and Unterwalden belonged to all the confederacies and so interlocked them. The primary motive of all these alliances, except perhaps the union of the forest cantons, had been to secure and to develop the independence of the contracting parties; the idea that their individual independence should be in any way reduced for the benefit of some federal whole was originally alien, and only very slowly and imperfectly did they become accustomed to it. Berne and Zürich had expressly reserved and consistently exercised freedom to make further engagements without consulting the other confederates; how little either of these towns felt herself bound by a general confederate will had received recent illustration. In the war of Sempach—however respectable her motives—Berne had failed her allies at the battle; in 1393 a treaty pledging Zürich to neutrality in an Austrian war of revenge against the forest cantons was cancelled only as the result of an internal revolution.

An institutional armature of the confederacy hardly existed. The need of it was felt the less because in ordinary times the confederacy was a mere potentiality, which was realized only when the individual *casus foederis* arose. If the members had matters to discuss there was no regular assembly in which this might be done; a conference had to be called *ad hoc*, at which only the members directly interested would be represented, and which remained powerless to reach or to impose a decision not accepted by the individual cantons. A great Swiss historian has put it thus: 'The confederacy . . . possessed no constitution, no regular representative assembly, no executive organs, no capital, no treasury, no chancery, no depository for documents, not even a seal of its own.' These deficiencies were rooted in the nature of the confederation whose members had come together, not with the conscious intention of founding a state, but because they had thought it expedient to take allies in order to defend their own interests. In this they did not differ from members of the leagues for the maintenance of the public peace which pullulated in Germany in the thirteenth and fourteenth centuries. Yet alone of all these unions the Swiss confederation did ultimately take on a permanent political character. Switzerland, though long remaining within the framework of the German kingdom—until the end of the fifteenth century in fact, until 1648 in law—did at last become an independent state.

Why this happened in Switzerland and nowhere else cannot be explained simply. Some obvious reasons present themselves: the singularly close union of the three forest cantons which went beyond the normal range of alliance and provided a steady centre for later and looser groupings; the accidents which made the confederacy a geographical continuum and united urban with rural communities; the absolute necessity of co-operation in order to pursue a successful war against the common enemy, Habsburg; the creative preparatory work which Habsburg itself, in its attempt to make a territory in the Swiss area, had achieved and which the confederates inherited. Ingenuity could excogitate further likely explanations of the fact: only the fact itself is indisputable. Even in the fourteenth century there were indications that the whole was to become something more than the sum of its parts; the beginnings of a federal law can be discerned. In the Priests' Charter (*Pfaffenbrief*) of 1370 the forest cantons and Zürich, Lucerne, and Zug declared that none of their inhabitants was to escape the jurisdiction of the communal courts by pleading that he was an ecclesiastic or a servant of Austria; the preservation of good order on the road from the St. Gotthard pass to Zürich was to be the general concern of all the cantons making the declaration. A clause was added which represents the first significant diminution of the sovereignty of the individual cantons: the arrangements of 1370 could be amended by a majority decision. In the Covenant of Sempach (*Sempacherbrief*) of 1393 general legislation was taken a step farther, this time with the concurrence of Berne: the attempt was made to state a common code of behaviour for the troops of the confederacy in the field and to prohibit any member from starting a war without reference to its allies. These were but the rudiments of a federal system, but they pointed the way to developments which would be found necessary early in the next century, when the administration of conquests made from Habsburg by joint effort—the common lordships—demanded decisions incompatible with complete cantonal sovereignty.

Despite the incoherences of its structure the confederation had achieved decisive success by 1394. But we must not too hastily salute in it the triumph of liberal or democratic principles. The freedom for which the cantons had fought was their own communal independence, not 'the freedom of the individual in the state and from the state'; its enjoyment did not exclude the acquisition of subjects, and, indeed, it implied the right to oppress those subjects. In this respect the record of the rural cantons is better than that of the towns. The former did encourage neighbouring peasant communities, in Appenzell, in Grisons, in the Valais, to be rid of their lords altogether, and did not, in general, attempt to impose a new lordship of their own in place of the old; even so, as late as 1755 Uri was to be embarrassed by a peasant rising in the dependent Val Leventina. The city states of the confederation treated their subject populations, which they were as eager to increase as any of the contemporary territorial princes, no better and sometimes worse than was the habit of the princes. For a country district the rule of Berne or Zürich or Lucerne did not mean the abolition of manorial servitudes; these remained alive, the cause of recurrent controversy, until the second half of the eighteenth century. And for a town to exchange the lordship of a dynast for that of a city state almost invariably meant some loss of control over its own affairs. Thus the transfer from Habsburg to confederate rule was by no means always felt to be a boon, nor did it necessarily bring an enlargement of freedom: the men of Grüningen, to the north of lake Zürich, who had passed from Austria to Zürich in 1408, by 1440 were complaining that their position had deteriorated under their new masters.

To turn from subjects to citizens: how democratic were the constitutions of the ruling communes? Here again there is an obvious distinction between the rural cantons and the urban oligarchies. In the former the sovereign was the *Landesgemeinde*, the assembly of the whole folk of the valley, which might delegate business to elected officials and executive committees, but which reserved the important decisions to itself. But, as Edward Gibbon pointed out in 1767, even in the rural cantons the making of policy can hardly have been left to the capacity of 'obscure peasants'; it is not among them that we are to seek the active agents of the unions of 1291 and

1315. In the early history of all the forest cantons there are traces of a directing *élite*, and sometimes of an aristocracy of birth, which was not ashamed to take advantage of the possibilities offered to capitalist enterprise by the St. Gotthard traffic. The nobles von Attinghausen held a predominant position in Uri from 1294 (at the latest) until 1357, occupying the office of *Landamman* almost by hereditary right; at the same period Schwyz had its great families —though they were not noble—Stauffacher and ab Iberg; the Waltersberg family exercised an Italianate tyranny in Unterwalden. About these men the evidence is scanty, but it is enough to allow us to suppose that it was they and their kind who animated and organized the confederation in its early years. Nevertheless, in the valleys the popular assemblies did in time rid themselves of these over-mighty families and take over the business of government.

There was little room for such popular movements in the towns. Neither in Lucerne nor in Berne were the gilds able to gain the power which they attained elsewhere in Germany. Attempts were made to broaden the basis of government in Lucerne in 1336 and again in 1343, but in effect, in Lucerne as in Berne, where a conspiracy to impose a gild constitution failed in 1368, the council which ruled was a self-perpetuating body of merchant patricians, tinctured by remnants of the town nobility. By the overthrow of such a regime in Zürich Rudolf Brun rose to power in 1336. Gild support had been necessary for his success, and his revision of the constitution gave the gilds seats on the council, but it was he who remained the real ruler of Zürich. And although the office of burgomaster lost much of its importance after Brun's death in 1360, democracy had made no striking progress in Zürich before the end of the century.

Yet desire for freedom, in the sense in which they understood it, was the inspiration common to all the confederates, supplementing their institutional deficiencies and bridging the diversities in their constitutions and in their external ambitions. By the end of the fourteenth century the last had become formidable: Schwyz and Zürich were rivals for the lordship over the Linth valley; the eyes of Uri and Unterwalden were already turning towards the southern slopes of the Alps, and those of Berne westwards towards the Jura. The abiding common interest was in freedom from Habsburg, to be secured by aggressive action.

That perhaps is the most remarkable characteristic of the young confederation—its offensive, warlike nature. 'A system of military alliances for the common exploitation of the warlike energies of the people': thus has an Austrian historian defined the young confederacy, and clearly that is how, beyond all others, the canton of Schwyz understood it. For by the leading part it played in almost every attack on Austria Schwyz justified the conveyance of its name to the confederation as a whole.

It is proper to allow due weight to the manifold preoccupations which prevented Austria from dealing thoroughly with the confederacy. They permitted no more than two large-scale expeditions against central Switzerland in 100 years. But both these expeditions were catastrophic failures. Analysis of the reasons for the confederates' success cannot usefully be pushed farther: they knew better how to fight than their opponents. That the Habsburgs could plan a campaign their general strategic schemes before Morgarten and Sempach are evidence. They were not incapable of tactical experiment; at Sempach the device of Duke Leopold III of dismounting his men-at-arms and ordering them to use their long lances as infantry pikes presented the Swiss with a problem which could be solved only by some prodigious heroism, of which the traces survive in the tales about Arnold von Winkelried. But Austria was hampered by the conservatism of her military organization; the mounted feudal array, even when braced by mercenaries from Italy and the Low Countries, was becoming obsolete against disciplined infantry, and was peculiarly unfitted for warfare in Alpine valleys: at Morgarten the Austrian army had been defeated before it was deployed. For the Swiss were no amateurs, no gifted improvisers in war. They were practised mercenaries in the thirteenth century; in 1289 a contingent of 1,500 men of Schwyz—not far short of the whole fighting force of the valley—had distinguished itself in the imperial army at the siege of Besançon. They fought on foot, lightly equipped, and so were capable of great speed in mobilization and in marching. Throughout the fourteenth century their chief weapon remained the halberd, the dreadful axe with hook or spike to the rear, swung two-handed by its 8-foot shaft; not till the Appenzell War of 1403–8 was it replaced by an importation from Italy, the long pike on which the later exploits of the Swiss infantry were based.

The equipment of the medieval Swiss armies can still be studied in the museums; we are less well informed how they fought their battles. For if the early chronicles are meagre, the later are often preposterous. At times the Swiss built fortifications across their valleys, but these dry stone walls, the *Letzi*, were perhaps intended less as an obstacle to be stubbornly defended than as a means of breaking the enemy's order as he advanced, and then as an anvil on which to crack him as he was forced back. The contemporary account of the battle of Laupen mentions that the muster of the men of Berne resembled a wedge, but it would be rash to draw conclusions from a single reference about the normal fighting formations of the confederates in the fourteenth century. It is only at Laupen that we hear of generalship, and it is not certain—though it is very likely—that on this occasion a noble, Rudolf von Erlach, did exercise supreme command. The strength of the Swiss lay, not in the refinements of science, but partly in their skilled choice of position and more in the irresistible impetus of their charge. For that they were fitted by their hard physical condition, the gift of the Alpine life, by their light accoutrement, and by a savagery which did not commonly spare prisoners. Not idly did the Austrians call them beasts: *montani bestiales*. Above all, their *moral* and their discipline were excellent. The whole male population of a valley came out in arms to illustrate the truth that a man fights better in the presence of his own relations and his wife's. From the habit of success the Swiss acquired unshakable confidence; in the fourteenth century the silk was never frayed by defeat. Perhaps there was one opponent who might have withstood them, but the test never occurred. For two centuries the Swiss did not have to meet intelligent missile tactics such as the reformed army of the English king might have shown them. Against an Austrian array they were at any time the masters. On that fact the permanence of the confederation was established.

VI

THE HEROIC AGE

The fifteenth century. Judged by the standard of political significance for Europe, the fifteenth century is the supreme age of Swiss history. Between 1415 and 1525 the confederation achieved greatness: the emperor was brought to realize that his nominal subjects had escaped from his authority, but could be induced to offer him help; the kings of France let no opportunity slip of improving relations with these rough German fighters, while Burgundy, Savoy, Venice, and, almost more than any, the papacy, watched anxiously the proceedings of the frequent, cumbrous, and usually inconclusive diets in which a slight approximation to agreed Swiss policy was reached. During the years of transition from feudal armies to national armies, the Swiss were better able to wage successful war than any other community in Europe. A threat, or apparent threat, to their independence, an appeal to the needs and greed of poor peasants, adroit flattery, successful invocation of the claims of religion, or even skilful bribery of the few men who knew something of Europe and of the management of their fellows, could bring out an armed force of disciplined brave men whose fire-power and weight of advance made them formidable beyond their numbers, which were considerable. It was only when artillery became a decisive factor in armed conflicts that war ceased to be the only profitable national industry of Switzerland. There was a moment at the beginning of the sixteenth century when the united cantons were a great power, and when decisive action might have made the confederation as influential as the kingdom of France, but, fortunately for humanity, unity and aggressive decision were alike lacking, and variety continued to be the characteristic and the attraction of these peoples.

Most of the energy of this most active of centuries was consumed in what would be described in English or French history as civil war. It was essential that between the Rhine and the Rhone there should be sufficient community of purpose to ensure that the homes and possessions of the valley-dwellers should be safe, if necessity or interest should call away the majority of the able-bodied males.

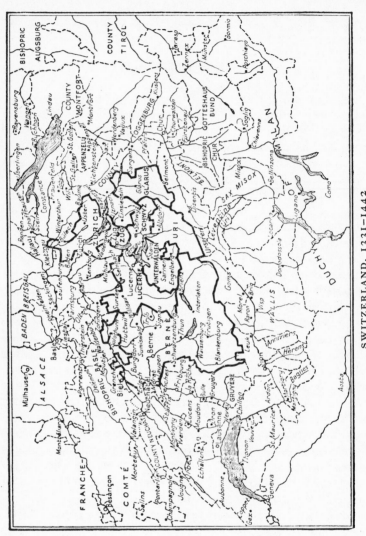

SWITZERLAND, 1331-1442

This was bound in the end to involve the subordination of the less well-organized communities to the better-organized ones and, in fact, led to the magnification of the cities and the predominance of Zürich and Berne. If the essentially trading oligarchy of the former could be brought into harmony with the semi-feudal aristocracy of the latter, a policy could at any rate be formulated for consideration by the proudly particularist peasantry who were linked by the waters of the lake of Lucerne and by the maintenance of the trade route to the south.

A great gap in the Swiss defences was stopped by the successful occupation of Aargau in 1415. Some insurance was thus effected against the danger of a Habsburg return and the price was worth paying, even if the administration of this area continued to be a source of division until 1848. The fact that the area was held, while later suggestions of advance into Swabia proved impracticable, is evidence that successful resistance to attack had become defence by aggression.

Much the same factor operated in the south-west. The house of Savoy was at no time after the thirteenth century as powerful as the house of Habsburg. The test of marriage-alliances is decisive in this regard; Chambéry was not a good enough home for the best heiresses, whereas Vienna was. At the beginning of the fifteenth century Sion, Geneva, and beyond, were districts almost as alien as France or Genoa to the men of Lucerne, but it was otherwise with German-speaking, imperial-minded Berne. The city of the Aare, once no mightier than Fribourg, had made itself what in England might have been known as the head of the honour of the Oberland. One by one castles had fallen, knights had submitted, territories had been acquired by lapse, purchase, and occupation. Berne was a powerful state, especially when in alliance with Savoy, and it was not until the failure of the escalade against Geneva in 1602 that Savoy finally abandoned all hope of seriously influencing, through Berne, the fortunes of the confederation.

The fifteenth century saw, too, the loose adhesion of the Valais and of the large and rather amorphous areas of the Ticino and of the Grisons to the confederation. The Grisons (*Graubünden*) was a generic name conveniently applied to the valleys of which Chur was the chief place, but whose inhabitants long exhibited by their diversity, variety, independence, and isolation, as well as by their forms of government, a Switzerland in miniature.

St. Gallen and Appenzell. The expansion which was so characteristic of the Swiss communities of the fifteenth century began
in the east and spread to the west. The monastery of St. Gallen had
steadily declined in spiritual and temporal prestige alike since the
thirteenth century, although its abbot maintained his position as
a prince of the empire and ruler of a considerable domain. Precisely what his rights over the abbey city of St. Gallen were was a
matter of constant dispute. The citizens were growing numerous
and wealthy: they knew how much had been achieved by the cities
of south Germany and by Lucerne, Zürich, Basle, and Berne, and
they restlessly demanded a greater measure of independence and
self-government. They wanted to judge their own citizens, to cease
paying taxes to the abbots, and to enter freely into leagues with
other cities.

These citizens found an ally close at hand in the inhabitants of
the inhospitable highlands of Appenzell. There the peasants owed
feudal service to the abbot of St. Gallen, but the nature of their
obligations was uncertain and the fourteenth century had seen
wide variations in the enforcement of these rights. An energetic
abbot, Kuno of Stoffeln (1379–1411) resumed authority formerly
exercised by bailiffs and agents and pressed for the full discharge
of ancient obligations. This was highly unpopular, coming as it
did at a time when ecclesiastical pretensions were meeting much
criticism in western Europe and when the success of the forest
cantons in obtaining complete practical independence had been
reinforced by the equally successful action of Glarus. Common
needs brought about common action: citizens and peasants joined
forces, and passive resistance to the monastic authorities soon led
to violence. The abbot had sufficient force available to enable him
to meet resistance in his city and in the immediate neighbourhood. This did not prevent the men of Appenzell from ravaging
monastic estates and defended positions but it drove them, for
protection, to seek help from Schwyz, help which was willingly
forthcoming in 1403. Moreover, the resources of the monastery of
St. Gallen, when mobilized, were considerable, and the abbot was
in a position to put up a good resistance to invading looters; yet,
even so, his army was turned back near Speicher (15 May 1403) by
a much smaller Appenzell–Schwyz contingent.

Further plundering followed. The abbot of St. Gallen now
appealed to Austria, a skilful move, for Schwyz was included in

the confederate truce with Austria,[1] and the cities of Lucerne, Berne, Solothurn, and Zürich were disinclined to advance the cause of another peasant hill-community. Only a bankrupt noble-man in peasant garb, Rudolf von Werdenberg, helped Appenzell. Even so, at Stoss, in June 1405, the Austrian–St. Gallen force was again driven back, and again the mountaineers looted to the gates of St. Gallen and beyond. These operations were all on a small scale and were outside the limits of the confederation save in so far as men from Schwyz shared in the occupation of a little territory. When the men of Appenzell and their allies reached Bregenz in January 1408 they were easily overcome and a peace or truce was arranged by Rupert, king of the Romans, on a basis of return to the position before the outbreak. But whatever the theory, in practice the men of Appenzell had obtained independence, and this was marked in November 1411 by the acceptance of Appen-zell as an ally (*Zugewandte*) of the states of the confederation excluding Berne. The men of Appenzell promised to assist their allies when called upon to do so, freely, and with all men avail-able; they would also make no alliance outside the confederation nor enter independently into any war. It was a position of pro-tected subordination and, until the recognition of Appenzell as a sovereign state (*Ort*) in 1513, it provided the classic example of an 'ally'. This in itself implied an enlarging of Swiss responsibili-ties, although only on a small scale. It led to an even more decisive expansion.

Occupation of Aargau

Rupert, king of the Romans, died in 1410 and Sigismund of Bohemia was elected emperor in 1411. These were years of great confusion—the Great Schism crippled the power and lowered the repute of the papacy, the renewal of the Hundred Years War be-tween England and France made matters worse, and the eclipse of the Habsburgs made Austria less powerful. The city of Con-stance, so well known to every merchant of eastern Switzerland, was chosen for the assemblage of a great international conference, to bring, in medieval fashion, unity to the church. The passage of rich ecclesiastics over the Swiss roads brought money and a sense

[1] See p. 100 above.

of importance, while the politics of the council offered an opportunity which was quickly taken.

The violent and debauched Pope John XXIII whom the council intended to depose was supported by Frederick of Austria, count of Tyrol (known as 'the Penniless'), and it was to Frederick's protection that John XXIII appealed when he fled on 20 March 1415 to Schaffhausen and vainly tried to dissolve the council. Frederick was put to the ban of the empire and Sigismund looked for help from the south. Between Berne and Zürich lay the Austrian corridor of Aargau, the last notable outpost south of the Rhine still in the hands of the traditional enemy. With Austrian forces in undisputed possession of the river fortresses of Zofingen, Aarburg, Aarau, and Brugg, a perfect bridgehead existed for a renewed attack upon the confederation. Berne now took the lead in an unprovoked but entirely successful assault upon the salient from the west, Zürich attacking from the east and Lucerne from the south. In spite of orders from Sigismund to desist when Frederick of Austria made his submission, the invaders pressed north to Baden, entering the city and securing the submission of its castle.

There had been little serious resistance, but if Aargau had been occupied easily it must also clearly be defended against a counter-attack, and this raised the questions of by whom and for whom? The continued occupation of Aargau not only marks a stage forward in Swiss history; it was also later to provide almost the only cement capable of holding the confederation together. For it was agreed that the area should not be partitioned but should be held in common. Together the conquerors would collect taxes and dues, arrange tolls, and appoint governors. The remaining states of the confederation would be consulted and thus 'a common lordship' was formed. It was one of those compromise solutions easy to arrive at at the moment, but with the most far-reaching implications only to be realized much later.

Valais and Ticino. The occupation of Aargau sealed the northern gap and also allowed some attention to be paid to the south. There the threat from the house of Savoy might prove as menacing as that from the Habsburgs. Between Berne and Savoy lay the rich valley of the Rhone, *the* valley, Valais, with the bishop of Sion as its most influential personality. When, as in 1400, the bishop was of the powerful local family Raron, the valley-dwellers themselves had to struggle to secure their liberties, including some guarantee that their magistrates would be local men, known to them. Lucerne, Uri, and Unterwalden were even more interested parties than Berne, and it was with their assistance that the independence of the inhabitants of Valais was somewhat precariously secured.

Adjoining the Valais to the east was the area forming the present-day canton of Ticino. Here local boundary disputes had been common since the twelfth century, and these became intensified as the power of the emperor declined and as Milan became a powerful duchy. The trade passing over the St. Gotthard was so considerable and so valuable to the communities round the lake of Lucerne that, if necessary, they, and in particular Uri, would intervene to prevent its interruption. The crucial point had long been the district around Bellinzona. The controlling power there was exercised by the Freiherr von Sax zu Misox, a petty impecunious nobleman who in 1419 parted with his rights for cash to Uri and Obwalden. Three years later Filippo Maria Visconti of Milan challenged this action, claimed Bellinzona (offering some money compensation which was refused) and sent an army north up the Ticino. The mercenary commander Carmagnola showed his gifts of strategy and organization to considerable advantage, advancing almost without opposition up the Eschental and Valle Leventina. Slowly and reluctantly a small indisciplined force from the lake of Lucerne came to meet the threat to their communications, then divided in order to forage and were defeated with some loss at Arbedo (30 June 1422). Finally, in January 1426, a peace was mediated by Basle, Berne, and others at Sion, the unsatisfactory and uncertain former conditions being restored. It implied the temporary abandonment of expansion to the south and it showed that effective co-operation in anything save defence against an obvious enemy was still to be desired.

Zürich and the Toggenburg inheritance. This was made even clearer in the valley of the Thur. From thence Count Frederick VII of Toggenburg (d. 1436) had improved his hereditary position by the acquisition of Uznach, Prätigau, and Davos, and, by pledge or grant from Austria, of Sargans and the Gastern valley. By 1430 it had become apparent that Count Frederick was likely to be childless and that his lands might become the prize of successful violence or intrigue. The competitors for control of the trade route involved were Zürich and Schwyz. Here was an historic rivalry that persists throughout the course of Swiss history—the town against the country-side, the intelligent and numerous artisans against the scattered and prejudiced peasants, the conciliar oligarchy of Zürich against the primitive democracy of one of the most ancient of freedom-loving communities, the whole embodied in and accentuated by the personal differences between Rudolf Stüssi, burgomaster of Zürich, and Ital Reding, chief magistrate of Schwyz. Count Frederick had been admitted a citizen of Zürich and he had also made a common law agreement with Schwyz, while the uncertainty of his position while alive was paralleled by the complexity and dubious nature of the disposition of his property revealed at his death in 1436. His widow agreed that Zürich might occupy Uznach, which was done, but any further advance to the Walensee and beyond to Sargans or in the Gaster region met with fierce resistance. Claimants to the inheritance multiplied and there was no way out but by the clash of armed force—no one would accept Sigismund's proferred imperial mediation. Schwyz and Glarus hoped for the whole area jointly or severally and rejected any suggestion that the confederation might arrange some partition, while the people in the southern (Grisons) part of the heritage formed a separatist local confederation known as the *Zehngerichtenbund*.

Hence, in 1436, the death of the count was followed by an immediate armed struggle. The force from Zürich which occupied Uznach pushed on beyond the Walensee to Sargans, an alliance with which relatively distant outpost was Zürich's chief gain from the war. Schwyz and Glarus resisted with determination every attempt at any further penetration by Zürich and succeeded in securing the friendship of the group of nobles who between them claimed most of the Toggenburg heritage. In addition they gained the support of Austria as well, which could put forward considerable claims in the area, and thus they were able ultimately to prevent Zürich from acquiring an area of subject territory in eastern Switzerland corresponding in size to that of Berne in western Switzerland. This failure, in the long run, deprived Zürich of the chance of becoming the 'capital of Switzerland' which must otherwise inevitably have been the case.

Efforts at mediation made in 1437 by the remaining members of the confederation resulted in failure. The men of Zürich, led by Burgomaster Stüssi, closed their markets to their enemies, a serious measure, for the hill-men found difficulty in obtaining the necessary corn in exchange for cattle-products elsewhere. Economic boycott finally led to an armed clash: Schwyz secured the help of Uri and Unterwalden, and they were also joined by individual adventurers allowed to come from Lucerne, Berne, and Zug. On the Etzel in 1439 and at Pfäffikon in 1440 the men of Zürich were driven back. Stüssi had failed to obtain the Toggenburg inheritance and the defeat was complete. There was no alternative but to reopen the markets and accept the setback.

Albert II, king of Bohemia and Hungary, died after a very short reign in 1439 and was succeeded in 1440 by the dreariest of the Habsburg emperors, Frederick III. An uninspiring personality Frederick may have been, but he was the inheritor of the Habsburg family tradition. His advisers could not fail to suggest that free communities of peasants ought not, whatever instruments signed in the past might say, to be permitted to live securely and independently on territory that had belonged to his ancestors. This could not now be regained by any force of arms that Frederick could muster, but he was not reluctant to try intrigue. Nor, equally, was Stüssi of Zürich, whose whole public life had been taken up with successful but risky and somewhat shady negotiations. By 1442 an understanding had been reached. The city of Zürich would join forces with Frederick III; the king of the Romans, with the help of his ally, was to regain the county of Kiburg, which had been lost something like a century previously, and in return Zürich would receive legal rights over the Toggenburg lands and, no longer part of the confederation, could edge out the other occupiers of Aargau which should form part of a greater state of Zürich. Sentiment and tradition apart, it was a masterly scheme, but sentiment and tradition were already of the very stuff of which the confederation was made. Frederick III could not in fact produce either money or men; Zürich could wield a powerful economic weapon if time were allowed for its operation, but Lucerne, Zug, Schwyz, Uri, Unterwalden, Glarus—and possibly Berne—could, if necessity forced it, produce at short notice a small force of halberdiers and pikemen such as Europe had not yet seen the like.

Otherwise Stüssi had worked well. He could put up a good legal case and he expected that economic pressure would do the rest. A request that Zürich should break with Austria was followed in

1443 by an ultimatum to this effect from the confederation which was ignored and was followed by an advance into Zürich territory by some 6,000 men. A scratch civic force, ignoring sound military advice from the Austrian representative, Türing von Hallwill, came out to meet the invaders and met with a decisive defeat (22 July 1443) not far from the city walls, near the hospital of St. James (St. Jakob an der Sihl). Stüssi was killed and Zürich agreed to an armistice, once more relinquishing her gains. While peace negotiations went on, application for further help was made to Frederick III, who had none to send. The armistice days ran out, Greifensee fell after a brave resistance, and on Midsummer day 1444, Zürich was besieged. Relief came from an entirely unexpected quarter. The emperor was at the moment on terms of friendship with Charles VII of France, who had now expelled all but the last remnants of the English and thus brought the Hundred Years War practically to an end. There was a truce with England and thousands of military adventurers in France were unemployed. It was a suitable moment for the Habsburg monarch to call on the French king for assistance on behalf of Zürich against the Swiss who were then almost entirely unknown in Paris. Charles VII saw an opportunity to rid his realm of the 'brigands', *écorcheurs*, Armagnacs, as the companies of ex-soldiers, wandering and looting in the south of France, were known. The dauphin, the future King Louis XI, then twenty-one years old, was placed in nominal command of a fighting force to help Austria. Thousands, probably more than 10,000, ragged, ill-disciplined but experienced ruffians slowly lumbered eastwards to the Rhine, plundering and devastating as they went. This was the help that the Habsburg could bring Zürich, far larger, and also far more unmanageable, than had been anticipated, with Antoine de Chabanes, count of Dammartin, as their effective commander.

St. Jakob an der Birs. His plan seems to have been to relieve Zürich, which was in no immediate danger, by effecting a junction with Thomas von Falkenstein, a Habsburg supporter whose castle at Farnsburg was invested by the confederates. Basle itself, a free imperial city where an oecumenical council was bringing its deliberations to a close, might well be in danger, more perhaps of a sack than of a permanent French occupation. The long columns of the invaders could be seen from the walls of the city passing south of it, while to meet them came a small body of less than 2,000 infantry. This Swiss contingent, small as it was, contained picked men drawn from every state of the confederation, and men from Solothurn and (perhaps) Neuchâtel as well, but received no serious support from Basle whose citizens, after a half-hearted sortie, seem to have watched what was happening, either hoping for immunity by neutrality, or else accounting every man necessary for defence in case of a siege. At St. Jakob an der Birs, all day, 26 August 1444, the Swiss, outnumbered by ten to one, and by professional soldiers at that, fought until they were overwhelmed by sheer weight of numbers. They were wiped out almost to a man. Nor had there been any token of or suggestion of surrender, and their discipline, their cohesion, their skill in the use of bow, pike, and halberd, had accounted for many times their own numbers.

The battle of St. Jakob an der Birs was one of those apparently insignificant events which, in fact, indicate a great deal. A small force of unknown warriors, after a gallant resistance, had been wiped out. Such a thing had happened before and was often to happen again. What gave it its special meaning was that it showed France, the greatest European power, the stuff of which these peasants were made. They were far from home; they had no natural advantages from the country or from special local knowledge as at Sempach and Näfels; they were involved in a war with the emperor on behalf of Swiss unity and the right to settle their own affairs in their own way and they faced, together and undaunted, overwhelming odds. If this was what an advance force could do in the plain, what might not be expected if the French moved eastwards towards the hills? The *écorcheurs* knew fighters when they saw them, and the leaders, and the dauphin himself, had cause for reflection. Even if the advance continued and Zürich were relieved, it would be at great cost in men and materials and would benefit only Frederick III who had done little to help himself and who was in fact potentially a far more dangerous enemy to the French than to the Swiss villagers. There was a pause, as it were for reflection, while the invading force foraged far and wide. Approaches were made to the council of Basle for the surrender of the city and were decisively, almost derisively rejected. The duke of Savoy, Louis's father-in-law, offered mediation, the Swiss abandoned the pressure on Zürich and Farnsburg, and the Austrian forces seemed as much disposed to attack the French as the Swiss. On 20 September 1444 an armistice was arranged and on

28 October the dauphin allowed his seal to be set to the peace of Ensisheim. It was the first of many such documents, and it implied recognition by France that a community existed near its frontiers with whom mutually advantageous arrangements might be made. For the moment a general guarantee of security of person and property, some facilities for trade and a promise of French assistance to bring about peace between Austria, Zürich, and the confederation, was all that could be obtained. The 'brigands' moved where they could loot best, into Alsace, and thus ceased to be a menace to the French kingdom, for the infuriated peasantry destroyed many, and others returned to become regular soldiers in the service of the French king. The dauphin was recalled, and Charles VII soon ceased to be on friendly terms with the Austrian monarch.

Further expansion

What the latter had been unable to secure with French help he was unlikely to obtain alone, while at Zürich the Toggenburg inheritance receded somewhat from the immediate picture. This, however, did not mean that the struggle was at an end; indeed, it rather intensified the local side of it, making it more clearly a civil war, a fight between closely allied peoples. Throughout most of 1445 there was desultory 'phoney' war, cattle-lifting, sieges, lake battles, and forays, working up in 1446 to a serious battle at Ragaz (6 March) when an army of just over 1,000 men, mostly from Glarus, defeated an Austrian force four times its size.

The victory was a minor one, but decisive. Clearly Austria, even with the support of Zürich, could not win back what had been lost for a century. Equally clearly, Zürich could not hope to obtain the whole of the Toggenburg inheritance and build up a great eastern state, larger and more powerful than Berne. The Austrian nobles began to weary of a struggle which offered little prospect of easy reward, while a prolongation of it might lead to their own tenants seeking Swiss help against them and attempting a revolt. The harm that Zürich could do by closing its markets to its neighbours recoiled upon itself and more and more citizens opposed an increasingly purposeless combat. Between the armistice accepted in 1446 and the peace mediated by Heinrich von Bubenberg of Berne in 1450 lay four years of cooling reflection. At the peace it was agreed that Zürich should renounce the Austrian alliance—a considerable blow to its pride—should be accepted once more into the confederation and should regain the places and land that had been taken from it. Schwyz gained control of positions on the lake of Zürich, thereby blocking the advance of the great city south-wards, and this at a time of general and energetic expansion. The first civil war had compelled a recalcitrant state to come into line with the others: all felt the shame that brethren should be in arms against one another, eastern Switzerland suffered loss and devasta-tion while, in the west, Berne prepared for yet further extensions of its influence.

Instead of the former enmity to the house of Habsburg, which was mainly directed against individual rulers, there now was hostility to the Holy Roman Empire as an institution and a deter-mination to obtain complete and real independence of it. Rela-tions with France had opened and were soon to be placed on a footing of increased intimacy; the fighters from the valleys were now conscious of their strength and an era of participation in con-flicts outside the confederation begins.

The abbot of St. Gallen was the first to recognize the new situa-tion and in 1451 became an ally, almost a member, of the con-federation. He was for the future for all time to be in *Burgrecht* and *Landrecht* with Zürich, Lucerne, Schwyz, and Glarus; he could count on their protection, but it was to be long before he or the city of St. Gallen were to be admitted to full rights within the confederation. Much the same was true of Appenzell (1452) and of Schaffhausen (1459), while Stein on the Rhine (1459), Rottweil (1463), and Mülhausen (1466) were also brought into alliance status. Rottweil was distant and isolated and in the end could not fulfil its obligations, and Mülhausen, although at one time almost accepted as a full member of the confederation, continued to occupy an unstable and somewhat uncertain position until the French Revolution. Appenzell and Schaffhausen painfully edged their way forward to the position of sovereign members of the Bund, but full recognition was long delayed.

One of the reasons why this was so was that the original cantons, jealous and self-important in any case, were about to embark upon further expansionist activities and were not prepared to share with any others the profits of such enterprises. Berne was independently setting an active example, making sure that Fribourg was not to be brought into such close relations with the duke of Savoy that there was any danger of the Savoyard duchy taking it into 'protective custody'.

A shooting match at Constance in 1458 led to a renewed quarrel with Austria, wantonly picked on a slight pretext and resulting in the acquisition of the strategically valuable position of Rapperswil as a semi-dependent ally by the three forest cantons and Glarus. An almost equally trivial, or at any rate irrelevant, matter led to the 'liberation' of Thurgau, the area to the west of the lake of Constance. Duke Sigismund of Austria, count of Tyrol, son-in-law of James V of Scotland, was excommunicated in 1460 by his former friend, Pope Pius II, because of his attempt to exclude Cardinal Nicholas of Cues from his bishopric of Brixen. This pretext, and the fact that he was first cousin of, and a possible successor to, the emperor Frederick III, brought a large force of warriors, mainly from Lucerne and Unterwalden, north. Without meeting any very considerable opposition, they swept onwards as far as the Rhine, occupying Frauenfeld but failing to take Winterthur which passed more unromantically to Zürich in 1467 by purchase. The peace of Constance, 1 June 1461, left Austria, once so menacing, almost without a stronghold south of the Rhine.[2] It meant that security had been achieved and that there was now no power which would risk interference with the peasant communities who had shown such singular powers of organization, such ferocious and disciplined bravery on the field of battle, and such clear capacity for further advance.

There was no tradition of neutrality, no sense of international obligations, not even, it is to be feared, any great inclination to observe treaties that they themselves had made if circumstances offered advantage to those who ignored them. Somehow, in the critical fifties and sixties of the fifteenth century, the members of the scarcely coherent Swiss confederation, without realizing themselves what was happening, passed from the allegedly defensive to the openly offensive. War had been forced on their fathers; the sons had come almost to enjoy fighting for its own sake. Life in the valleys was hard. There was too little sun and too little depth of soil for it to be possible to feed a growing population, nor could cheese and milk products alone provide sufficient exchange-value for other necessities. There was, indeed, a source of income from the tolls levied on goods coming over the St. Gotthard, but neither

[2] Rheinfelden and Laufenburg were the chief exceptions.

these, nor the profits of carrying them northwards, could amount to very much. Zürich was the centre of a silk and wool industry, but the two wars in which the city was engaged had done much to ruin this. 'How can our young men find a living?' This has been the age-long question for the Swiss, and in the fifteenth century the answer was as obvious as hotel-keeping was in the early twentieth century—by war. What could not be obtained by labour could be, almost must be, obtained by loot. They had seen and defeated, almost easily, knights and foot-soldiers from the empire, from France, from Savoy, from Milan. They had learnt that if they could but keep together, land, stores of food, cities, and gold were theirs for the taking. To the ethics of the situation they paid no more heed than did Elizabeth's seamen beyond the line a century later. Their necessities were their excuse and their successes their justification.

Renewed expansion: Mülhausen. The struggle with Austria had been mainly carried on by the forest cantons and their allies. Berne had been less interested save when it was apparent that a common danger must be met by common precautions and also when the chance came for securing the whole of the valley of the Aar by well-planned aggression. The Aar joins the Rhine near Waldshut which, with the country round (the Fricktal) and the 'Rhine towns' of Säckingen, Laufenburg, and Rheinfelden, was now under the control of Duke Sigismund. Berne and Solothurn were in close alliance and knew that at least a benevolent neutrality could be assumed on the part of the great free imperial city of Basle, well able to look after itself. But north of Basle, almost on the Rhine and commanding the too famous Belfort gap, lay another free imperial city, less sure of its defences, Mülhausen. The independence of this little walled town was precarious. Its trade depended upon communications which were constantly in danger of interruption, for it was set in a border country-side which knew no effective master, it had suffered from the ravages of the *écorcheurs*, it had not administered its own internal affairs with special prudence or foresight, and both its revenues and its position were coveted by the dukes of Austria and by the local nobility. The city—or some of its leading citizens, for it is unprofitable to differentiate—was in debt to various creditors. It was at this juncture that Sigismund, duke of Austria, joined forces with certain local landowners to threaten the city with an assault or a

siege. The citizens looked round for help and in June 1466 concluded a defensive alliance with Berne and Solothurn for twenty-
five years. This could easily be regarded merely as one of the many
inter-civic alliances which were so frequent in this century, particularly among the cities of south Germany, but, in fact, it turned
out to be something different. Berne in 1466 was the most powerful of the cantons of the confederation, Zürich being temporarily
eclipsed after the Toggenburg War. Reasonably secure from the
south, Berne was in a position strong enough to hope for security
by expansion elsewhere.

In 1467 and 1468 efforts were made from Basle (both by the
bishop and the city) and Berne to arrange an agreement between
Mülhausen, Sigismund, the Alsatian nobles, and the city's creditors, no easy matter, particularly in view of the traditional Swiss
fear and dislike of Austria and also in view of further uncertainty
about the position of Schaffhausen where a knight, Bilgeri von
Heudorf, an old enemy of the cantons, was threatening an attack.
The Austrian agent in the Sundgau, Türing von Hallwill, violently
renewed the threat to Mülhausen, investing the city and destroying
crops and vines outside the walls. Berne and Solothurn sent a force
to the relief of their ally in May 1468 and, finding this insufficient,
turned to the remaining members of the confederation, where,
almost unexpectedly perhaps, the appeal for assistance met with a
willing, although not numerous, response. A Swiss army streamed
north past neutral Basle, meeting with no resistance, looting and
burning noble castles. At Ochsenfeld, near Thann, more Swiss
warriors joined the main body, presenting in all so formidable a
front that the followers of the opposing landowners made no
attempt to accept battle. Thus the Swiss march had been successful; Mülhausen remained a free city and an ally; the armies had
looted freely and continued to do so on the return journey, satisfied with the campaign. The states were proud of their warriors
before whom the enemy had fled. It seemed as if such enterprises
might be highly profitable and not too formidable: it might even
be that the remaining Habsburg dominions in south-west Germany were breaking up.

Berne, at any rate, was determined to profit by the situation
and to establish a claim to effective control over much of Aargau.
There seemed nothing to resist this. It was, however, rather a different matter from assisting an ally, and the eastern states were

not likely to forward attempts by Berne to become more powerful. The recent advance to Mülhausen, too, with its accompanying devastation, had left a bad impression on the country-side. To be successful the Bernese must occupy the four Rhine towns[3] of Rheinfelden, Säckingen, Laufenburg, and Waldshut. The latter became in August 1468 the immediate objective, and part of the force returning from Mülhausen appeared outside its walls anticipating an easy entry. But the inhabitants of Waldshut saw no reason for exchanging an amiably inefficient local Austrian control for a distant, probably unsympathetic, Bernese one, while Duke Sigismund was not prepared to abandon his possessions without a struggle. The Austrian nobles, including Bilgeri von Heudorf, with a friendly city supporting them, were here in a different position from that in which they were in the open country outside hostile Mülhausen, and a defended fortress on a great river is favourably situated for supplies in the event of a siege. For five weeks the Swiss forces besieged the town, which showed no signs of capitulation, and when the Bernese commanders called for a frontal attack to storm the defences, the men from other states, with good reason, shrank from committing their lives to an enterprise with which they had little sympathy. The bishop of Basle, the city of Basle, and the duke of Bavaria, were ready to act as mediators, and Sigismund of Austria was willing to listen to suggestions. Berne, Solothurn, and Fribourg acquiesced. The peace of Waldshut (27 August 1468), cheerfully accepted by Sigismund, was, on the face of it, simply a return to the situation as it had existed for the last seven years, including commercial and administrative freedom for Mülhausen. In addition, Sigismund promised to pay to the Swiss 10,000 gulden before 24 June of the following year, with a guarantee that if the money were not forthcoming in full the Swiss might occupy Waldshut and the Black Forest forthwith. From this simple promise enormous consequences were to follow.

Treaty of St. Omer. Enough was known of the Swiss to make it certain that the money must be forthcoming and in good time. Sigismund was in no position to put down 10,000 gulden and Frederick III was unable to help him. The duke turned for assistance to Louis XI, at whose court the influential Bernese citizen,

---

[3] Or forest cities (*Waldstädte*)—not to be confused with the forest cantons (*Waldstätte*).

Nicholas of Diesbach, happened to be, but the king of France was notoriously careful about money matters, even if open to a profit-able investment, and still more careful about keeping clear of engagements which might involve his country in war. He there-fore listened readily enough to Diesbach's arguments opposing any help to Sigismund whom the king refused to see in spite of the fact that Sigismund was married to Eleanor of Scotland, Louis's sister-in-law. The duke of Austria therefore turned to the only other obvious source of supply, Charles the Bold, duke of Burgundy. This ambitious prince, having failed to overthrow Louis, was now concentrating his efforts upon linking up his dominions and form-ing a unitary state along the left bank of the Rhine from which he might menace, or secure, the Empire. He had, indeed, formerly refused any accommodation, but in May 1469 he accepted the re-newed offer. He would take Sigismund into his alliance and under his protection; he would pay at once the 10,000 gulden due to the Swiss and would advance a further 40,000 gulden for Sigismund's needs within six months, receiving in return all Sigismund's rights over the landgraviate of Upper Alsace, the county of Ferette, and the four Rhine towns Waldshut, Säckingen, Laufenburg, and Rheinfelden, the latter being traditionally under the protection of Basle. With all this the duke likewise took over debts due to Sigismund from his Alsatian subjects or their creditors, the forti-fied city of Breisach, and all the vaguely defined Austrian rights and privileges in the area. Further, Charles received permission to redeem, wholly or in part, mortgages already raised on these lands (valued at 180,000 gulden) and the right to repair and build necessary fortifications. Sigismund reserved to himself only the right to redeem all this by repaying the whole of what was bor-rowed or due, in one lump sum at Besançon. Such were the essen-tial terms of the treaty of St. Omer (2 and 9 May 1469).

The Burgundian War

They implied and were accompanied by an alliance together with rather vague promises of mutual assistance. Sigismund seems to have been left with the impression that he could be sure of Burgundian help against the Swiss and thus secure once again former Austrian possessions across the Rhine. This was not the intention of Charles the Bold who had inherited, and wished to retain, Swiss friendship. But Charles also wanted, indeed needed for the fulfilment of his wide schemes, Alsace and the pledged territories. He was thus almost bound to come into conflict with the confederation and with Berne in particular. A Burgundian watch on the Rhine might be more dangerous than an Austrian one to Swiss liberties and, in any case, a great power, for such Burgundy was, could and would resist the northward thrust and the expansionist policy that had been favoured by the Swiss for the past three decades.

The danger was not immediately apparent. It is true that Burgundian commissioners made a symbolic entry into the Alsatian lands in May 1469, and Rheinfelden and Ensisheim accepted their new master in June and July, but this made little immediate difference to the actual situation, while Sigismund was manifestly deferring the transfer of Breisach as long as possible. Somewhat suspiciously, if also ineffectively, the emperor at the same time declared the treaty of Waldshut null and void. Charles the Bold lost no time in showing how he interpreted his arrangement with Sigismund. He assumed from the first that the loan would never be repaid, and he redeemed mortgages as fast as possible in order that the amount due in cash might be even more beyond Sigismund's power to repay and in order that Burgundian overlordship might become more of a reality. These redemptions, and the administrative reforms in Alsace which accompanied them, were perfectly legal, but were resented none the less in that they disturbed vested interests sometimes of more than a century's standing and pointed to the likelihood of an efficient modern centralized government where no government had been known for generations. There was, therefore, reason for a little alarm among the Swiss, intensified when Rheinfelden and Mülhausen, closely linked with Basle and Berne respectively, were threatened.

The Burgundian agent, 'Grand Bailiff of Ferette', appointed in September 1469, was Peter von Hagenbach, an obscure nobleman of proved efficiency and ruthlessness, admirably suited to tame wild men in a wild country-side. He believed in the ideal of Burgundian greatness, he was not afraid of illegality (although so confused was the situation which he inherited that he could claim to be within his rights in all that he did), and he had to extract the means for efficient rule from the country-side. Hence unpopular taxes and the inevitable linking of justice with extortion. Hence, too, pressure upon the independent and embarrassed

Mülhausen. In 1470 the Swiss diet was warned of the existence of danger to Berne's ally and invited Hagenbach to turn his attention elsewhere. The threat was dropped only to be renewed, and in 1471 and 1472 Hagenbach made himself more feared than ever, secured a potentially considerable revenue from the 'Bad Penny', an excise on wine, and practically broke up the little Alsatian civic league known as the Decapolis. Queer stories of the violence of the grand bailiff circulated south of the Rhine and were embodied in the popular songs of the peasantry. In Basle they were well known, for the independence of this great city was scarcely secure if all Alsace were united and joined with the Burgundies proper.

Sigismund was ready to urge Charles against the Swiss; Louis XI, guided by Diesbach, encouraged resistance without in any way seeming to intervene and did this so successfully that by 1474 Sigismund had been forced into a complete *volte-face*. He unwillingly perceived that, in fact, he had made the treaty of St. Omer with Charles almost in vain; the money was spent, Alsace was fast becoming a Burgundian province, and not an inch of ground was regained from the Swiss nor a single soldier sent to back up the Austrian claims. Lorraine, too, was fast going the way of the other neighbours of Burgundy and the ambitions of the great duke were confidently believed to include a kingdom for himself and the succession to the empire for his family.

The general alarm was intensified in 1473 by a renewal of the threat to the liberties of Mülhausen. Swiss dilatoriness, pacificism, and preoccupation with Milan, prevented action, whereupon the parties most immediately threatened formed a 'Lower' Union of their own including Basle, Colmar, Mülhausen, Schlettstadt, and Strassburg, with some episcopal and noble support. Defence could not be merely passive: assistance must be given to Mülhausen to liquidate outstanding debts, while Sigismund was open to receive offers, within the limits of the treaty of St. Omer, to redeem some or all of the territories he had pledged. Charles at once became alarmed at the very suggestion, having a few years earlier seen Louis XI regain the Somme towns in similar fashion. He noisily proclaimed that he would defend his ally Sigismund against all aggressors, but a little later made rather more friendly gestures towards the confederates. The Lower Union had continued to gather money or promises for the redemption. Sigismund had given up hope of Burgundian assistance and the majority among the governing body at Berne had decided where its interests lay. Led by the Diesbach family, Berne recognized in Charles the Bold the true danger to its future, and therefore in France the ultimate hope of salvation and expansion. Louis XI used every indirect means at his disposal (and they were not a few) to unite the many divergent interests against Burgundy. Accident and design were astonishingly successful and in March 1474 the extremes had met; Sigismund and the majority of the Swiss cantons sealed a perpetual understanding. There was to be free trade, a frontier settlement, arbitration in case of disputes, and mutual support. The Austrian duke had also secured, illusorily as it turned out, the money necessary for the redemption of his property and therefore for the denunciation of the treaty of St. Omer which was promptly signified to Charles (April 1474). The duke of Burgundy, although fully occupied in a quarrel with Cologne and in preparations for a siege of Neuss from which he confidently expected to extend his influence over the Rhineland, took up the challenge. He refused to acknowledge Sigismund's right to break his compact, insisted that the compensation offered him for his redemptions and improvements in Alsace was quite inadequate, that it did not even keep the precise terms of the agreement about repayment at Besançon, and that Alsace would remain his. He seems to have failed to realize both that the offer was, in fact, a Swiss declaration of war, and that Louis XI and Diesbach were behind the resistance of the forest towns, Breisach and Mülhausen. Hagenbach likewise failed to undeceive him. This faithful warrior had also visited his master, had received a vague promise of support, and had returned to continue the work of centralization and efficiency. A popular disturbance led to the arrest of the grand bailiff on 11 April 1474, followed by a trial before a semi-popular, illegal tribunal. Hagenbach was tortured, found guilty of oppression, moral delinquencies, and of plotting to exterminate the inhabitants of Breisach: his execution on 9 May was acclaimed with delight in Alsace and farther south.

It was a significant event, for it was a public challenge to Burgundy which could not be ignored. Charles the Bold, with singular maladroitness, succeeded in alienating Germans and Swiss, imperialists and independents at the same time, since all felt the same sense of menace, so that it was relatively simple for Louis XI to unite these enemies. While Hagenbach's younger brother Stephen led a punitive raid into Alsace, Louis, in September 1474, promised at a diet at Lucerne 80,000 livres as an annual subsidy to the Swiss cantons if they upheld the emperor in the war against Charles: the acceptance of this, together with an admission of French recruiting rights, implied action for which the confederate fighters were ready, and indeed eager, but whose final outcome was hardly suspected.

Charles possessed one ally who believed in the likelihood of Burgundian success, the ruler of Savoy. In this duchy, Yolande, sister of Louis XI, was acting as regent for her son Philibert I, and was influenced powerfully by her brothers-in-law, Philip of Bresse, and Louis, count of Romont. She was chiefly anxious for security, and to be able to resist the southward pressure of Berne. After some complicated intrigues, in which both Fribourg and Nicholas of Diesbach were involved, she accepted, on 30 January 1475, the treaty of Montecallerio. By this Savoy provided the link in an alliance between Burgundy and Milan (under Galeazzo Maria Sforza) which was to oppose a solid western barrier to any further expansion by Berne. In the event hardly anything turned out as planned. Charles could not, or would not, deal with his southern foes until he had forced the submission of Neuss, Sforza would not move a man or a horse until Charles came south in person, but his known adhesion to Burgundy alarmed the forest cantons, especially Lucerne, whose interests in the south had in the past come into collision with those of Milan. In February 1475 a diet at Lucerne was prepared to support Berne, and Berne had already informed Charles the Bold of its obligations, as part of the empire, to advance to the help of Frederick III. At the suggestion of Nicholas of Diesbach, reinforced by French gold, the Lower Union, with powerful individual Swiss support, had sent a force into Franche-Comté via the Belfort gap, and had laid siege to Héricourt (November 1474). A Burgundian force under Blamont advanced to its relief and was easily, but unexpectedly, defeated, leaving much welcome loot in the hands of the invaders. Alsace was thus saved at the outset and the victorious soldiers returned to act as the best recruiting sergeants for a campaign in the following year.

In 1475 the confederation was threatened with no serious danger, Charles the Bold being fully occupied first with winding up his affairs at Neuss, secondly with encouraging Edward IV to invade France, which he did profitably but pacifically in August, and then with an advance into Lorraine following the arrangement of a marriage of his daughter Mary with Maximilian, only son of Frederick III, in September, accompanied by a truce with Louis XI. Bernese forces had, all this spring and summer, been moving westward; had secured Grandson, Orbe, and Jougne, the castle of Blamont (Nicholas of Diesbach dying nearby and leaving the direction of Bernese policy to the less capable Nicholas of Scharnachtal), and much of the Vaud. Thus the policy of expansion was deliberately continued, and the inevitable clash with the Burgundian enemy was deferred until the following year when the strain was taken by the Swiss alone, unsupported from France or the empire.

Charles had come south at the beginning of 1476 with a fine army, its efficiency and equipment perhaps a little exaggerated by chroniclers anxious to magnify the greatness of its defeat. Well aware of the danger, Berne had moved men into the Vaud and had garrisoned various strong points including the castle of Grandson near the lake of Neuchâtel. This fortress was captured by the enemy in February and its garrison was put to death according to the custom of the age. Two days later (1 March 1476) a Swiss relieving force, gathered by Berne from every part of the confederation and from cities of the Lower Union, hardly inferior to the Burgundians in number and vastly superior in discipline, appeared prepared to offer battle. Charles advanced along the low ground by the shore of the lake, eager to meet an untried force of pikemen. He had reason to anticipate victory—in artillery and in cavalry his force was manifestly superior—and he was prepared to abandon a strong defensive position to come to grips with the enemy. This enemy had in any case divided its forces, part moving along the low road, part threading its way towards Grandson high up the hill-side. When, therefore, the Swiss soldiers knelt for a moment in prayer before the onset the duke thought this a sign of surrender and, when undeceived, ordered his artillery to open fire. The Swiss, unbroken, recoiled a little, and Charles, anxious to complete the overthrow, withdrew his main force somewhat in order to allow his gunners and archers freer play. This backward movement, unplanned and misunderstood, coincided with the appearance of the second Swiss detachment coming down noisily and defiantly from the hill. The whole Burgundian force promptly retreated in complete disorder in spite of Charles's efforts to rally it, leaving what seemed fabulously rich loot in the hands of the peasants. Overjoyed at an easy and complete triumph, a large number returned home laden with booty, ignoring suggestions from Berne that the Vaud should be permanently occupied. Neither side realized fully what had taken place. For Charles, accident had deprived him of a victory, but his army had not been destroyed, and at least nine men in ten escaped. He would rally his forces at Lausanne and resume the attack, surer than ever that Berne was his obvious objective and that he could attain his ends by one decisive blow. For the Swiss, their fellows had been avenged and their territory was in no immediate danger. Expansion towards the west was not popular with German-speaking easterners, and it was almost with reluctance that parties remained at Morat (Murten) and Fribourg to guard the western approaches to Berne.

Morat, a well-defended position, was garrisoned by Adrian von Bubenberg with 2,000 Bernese. The duke of Burgundy with great deliberation and some caution appeared outside its walls with 20,000 men on 9 June. There was no hint of surrender; the walls could not be destroyed by cannon fire quickly enough to be effective and attempts to storm a way in were relatively easily beaten off. The defence, which could not, of course, have lasted very long, enabled Berne to gather another incomparable infantry force, men streaming in from the north (Basle and the Lower Union) and from the east (including a belated Zürich contingent under the ambitious Hans Waldmann). This time there was no accident. Upon the issue of a battle, deliberately sought and accepted, depended the future of western, and probably also northern, Switzerland. The emperor had declared his neutrality and the emperor's son had been formally betrothed to Charles's daughter and heiress. To the new French danger—for Charles was rightly regarded as a French noble even if a rebellious one—was added the old fear and hatred of Austria.

The tactics of the battle of Morat (22 June 1476) have often been expounded: the duke's fear of a sortie from the garrison of the town, the rain followed by sunshine, the steady Swiss advance and the decisive flank attack. The Burgundian army was destroyed as a fighting force; thousands of the infantry were killed in battle, drowned in the lake, or shot 'like birds' in the trees into which they climbed. It was no accidental rout: the greatest military power in Europe had put forth all its strength and had been overthrown. The Swiss confederation now demonstrably possessed the finest striking force in Europe provided it could be brought together with an agreed objective in view. The battle of Morat and the episodes of the fifty years that followed it secured the independence of Switzerland, made the Swiss soldiery the potentially decisive force in the struggle of Habsburg and Valois, and saw the chance of power in Europe thrown away for the sake of money reward. With the development of field artillery in the sixteenth century the invincibility of the Swiss pikemen came to an end and by that time, in any case, religious differences had made united action impossible.

After 1476 the Swiss confederation lost the great unifying influence of fear of an external enemy. Annexations by individual cantons, protracted negotiations to secure common action, and the rise in the general standard of living, in part due to loot and pensions, provide sufficient explanation of the events that attended the coming of the sixteenth century. Immediately, however, in 1476 Charles the Bold was still alive, and, turning his back on Berne, was in pursuit of his former unwilling ally who had now joined his enemies, René of Lorraine. Savoy had hurriedly and gladly accepted French mediation, while the men of Valais had easily repulsed at Sembrancher a contingent of north Italians who rather half-heartedly came to join forces with Charles. René of Lorraine was encouraged to recruit soldiers at standard rates of pay from the Swiss communities, and hired a useful force under Hans Waldmann from Zürich, so that it was a mixed body of men from Lorraine, from the Lower Union, and from the Swiss valleys, that faced Charles the Bold in January 1477 at Nancy. Here the 'great duke of the West' met an obscure death in an unnecessary battle which, in fact, served only to crown with success the persistent and subtle 'cold war' that Louis XI had long waged against him, using every means but fighting and every ally who could be bought to secure French security and strength.

External allies and internal rivalries. The death of Charles the Bold, and the partial dismemberment of his dominions which followed, left a vacuum in Europe comparable in many ways to the disappearance of the Austro–Hungarian empire in 1919. That empire, indeed, was itself in some measure built on the ruins of the Burgundian edifice. The marriage of Maximilian, son of the emperor Frederick III, to Mary, only child of Charles the Bold, made possible the future career of Charles V and all that followed from it. It was fortunate for the Swiss that they were able so to secure their position in the forty years between the battle of Nancy and the election of Charles V that they were by then reasonably safe from reabsorption into the Habsburg dominions, although this was due as much to events over which they had no control, such as the alliance of France with the Ottoman Turks or the preaching of Martin Luther, for example, as it was to their own efforts.

The battles of Grandson and Morat had been fought because the Swiss homeland was in manifest danger. It became a very different matter to persuade villagers to leave families and cattle in order to assure by offensive action their continued security. The attack had come from the west and had been defeated essentially under the direction of Berne. This now powerful state had great ambitions, ambitions which involved the permanent garrisoning of much of Savoy and Franche-Comté. The fulfilment of these purposes would not only upset the balance of power within the confederation, it would also ultimately involve the absorption of considerable French-speaking populations different in outlook and tradition from those who had laboured and bled for safety in the mountains.

The men who had formerly struggled against political dependence and economic insecurity were now free and relatively prosperous. The years after the Burgundian war in fact developed into an internal contest between centrifugal and centripetal forces in which some substitute had to be found for the fear of Austria, and then of Burgundy, which had obliged communities to co-operate to resist a common danger. So long as there was some sort of agreement about the administration of lands held in common by more than one state—a rather important exception—there was no need for co-operation or joint action. The age-long rivalry of country and town, of the hill-men and the dwellers in the plain, was intensified by strong valley patriotism and by powerful family feuds and groupings. Tradition and interest now brought long-standing differences to the surface, so that local, sectional, and often selfish interests received free play. Spokesmen had to be found for these interests, men like Nicholas of Diesbach in Berne, Jost of Silenen,

Hassfurter, and Hertenstein in Lucerne, while the most notable statesman with an outlook which was wider than that of any one locality was Hans Waldmann of Zürich and, on a different plane, this was possessed by Niklaus von Flue.

In the resistance to Burgundy Berne had received indispensable help from the neighbouring cities of Fribourg and Solothurn. These two centres were now (May 1477) brought by Berne into league and co-citizenship with Zürich and Lucerne; when they should also obtain admission to the confederation there would be five city cantons (Berne, Lucerne, Zürich, Fribourg, and Solothurn) to balance five country cantons (Uri, Schwyz, Unterwalden, Glarus, and Zug). The latter, of course, had no special desire to be 'balanced' but were bound to be affected by the existence of powerful potential allies, while geography placed Lucerne in a specially influential position in regard to both.

Chroniclers and popular songs alike celebrate the immense amount of booty that had been obtained from the defeated Burgundians—arms, armour, clothes, jewels, weapons, and valuables of every kind. The problem of fair division of prize-money has never been an easy one to solve even in a modern unitary state; among loosely united allies and friendly communities disputes were bound to arise which no machinery existed to settle by arbitration. To the problem of the distribution of the loot must be added that of pensions. Louis XI, Sigismund of Austria, René of Anjou, and others had not only hired men, they had also, in accordance with the custom of the age, offered and paid sums of money to public men who could secure a following or offer some advantage. This practice, too, bred jealousy and rivalries. Some received more than others, none knew quite what was paid, or to whom, or on what principles. There were ransoms to be negotiated without much knowledge of the amounts to be demanded or the nature of the shares due to more than one beneficiary. Recruiting officers from neighbouring states were busy, but any common rate of pay or terms of employment did not exist. Thus were divisions fostered and increased.

No one clearly saw the possibilities of Swiss greatness until the days of Zwingli, and then it was too late. In more than one state it was difficult to maintain public order or even, while 'easy money' was available from foreign powers, to get the crops tended or the soil tilled. Instead, in 1477 there had been a wild spontaneous plundering raid from Schwyz into the Vaud which did not return until Geneva had paid blackmail money. There was also an expedition against Milan in a renewed effort to secure and enlarge the control over the St. Gotthard route southwards and to retaliate upon the Milanese for help given to Charles the Bold. The pope, Sixtus IV, for political reasons, blessed and supported this enterprise which was mainly urged on by Uri and which, after the main force had returned, resulted in December 1478 in a Thermopylae victory at Giornico. Reputation, cash, and further assurance against attack were indeed gained, but little political advantage, while certain events of the battle increased the tension between Zürich and its southern neighbours.

Even while the Milanese War was in progress, disputes about the future of the Vaud, about the relations of the forest towns on the Rhine (Laufenburg, Rheinfelden, Säckingen, Waldshut), about the relative powers of the abbot and the city of St. Gallen, about the extent of the jurisdiction of the bishop of Constance in Thurgau, were causing growing internal disharmony. Behind all the local differences lay the whole issue of the continuance of the confederation, for the pact with Fribourg and Solothurn, unless accepted by the country states, must either be denounced or else enlarged. The right (and conditions) of accession to the confederation manifestly needed definition, for the alternative clearly threatened by Unterwalden at Entlebuch was bitter and prolonged civil war. This was avoided by lengthy negotiations, compromise, and by the dramatic intervention at the last moment when agreement seemed impossible of the hermit, Brother Claus (Niklaus von Flue).[4] The agreement of Stans[5] (22 December 1481) is notable rather for the fact that an understanding was reached at all than for the clauses of the document that was sealed on behalf of the eight states. Their sovereign authority was left undiminished, the earlier agreements, the Priests' Charter and the Covenant of Sempach,[6] were confirmed and extended, arrangements were made about the division of plunder, mutual assistance facilitated a little, and unlawful assemblies were forbidden. In practice, although not yet in theory, Fribourg and Solothurn were admitted to the confederation. It was a victory, but a very qualified victory, for the

Controversy and uncertainty still cling to the career and influence of this figure.   [5] Stanserverkommnis.

[6] See p. 102 above.

country states. The spirit of union was maintained and even intensified, while at the same time, states' rights were fully upheld.
Indeed, it is clear that it was the federal principles that triumphed
at Stans and that at a critical moment. The confederation was still
fluid, and if war had been the outcome instead of a mediated agreement, the centralizing tendency, already foreshadowed, might
have gained an unwelcome victory.

With the conclusion of the agreement of Stans there intervenes
another of those generations in Swiss history, in which the whole
seems less than the sum of the parts, and in which east and west
seem to become separated. Before the fifteenth century was out the
last links binding Switzerland to the empire had been snapped.
This consummation was, essentially, the work of Zürich and signalled the returning pre-eminence of that state in the confederacy
and the temporary eclipse or subordination of Berne. The Burgundian repulse was engineered from the west, the imperial pretensions were rebuffed from the east.

Hans Waldmann. Among those who had shared in the victory
over Charles the Bold was the leader and inspirer of the Zürich
contingent at Morat, Hans Waldmann. This pious warrior, orator.
artisan, business man, politician, son of the people, born of insignificant parentage in 1435, almost the richest and most powerful man
in his country in 1479, illegally condemned and executed in 1489,
helped powerfully to settle both the boundaries of his country
and to ensure a semi-aristocratic constitution for its chief city
during the following two centuries. His astonishing combination
of military and forensic abilities secured for him the office of
burgomaster of Zürich in 1483, whereupon he overthrew the old
aristocratic families championed by Heinrich Göldli and made
himself, although less obviously than Rudolf Brun a century
before, dictator of an expanding state.

Before long, half the countries of Europe were prepared to buy
his support at his own price. He alone understood how to maintain his civic pre-eminence among jealous rivals, how to intervene
successfully in what may almost be described as the Swiss anarchy,
and how to enunciate a national foreign policy of expansion, security, and profitable export of trained warriors. Against the Italian
cunning of the rulers of Milan he was only moderately successful,
and his efforts to support Matthias Corvinus of Hungary and the
king of France against the emperor Frederick III, while at the

same time securing advantages as against Sigismund of Austria, required the talents of a genius as well as the resources of a great state. The latter, at any rate, he did not possess.

With great adroitness, much money that should have gone to the common soldiers was diverted to Waldmann's private purse: the richer he became, the more powerful he became, and the more influential he was, the more willing were foreign rulers, and especially Louis XI, to buy his aid at his own price. In 1483 the election of Waldmann as burgomaster of Zürich came at a favourable moment; civic industries were improving, the wealth of the country-side included in the state was increasing. By purchase, by exchange, by inheritance, by redemption, by occupation and by chicanery, the possessions of the state were being widened. The new burgomaster fitly embodied its ambitions. He attacked ruthlessly, relentlessly, and successfully, the spokesman of the old aristocratic families who proposed to rule the city in the manner consecrated by tradition, Heinrich Göldli. Raising himself to power by use of the gilds (the distant relations of the modern trade union), whose leaders he enabled to rival and then partly to displace the city councillors, Waldmann engineered a constitutional revolution. Unity and efficiency were secured at the expense of antiquity: by 1486 his personality, sometimes on the stage, sometimes behind the scenes, was supreme. He lived like a prince and conceived the notion, also to occur momentarily to Zwingli, of becoming the chief figure in the confederation. This implied a conception of unity that could not be translated into practical politics without a victory of the cities over the country-side, of the influence of Zürich over that of Berne, and of centralization over democracy. This could not be, and when Waldmann failed to secure either help or even reasonable terms from Milan, and at the same time quarrelled with Lucerne, where an active but much less able man, Frischhaus Theiling, was in power, his fall was imminent. He brought his rival low first, Theiling being illegally executed in·1487 because of earlier public criticism of Waldmann's rule. More than a clash of personalities was involved in this, and Lucerne, well knowing that it had the support of its immediate neighbours, awaited the opportunity for a counterstroke.

It soon came, partly because Waldmann saw much farther into the future than did his opponents. In 1487 Sigismund of Austria, ever impecunious, sold his rights in southern Germany, including the four Rhine towns, to the dukes of Bavaria. This was accompanied by the organization of the rulers, cities, and localities of Swabia into a league for the preservation of peace which implied resistance to further Swiss expansion. Waldmann alone recognized the seriousness of the change that the removal of Charles the Bold had brought about in the position of the Habsburgs and the south German states alike; he tried to arrange an advantageous treaty, failed, owing to factious opposition, and returned to Zürich to face a petty local dispute said to have arisen out of the shooting of some savage dogs. The peasants, who objected, found friends within the city where Waldmann's ostentation had increased his growing unpopularity; he was illegally arrested, tortured, and finally put to death on 6 April 1489. To bring about his overthrow the civic constitution had been strained or violated, and the effects of his execution were far-reaching. It meant that at a critical moment the city had capitulated to the country-side, that there was no one capable of leading the Swiss states, Zürich having fallen into anarchy and Berne obstinately refusing to face the fact that eastern affairs interested her future. Thus the confederation was a ship without rudder or captain.

Maximilian

In 1493 the emperor Frederick III was succeeded by his adventurous son Maximilian, the husband of Mary of Burgundy, and in 1494 Charles VIII of France, whose agents had previously been busy in Switzerland, moved impressively southwards on that unresisted march to Naples which was to have such notable consequences in Italy and elsewhere. The significance of these events was only slowly apparent. Maximilian had immense ambitions. He would secure for the whole of the empire freedom, by agreement, from civil war; he would make the Imperial Supreme Court (*Reichskammergericht*) the final court of appeal in all causes and he would raise taxes throughout his dominions in the same way as the Tudor kings in England and the Valois kings in France were doing. Secure in Germany, with the Roman law received as the pattern and basis of jurisprudence, with the imperial chancery directing the machine of government, he could assemble an army which he could pay and with it assert ancient imperial claims in Italy. These were ambitious projects, but they had not, in fact, the indispensable support of the German princes, and they brought Maximilian into collision with France, the greatest power of western Europe.

The small, greedy, and quarrelsome Swiss communities can, presumably, scarcely have appreciated the wider implications of these proposals made at the Diet of Worms (1495). Certain simple facts, however, were obvious. Maximilian was the acknowledged head of the house of Habsburg, the age-long enemy of Swiss liberties. An energetic Habsburg who had united the direct possessions of his house, including the Tyrol and Vorarlberg, provided a visible threat from the north and the east, and the claim to raise taxation from the whole of the empire seemed to imply a renewal of the tribute, the payment of which had been successfully resisted at the cost of so much vigilance, effort, and bloodshed. French money had been circulating freely, a little too freely perhaps, since 1477, and the cessation of French subsidies would be unwelcome to the families who had come to rely upon them for personal luxuries and for the means of securing themselves in power. In November 1495 the 'friendship between the French Crown and the Confederates' was explicitly renewed, with the clear expectation of military employment. Maximilian replied by pressure, entirely legal, from the east. He allowed appeals concerning St. Gallen to be heard in his court; he secured possession of the city of Constance; he vainly summoned Swiss representatives to a diet at Freiburg im Breisgau. In reply the eastern Swiss cantons drew nearer to their neighbours, the Grey league (Grisons: *Graubünden*). The Grisons formed a miniature Switzerland within Switzerland. The inhabitants of the land round about Chur, partly to limit the too great authority of its bishop, had formed themselves into a league of God's House (*Gotteshausbund*), while on the Upper Rhine an Upper or Grey league (*Grauerbund*) existed and in 1436, after the break-up of the Toggenburg inheritance, the third partner, the League of Ten Jurisdictions (*Zehngerichtenbund*) acted as an independent unit. These isolated and sparse communities had hitherto scarcely concerned themselves with neighbouring states and had little capacity for co-operation even among themselves. Thus, in 1489, only the League of God's House had supported St. Gallen and Appenzell in an attack on the monastery of Rorschach, an action condemned by the confederation. Out of this local aggression had come an appeal to Maximilian and a closer alliance in 1497 and 1498 of the eastern cantons and the Grisons. The geographical position of these latter in relation to the Austrian possessions made them important, for they protected the flank of their allies where protection was badly needed.

The Swabian War

Maximilian had reason to believe himself to be in a strong position. He was secure in the allegiance of Constance, and he found ready to hand the Swabian league, a union of south German cities and nobles, originally directed against Bavaria, but at the end of the fifteenth century the protagonist of German jealousy of Swiss independence and success. 'The Swiss, too, must have a master' became a German slogan and with the opening of 1499, dynastic, local, personal, economic, and political rivalries led to open war. A Tyrolese attack on the Benedictine nunnery of Münster in the Münstertal brought the Grisons to its defence; the Grisons called on their Swiss neighbours for support, which, although at first a little reluctantly forthcoming, was fanned to eagerness to fight by Austrian insults. By February 1499 the Swabian War, the last war of Swiss independence, was in full course all along the Rhine from Basle to the Vorarlberg. Berne, Solothurn, Zürich, and their allies were at once involved.

The Swabian War lasted less than nine months but led to fierce engagements at many points. A Swiss victory at Triesen (9 February 1499) led to the burning of Vaduz; there were battles at Hard on lake Constance, at Bruderholz near Basle, at Schwaderloch 2 miles from Constance, at Frastenz, on the Ill near Feldkirch, all of which were confederate successes. Neither the personal appearance of Maximilian, nor proclamations appealing to class prejudice and indicting the Swiss as peasant clodhoppers, the enemies of nobles and nobility everywhere, had any serious effect. On the river Calven the Grisons warriors lost a valued leader, Fontana, in a bloody conflict, and there was a good deal of village-burning; but, especially after the Swiss victory at Dornach on 22 July, on the balance the German–Austrian attack was everywhere a complete failure. Ludovico il Moro of Milan hastened to mediate, and the peace of Basle, 22 September 1499, ended the war.

Like some greater instruments, the peace of Basle was chiefly notable for what it did not say. Actions begun against the Swiss in imperial courts were to be broken off, the agreements between the eastern cantons and the Grisons were to remain, there were to be no appeals to any external authority in matters that concerned Austria, Swabia, and the confederation. In other words Maximilian abandoned his plan for imposing the decrees of the Diet of Worms upon Switzerland and in fact, but not in name, recognized Swiss independence. External recognition was accompanied by internal consolidation. Within two years of the conclusion of the treaty, Basle (on 9 June 1501) and Schaffhausen (on 10 August 1501), key positions on the Rhine, had become full members of the confederation. At the turn of the century, when the medieval world conventionally becomes the modern, Basle, the free imperial city, made the vital decision to throw in its lot with the freedom-loving Swiss. The city fathers who decided this in their new Rathaus can scarcely have realized that they thereby secured future generations from incorporation in France, even if they knew that an immediate prospect of industrial and commercial advance opened before them. The authority of the bishop of Basle, already diminishing, became less; the connexion with Berne on the one hand and with the Lower Union of Alsace on the other was notably strengthened; the keys to the gateway to Switzerland were now in Swiss hands. Schaffhausen was accepted, a little unwillingly, along with Basle, for defensive reasons, the 'country' cantons showing great uneasiness at the strengthening of the 'city' element among them implied in the two new acquisitions. Perhaps it was as a kind of offset to this that the backward, rural district of Appenzell was accepted as a full sovereign member of the confederation, in the teeth of opposition from the abbot of St. Gallen, on 17 December 1513. There were now thirteen independent states[7] joined in a Federal Union, and the number remained unaltered until the French Revolution and Napoleon pulled the whole antiquated structure to pieces.

[7] Uri, Schwyz, Unterwalden, Zug, Glarus, Appenzell (rural): Berne, Lucerne, Zürich, Fribourg, Solothurn, Basle, Schaffhausen (urban).

VII

REFORMATION AND
COUNTER-REFORMATION

An inscription over the door of the great minster church of Zürich
records the fact that the gospel was first preached there on 1 January 1519—a rare example of an exact and accurate date for the
beginning of a long process. On 3 September 1494 Charles VIII of
France, at the head of a fine army, had entered Italian territory.
In the twenty-five years between these two decisive events the
political as well as the psychological and ecclesiastical prelimi-
naries of the Swiss Reformation were accomplished. After the overthrow of the duke of Burgundy, and still more after the successful
resistance to Maximilian, the confederation found itself courted
by every great ruler of the day, and proved itself as vulnerable to
bribes and flattery as it had been impregnable against violence and
invasion.

Mercenaries. The European situation was never more favourable
to the Swiss than at the moment of the French incursion into Italy.
The duchy of Milan, whose uncertain northern boundaries had
already provoked more than one expedition, was now the key position to the whole future of France and the empire. If France ruled
in Milan, French pressure on the pope would be irresistible and all
Italy might become a French dependency. If the emperor ruled
there, both ends of the north–south route of Swiss commerce would
be in the hands of a Habsburg. Further, the marriage in 1496 of
Maximilian's son, Philip, with Joanna, daughter of Ferdinand of
Aragon, indicated a future Spanish interest in a country where
the ruler of Naples was already Aragonese. The popes were
anxious chiefly for real independence in a state which had been
theirs for hundreds of years, always realizing that this could not
be if Milan and Naples were in the same hands. Fifteenth-century
conditions also meant that papal independence must be assured by
the same means as were used by the other Italian states, including
the employment of mercenaries.

Machiavelli, who knew the situation intimately, was of the
opinion that mercenaries were often either useless or else danger-

ous. The prince, he insisted, who relied upon such men could never feel entirely safe or secure, for they were usually disunited, ambitious, and undisciplined. Bold among their friends, cowards in the face of the enemy, they neither feared God nor kept faith with man. The Swiss mercenaries were different. After Grandson and Morat no one could doubt either their discipline or their courage. The young men liked military service. The problem facing the Swiss states in the sixteenth century was not how to get men into the army but how to keep them out of it. The promises and payments of the French government combined with the loot of the Burgundies had shown the villagers that by risking their lives in a short campaign they could be sure of generous payment and had the chance of fabulous prize-money. In each Swiss state, too, there were officials, notables, and heads of ancient families at whose command or suggestion well-armed, orderly companies would go forth to serve others, and large rewards remained with those who sent them. It was thus possible to hire, buy, or corrupt high and low; the wisdom or justice of the quarrel mattered little in comparison with its proceeds. There were, indeed, a few who were uneasy about the acceptance of foreign subsidies almost from the start, but their voices were lost amidst the willing clash of arms.

The Swiss confederation was, in origin and essentials, a voluntary league of states for mutual defence. After 1499, union for this purpose was hardly necessary, for the traditional Austrian enemy ventured no more across the Rhine, while the French government was long occupied with greater matters than the intimidation of fierce German-speaking peasants. Swiss diets might agree that foreign service was inadvisable, but such decisions could not be enforced. The famous march of Charles VIII to Naples was practically unresisted partly because of the fear felt for the 8,000 Swiss in his pay. It was with their help, too, that the hurried French return in 1495 was made possible and the way cleared at Fornovo. There were, moreover, indications of trouble in Milan also which came to a head when Louis XII invaded the duchy in 1499. This time both the king of France and his antagonist, Ludovico il Moro, had recruited Swiss and there was a moment when it seemed as if there might be a clash at Novara. This did not take place, chiefly because Swiss would not yet fight Swiss, and Ludovico il Moro was betrayed by one of his own hirelings. In this campaign charges of indiscipline, greed, faithlessness, and heartless cruelty were brought against the Swiss, and it is to be feared that some of these qualities were to be exhibited again before the Italian wars were over.

Expansion south. The northern parts of the duchy of Milan, the valley of the Ticino, Locarno, Lugano, Bellinzona, were points of great concern for the eastern states of Switzerland which had relatively recently offered a measure of guaranteed security to the men of the Grisons. Louis XII, as duke of Orleans and claimant to Milan, had promised the Bellinzona area to his Swiss allies; after becoming king of France in April 1498 and recovering possession of Milan in 1500, he refused to honour his promise. The men of Uri, in particular, were not prepared to retire from their outposts, and reinforcements streamed over the St. Gotthard early in 1503. Fearing the effects of an advance into Lombardy, the king hurriedly came to terms, and by the treaty of Arona (11 April 1503) agreed to hand over Bellinzona and the Blenio valley to Uri, Schwyz, and Nidwalden. This implied that the centre of interest in Switzerland was not, at that moment, the west, but the south; and, although events in Italy, far from being controlled from the Alps, depended upon decisions taken in Venice, Naples, and Rome, the Swiss southward pressure continued, and interest in the Valais and the Grisons was long maintained.

The actions of Louis XII, too, were undermining that good understanding between France and the Swiss diets which had existed since 1474. Just when France most needed foreign infantry to strengthen its own magnificent cavalry, this threatened to be inaccessible. At a diet at Baden, 21 July 1503, representatives of all twelve cantons and of St. Gallen and Appenzell formally renounced military service with foreign powers and the acceptance of pensions, gifts, and similar inducements to recruiting. It was a notable act of self-denial and for four years was intermittently operative, but, in fact, a diet could not control the separate states, and the governments of the separate states scarcely controlled their own citizens, while the lure of easy money was soon to prove irresistible. After five years' trial, the Baden resolutions were admitted to be Utopian, although still upheld by a minority of thinking men.

Cardinal Schinner. Military service in the pay of the pope could, in a sense, be regarded as having the approval of the church, a fact that seemed to some to call for reflection. The pope from 1503 to 1513 was the mighty Julius II, strong-willed and politically minded, determined to drive the French out of Italy and to lower the pride and power of Venice. His agent in Switzerland was the able and masterful bishop of Sion, Matthew Schinner. This eloquent patriot hated the French, turned opinion against them, and was able in 1511–12 to use the murder of two Swiss envoys by some Frenchmen at Lugano to bring 10,000 men south to the help of the Holy League. In spite of Gaston de Foix's brilliant victory at Ravenna (Easter day, 11 April 1512), before that summer was over, Swiss and Venetians, acting together, had driven the French out of Verona, Pavia, Milan, and the whole of Lombardy. Bologna was restored to the pope, Genoa regained its ancient independence. The Swiss were masters of the situation and treated the Spanish envoys from Naples as clients. Domodossola, Locarno, Lugano, and Mendrisio were now securely in the hands of the three forest cantons, the Valtelline, Bormio, and Chiavenna were under the control of the Grisons, and Berne, with its friends, had reduced Neuchâtel temporarily to the status of a common lordship. A united confederation at this juncture might look forward to securing the duchy of Milan as an allied member and to becoming the decisive factor in the destinies of the Italian peninsula. A guarantee given to Maximilian (Massimiliano), son of Ludovico il Moro, as duke of Milan, almost implied protection.

1513 was a brilliant year. The aged Julius II died in February to be succeeded by Leo X, the pope of many problems and little purpose: Venice joined France; Louis XII invaded the Milanese. To secure the capital he had to take Novara which was defended by a Swiss garrison. The siege was pressed with vigour and answered by a defiant defence. When a relieving army arrived, the French chose the ground on which to meet them. The main body of the Swiss attacked a strongly defended position, advancing in spite of artillery and small-arms fire on 6 June. There was a moment when the bold advance seemed to have failed and a French cavalry attack was penetrating the main formation. Maximilian Sforza fled, believing the day lost, but, as at Grandson, an unexpected flank attack proved overwhelmingly successful and only the enemy horsemen escaped, since the Swiss infantry were unable to follow them fast enough. The duchy of Milan was soon clear of the French who did not seek another such combat; Henry VIII landed a force which won the battle of the Spurs in northern France—the Scots losing at Flodden at the same time—and in September a very large Swiss force, 30,000 strong, was passing through Besançon on the way to Dijon, chief town of the duchy of Burgundy. Dijon capitulated. Its governor, La Trémouille, accepted terms which included the complete evacuation of Lombardy by the French and the payment to the Swiss of 400,000 crowns. Exulting, greedy, and simple, the warriors returned home without waiting for king or diet to ratify the agreement. Louis XII, in fact, delayed until it was safe to repudiate his agent and then refused to sign. 1513, and then 1514, came to an end amid great uncertainty; the pope playing fast and loose with all, even Cardinal Schinner, the confederates uncertain as to what either honour or interest required of them.

The accession in 1515 of Francis I, determined to regain Milan, intensified the difficulties. Cardinal Schinner opposed the French demands, the pope hesitated, Berne and its allies were not very much concerned about Swiss ultramontane interests or the rights of Maximilian Sforza, and the other Swiss states were anxious chiefly for loot. When, therefore, in July 1515 a splendid French army appeared on the Italian plain by the unfamiliar Col de l'Argentière route, Maximilian Sforza called on his northern allies for help. Pay was short and plunder in a country you are defending is always difficult. At Gallarate, in September 1515, the men of Berne, Fribourg, Solothurn, and Valais allowed themselves to be bought off with promises of a million crowns and returned home. The remainder, however, from the eastern cantons, were persuaded by Schinner to continue the fight. At Marignano the Swiss eastern army, with some papal and Milanese supporters, attacked Francis I in a position strongly fortified by ditches, earthworks, and artillery. Against superior numbers, on the plain, and opposed by skilfully handled guns and cavalry, the hitherto invincible Swiss phalanx marched in vain. After two days of bitter combat they were forced to withdraw, carrying their wounded, to Milan, and thence back home. They had lost over 8,000 men, a severe blow to a small country; they had lost the reputation of invincibility and they had shown that the confederation was not united. Eight cantons[1] again

---

[1] Berne, Fribourg, Solothurn, Lucerne, Unterwalden, Glarus, Zug, Appenzell.

agreed to the Gallarate terms, but the remainder gathered another army, joined the emperor Maximilian, who was in alliance with the pope and unwilling to abandon Milan altogether, and prepared to continue the struggle. The imperial forces, however, did not really mean business; the duke of Milan feared for his own safety, there was no pay for the Swiss, and the enemy was in a powerful position. Finally, the king of France was willing to be more than reasonable. The million crowns were still available for distribution and Francis was willing to give up any claim to Bellinzona, Lugano, Locarno, Mendrisio, Bormio, Chiavenna, the Valtelline—everything in fact that the confederation and the Grisons had claimed except Domodossola. On these terms the Swiss diet agreed, by the Perpetual Peace of 29 November 1516, not to support the enemies of France.

Ulrich Zwingli. The victory of Novara and the defeat of Marignano had both been witnessed by the young Catholic priest from Glarus, Huldrych (Ulrich) Zwingli. The Swiss reformer, born on 1 January 1484, a few weeks after Luther, came of substantial peasant stock of Wildhaus in the Toggenburg district. Brought up in an entirely rural atmosphere, taught a little Latin by an uncle, Bartholomew, priest at Wesen am Walensee, the boy was intensely musical and unusually intelligent. Taught grammar at Basle and at Berne, sent down as an undergraduate from the university of Vienna, possibly visiting Paris, his regular academic studies were undertaken in the small and relatively new university of Basle between 1502 and 1506.

Basle at the beginning of the sixteenth century was a wonderful city. Situated at the critical bend of the greatest river in Europe and accessible therefore to all, with a tradition of freedom and self-government in no whit diminished by its acceptance as the city of a sovereign state into the confederation, Basle was the home of warriors, traders, artisans, and scholars, with a renowned cathedral, churches, and monasteries, and with the printing presses of Amerbach and Froben which were later to attract the patronage and the person of Erasmus. The university had been founded by Pius II in 1459, embraced some 300 masters and scholars, and was closely connected with the German universities, particularly Luther's university of Erfurt.

The teaching at Basle, as elsewhere, was based upon translations of Aristotle, owing much to the 'old way' (*via antiqua*), to Aquinas and to Duns Scotus, the writings of the latter, newly printed in 1503, influencing Zwingli considerably. It was to Basle that Erasmus was soon to come to find the amenities, leisure, and respect that were denied him elsewhere. The atmosphere there was one of German humanism, a little heavily serious, like one of Froschauer's book lists, but healthy, learned, and religious: it suited Zwingli admirably. By the time he had become Master of Arts (1506) he was well known as a Latinist, able (and eager) to correspond on equal terms with the rather select company of those who tried to write passably correct classical Latin, and he had learnt something more than the rudiments of Greek and Hebrew. These were unusual achievements for a boy from a Toggenburg village and were not attained without much labour and thought.

In 1506 the renowned young humanist, for such he appeared locally, was invited to come as parish priest to Glarus. He was not yet in priest's orders and had not preached a sermon, but these were removable defects and he celebrated his first mass at his home church of Wildhaus on 29 September 1506. For ten years he enjoyed the cure of souls at Glarus, orthodox enough to all outward appearance, reading widely, writing a little, tolerating indulgences without protest, making a pilgrimage to Rome and accepting the titular office of papal acolyte, above all accompanying his parishioners on their most important business journeys as mercenary soldiers to Pavia, Novara, and Marignano. There he learnt what such adventures implied—the loss of life, the hardships, the unfair distribution of the rewards and profits, the use of brave men to shed blood in causes which did not concern them, the demoralizing violence of camp life. Although by no means unappreciative of the military virtues, he hated what he saw and returned to advocate the abandonment of mercenary service. He had seen how irresistible a united Swiss force could be and, at Marignano, he had seen the fatal effects of disunion. Erasmus, whom he so much admired, wrote in favour of pacifism, and some early writings of the young Swiss humanist breathed something of the same spirit.

In November 1516, installing a vicar at Glarus, Zwingli accepted a benefice in the village that had grown up round the monastery of Einsiedeln where pilgrims constantly resorted to pray before a renowned image of the Virgin. In this milieu the dissatisfied young man began to read the New Testament, just published in the original Greek with a new translation by Erasmus. It set him thinking about the conditions of the early church and contrasting these conditions with what he saw and knew of the religious society around him. A pious peasant population was grouped, ecclesiastically, into the dioceses of Constance, Basle, Chur, Lausanne, Sion, and Geneva, none of which rather unmanageable areas corresponded at all closely with Swiss states or groups of states. Effective episcopal supervision was thus difficult and was not in fact exercised. Institutionally, church affairs were very much local affairs, the cantons being accustomed to some general oversight over the observances of their citizens. The territorial rights of the churches were unpopular and those of the monasteries were even more so; tithes were paid reluctantly by poor country people; but there was no heresy, the pope was a friendly employer, the parish priests, if often corrupt and concubinary, were accepted as the rather mechanical performers of prescribed ceremonies which were ill understood and sometimes regarded almost as innovations. In such conditions it would not be hard to bring about a religious revival, and in this the rediscovery of the Bible, for it almost amounted to this, played a large part. It was important negatively, for a precedent-loving people could find therein no authority for much that had been assumed to be of immemorial antiquity; prayers for the dead, obits, images, pictures, devotion to the saints were not known in the days of the New Testament. Nor did the study of the early Fathers of the Church, in great new folio volumes recently published, and eagerly read by Zwingli, the record of Jerome, Origen, Augustine, and Chrysostom, justify any more clearly the innovations. Nor, too, was the superstition of the ordinary parish priest often accompanied by any notable personal sanctity or exemplary good conduct. Zwingli himself had not been entirely discreet in his private life at Einsiedeln, as he engagingly admitted when he applied for and was elected to, in December 1518, the office of people's priest in the Grossmünster, principal church of Zürich.

The Reformation in Zürich. He was now at the heart of affairs. Zürich was the greatest city of the confederation, more German in outlook than Berne, its rival, more democratic too, although to apply the word 'democratic' to a city government which was in the hands of a few aristocrats who consulted with a few more leading trade unionists, is to misuse terms. It was an industrial city, with a large and recently acquired cantonal jurisdiction, accustomed to manage its own affairs, including church matters, with little reference to the bishop of Constance. The artisans were active, alert, and much interested in public affairs, political and religious. In January 1519, then, a considerable congregation gathered to listen to the new preacher, the well-known scholar, pacifist, opponent of the French. Abandoning the prescribed lessons (Pericopes) Zwingli now expounded the gospel according to St. Matthew from the beginning, and the originality of his matter and the homely eloquence of his style won him wide support. When Bernard Samson came in February with an indulgence to offer he was turned away: when in June the 'German' Charles V was elected emperor rather than Francis I, Zürich rejoiced.

The Conservatives soon put it about that Zwingli was a Lutheran. Like Luther he had read widely in the works of St. Augustine, like Luther he appealed to Holy Writ, but he did not want to be excommunicated, or involved in possible civil disabilities, and he indignantly repudiated any suggestion of discipleship: 'I have not learnt the teachings of Christ from Luther but from the very word of God.' After preaching for a year, in 1520 Zwingli began to call for action. Tithes, he said, to the delight of the agriculturalists, should be voluntary; the service-book of the Grossmünster should be simplified; there was nothing in the Gospel that demanded abstinence from meat. At the beginning of Lent, 1522, in company with his friend Froschauer, the printer, Zwingli ate in company a small piece of sausage. It was a deliberate challenge to the authorities. The state at first upheld the law of the church, Zwingli justifying his action in a pamphlet, and the bishop felt obliged to make it a disciplinary matter. In May, complaints, in general terms, were brought against 'presumptuous preaching' at a confederate diet at Lucerne, and the wider issue of clerical celibacy, ill-observed in the valleys in any case as all knew full well, was raised in a petition of ten priests to be allowed to marry. Before 1522 was out Zwingli had stated his theological position of exclusive reliance upon the Bible in *Archeteles*, had secretly married a young widow and had resigned his position at the Grossmünster to receive a similar preaching appointment from the city council. There was also arranged for

29 January 1523, in the town hall, a public debate on sixty-seven conclusions put forward by Zwingli, developing a little further, or a little more clearly, the implications of freedom for the individual in exclusive reliance upon the text of the Bible. The assembly was not a very representative one, although the bishop sent observers. Zwingli was, however, judged to have established his case, which meant that he now became the official adviser to the city council in matters of religion, and that various ceremonies were dropped. The cup was granted to the laity, monks and nuns allowed, almost encouraged, to leave their cloisters, and a reform of the Grossmünster was undertaken. It was not until April 1525 that the mass was abolished, by which time images, pictures, and crucifixes had been removed, relics buried, chrism no longer consecrated, and extreme unction discontinued. At the end of 1524 the abbess of the city nunnery, the great Fraumünster, founded by Louis the Pious and formerly owner of the city, gave her foundation to the state in exchange for a large pension. The moneys received from the sale of this property and from the voluntary dissolution of other convents, and from a radical reorganization of the Grossmünster enabled the city council, still at Zwingli's instigation, to enact a generous Poor Law and to make extensive provisions for education, culminating in a kind of theological college. Further, in Leo Jud, Grossmann, Ceporinus, Pellican, and Myconius, he found valued and enthusiastic assistants, while his own writings multiplied his influence and clarified his thought.

All this was not accomplished without opposition. Zwingli kept his feet firmly on the ground; he was content to advance slowly, to consolidate one position before attacking the next, to keep ahead of, but not too far ahead of, the public opinion of the city, to make each step appear the inevitable result of the former, and his opponents as ignorant and unpatriotic. Each religious advance was also a political advance, as the Lucerne chronicler Salat noted when he said that Zwingli was burgomaster, town clerk, and city council of Zürich. He was never quite this, but as his influence grew his enemies multiplied: good Catholics, notable aristocrats, jealous politicians, easy-going merchants, and former ecclesiastics formed a solid opposition. Still more troublesome were the extremists who insisted upon pushing Zwingli's arguments to what they could allege were their logical conclusions. These included some of the inhabitants of the villages along the lake of Zürich such as Zolliken, Witikon, Höngg, and Rapperswil, always jealous of the preponderating influence of the city, and foci of peasant grievances such as flared up in the German Peasants' Revolt. Here and elsewhere communists were attacking private property, rent, interest, and feudal dues; pacifists denounced the use of armed force of any kind; others refused to take solemn oaths when required. These tendencies were focused in the rejection of infant baptism by the Anabaptists. Zwingli acted, in this matter, with great circumspection. He rejected both the Catholic and the Lutheran views of baptism as a sacrament, freeing the recipient from original sin, but he declared the service to be necessary as a sign of membership of a Christian community, a promise of Christian upbringing, and a requirement that could properly be demanded by the community. The authority of the Christian magistrate, lawfully appointed, must be upheld, and it was with Zwingli's full knowledge that the death penalty against Anabaptists was decreed and in some cases enforced. By 1529 the Anabaptists had ceased to be dangerous anywhere in Switzerland; the Zwinglians, like the Lutherans, had rejected them as fellow travellers and their faith remained technically proscribed in every canton until 1798.

While Zwingli tirelessly and independently thought, wrote, and administered, his growing renown brought growing antagonism. To the Catholics he and his followers were heretics to be exterminated. Erasmus, after expressing polite rejection of his views on free will, turned decisively against him when he welcomed the fugitive Ulrich von Hutten. Luther manifested a growing jealousy and hostility. It had been hard enough for Catholic Zürich under Waldmann to co-operate with the country states; how could they continue to act together when to economic jealousy was added religious difference and when the foreign service which alone saved many young men from misery and starvation was being denounced?

Trouble seriously arose over a Zürich religious enthusiast who had been expelled from the city for iconoclasm, Klaus Hottinger. He had gone to Baden where, in spite of the fact that it was a 'common lordship' in which Zürich shared jurisdiction with other states, he was arrested, taken to Lucerne, and put to death in March 1524. In the summer there was iconoclasm at Stammheim in Thurgau, the burning of a Carthusian monastery at Ittingen on the border of Zürich territory, followed by further arrests and executions. At the same time Uri, Schwyz, Unterwalden, Zug, and Lucerne formed a union at Beckenried to resist the new faith, but efforts to extend this soon demonstrated that Zürich was not as isolated as they hoped. Berne, Basle, and Schaffhausen were wavering. An effort by Luther's opponent, Dr. Eck, to lure Zwingli to Baden to a disputation was unsuccessful, but the Protestant case was ably maintained by Oecolampadius (May–June 1526) who was not molested.

Luther and Zwingli. Early in the autumn Luther publicly dissociated himself from Zwingli whom he classed with Carlstadt and the revolutionary Anabaptists. Zwingli had, in fact, given much thought to the question of the eucharist and had studied carefully the opinions of ancient and modern authors, including those of Luther himself. Luther had rejected the teaching of the Catholic church about transubstantiation and the mass and had put forward his own doctrines, accepting the divine presence to the faithful in the consecrated elements in a manner that came to be given the name of consubstantiation. Partly as a result of his university training in logic, and basing his arguments upon the Gospels, the Epistles, and the practice of the primitive church, Zwingli concluded by rejecting entirely the conception of the Last Supper as a sacrament, a word, he said, that he wished had never been invented. The communion in bread and wine was symbolical only, a memorial meal, a conception which, more radical than that adopted later by Calvin, made the Swiss Reformer the revolutionary theologian of the Reformation. Luther had arrived at his own position after considerable intellectual struggles, and he could not admit any flaw in his arguments or be attracted by the efforts of theologians like Haner, or even the persuasion of so powerful a territorial prince as Philip the Magnanimous of Hesse, to think of any compromise. The more Luther learnt of the Swiss theologians the less he liked them, and he said so in unmistakable terms.

Spread of the Reformation: Schaffhausen; St. Gallen; Appenzell

Philip of Hesse was an interested party because Zwingli meant Zürich, and an alliance with Zürich might mean one with the most powerful elements of the Swiss confederation. These were accepting the gospel as expounded from Zürich with varying degrees of willingness. Schaffhausen, for example, was geographi-cally exposed to both Lutheran and Zwinglian propaganda, several of its young men, like Oechsli and Peyer, studying at Wittenberg. They were encouraged on their return to expound the new doctrines by Johannes Müling (Adelphus) and Michael von Eggensdorf, but the most active gospel preacher was the former Dominican, Sebastian Wagner or Hofmeister (Oecono-mus). He had met Zwingli at Zürich and had been converted; back at Schaffhausen in 1523 he set forth the new teaching about prayers to the saints and about the mass; his words were welcomed by the city council and by many others so that very soon another outpost was lost to the Catholics. The city of St. Gallen, similarly, anxious to free itself from the control of the great abbey to which it had owed much of its earlier prosperity, allowed the humanist Vadian, with Miles and Burgauer, to preach the gospel between 1521 and 1523, by the end of which year the city had accepted the new doctrine. Appenzell followed a like course at the same time, chiefly owing to the efforts of Bartholomew Berweger, while Glarus and the Toggenburg, Zwingli's own country, had been won over by 1523, a considerable Catholic minority remaining unconvinced in each of these areas.

Grisons

The evangelization of the allied federations of the south-east, the Grisons, the League of God's House, and the League of Ten Jurisdictions, was a partial, unsatisfactory, and complicated busi-ness like much else in that area prior to the nineteenth century. There was a fertile soil for the seeds of reform: traditional opposi-tion to the bishop of Chur, notorious ecclesiastical corruption, support for refusal of pensions and military service. There was also Catholic Austria (specially interested in the League of Ten Jurisdictions) to the east, with Milan and Venice to the south. None the less, reformed preachers in the valleys, carrying little bundles of newly printed literature, won over Fläsch, St. Antönien, Igis, Malans, and Davos, between 1521 and 1524. An attempt by the first articles of Ilanz (4 April 1524) to regulate the situation by a measure of toleration failed; public debate, the Ilanz disputa-tion (7 January 1526) led to further conversions and an arrange-ment by which each rural community decided its own form of worship. This in turn was followed by evangelical advances and even by the conversion of whole monasteries, which led to the rejection of episcopal, and therefore of Catholic, jurisdiction altogether by the second articles of Ilanz (25 July 1526). The acceptance of the Reformed faith by much of the Grisons meant that the consistently Catholic states of the original confederation must always be on their guard against a stab in the back.

Basle

At the opposite corner, in Basle, there was an intellectual community in the university and city better acquainted, perhaps, with the thought and writings of the humanists, particularly Erasmus, and later with those of Luther and Melanchthon, than any similar group in Europe. Pellican, Sündli, Capito, and others were popularizing the new teaching from 1520 onwards, and in 1522, copying Zwingli, there was an outbreak of flesh-eating in Lent. Basle, however, was not Zürich. It was an episcopal city with a resident bishop; it was a frontier state, nominally within the dominions of Charles V and actually surrounded by Austrian possessions. The city council, which had no love for the bishop, was cautious. In November 1522 there came to the city John Hussgen of Weinsberg, a priest and Hebrew scholar who had studied at Heidelberg and had helped Erasmus with his edition of the New Testament, adopting the name of Oecolampadius. An eager correspondent with Zwingli, popular as a university lecturer, and as preacher at St. Martin's, he helped to secure the permanent retirement of the bishop to Porrentruy (Pruntrut) in 1523 and arranged more than one public debate on religion of the kind then common. The new preaching was very acceptable, particularly to the artisans, who were jealous of the influence of the cathedral and of the monasteries. Basle was a merchant city which showed some of those leanings to Protestantism characteristic of sixteenth-century capitalism, and when Oecolampadius announced his marriage the city council invited him none the less to continue his preaching. From this it was an easy transition for the city council to proclaim a measure of toleration, citizens being free to attend or to stay away from mass as they wished. But this was an unnaturally modern solution even for the home of Erasmus, and in February 1529, responding a little unwillingly to trade union pressure and the demands of a public meeting in the market place, the city council replaced it by the exclusive recognition of the Zwinglian worship. Erasmus, together with some friends and most of the episcopal officials, reluctantly left the city which, from that date, remained an outpost of the Protestant cause. This was not unimportant, as is apparent when it is recalled that the canton of Basle alone, in the sixteenth century, was richer than all the Catholic cantons put together.

Berne. More powerful than Basle was the mighty and aggressive state of Berne, agricultural rather than mercantile, with a tradition of government by ruling families, the artisans being almost powerless. Having been an imperial city, in the sixteenth century Berne was free to turn in any direction, as interest or conviction should dictate. When Charles V became emperor, and especially after his victory at Pavia (1525), Berne became almost passionately anti-imperial (which meant also pro-French) and the facts that the emperor was identified with hostility to Lutheranism and was the chief support of the Catholic church were not overlooked in the city on the Aar. When Charles V was found in close alliance with Duke Charles of Savoy, the opposition, based on apprehension, became intensified.

These, however, were political and military considerations. Berne was singularly free from direct ecclesiastical oversight; there was no great abbess as at Zürich, no bishop as at Basle, no abbot as at St. Gallen. There had been little or no trouble in the high middle ages; churches and monasteries were built, the normal services held, pious gifts received for the souls of the faithful departed and for the poor. There were some complaints that money went to Rome or to the distant and semi-alien Lausanne and Constance, the city of Berne itself being in the former diocese but its neighbours east of the river being in the latter. Some of the monasteries in the country-side were considerable and wealthy landowners and were naturally regarded with some jealousy; men complained of the pride of the monks, of the idleness of the friars, and of the prevalent concubinage of the secular clergy.

These things of themselves were far from being enough to bring about a religious revolution in a conservative state. And yet, between 1523 and 1528 this happened. One of Zwingli's disciples and admirers, the Swabian Berchtold Haller, obtained a stall in the collegiate church (Münster) of Berne in 1520. His preaching, circumspectly moderate, was of the reformed pattern and was acceptable to his hearers. He found an unwelcome but influential ally in Nicholas Manuel, a coarse and clumsy satirist who in 1522 arranged two Christmas plays or pageants, *The Pope and his gang of priests* and *Pope and Christ in opposition,* in which ecclesiastical pomp and luxury were crudely contrasted with the poverty and suffering of Christ and his true followers. These representations were received with acclamation, were soon put into print, and achieved a large and ready sale. Other equally popular and equally scurrilous pamphlets followed. The aristocrats, who dominated the Small Council, were displeased at any suggestion of any disturbance of a *status quo* which they had by now manipulated to their satisfaction; the Great Council, on the other hand, contained representatives of the artisans who were ready for a measure of spoliation of church property.

The preaching of the Gospel was explicitly permitted in 1523 provided Luther's name was not mentioned. When, therefore, Berchtold Haller declined to celebrate mass any more but confined himself to preaching, and was in consequence suspended by the bishop, the mandate of the latter to this effect was refused admission to the city. Events were thus obviously moving fast. The elections of 1527 brought to both councils a larger number of those who favoured reform and, as a result, it was agreed that a public debate about the Catholic faith should be held early in the new year. The bishops declined to be represented and the Catholic cause was left in weak, inexperienced, and insignificant hands, whereas the evangelicals, more alive to realities, brought in their ablest advocates. There came to the support of Haller, Zwingli in person, accompanied by an armed escort from Zürich, Bucer from Strassburg, and Oecolampadius from Basle. Before such a team the orthodox put up a very unconvincing case and the debate of January 1528 was decisive for Protestantism.

All that had been done in Zürich slowly was done in Berne hastily. The authority of the bishop was declared at an end and all clergymen brought within the laws of the state. The monasteries were dissolved, provision being made for the occupants; and superstitious objects, images, crucifixes, vestments, organs, and windows were destroyed. Mercenary service and the acceptance of foreign pensions were denounced. In addition to the city, Berne also ruled over a considerable and relatively recently acquired territory in the Oberland. Here there was reason to fear lest the

little finger of the state would be thicker than the loins of the
bishop; and the peasants, aided by men from Unterwalden,
offered armed resistance to the abolition of the mass. It was quite
in vain, and the Reformation was forcibly imposed on them by
the city. Indeed, it had more readily become state policy because
of the opposition thus encountered. It meant greater authority
for the city council and it also inserted a permanent confessional
wedge between the peasants of the Oberland and their otherwise
natural allies, the peasants of the forest cantons. Much of the
money from the church property enriched and strengthened the
power of the Bernese aristocrats, for little of it, in contrast to what
had happened in Zürich, was diverted to education or to the
relief of the poor. Thus, almost casually and as it were by default,
Berne became Protestant. The results were notable. Without a
Protestant Berne and Vaud, Geneva could not have retained its
independence; and without the inspiration, leadership, and men
that came from Geneva, the Reformed faith could hardly have
withstood the onslaught of the Counter-Reformation anywhere
in Europe save, perhaps, in Scandinavia and in Scotland.

By 1529 it had become clear that in Switzerland, as in Germany,
politics and religion could not be kept apart. The Swiss constitution, compact of uncertainties and contradictions, was not made
to take the strain of religious differences. It was easy to apply
the obvious and simple rule that each state should decide and
enforce its own form of religious observance—*cuius regio eius
religio* operated here long before the peace of Augsburg—but
how this could apply to lands in common ownership whether of
the confederation or groups of cantons, and how the discussions
at the frequent traditional diets could be carried on with one side
abhorring the other as heretics it was difficult to imagine. To
this was added a growing divergence between Lutherans and
Zwinglians.

The Christian Union

To the suggestion that the inhabitants of the common bailiwicks should be free to do as they wished in matters of religion
while remaining under the political control of their lawful joint
rulers, the Catholic cantons, Zug, Uri, Unterwalden, Lucerne,
and Schwyz, replied with an emphatic negative. Their agents
would, and did, continue to persecute and burn in the Rheintal,

the Thurgau, Toggenburg, St. Gallen, and Baden. Zürich, confident and aggressive, the ally of Constance, was determined to secure an expansion of religious freedom at least, and gave evidence of this by arresting and executing the most vigorous of the persecuting Catholic officials in Thurgau, Marx Wehrli. Unable to make any effective reply and fearing lest Zürich was aiming at the incorporation of Thurgau, the five Catholic cantons accepted at Waldshut on 22 April 1529 a 'Christian Union' with Ferdinand of Austria. The ancient enemy of the Swiss was now in the opposite camp from Zürich; the Habsburgs could hope to regain their ancient possessions by bringing in Catholic Switzerland on the side of Catholic Germany and thus striking a shrewd blow at the Lutheran princes. The chief of these, Philip of Hesse, recognized at once the danger and the possibilities. The Swiss soldiers were the finest in Europe: Zürich, Mülhausen, Biel, Berne, St. Gallen, could themselves raise a formidable force, and they might by persuasion or pressure bring in others. In any case, now that the Catholic states were forming a Christian Union, the Protestants must adhere more closely. Philip therefore tried to bring together Zwingli and Luther.

The first religious war. While letters were passing, the Catholic states forced the pace by extending their union to embrace Valais and Fribourg, and arrested an evangelical citizen of Zürich, Jacob Kaiser, as he preached the gospel at Uznach, a place within the common jurisdiction of Schwyz and Glarus, burning him forthwith as a heretic. Ten days later, 8 June 1529, Zürich declared war on the Catholic states, called on its allies for their covenanted assistance, and moved a powerful force against Zug. Zwingli was in command; the plans had been carefully laid and the opposition was certain to be defeated before its Austrian or Savoyard supporters could come to its help. This very fact, however, helped to save them. Zwingli, triumphant master of the heart of Switzerland, would be irresistible. Zürich would call the tune for the confederation, and Berne, Basle, and the others, who had fulfilled their obligations with some reluctance, would take a subordinate place. Hence they hoped for a settlement, while the rank and file of the army were conscious of little but friendship for fellow countrymen, even if unenlightened ones. When, therefore, the *Landamman* of Glarus, Hans Äbli, called for an immediate arrangement, and at the same time the opposing forces at Kappel were drinking soup together, each on its own side of the line, an agreement was inevitable. Berne made it clear that it would support Zürich only in a manifestly defensive war and this declaration made a compromise imperative. Against Zwingli's advice and better judgement—'the peace you want means war' he said 'the war I call for means peace'—terms were arranged on 26 June. The union with Ferdinand was denounced publicly, freedom of worship promised in the common bailiwicks, and a recommendation advanced against the acceptance of further foreign pensions. It was a notable achievement to have secured this without striking a blow. Basle, Strassburg, Berne, Constance, St. Gallen, Biel, Mülhausen—all supported Zürich and its all-powerful spokesman. It is true that Berne, in particular, had other ambitions that were scarcely compatible with the aims of Zürich, but on the surface the Catholics had capitulated and Zwingli could go to Marburg almost as if he were the foreign minister of a great power.

The Marburg conference

For ten years Zwingli had respected Luther as a fellow labourer and religious writer; he acknowledged his indebtedness to some of his writings while stoutly maintaining his own independence of judgement and conclusions. Luther was jealous of Zwingli's abilities and success. He treated the Swiss reformer as a sectarian, an enthusiast, to be classed with the Anabaptists. In September 1526 Luther had attacked Zwingli's eucharistic teaching with violence that soon became abusive. It was difficult to find a compromise between consubstantiation and the concept of the eucharist as a commemorative evening meal and in the end those who tried to do so, such as the ingenious Bucer, had to admit failure. However, in 1529 an arrangement, if not a compromise, was politically almost indispensable after the Diet of Speyer; and Philip of Hesse was sufficiently important to be able to bring the contestants together. On 3 September 1529 Zwingli, almost secretly, left Zürich for Brugg and Basle on the first stage of his journey to Marburg, a journey which might end in a Protestant coalition capable of overwhelming the emperor and his brother and uniting all Europe north of the Alps. He was joined on his way by Oecolampadius, Hedio, Bucer, Sturm, Frey, and others, and in Marburg castle Luther, attended by Melanchthon, Justus Jonas, Myconius, Osiander, and Stephen Agricola awaited him.

For four days (1–4 October) the discussions continued, Philip of Hesse urging some agreement, Luther, with *Hoc est corpus meum* written before him, refusing to give way on the essential issue. Finally, like many other international conferences which fail to reach agreement, the Marburg discussions ended with a report, a 'confession' of fifteen articles signed by the participants, agreeing upon communion in both kinds and the rejection of the mass as a sacrifice, but wrapping up essential divergencies in theological verbiage which deceived no interested party.

Zwingli returned to Zürich on 19 October to arrange an alliance with Basle and Strassburg and Hesse and to expound his faith again in the pulpit and in writing. The Catholic cantons were in touch with Charles V who had now arranged for his coronation by the pope but whose position was far from strong. Against him there was a chance that France, well disposed to Reform by Margaret of Navarre and the group of Meaux, Wurtemberg, where Duke Ulrich was to be restored, Constance and the Swiss allies might co-operate. Where Marburg had failed Strassburg tried its hand. Bucer produced a compromise plan known as the *Tetrapolitana*[2] but this time it was Zwingli who would have none of it, as indeed he must, since he could not accept the possibility that there could be, at any rate for unbelievers, any Real Presence in the eucharist.

Further theological discussions and a projected common front with the Schmalkaldic league were interrupted by news from the south. In March 1531 an Italian adventurer, Gian Giacomo de' Medici, who operated from his castle of Musso on lake Como and who had been a thorn in the flesh to the inhabitants of the Grisons since 1525, murdered one of their envoys returning from Milan and then invaded the Valtelline, seizing the town of Morbegno. The Grisons appealed to their allies for help which was refused by the Catholic cantons but forthcoming from the remainder, particularly Zürich, where the attack by Musso was believed to be part of a general offensive arranged by Charles V. Musso capitulated, and the duke of Milan recognized the rights of the Grisons over Chiavenna, Bormio, and the Valtelline. It was a small episode, but it had striking consequences. It revealed that in a matter of external policy the confederates would not co-

[2] The joint work, supposedly, of the four cities of Strassburg, Constance, Lindau, and Memmingen.

operate and a case could be made for the allegation that the Catholics had failed to fulfil their obligations.

This could not be allowed to continue, and when renewed disputes about the common lordships and allegations that Zürich was forcibly helping Protestantism in Thurgau were brought forward, Zwingli insisted that the Kappel agreement had broken down and that armed coercion of the Catholics was unavoidable. He had a bold and statesmanlike plan in mind. The common lordships should be abolished. The five Catholic cantons should become subordinate, at any rate so far as external policy was concerned, to Zürich, while Berne should obtain a similar hegemony in western Switzerland. Basle and Constance would enter this system as friendly secondary partners and the Swiss confederation would be governed by the Reformed dyarchy of Zürich and Berne. Zwingli was also convinced that if the gospel could be freely preached in the five cantons it would prevail there.

The second religious war: death of Zwingli. These ends he believed could be secured by economic sanctions. If no provisions reached the forest cantons from the north and the markets under the control of Zürich were closed to them they might capitulate. In fact, naturally, they preferred to fight, and the blockade was not effective since grain and salt could come, a little expensively, from the south. Zürich had for some years neglected and saved money on its armed forces and at the same time there were some complaints of Zwingli's dictatorship which were silenced by his offer to resign his position as people's preacher, an offer that was refused. Quite unexpectedly, on 4 October 1531, the five Catholic cantons declared war on Zürich at Lucerne, accusing her of having broken the Landpeace and of having brought in the foreigner from Constance and Strassburg. Eight thousand determined men marched north from Zug to Kappel. In Zürich there was strange confusion and divided counsels. No armed men were ready and it was with difficulty that some 2,500 volunteers were mustered under Jörg Göldli. With them marched Zwingli in person. The numbers were inadequate, the artillery badly used and Göldli was an incompetent tactician. On 11 October, at Kappel, the Zürich force was taken in the flank and overwhelmed, Zwingli being killed. He was only 47.

Although the battle of Kappel was little more than a skirmish, the death of Zwingli made it a turning-point in Swiss history. His great concept of a united Switzerland, a great European power, allied with Venice and the German Protestant princes, opposing Austria and the Catholics from Denmark to the Adriatic, died with him. In Zwingli, humanist, preacher, theologian, statesman, was seen the best that sixteenth-century Switzerland could offer. His death was a disaster to Protestant Europe, and it was followed by three centuries of Swiss disunion, the effects of which are still apparent.

Bullinger

The (second) peace of Kappel marked the decline of Zürich, for although it lost no territory its influence was mightily diminished. Each state was to decide its own form of religion, and evangelical preaching in Catholic states was forbidden. In the common lordships the *status quo* was to remain undisturbed, Catholic minorities being protected. Various indemnities were arranged which, indirectly, resulted in Solothurn and Glarus becoming Catholic. The free bailiwicks (*Freie Aemter*) in Aargau were regained for the Catholic faith, together with other places,[3] among them Bremgarten, from whence Heinrich Bullinger, a gentle humanist and warm admirer of Zwingli, was driven to Zürich. Here he came as Zwingli's religious, but not as his political, successor. He expounded and developed the Zwinglian creed, maintained a considerable correspondence with the supporters of the Reformed faith in England (where he had considerable influence), did much to receive the Marian exiles in Zürich, and was powerfully instrumental in bringing about the doctrinal compromise which united the Swiss reformers. He was not a man of notable original thought, nor, perhaps, of strong character either, but he had an eloquent and persuasive tongue, was untiring in the service of the church of Christ, and as an organizer, administrator, and host his services were invaluable.

Berne and the Vaud. The overthrow of the Zürich forces at Kappel was in part due to the failure of other Protestant cities to come to its assistance in time of need. This inaction was due in part to the speed of the war, hurriedly declared, soon over: so far as the greatest state was concerned, Berne had ambitions in the west which were not compatible with an internecine war in the east, and there may possibly have been, too, an element of jealousy of the

---

[3] Mellingen, Rapperswil, Toggenburg, Gaster, Wesen.

potential greatness of a victorious rival. The policy of the Bernese aristocracy was relatively simple in the sixteenth and seventeenth centuries and it explains much that happened from 1530 onwards. Self-preservation was necessarily always present, and self-preservation implied the maintenance of the authority of the city council (which meant in fact the will of a few ruling families) over the nobles and peasants of the country-side and over the artisans of the city. Berne was the consistent upholder of the 'perpetual' alliance with France which brought money to the magnates and made possible further expansion by land. Perpetual vigilance was the price of Berne's freedom of action, and in all its policy defence shaded off imperceptibly into aggression. Berne was almost a frontier city, and very much a frontier state, in the sixteenth century, and its safety was closely bound up with that of Fribourg, Solothurn, Geneva, Lausanne, and Neuchâtel. The defeat of Charles the Bold had opened the whole question of the future of Franche-Comté and of the Vaud. The actions of Louis XI and of Maximilian, combined with the understandable desire of the victors to dispose of their plunder had, in fact, lost Franche-Comté for all time, a fact which in itself directed attention to the uncertain position in the area between the Jura mountains and the lake of Geneva.

The Vaud had formed part of the Holy Roman Empire over which the emperor exercised singularly little authority. His chief feudal vassals were the bishop of Lausanne (in whose diocese, but not in whose feudal domains, Berne and Solothurn were), and the duke of Savoy, himself overlord of numerous lesser nobles. There were also a number of independent, castle-owning barons, and the abbeys of Bonmont, Hautcrêt, Lac de Joux, Romain-môtier, Payerne, and others controlled considerable territories. The bishop of Lausanne claimed to be count of Vaud, but his authority was everywhere flouted, even in his episcopal city; the duke of Savoy claimed to be imperial vicar, representative of the emperor with sovereign rights of appellate jurisdiction, but little notice was taken of this claim either. In spite of the efforts of the dukes to introduce, through the estates, some degree of centraliza-tion, twenty codes of customary law and twenty sets of weights and measures were said to operate in the area.

The city of Lausanne was in alliance with Berne and Fribourg and pursued its own external policy; Orbe and Grandson were under the direct control of these same two cities, while in 1519 Geneva joined in a pact of co-citizenship with Fribourg, both cities then, of course, being Catholic. The danger feared by all was not the aggression of Berne but the reassertion of ancient or pretended authority by Duke Charles III of Savoy. He was strong enough to insist upon the Genevese abandoning their arrangement with Fribourg (whose force had occupied Morges) while, in 1517, the citizens of Lausanne had requested his protection against their bishop. After an interlude of co-operation with France, Charles of Savoy, anxious, like all his house, to be on the winning side, after Pavia supported Charles V, and the struggle for the Vaud became, in part, one of the many issues fought out between Habsburg and Valois. After 1528, too, this struggle was closely connected with the progress and then with the survival of Protestantism. For the acceptance of the Reformed faith by Berne meant its imposition—a singularly gentle imposition, as it proved—upon lands conquered by Berne in the Vaud where the Catholic prelates and ecclesiastical landowners were as notorious for their rapacity as the priests and monks were for the laxity of their morals and neglect of their religious duties. Further, if the Vaud had not been forcibly occupied by Bernese forces, Geneva could scarcely have maintained its precarious independence and, without Geneva, Protestantism itself could hardly have survived in its historic form.

Geneva. While Guillaume Farel and his companions were preaching the gospel of the open Bible in the villages of the Vaud, the city of Geneva was in a state of uncertain hesitancy. In the city the temporal authority of the bishop had long ago been reduced to relative insignificance, although the rights of bishop and duke were not entirely negligible. The city was ruled by the usual complicated system of councils in which the friends of Savoy (the so-called Mamelukes) struggled for the mastery with the republicans who favoured closer relations with the confederation. The leader of the latter, Berthelier, was put to death on St. Bartholomew's eve, 1519, and his successor, Besançon Hugues, sought salvation in flight. Yet the economic interests of the markets and the natural sympathies of a French-speaking city state on the lake, supremely anxious to retain its self-government, were all with the communities of the Vaud and therefore with their protectors. The league of Berne and Fribourg in 1526 decided the Genevese, at the instigation of Hugues, to accept the protection that this offered and to join (as Lausanne had done) for twenty-five years. Four years later, in 1530, the danger of a renewal of episcopal and ducal rule seemed so great that a force from Berne, Fribourg, Solothurn, Neuchâtel, and Payerne entered the city and obliged the duke to accept the peace of St. Julien, (19 October 1530), pay an indemnity, and allow the occupation of the Vaud as a pledge for the safety of the city. Geneva, it must be emphasized here, remained an independent republic until 1798, but its relations with Berne in particular, and through Berne with the remaining Swiss states, were so close that its history is manifestly also that of Switzerland.

Two years previously Berne had accepted the Reformation, so that a Geneva under Bernese protection could not fail to be visited by preachers of the gospel, the experienced and tireless Farel chief among them. The conversion of Geneva was not an easy matter. There were numerous priests and monks to uphold the traditional doctrines against what could be regarded as German heresy and as a sign of Bernese domination. Fribourg and Solothurn were not reformed, and it was certain that Berne's policy of western expansion was not popular in the confederation. Farel made such headway as he could, succeeded in the summer of 1535 in proclaiming his faith from the pulpit of the cathedral, in securing the abrogation of the mass before the end of the year, and in May 1536 the acceptance of the new faith. There were, however, many who disapproved or wavered and who pointed to the blockade in operation from the Savoyard territories all round them. The situation was saved by the armed forces of Berne and the genius of Calvin.

The announcement that the lord of Musso[4] had joined forces with Savoy was sufficient to prevent the Catholic cantons from intervening when Hans Franz Nägeli led 6,000 well-equipped warriors into the Vaud in January 1536. Such half-hearted resistance as there was was easily overcome, Geneva relieved, and the advance continued round the south shore of the lake into the county of Chablais. In order to save this area from evangelization, the men of Valais, supported by the bishop of Sion, joined with the Bernese against Savoy. By the beginning of March the campaign was over; the castle of Yverdon, the most notable obstacle,

[4] Cf. p. 160 above.

had capitulated and the Bernese army returned in triumph. There were certain difficulties with Fribourg to be arranged (which it was easy to do), mediation by Zürich, and a renewed expedition in March, again under Nägeli, against the bishop of Lausanne whose castle of Chillon was taken in two days and Bonivard set free. Berne thus succeeded to all episcopal rights in Lausanne and made full use of them. Valais shared in the proceeds of successful aggression and, after considerable adjustments of detail, Bernese governors controlled for the benefit of the canton, Yverdon, Moudon, Vevey, Lausanne, Thonon, and Ternier. After a public debate of the now familiar pattern held in the cathedral church of Lausanne in October 1536, public observance of Catholic services ceased throughout the Vaud.[5]

John Calvin

Exactly at this juncture a French preacher, twenty-seven years old, visited Geneva on his way north to Strassburg. Although relatively young, John Calvin had already achieved some degree of eminence. A Picard from Noyon, son of a hasty tempered ecclesiastical lawyer who died while his son was still a student, he had had his own way smoothed by church preferment and had studied at Paris, Orleans, and Bourges under some of the ablest professors that Renaissance France possessed. A studious, asthmatic youth, life in childhood and early manhood had not been easy. The severities of the Collège de Montaigu, the endless disputations, the arid logic, the painful acquisition of a good Latin style and a more than ordinary knowledge of Greek and Hebrew, interwoven with the study of civil and canon law and a comprehensive understanding of the essentials of the Catholic faith had bred a keen mind, orderly, acute, and subtle. His hard legal studies taught him that enduring institutions must rest on clear, explicit written statutes, while his classical knowledge opened to him the Greek text of the New Testament and an independence of judgement in approaching the study of it. A youthful commentary on Seneca had brought him to the notice of the learned world, where he made many friends, and contact with some of the Lutheran thinkers who had gathered round Lefèvre d'Etaples and the

---

[5] Chablais and Gex were abandoned by Berne in 1564. The district of the Vaud in the sixteenth century is not identical with the nineteenth-century canton of this name.

bishop of Meaux had set his active mind considering the issues raised by them. There was no profound psychological tumult such as sent Luther to a monastery and then out of it, no sudden revelation, no religious crisis. Calvin thought out for himself the implications of the revelation of Christian truth. He became convinced by cold reason that the teaching of the church of Rome was wrong and he knowingly chose the path of heresy.

The France of Francis I, after that monarch had come to terms with the pope, was no place for an avowed heretic, and to save his life, Calvin went to Basle. There in 1536 he stated his case, prefaced by an uncompromising letter to his monarch, in *Christianae religionis institutio,* 'the most influential book ever published by so young a man'. The church of Christ, as he saw it, one and undivided, was obliged, by the working of Satan, to act in many groups of true believers scattered over the face of the Christian world. It was their duty to spread the teaching of God's word, established for all time in the canon of the Scriptures. Like Zwingli, Calvin rejected tradition and would accept no doctrine that was not to be found in, or clearly and manifestly deduced from, the Bible. The sacrifice of the mass, the mediation of the saints or of the Virgin Mary, the cult of images and relics, the monastic vows, auricular confession, and much else were as decisively rejected by the Frenchman as by the German. There was no need for bishop or priest; the minister of God's word was chosen by his hearers to lead them in prayer and to expound methodically, reverently, and regularly the duties and obligations of the Christian. Baptism was the necessary token of regeneration in Christ and of membership of his church and the commemoration of Christ's death in the Last Supper was indispensable. The 'outward and visible sign of an inward and spiritual grace' implied a Real Presence for believers, and Calvin's view of the communion, rejecting Catholic transubstantiation, Lutheran consubstantiation, and Zwinglian bare symbolism, came to be widely accepted later.

Influenced, as few students of such things can fail to be, by the penetrating teaching of St. Augustine, Calvin assured the elect, who could know by manifest signs that the finger of God was upon them, of their eternal salvation. The few chosen must fulfil the purposes of the Almighty; among the many there would be those to whom ultimate salvation was denied, although in this life, none could know who they were.

Farel was deeply impressed by the profundity and incisiveness of his younger friend's book; and when the pale, devoted preacher reached Geneva in 1536 he invited him, adjured him in God's name, to stay. Calvin accepted, a decision that changed the history of the world. For here was an organizing genius who knew exactly what he wanted, who was realist enough to accept, assess, and use the political and personal factors of the time and place in which he found himself and who was idealist enough to scorn selfish ends or personal power. Like Zwingli, he won the confidence of, and dominated, the city councils, and he at once set about the arrangement of church government in orderly, logical fashion.

Within a year, Geneva learnt what the following of Christ under such a leader meant. Stark austerity, self-discipline, a life praising God with prayer and preaching, sin, vice, and self-indulgence publicly rebuked, the young instructed by a French Catechism, the older by the Consistory of pastors and elders, the externals of dress and behaviour made to conform to the new spirit. Calvin was very much in earnest and lacked a sense of humour; sixteenth-century methods and earlier traditions account for the sumptuary and ethical regulations which were strictly enforced. Like other religious and social reformers he went too fast and too far. Early in 1538 an opposition, called by the Godly the 'Libertines', had organized itself under Jean Philippe and Richardet and had obtained a majority on the governing bodies of the city. Farel and Calvin were informed that their services in the pulpit would not be needed further. 'Had we served men', Calvin replied, 'this would have been a poor reward for our labour, but we have served a greater Lord who will not be unmindful of what is due to us.'

Calvinism at Geneva

Farel went to Neuchâtel, Calvin to Strassburg, where he met Bucer, continued his writings and studies, and made a happy marriage. Through Bucer he became better acquainted with German Protestantism, developing and modifying his own thought somewhat. In Geneva there were violent faction fights in the councils, there was threat of a renewed Bernese occupation and the clearest signs that instability would mean permanent loss of independence. In these circumstances it was resolved to invite Calvin to return, which he did, unwillingly and on his own terms, in September 1541. From that date until his death in May 1564, inspired more passionately than ever with the conviction that he was fulfilling God's purpose, he ruled Geneva almost as autocrat. Endowed with a marvellous memory for facts and faces, a splendid judge of men and able to inspire them with his own singleness of purpose, he made Geneva a model Christian polity, the chief school and seminary of the reformed doctrines. That there were ludicrous extravagances is well known. The Consistory carried out his wishes and exercised an almost inquisitorial oversight over the lives of the citizens; men and women were rebuked and punished for the slightest sabbath breaking, for wearing unsuitable clothes or hair done in an unusual fashion, for absence from church on weekdays as well as Sundays, for infringements of Mosaic commandments, for laughing during sermons, for dancing or frequenting taverns, for light words or for phrases that could be interpreted as criticism of the administration.

Church and state were not identical. Calvin was indeed the moving spirit in the city councils, and he entirely understood the complicated system for administrating civil affairs, but the duty of the state was the government of men, while the purpose of the church was the salvation of the sinner. In a godly society, however, the state upheld the minister of the gospel who had been trained, tested, accepted, and ordained by his fellows. To criticize him was to attack the government, and this, in the sixteenth century, was visited with heavier penalties than in more recent times. Geneva was a frontier state, a besieged garrison, in danger alike of falling under the physical control of Savoy and the spiritual control of Rome. Hence some of the restrictions. It must not be forgotten that neither good music, good cooking, nor good wine were prohibited, that the sick and the poor were cared for diligently, and that an admirable system of public education rivalled anything that the renowned Jesuit schools could produce later. The boys of Geneva, well instructed in Latin, knowing the meaning as well as the words of the Catechism, taught from earliest days and shown by example that the highest and best service to God and his people was the ministry of the word, naturally became missionaries and preachers. Speaking French, they tended to evangelize France; and the French wars of religion, the triumph of Henry IV and even, in some measure, the failure of Louis XIV, were their doing.

Geneva was also the principal and obvious city of refuge for those fleeing from religious persecution by Catholics. Refugees, mostly French, arrived almost daily and, while accepted as residents rather than as full citizens, strengthened the hands of the administration. Evidence that some of the older families disliked the new system was clearly seen in 1546 when Pierre Ameaux, a propertied city councillor, had to do public penance for words critical of Calvin spoken in his private house after dinner. A preacher, for some similar criticism, was forbidden to occupy the pulpit. In 1547 Jacques Gruet provided a sterner example. Politically he had been consistently in opposition. When he, too, publicly and in writing criticized the preachers, his house was searched, and papers in his hand, showing disbelief in the Pentateuch and denying the immortality of the soul, were discovered. Tried, found guilty of heresy and treason, he was beheaded. A minor reign of terror followed in which, less dramatically and without bloodshed, members of the renowned Favre and Perrin families were struck down.

When Charles V triumphed over his enemies in Germany, when Luther was dead and his followers tempted to accept the compromise known as the *Interim* (1548), it was necessary for Calvinism to demonstrate that it was not a negative creed of sweetness and light or vague Deism but a defined and exact system of beliefs and practices. Jerome Bolsec, doctor and ex-monk who had been converted but who could not accept the rigours of predestination, was declared a dangerous heretic and was lucky to escape, with some help from Berne, into perpetual banishment.

Servetus. The classic case, however, was that of Servetus. This bold Spanish scholar, whom the Inquisition would have removed had he been in Spain, professed a mild Unitarianism and was unsound on the subject of infant baptism. Calvin knew his tenets, and pursued him with relentless hatred; he would have delivered him to the French authorities if he could. If he should ever come to Geneva he would not easily escape. And, early in 1553, he was unwise enough to pass through Geneva on his way to Italy. Arrested, he was brought before the city council where Calvin's opponents attempted to save him. Their efforts were in vain, for the heterodoxy of the man was notorious and a belief in the Trinity was an indispensable article of faith upon which all were agreed. The case was thought sufficiently notable for the four Protestant cities, Berne, Basle, Zürich, and Schaffhausen to be sounded for their opinion and to be made accessories to the Genevan action. On 27 October 1553 the Spaniard was publicly burnt to death. It was, in Acton's memorable words 'one of the great days in the Church history of the century . . . the charge of human freedom passed from the churches to the sects'.

It was after this judgement that a number of Calvin's opponents left Geneva which henceforward assumed something of the detached and semi-international character so often regarded as its characteristic. It was also a city of God: John Knox stayed there in 1556 and described it as 'the maist perfyt schoole of Chryst that ever was in the erth since the dayis of the Apostillis'.

After 1559 Viret and Beza lectured on theology to considerable audiences at the Genevan academy, while the Zürich Agreement (*Consensus Tigurinus*) of 1549, made between Calvin and Bullinger, was ratified, modified, and enlarged in 1562 as the 'Second Helvetic Confession' with which Zwinglianism as an independent form of belief was absorbed and disappeared throughout the Swiss area. Calvin's writings were read widely in France and the Empire, but the best exponents of them were to be found where independence and freedom were most highly valued—in Scotland, in the United Provinces, and in New England. There were indeed elements in the doctrine which were favoured by the rise of capitalism, particularly the recognition of the lawfulness of reasonable interest-payments for the use of borrowed capital. It was not usury, however, that brought wealth and advantage. Simplicity and moderation of living, personal uprightness and honesty, a quiet austerity that often accompanied deep religious convictions, made for business success, and many private family fortunes quietly accumulated.

Genevan independence and Calvinistic thought likewise tended to favour republicanism and upheld resistance to authority if this should be in the hands of or act on behalf of ungodly men. The misrule of unrighteous kings and princes was not to be suffered meekly as the will of God, for the oppression of true believers and opposition to the preaching of the gospel could not be acceptable. And it was not wrong to take up arms on behalf of God and His angels.

Geneva's successful struggle for security. Geneva, at any rate, was still prepared to do so. On Calvin's death (27 May 1564) Beza took his place, just as, similarly, at Chambéry, Duke Charles III had been succeeded in 1553 by Emanuel Philibert. At Cateau-Cambrésis (1559) France and Spain joined forces on behalf of Catholicism, and at Lausanne, in 1564, Berne abandoned to Savoy Gex and the territories south of the lake of Geneva. Although sure, for interested reasons, of help from Berne, Geneva had no alliance with the Swiss confederation as a whole. The Catholic cantons vetoed this suggestion every time it was made: Lucerne indeed was entirely prepared for the reoccupation of the city by Savoy. Zürich, however, was prepared to add its weight to that of Berne, and the three cities were linked in a perpetual league in 1584. Henry III of France also, in 1579, before he had fallen entirely under the influence of the Guises and the Catholic league, had made a pact with Geneva, promising support against aggression, Savoy being a Habsburg satellite. In 1589 this help was needed, for France and Savoy were at war, and a large French force was operating from Geneva. Berne was thus drawn in, but without enthusiasm when it was apparent that all the advantages to be gained were for a France well able to look after itself. At Nyon, in 1589, Berne agreed to stand neutral if the duke of Savoy should again attack Geneva, but the agreement raised a storm of protests from Basle, Schaffhausen, Zürich, even from Elizabeth of England, and it was not ratified. Geneva was, therefore, not included or mentioned in the treaties of Vervins (1589) or Lyons (1601) when Gex became a French possession.

In 1602 Duke Charles Emmanuel made his last great effort. Urged on by Pope Clement VIII, vigorously supported with men and money by Philip III of Spain (and Milan) he planned a sudden assault. Two thousand paid soldiers, Italian, Spanish, Savoyard, and French, under Charles d'Albigny, moved in secrecy to attack the city on the night of 22 December. The surprise attack failed. Although the outer walls were scaled, Isaac Mercier guarded the New Gate against all comers, the alarm was sounded, the ladders adroitly shot down and the attackers withdrew, having lost sixty-seven men as against seventeen on the side of the defenders. The 'Escalade' was a trifling affair, but it would have been far from trifling had it succeeded. By the second peace of St. Julien (21 July 1603) the duke of Savoy recognized the independence of the Protestant city, accepted a trade agreement, and for almost 200 years Geneva was undisturbed.

Catholicism and the central cantons. What Calvin accomplished in person at Geneva his Spanish counterpart, Ignatius Loyola, carried through by deputy at Lucerne. The same factors operated in bringing about the so-called Counter-Reformation in Switzerland as in Germany or France. The purification of the papal *curia*, the elimination of the more scandalous appointments to the college of Cardinals, the marked alteration in the character of the Supreme Pontiffs themselves could not be lost upon a people whose ultramontane contacts and interests had for so long been so valuable and intimate. The activities of the new societies and orders, the Oratory of Divine Love, Theatines, Servites, Barnabites, above all the Capuchins, were soon well known in the villages and towns of the southern valleys of Switzerland.

The Inquisition, it is true, was seldom used in this country, although some of its more notorious methods of obtaining information lingered on until the days of the French Revolution, and the Index of Forbidden Books served only as a guide in the Catholic cantons to the literature, the discovery of which in the possession of a suspect could be used as evidence for his unreliability. The Council of Trent, on the other hand, attracted a considerable amount of notice. The bishops of Constance, Chur, Basle, Lausanne, and Sion were present at its deliberations; it was held, save for the brief period at Bologna, almost on the soil of one of the allies of the thirteen cantons, and many visitors to the Council used the Swiss roads and passes. The reforms, too, that were accepted by the Council were, for the most part, remedies for the chief abuses that had been most apparent in Switzerland. The provision of seminaries diverted the ordinands from the heretical and unsettling atmosphere of the university of Basle and made them less likely to read the satires of Erasmus. The issues about which Erasmus had been most eloquent were raised and settled. The bishops were obliged to reside within their dioceses and thus exercise that personal supervision that had been so often lacking before. The parish priests were obliged to assume outward respectability at least and unabashed public disregard by them of the laws of the church ceased. Thy had an authoritative Vulgate, easily procurable and a revised liturgy which use made popular. The itinerant indulgence vendor no longer appeared with his misleading documents to take money and produce from poor peasants. Tradition was now known to be binding, the seven sacraments affirmed, clerical celibacy enforced, transubstantiation and communion in one kind accepted, and defined doctrines made the line dividing Catholics from Protestants as sharply defined as a ridge of mountains. When the Gregorian calendar was issued, the very dates of the year emphasized the divergency. And behind the council and its reforms was the might and wealth of Philip II of Spain, who was also ruler of Milan, and the ever-present threat of the Austrian Habsburgs.

Constitutional arrangements. The second peace of Kappel, hastily concluded in November 1531, indicated the essentials of the constitutional set-up of the future. The Catholics had as decisive a preponderance in the number of states as the Protestants had in the number of inhabitants. Zürich, Schaffhausen, Basle, Berne, stood on the one side; Fribourg, Solothurn, Uri, Schwyz, Unterwalden, Zug, and Lucerne on the other. The Catholics were secure in, if somewhat embarrassed by, the alliance of Valais, while their opponents could count on Geneva and the Grisons. The future of Glarus, Appenzell, St. Gallen, the Italian valleys that were to be compressed into the Ticino, the common bailiwicks, and much else remained in doubt. The preacher might convert, the soldiers might constrain and compel, tradition, economic interests, foreign rivalries and alliances, pulled this way and that. In Germany and in France, where men fought about religion, Swiss volunteers were to be found on either side, helping to prolong the struggle and preventing a decision by destruction or unconditional surrender. The forcible imposition of Catholicism on Strassburg and on Constance, robbing Switzerland forever of this latter city which might otherwise so appropriately have adorned the confederation, was reluctantly accepted. When, however, there was no question of foreign intervention, as in the case of the inheritance of the counts of Greyerz (Gruyère) on the Upper Saane, Protestant Berne and Catholic Fribourg were able to arrange a peaceable partition.

Arrangements between individual cantons were relatively easy to make, and arrangements between the confederation and external powers were possible, provided the matter was a relatively uncontroversial one. But co-operation after 1531 between Swiss Catholics and Protestants in the management of their own common affairs was exceedingly difficult when politics could not be separated from religion and when the future of considerable territories was involved. When Zürich or Basle objected to taking the federal oath 'by God and the saints' and the old cantons refused to take it or accept it as taken in any other fashion, another link with the heroic age was broken, although necessary business could still be transacted.

Part of this involved Aargau, conquered territory commonly administered. There, by treaty right, the Catholics were unmolested; and the most strenuous, and largely successful, efforts were made by them to add to the number of converts. For Baden separated Zürich from Basle and from Berne, and south of Baden was Lucerne and the Catholic *bloc.* Across the St. Gotthard lay the southern group of common lordships, again separating the Reformed Grisons from the Valais. Here there was a majority of Catholics, but in some of the larger towns clustered round the north of the Italian lakes there were considerable Protestant groups, proselytizing in tendency. The most important of these, some hundreds strong, was at Locarno. Such a nest of heretics could not be allowed after the Council of Trent had met, and the Catholic states proceeded to order their expulsion. Zürich protested but protested alone, and the exiles, taking with them such property as they could realize, moved northwards. Like the French Huguenots a century later, they brought with them a little capital and considerable industrial skill and commercial knowledge. Names such as Pestalozzi and Orelli indicate to later centuries something of the debt that the textile industries of the lake of Zürich owe to the intolerance of the forest cantons. At the time, actually, the action was regarded as a victory for the Catholic cause, and a belt of Catholic states from the Rhine to lake Maggiore divided the east from the west.

Glarus. With the acceptance and promulgation of the decrees of the Council of Trent by the Catholic cantons, and with the appearance of Jesuit-trained apologists, went an ideological attack upon the wavering canton of Glarus. Zwingli had a special affection for the Glarner and had won many adherents there. But a fellow humanist and scholarly patriot, Aegidius Tschudi, regained for the old faith much that had been lost. When reason and argument failed, forcible pressure was brought to bear upon the Protestant congregations who refused to accept the ministrations and services of Catholic priests. In 1556 the popular assembly of Glarus was induced, almost forcibly, to agree to the expulsion of the remainder of the Reformed pastors, but the decree was only partially enforced, and considerable 'heretical' pockets remained.

Tschudi used more than learning against these; with the approba-
tion, expressed or implied, of emperor and pope, he intrigued so
successfully in the neighbouring states that in 1560 the five cantons[6] were refusing any recognition of the evangelical part of
Glarus, while Schwyz and Unterwalden had armed men ready on
the frontier should any such help be needed. For four years,
Tschudi's War, as it was popularly called, went on, Glarus being
threatened with exclusion from the common affairs of the confederation until in 1564 Zürich and Berne persuaded Lucerne and
Zug to join them in restoring Glarus fully to its own rights and in
thus securing recognition and reasonable security for the Protestant minority. Tschudi himself, after a sojourn at Rapperswil,
returned to Glarus to become archivist and diplomatic adviser
and also to write the *Chronicon Helveticum* which remained the
best guide to confederate history before 1470 until the appearance
of the equally uncritical work of Johannes von Müller.

Melchior Lussy. Pope and Catholic Swiss had need of one
another in the second half of the sixteenth century. Although
Italy had ceased to be the battle ground of France and Spain, there
were still disputes between the independent states of the peninsula,
of which Venice and the states of the church were the chief. Good
soldiers were still in steady demand and the popes knew where
they could be hired. There was money available in Rome, and
there were some who could offer what was needed in exchange for
it. Among these was Melchior Lussy, born at Stans and destined to
spend his later life in the cause of the Catholic cantons. Fairly well
educated, knowing Latin, Italian, and German, he gained a reputation for courage in the wars against Spain while fighting under the
command of Montmorency. Pope Paul IV, the stern and bitter
Caraffa, hated and feared the power of Spain, with Philip II ruling
in Milan and Naples. He forwarded the Counter-Reformation in
Switzerland by sending to Lucerne Ottaviano Rovere, bishop of
Terracina, as papal nuncio. Among those who went to Rome to
thank the pope for this action and to negotiate about a good deal of
concomitant business, including the arrangements for a seminary
at Lucerne, was Lussy, representing his native canton of Unterwalden. The manner in which he obtained wealth and honours
from the pope, in exchange for a company of men whom the pope
called his legion of angels (the ancestors, in some measure, of the

_____
[6] Lucerne, Uri, Schwyz, Unterwalden, Zug.

modern papal guards, always Swiss, and with unaltered Renaissance uniform), his temporary and lucrative employment by Venice, followed by successful appearances before Pius IV and Pius V, made him, in the years before his death in 1606, one of the most influential and wealthy men in Catholic Switzerland.

Here, then, is one reason for the consistent Catholicism of the old cantons. The pope and the rulers of France and Spain had money to spare, while the growing population around Lucerne had little option but to seek their fortunes in the most obvious field of foreign service. There were no tourists and hardly any foreign visitors, the export of milk products had not begun, and starvation stared strong healthy men in the face every winter. *Pas d'argent, pas de Suisses,* first used by the Swiss themselves because France was notably in arrears with pay and subsidies, became a proverb, because, before the nineteenth century, the mountain-dwellers had little but their bodies to sell and naturally bargained for the highest price. Fortunately, the long rivalry of France and Spain, and, later, the opportunities for service paid for by British gold, prevented Switzerland from becoming the purchased French province that seemed at one time likely.

Corrupt, undoubtedly, many Swiss statesmen like Lussy and Ludwig Pfyffer of Lucerne were, but they seldom deserted the religion of their parents. Those who fought so effectively for the Huguenots and helped to secure the throne for Henry of Navarre were from Protestant or semi-Protestant states; those whose assistance to the Catholic league was so powerfully influential in preventing France from becoming a Protestant state were themselves good Catholics. That these latter were so was in large measure due to the Swiss Catholic revival initiated by St. Carlo Borromeo. Nephew of Pius IV, cardinal and archbishop of Milan before he was 23, the career of the Italian saint has much in common with that of Charles of Guise, cardinal of Lorraine. Both justified by their lives family patronage otherwise entirely unjustifiable. By personal example first of all, the archbishop of Milan purified his province. Devout, ascetic, constant in prayer, an eloquent preacher who secured the almost fanatical devotion of his female hearers, he was a tireless organizer with a defined programme, that of the Council of Trent, and with the prestige and wealth of Milan behind him. His conscientious visitation of the whole of his diocese brought him north of Locarno to the valley of the Blenio and thus into direct official contact with the Swiss protecting cantons. The pope named him *Helvetiae Protector*; he corresponded with Lussy and crossed the Lukmanier pass in person to honour the relics at the Grisons monastery of Dissentis and make this once more a centre of religious activity. He showed how heretics in the common lordships, against whom the civil power could not proceed on religious grounds, could be removed as necromancers or witches, thus taking advantage of that literal acceptance of Old Testament teaching by the Reformers which allowed such discreditable persecution. The fillip given to the Catholics by the well-advertised visits of the cardinal archbishop was paralleled by his acute perception of the needs and character of the people with whom he had to deal.

The Capuchins were encouraged by him to seek (and to find) fertile soil for their labours, and from a central point at Altdorf, in Uri, they sent many earnest exponents of the new Franciscan spirit into the villages. Two notable Jesuit centres likewise became, under his initiation and guidance, homes of scholars and priests who could demonstrate that the intellectuals of the Protestant cities had no monopoly of biblical knowledge, Latin scholarship or powers of argument. The Jesuit college in Lucerne, opened in that city's finest building in 1577, instead of being erected, as had at first been suggested, at Constance, established the moral right of Lucerne to call itself the capital of Catholic Switzerland. In 1580 this college was supported by another, erected by Pope Gregory XIII at the instance of Peter Canisius, at Fribourg, thus establishing a firm outpost in the west. The fortunes of Berne and Fribourg were, however, necessarily so closely intertwined that co-operation in many matters continued to be necessary, and provided a kind of norm or model for the much more difficult co-operation of the Protestant and Catholic states within the Bund.

St. Carlo Borromeo's last great work for Catholic Switzerland was to find a way of overcoming the difficulty presented by its five dioceses which, together, were not co-terminous in their boundaries with the confederation. The pope, in 1579, appointed an Italian student-friend of the archbishop of Milan, Giovanni Francesco Bonhomini, as papal nuncio and visitor for the whole of Switzerland. In the same year the opening of the Helvetian college, also at Milan, provided a papal institute of higher education where boys could learn Latin, Greek, and Hebrew without the need to resort to Basle or Germany, and where future priests could receive the long training in theology, philosophy, apologetics, and in the hearing of confessions and the assessment of penance which the Council of Trent required.

The Borromean league. All this gave the forest cantons greater confidence to pursue their own policy. Nothing more is heard of the iniquity of foreign service and very little of co-operation with German Protestants. The willing acquiescence in the occupation of Constance by Austria would have been accompanied, but for the resistance of Berne and Valais, by an equally willing acceptance of a Savoyard annexation of Geneva. An appeal in 1585 by Berne, Basle, Schaffhausen, and Zürich for a united federal front was answered by a demand that they should abandon the Reformed faith. Even the 'perpetual' friendship with France was abandoned in the following year when the seven Catholic cantons[7] formed a Christian alliance, known later as the 'golden' or 'Borromean' league. It was the work of Ludwig Pfyffer, bailiff (*Schultheiss*) of Lucerne more than of anyone else, and it implied practically the break-up of the confederation. The wonder is that it did not lead at once to a civil war in which the wealth of Zürich and Basle and the man-power of Berne must have been decisive. The text of the league, however, was skilfully drafted so that it was apparently reconcilable with preceeding arrangements, although the implied violent hostility to the Calvinists was clear enough. One result was the division of Appenzell into the two exclusive sections, for all practical purposes independent states, of the Inner (Catholic) and Outer (Protestant) Rhodes, an enduring monument to sixteenth-century intolerance.

The significance of the Borromean league became apparent when, on the impending accession of Henry IV to the French throne, the allies, with the exception of Solothurn, signed a treaty with Philip II of Spain, promising soldiers at the usual rates and free passage over territories under their control. Since Philip ruled in Milan and in the free county of Burgundy, the danger to France was apparent; still more apparent was the fact that a people which at the beginning of the century had been courted as the equal of the great powers, at the end of it had ceased to be feared and had become an item in Spanish and French budgets.

[7] Uri, Schwyz, Unterwalden, Lucerne, Zug, Fribourg, Solothurn. For the perpetual friendship' see p. 146 above.

It is thus remarkable that independence was retained for two centuries, that the threatened civil war did not take place, and that the confederation received European recognition in 1648.

Henry IV overcame all his enemies, made peace with Spain at Vervins (1598) shortly after which Philip II died and it was apparent to the Swiss Catholics that they must accept the re-converted Bourbon as ruler of France. Moreover the Spaniards, although fertile in promises, had been behindhand in payment, which the French kings had seldom been. With the end of the war, the Catholic league with Spain ceased to be needed and Henry IV was able to bid for a renewal of the 'perpetual' agreement between France and the whole confederation. After long negotiations conducted with the utmost adroitness by de Vic, accompanied by plenty of hard bargaining, the alliance was renewed in 1602 on favourable terms. An embassy not unlike that sent to Louis XIV and depicted in a renowned tapestry, was received with lavish hospitality in Paris. Service for France, payment by France, and protection from France were secure until the Revolution.

The Grisons. While Henry IV was thus successful in his dealings with the Swiss confederation, notwithstanding the confessional difficulties, his ally, Venice, was equally so with the miniature Switzerland of the three leagues, one Catholic and two Reformed, which it is convenient, if a little misleading, to speak of as the Grisons.[8] Venice had recruited mercenaries there, and elsewhere, since the early fifteenth century and, when the Valtelline was occupied, Venice had a common frontier with the Grisons. Although Catholic, Venice was critical of the papacy, disliked the Tridentine decrees and allowed forbidden books to issue from its printing presses. Far less wealthy and powerful at the end of the sixteenth century than it had been at the beginning, the decline was adroitly concealed, the trading city was still important and the skill of its ambassadors world renowned.

Spain desired above all things to keep Venice and the Grisons apart. In alliance they menaced Milan and offered little comfort to the Counter-Reformation. The factors that brought about an understanding between them were the power and greed of the proud Grisons aristocracy, the money lavishly bestowed upon

[8] *Bündner* is a more satisfactory word than Grisons, but less familiar to English readers.

them in the right places and at the right times, the anxiety of both sides to keep the passes open, and the finesse of Venice's master diplomat, Giovanni Battista Padavino. In August 1603 the treaty of Davos was agreed: mutual defence, soldiers for the Venetian army at high rates of pay, freedom of trade and facilities for transport. The Spanish governor of Milan, the count of Fuentes, tried by every means to undo the agreement. These included economic pressure by cutting off supplies, a military threat by building a fort named after himself, and diplomatic protests from Madrid itself. Henry IV countered with all the resources of his Foreign Office and shortly before his untimely death had succeeded. The Grisons did not give way to Spanish threats, and it was left to Louis XIII and his able minister to deal with the Valtelline question in relatively favourable circumstances.

After ten years of effectiveness, the alliance between the Grisons and Venice was not renewed in 1613. This was in large measure due to the arguments and inducements offered by the French envoy, Gueffier, and to the anxiety of the Protestant ministers lest the growing influence of the Catholic states should render the already precarious position of the southern Reformers worse. When, in fact, a Reformed synod met at Bergün in 1618 and declared Spain to be a serious danger to the Grisons, the considerable discontented elements in the Engadine revolted against their aristocratic masters, particularly the powerful Planta family. Unable to obtain any encouragement or help from the Swiss states, Rudolf Planta appealed to the Austrian Habsburg monarchy, the ally of Spain and itself having hereditary claims in the Engadine and Münstertal. Thus began a series of movements in the Grisons of which outside powers took advantage. The Catholic subjects of the Grisons in the Valtelline, occupying a position of renowned strategic importance between Milan and the Tyrol, were badly misgoverned by bailiffs whose chief object was to secure the profits of jurisdiction, having paid heavily for their offices. Within the Grisons themselves, two states only were Protestant, the third, the Upper League, being Catholic and hoping with Valtelline support to alter the religious balance of power.

The Valtelline. When, then, in 1620, the people of the Valtelline turned on their Protestant fellows and killed or drove away many of them, the Grisons states, aided by men from Berne and Zürich, lawfully intervened to punish the insurgents. The latter appealed to Spain, whose forces repulsed the Swiss at Tirano, while the Catholic cantons declared their solidarity with their co-religionaries. The exiled Planta family took the opportunity presented by the civil war to return, to be again attacked in 1621 by Georg Jenatsch, the Protestant pastor now turned soldier and politician.

This offered Austria a further opportunity for intervention, and 8,000 Austrian soldiers occupied the Lower Engadine and Prätigau, while the hold of the Grisons over the Valtelline was entirely relaxed apart from Chiavenna. Indeed, the Austrian commander, Baldiron, was practically master of the whole of the eastern Grisons and threatened Chur and Maienfeld, while forcibly imposing the Catholic religion on the occupied lands. Temporarily displaced by a popular rising in 1622, Baldiron was back with more Austrian infantry in 1623, and the independence of the Grisons seemed at an end. Austria ruled over the Münstertal, the Lower Engadine, the whole of the League of God's House, and most of the League of Ten Jurisdictions.

This could not be allowed, and in 1623 France (i.e. Richelieu), Venice, and Savoy agreed at Avignon to restore the *status quo*; a French army under the Marquis de Coeuvres expelled the Austrians, freed the Lower Engadine, and returned Bormio and Chiavenna to Grison control.

The Catholic subjects in the Valtelline were now, by the treaty of Monzon (5 March 1626), placed under papal protection, papal troops occupying the valley, and they were allowed complete self-government provided they paid tribute to their Grison overlords. Thus, temporarily, Spain was nominally excluded.

The war of the Mantuan succession in 1629, in which Austria and France were again in conflict, led to the Grisons being involved because Austrian forces crossed and recrossed their territory with impunity. Again they looked to France; Richelieu allowed French troops to go to their aid and turned a blind eye when Henry duke of Rohan, the Huguenot leader, offered them his services. After the imperial victory at Nördlingen (September 1634) over the Swedes, a victory made possible by the presence of 12,000 Spanish infantrymen who had marched up the valley of the Adda, France declared war on Spain. And, although Rohan successfully won a brilliant campaign in the Valtelline, Richelieu ignored him and treated the Grisons as of no account.

Whereupon Georg Jenatsch, having been for political reasons converted to the Roman Catholic faith, went over to the side of the emperor and persuaded his followers to renounce the French alliance. This secured, in the end, their independence, but Jenatsch did not live to see it for he was murdered at Chur in 1639. By the 'perpetual' peace with Spain of 3 September 1639, the southern bailiwicks returned to Grison control, but the Protestants received three months' notice to leave, the alliance with Spain was confirmed, and in 1649 Austrian rights in the Münstertal and the Lower Engadine were bought out for cash.

The return of the Valtelline to the Grisons is sometimes represented as a triumph for the diplomacy of Richelieu. But if so, it was a barren victory, leaving the enemy almost in as strong a position as before. Richelieu's real victories were won elsewhere, on the plains of Germany.

The Thirty Years War. The Thirty Years War, indeed, altered the whole face of Europe. Beginning as a war about Bohemia and about religion, it developed into a trial of strength between France and the Habsburgs in which France won at the expense of the German people. As the war spread beyond the confines of Bohemia, it seemed inevitable that the Swiss confederation, part of the empire, and a great reservoir of armed men, must be brought in. Yet this did not happen, and with this war, out of which the confederation obtained European recognition at last, the policy of Swiss neutrality, envisaged earlier, was strengthened to last until the twentieth century. In Germany, at first, the Catholics were victorious and the 'winter king' melted in the spring as the Jesuits said he would; the Catholic cantons naturally welcomed another Catholic victory, but they were even then conscious that a too-victorious emperor might think of the castle of Habsburg and of the Swiss land that once belonged to his family. The Protestants rejoiced at the later triumphs of Gustavus Adolphus and of the French, but reflected that Swiss methods of warfare were out of date compared with Swedish speed and artillery, and that their cities could not withstand a battering such as had reduced Magdeburg.

The young men of the cantons were brave and warlike enough, and large numbers of them went off to the wars, grimly fighting for pay on either side, many of them never returning. The religious disunion of their country prevented the confederation from having any official policy save that of doing nothing. It was, indeed, no easy task to save their own lands from invasion when the Alpine passes and Swiss roads offered such convenient routes for the belligerents to use for attack or retreat.

Defence of the frontiers alone was insufficient guarantee of Swiss independence and, in fact, this was largely secured by the unsatisfactory outcome of the prolonged war. Had Gustavus Adolphus been overwhelmingly successful and his *corpus evangelicorum* become paramount in central Europe, a revision of the second treaty of Kappel would have been called for and Zürich and Berne could hardly have failed to obtain overwhelming predominance in the confederation. On the other hand, had the emperor Ferdinand's Edict of Restitution (1629) been applied, as in strict law it unquestionably should have been, to the bishoprics of Basle and Constance and to the abbey of St. Gallen, the balance of power would have been shifted decisively in favour of the Catholics. In spite of threats, and of short cuts across Swiss territory taken by soldiers of either side, neutrality, and even mediation between the combatants, remained the clear policy of the Swiss diet. The war brought much suffering, for plague, crowds of refugees, debasement and counterfeiting of the coinage, and high prices of food were attributable to it. The cost of defence was considerable and was assessed by the 'Defensionale' of Wyl (1647) which became a further bond between the cantons and, with modifications, lasted until the French Revolution. Furthermore, something was gained in that soldiers and materials, salt, grain, and cattle exports fetched high prices in the belligerent markets. When the war came to an end, Switzerland not only survived in good heart, but also obtained from the emperor Ferdinand III, on 19 October 1647, an explicit recognition of the permanent separation of Basle and the other Swiss cantons from any dependence, legal or otherwise, on the empire. It was long overdue.

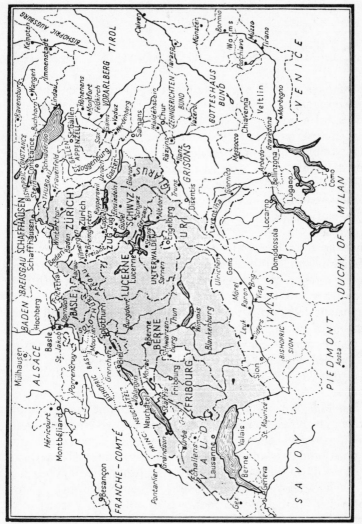

SWITZERLAND, 1442–1797

VIII

PEACE AND SELF-GOVERNMENT 1648–1789

FROM the peace of Westphalia to the French Revolution, the Swiss people managed their own affairs in their own way, variegated, conservative, and attractive. More and more foreign visitors came and reported on what they saw, although few troubled to understand fully the infinite complexities of the relationship of the various communities with one another. Every kind of government existed within these borders. In Neuchâtel and in the dominions of the prince abbot of St. Gallen there were autocratic rulers as irresponsible, authoritative, and enlightened as Louis XIV or Frederick the Great; in Berne, Fribourg, Solothurn, and Lucerne an aristocracy based on birth and inheritance ruled as graciously and corruptly as the great whig nobles did in England. In the forest cantons, most obviously in Schwyz and Uri, pure democracy was the rule, for all officials were elected, and all important decisions ratified, by the open-air meeting of all adults capable of bearing arms. The habits of such gatherings were, in fact, extremely conservative and traditional; departures from the settled routine of precedent and the choice of any other than members of well-known families for office were extremely rare.

Economic life. In such an atmosphere economic change was unlikely to be rapid, and, in fact, agriculture, based on small family holdings and on communal agreements about pasture, the rearing of beasts and constant attention to the cow and to milk products, filled the life of the country-side. Much greater attention began to be given to trees and forests; the wanton removal of these, almost unchecked in the middle ages, was so obviously destructive of soil and favourable to avalanches that communal action for their preservation was early taken, willingly accepted, and rigorously enforced. Technical improvements in seeds, rotation of crops, new grasses providing better crops of hay which was so much needed for the winter, manures (copied, where applicable, from England and from Germany), all helped to make the Swiss soil a little more productive, but, even so, it was impossible for food supplies to keep pace with the steadily growing population, even when this was thinned by armed service abroad.

In the eighteenth century an interest came to be shown in the peasant and his life that had been unknown before. This was due, in part, to the general acceptance of the ideas of the French *philosophes,* and to the new respect for nature, a movement which found its reflection also in the fashionable make-believe of the shepherdesses and milkmaids of court plays and imaginative literature. Switzerland, almost entirely rural, could not fail to be affected by this tendency. When, therefore, Hans Kaspar Hirzel of Zürich published in 1761 *The economy of a philosophical peasant* it had an immense sale and helped to popularize a 'back to the land' movement. In Basle, Berne, and Zürich agricultural societies reflected the tendency of the age, the interest shown by Berne providing evidence that the old fear and mistrust of the exploited countryman was giving way to a friendlier wisdom based on security. None the less, oppressive taxation of the peasant's few necessities was not relaxed, and so he later looked on, in sullen indifference and disapproval but without active opposition, when the enemy overran his lands in the name of liberty.

If agriculture changed relatively slowly after the Thirty Years War, manufacturing underwent much more rapid and far-reaching changes, so that it may be said that the industrial revolution in Switzerland preceded that in England. To speak, however, as many Swiss writers perfectly correctly do, of their country as the most highly industrialized corner of Europe, may easily leave a false impression. Rural life, the routine of the farm and the field, remained predominant in Switzerland as it did in England at the time of Jane Austen or even of Cobbett. None the less, like Great Britain in a later century, Switzerland must either export or decline, but unlike Great Britain, there were no large coal measures or mineral deposits, and, until the advent of electricity, heavy industry was out of the question. The desirable ideal was an exportable commodity requiring considerable workmanship, little application of heat, and little raw material. The Protestant Switzerland of the plain was in general more suited to industrialization than the Catholic mountain villages, although in the winter there was a reserve of labour here which could be, and was, used for domestic craft industries.

Again, after 1648, road and water transport was a good deal

safer than previously, and organized post services began to run. They were exploited, as the industrious people were, by capitalist employers, whose prosperity or good fortune was believed by Calvin's followers to be a sign of divine favour. Gold had come in some quantity to Switzerland when the Continent was at war, and rich men were not expected to live ostentatiously but to invest their capital for their own and the public good. In this regard they were only moderately successful in the greater cities, where, particularly in Zürich and Basle, an elaborate gild organization had long attempted to regulate conditions of employment. While this chiefly affected the ancient trades, builders, carpenters, shoe-makers, tailors, bakers, flayers, and butchers, it was the weaving industry, wherein new fortunes were to be found, which made the most noticeable advance.

Textile industries. Wool could be had wherever there were sheep, even if the quantity to be obtained from mountain sheep was not very considerable. Hand-spinning of wool had been practised from the middle ages, but with improved mechanical methods the industrious, if not very inventive, Swiss worker could go far. It was the foreigner who purchased these products of Swiss industry, especially the French, with whom free trade was guaranteed. And it was largely the French refugees from religious persecution who brought what was so invaluable to the seventeenth and eighteenth centuries, knowledge of new industrial processes. It was in this way that the silk and, later, the cotton, textile industries came to, or were revived in, Zürich, where factories could be built round the lake and where there were men rich enough to provide the necessary raw materials, the machinery, the access to distant markets, and the financial reserves that could meet the vagaries of fashion or the accident of trade depression. Equally necessary was knowledge of where foreign markets were to be found, and this was among the chief benefits brought back by those who served in foreign armies and visited many lands and peoples.

There was no lack of cheap labour, for every year a surplus of countrymen had to find employment where they could or else starve. Therefore anyone who offered regular employment at home in knitting, embroidery, lace-making, spinning or weaving, was regarded as a benefactor to young and old alike. The newer industries, silk- and cotton-weaving and fabrication in many forms, were less subject to traditional restrictions than others, and the use of immigrants who were not full citizens added to the flexibility of these employments. Dutch imports from India, brought up the Rhine, showed what was wanted; the art of simple dyeing was easily learnt, and Zürich-made, and later St. Gallen-made, cotton wares had a wide market in Europe until they were finally ousted by the products of the power-looms of Lancashire.

Certain natural advantages for the growing of flax, some local skill which was an inheritance from the middle ages, and the existence of a large number of villages whose inhabitants were extremely anxious to do paid handwork at home, led to St. Gallen becoming the leading centre of the linen industry. There were here no civic or cantonal regulations or restrictive practices to protect or impede the free exercise of competition and individual effort. The middle-man, who brought the prepared flax and received and paid for the roughly completed linen was for long a familiar and accepted figure. In the city of St. Gallen itself, the final bleaching, finishing, and packing was carried out, and from thence the completed articles were sent to France (chiefly to Lyons), Austria, and Germany. While Europe was content with a rather coarse but durable fabric, the industry constantly increased, but the growing insistence upon greater fineness and elegancy in the eighteenth century, together with changes in fashion, caused a persistent decline in the demand for this linen.

Cotton goods, softer and more attractively made up, began to displace linen, whereupon St. Gallen accepted the changed situation and turned with equal energy to cotton-spinning, weaving, and dyeing. These manufactures, enhanced by fine muslin, ingenious cotton mixtures, and beautiful embroidery regained for St. Gallen its former repute. The amount of patient hand-embroidery that must have gone on in ill-lit, wooden, peasant-dwellings is enormous and in our admiration for the patient activity of the needlewomen, and for the beauty of the finished products, it is not possible also entirely to overlook a background of sweated female labour and ruined eyesight.

Knitting was, equally obviously, a suitable occupation for active hands. The introduction of Lee's stocking-frame in the seventeenth century and the substitution of breeches and stockings for hose, brought work and some money to Basle and its country-side as far south as Solothurn and Biel. But the city gilds were opposed to the machines and to the new methods; neither the wool textile industry in Basle, nor the ribbon-weaving which partly escaped regimentation, were comparable in importance to the cotton and silk from the east. There was also in this city—in which smoking in public was nominally prohibited—a considerable tobacco manufacture, the leaf coming from Alsace.

Industrial development: clocks and watches. Berne played a relatively minor part in Swiss industrial development. A small and much regulated city, with a large agricultural hinterland of which it was extremely proud under its control, Berne was almost too aloof to try to compete with Zürich. Few refugees arrived within its walls and they received, generally, a cold welcome; when the physiocrats made agriculture seem a proper interest for aristocrats, Berne rejoiced. A certain amount of fine lace, hand-made in the villages of the Jura, was collected and distributed by Berne, but the quantity was not very considerable.

In general, the industrial development of Switzerland may be thought of as arising first in order of time and importance, from the textile manufacturers of the east, and then secondly from the watch- and clock-making of the west. Genevan timepieces were renowned for accuracy and elegance from the sixteenth century onwards, but a rather close trade union restricted the profitable industry to the city of Geneva and to certain groups of families in it. Jewellery, likewise, was made for export separately from or in conjunction with watch-making, the combined industries accounting for one third of the employed persons in the city. This trade spread to the Jura, or, perhaps, started there independently. From La Chaux-de-Fonds and Le Locle, watches, at first copies of London productions, made their appearance. Simpler and more standardized than the beautiful and elaborate productions of Geneva, they were cheap, and were, possibly, the real origins of what was later to be Switzerland's best-known contribution to the world markets. The marine chronometer owed much to Swiss talents, while, on a lower level, from the hill-sides of the Jura came the musical boxes and automatic machines that surprised the world.

Peace of Westphalia. These notable economic developments could have taken place only in an area where peace and security ruled and where the authority of the state was capable of enforcement. Swiss neutrality during the Thirty Years War was rewarded by the recognition of independence secured at Münster, mainly by the efforts of the Basle burgomaster, Johann Rudolf Wettstein. At the great peace conference he counted as one of the Protestant mediators and was highly respected and influential as such. After the peace of Westphalia, an attempt was made by the emperor to bring Basle under the appellate jurisdiction of the imperial *Kammergericht* at Speyer, and it was Wettstein's second great achievement to bring about, with Catholic help, the abrogation of this claim. For all practical purposes all connexion with the Reich was now severed. Together with this success went the acceptance of Mülhausen as an ally of the Protestant cantons alone, although the city very nearly became a full member of the confederation and was, in any case, saved by Swiss protection from falling into the greedy clutches of Louis XIV.

Religion. The religious division was fundamental. A man was born into either a Protestant state or a Catholic one; conversions were very rare, and the outlook of ordinary men and women was limited by the boundaries and opportunities of their little state. The diets of the whole confederation came to be merely formal affairs concerned only with the administration of the common lordships and with any direct threats to the common peace and security. Such threats were rare, and religious disunion caused them to be interpreted as narrowly as possible. In 1668 a new defence agreement made the obligations of each member of the confederation a little more explicit, but no common guarantee of protection for Geneva or the Vaud was ever collectively secured before the nineteenth century.

The Catholics possessed seven out of the thirteen effective places in the diet and the Protestants acquiesced in thus being in a numerical minority because of their obvious economic and military superiority which guaranteed attention to their opinions. Neither the Valais nor the Grisons cared much about their separate representation at the diet; St. Gallen, on the other hand, was in time willingly included because city and abbot, often hostile, tended to cancel one another out. Behind all lay the alliance with France, giving French envoys a preponderating voice in the offer of advice, but also bringing security, freedom of trade, and plenty of paid foreign service and protection. In addition to the full meetings of the formal Swiss diet, there were separate diets of Protestants and Catholics meeting at Aarau and Lucerne respectively, the Protestants showing themselves generally the more energetic and far-seeing, the Catholics the more cautiously conservative and defensive.

Subjects. Collectively or separately every state had subjects over whom it ruled by right of conquest. Thus twelve of the thirteen *Orte* (Appenzell was the exception) ruled the Italian possessions, the Sotto Cenere—Lugano, Mendrisio, Locarno, and the Val Maggia; nine states ruled the Rheintal; eight Thurgau, Sargans, and the upper Freiamt; Zürich, Berne, and Glarus ruled Baden, Bremgarten, and Mellingen; Schwyz and Glarus ruled Gaster and Uznach; Uri, Schwyz, and Nidwalden ruled Bellinzona and the Riviera; Berne and Fribourg ruled Schwarzenberg, Orbe, Grandson, Morat, and Echallens. The complicated task of administering this miniature empire was made possible by the existence of understandings between the various states about the employment of agents for limited periods only and about the order in which they were to be nominated. These agents naturally made the best use of their opportunities to make small fortunes at the expense of the subjects over whom they ruled without, apparently, any marked loss of popularity.

Allies. The position of the allies (*Zugewandte*) was equally elaborately established by many agreements and long tradition. They varied from the insignificant, such as Gersau, Engelberg, Payerne, Neuenstadt, Rapperswil, Münstertal, and Erguel, to those included by name in official treaties, Toggenburg, Gruyère, and Saanen, and then the greater allies, the abbey and the city of St. Gallen, the bishopric of Basle, Mülhausen, Rottweil, Biel, Geneva, the Grisons, and Valais. With such groupings, as indefinable in their obligations and relationships as the British Commonwealth, the Swiss could feel a sense of stability and security.

This very security allowed, and at times almost encouraged, internal discontent. The tradition of obedience to duly constituted authority was, indeed, strong, and, in the cantons dependent upon a capital city, the city council expected to interfere with the daily lives of its citizens and to be obeyed unhesitatingly. As in Italy, the cities tended to oppress the country-side and the peasantry to be interested only in local affairs and to exaggerate local grievances. With the end of the Thirty Years War many, who had to come to live in Swiss villages for safety, went away and their payments were missed; prices fell rapidly when the war demand was over and many who had borrowed or mortgaged on the assumption that prosperity would continue indefinitely were in dire straits. More state officials had been appointed and their vigorous exaction of dues and tithes was felt to be oppressive. A general devaluation of the various currencies was also necessary, for much 'bad' money had circulated in war-time and was now being eliminated by drastic methods.

Discontent and rebellion. Discontent was first violently manifested in the Catholic canton of Lucerne, where, in January 1653, the Entlebuch was in an uproar following addresses at Schüpfheim by a well-to-do peasant, Emmenegger. Before January was out, most of the villages of the canton of Lucerne were clamouring for a reduction of taxation and of mortgages, for a more stable currency, and for the right to pay tithe in kind. Lucerne itself was soon besieged by peasants demanding redress of grievances. The city appealed to its neighbours for help, and Zwyer of Uri was accepted as mediator. He promised to secure for the peasants their ancient rights; the city on 1 April 1653 agreed to some reduction of tolls, dues, and demands, and the peasants went home.

The rebellion, however, had spread to neighbouring states. The Swiss diet was now concerned to secure its suppression everywhere and steadily brought together, appealing to the agreement of Stans,[1] the co-ordinated forces of the cantons. Berne was especially alarmed. Its wide territories had to be kept obedient at any cost, lest memories of ancient independence should revive. Rebel emissaries, particularly one Samuel Tribolet, were exploiting the ignorance and the needs of the peasants and rousing violent resentment against the city. The example of the Entlebuch was copied across the frontier in the Emmental and in the Oberaargau. The country folk divided into 'hards' and 'softs', enemies and supporters respectively of the governments, the 'hards' coercing some who hesitated by cutting off the beards or ears of the 'softs'. Soon an organized Peasants' Union stood over against a Lords' Union in Solothurn, in the Freiamt, in Aargau, and in the countryside of Basle. The core of the revolt remained in the Entlebuch, and its chosen head, Nicholas Leuenberger, was a man of some property and local renown. No great leader, somewhat lacking in fire and determination, he was highly popular and thousands from all sides gathered round him. Appealing to the ancient

[1] See p. 133 above.

traditions of Swiss self-government, he demanded more consideration for the rights of the tenant and subject, provisions for appeal
from the state governments to the confederation, and wider local
autonomy. By May 1653, 16,000 men were ready to fight for this
vague creed and moved against Berne which hastily promised to
consider their grievances. Turning north they met, on 3 June, at
Wohlenschwil, the federal forces who were in excellent order and
who outnumbered them. They were easily defeated, and by
8 June the rising was over, the peasants surrendering on terms
which were later denounced. Another party of peasants was
crushed at Herzogenbuchsee and terribly severe punishments
followed. Basle, Solothurn, Zürich, and Berne agreed in the
elimination of the leaders and in making an example of their
principal supporters before considering any redress of grievances.
A large indemnity was charged on the insurgent country-side
and the dependence of the peasant was made more obvious as
well as being more strictly enforced than before. None the less a
little was gained. After the rising, Berne took certain precautions
to prevent undue extortion and severity on the part of its bailiffs,
and taxes were, where possible, reduced. The old confederation
never again had to deal with a general revolt.

First Villmergen War. The religious question, on the other hand,
it could in no way resolve. The second peace of Kappel[2] had been
a hurried and most unfortunate agreement and the Catholics lost
no opportunity of interpreting it narrowly and harshly when it
suited them. Attempts to alter it or to modify the federal constitution failed, and, even after the Thirty Years War, religious hatreds
ran so strong that Catholics were again joining forces with Savoy
so that the Protestants, remembering those

> slaughter'd Saints, whose bones
> Lie scatter'd on the Alpine mountains cold

sought the alliance of Cromwell and the United Provinces. A
trifling incident led to the so-called First Villmergen War (1656).
The Zwinglian reformation in its early days had penetrated
to Arth, on the lake of Zug, and when, after 1531, the canton of
Schwyz determined to retain the Catholic faith, a few Protestant
families continued quietly and unostentatiously to practise their
own form of worship there. Threatened with suppression in 1655,

[2] See p. 162 above.

some thirty-seven Protestants took refuge in Zürich where they were received in very friendly fashion. A score or so who remained in Arth now suffered severe persecution from the government of Schwyz, three being handed over to the Inquisition at Milan. Zürich retaliated by demanding that the property owned by the refugees, or its value, should be restored to them. This was refused by Schwyz which in turn called for the repatriation of its subjects. This issue might reasonably have been submitted to arbitration, but bound up with it was the future position of Catholicism in the confederation about which no compromise was possible. It was soon apparent that while the unnecessary and overbearing violence of Schwyz was nowhere popular or even seriously upheld, the law as it stood was with the canton, and Zürich could depend only on the half-hearted support of Berne. Even so, if it came to an armed conflict, Zürich might easily overbear its neighbour, as the French ambassador, La Barde, clearly indicated in his reports.

No arrangement was possible, and in January 1656, Berne and Zürich declared war on the five Catholic states—Uri, Schwyz, Unterwalden, Lucerne, and Zug—sending a force at once to besiege Rapperswil. The Zürich Protestant soldiers were unsuccessful in their efforts to storm its castle, while a Bernese force which advanced light-heartedly into the Freiamt was repulsed by Christopher Pfyffer at Villmergen (24 January 1656) with the loss of 1,000 men. Peace followed on 7 March at Baden, upholding the Catholic cause, insisting on the authority of each canton to maintain its own religion exclusively, and requiring each party to the conflict to pay its own costs. The religious division within the confederation was more sharply apparent than ever.

Neither the second peace of Kappel nor its substantial reassertion in 1656 corresponded to realities. The Protestant defeat in each case had been due to temporary, local, and accidental causes: in fact, the Protestant states were far more powerful in numbers and in wealth than their opponents, and this was bound in the end to tell. As Switzerland became more dependent on exports, which came chiefly from the industrial cities, a revaluation of political power was bound to come. When it should do so, merely by the exercise of a blockade, 'economic sanctions', Zürich, Basle, and Berne together could scarcely fail to win.

There were constant threats of a renewal of the religious struggle. In the councils of the common lordships Catholic preponderance, while unable to suppress the heretics, led to the creation of difficulties for them at every turn, particularly where mixed marriages and the education of children were concerned, and resentment steadily grew. There was nearly a war in 1664 when six soldiers from Lucerne, marching to Frauenfeld, were killed by some Protestant peasants in a fight near Wigoltingen in Thurgau and when, in spite of appeals, severe punishment was imposed. In 1694 the protection given by the bailiff appointed by Schwyz, Reding, to the celebration of mass in the Protestant township of Wartau caused further discontent. In 1697 the assertion of a Catholic claim to have the cross carried upright in procession through the streets of the city of St. Gallen was strenuously and effectively resisted.

Second Villmergen War. The conflict came about, finally, over a road. A Catholic highway from Schwyz, running *via* Uznach and Wattwil to the boundary of Austria, was projected in order to maintain economic security of transport and communication and in order to cut off Zürich from the Protestant portion of Glarus. Leodegar Bürgisser, abbot of St. Gallen, ordered the inhabitants of Wattwil in 1712 to provide labour on this highway, which they refused to do, having long since secured exemption from compulsory labour services. The abbot tried to coerce them into obedience, whereupon the whole of the Toggenburg declared its solidarity with the resisters and was supported by Zürich and Berne. The abbot refused to agree to arbitration, whereupon the Toggenburgers, led by Nabholz of Zürich, renounced all dependence upon him, drove away his agents, and blockaded some monasteries and castles. Zürich and Berne came to their aid and declared war on the abbot who, in turn, was supported by the forest cantons. This time the uniformed armies of Berne and Zürich co-operated well. Wyl was occupied, the monastery of St. Gallen was invested, the abbot, with his monks, taking refuge in Germany. Skirmishes at Mellingen and Bremgarten favoured the Protestants; Baden fell, supplies in the forest cantons ran short, and Lucerne received much blame.

Peace negotiations were opened in July at Aarau, where Lucerne and Uri indicated their readiness to agree to terms. The Protestant soldiers began to go home, believing the war to be over, but the pope denounced the suggested agreement and Catholic attacks in the Freiamt were renewed. Their success caused the explicit rejection of the preliminary peace agreement and a violent frontal attack on the Bernese army at Villmergen (25 July 1712) opened a hard-fought, mostly hand-to-hand struggle under a pitiless July sun, accompanied by serious casualties and ending in a Bernese and Protestant victory. The peace of Aarau (11 August 1712) regulated the position in the common lordships, securing real parity of religious rights and the setting up of mixed tribunals of equal numbers for the settlement of disputes. Zürich and Berne appreciably increased the territories over which they had control, thereby giving great offence to those who upheld the principle of the inviolability of the territorial settlement of the old Bund. Later, the abbot of St. Gallen promised, and secured, greater political and religious freedom to the Toggenburg, thereby completely ending the unnecessary conflict.

Louis XIV and the Swiss

In some respects this religious civil war was dependent upon events elsewhere. It was the victories of Marlborough and the Dutch that prevented direct French or Spanish intervention on behalf of the Catholics, and it was Louis XIV who skilfully gained all the advantage he could while not giving his enemies any opportunity to intervene. Throughout his reign the influence of the *roi soleil* was indeed powerful in the cantons, so powerful that it outshone much else. Without French salt, corn, iron, and silk, without service in the French armed forces, without subsidies from Versailles, without unimpeded access to French markets, seventeenth-century Switzerland would have found life unbearably hard. And, too, Swiss independence and neutrality were possible only while France was balanced by Austria, Spain, and Great Britain. If the war of the Spanish succession had ended in an overwhelming victory for Louis XIV, the Swiss confederation must have come entirely under his influence.

The French ambassador was, throughout his reign, incomparably the most powerful foreigner in Switzerland, and Louis's envoys, particularly Jean de La Barde, were able and well chosen men. They could bring much pressure to bear on the confederates. When Franche-Comté, and then Strassburg, and with it practically the whole of Alsace, fell into Louis's hands (thus leaving Mülhausen now as hopelessly isolated as Rottweil had been), when great guns were mounted at Hüningen expressly to overawe Basle, when Spain became France's ally and the Dutch retained a precarious independence chiefly through British support, when Austria could hardly face France alone and feared attack by a revivified Turkey, little wonder the Swiss felt insecure. Swiss soldiers fought in all Louis's campaigns, sometimes, as at Blenheim, against their own countrymen, and French pensions were readily accepted by leading Swiss citizens. On the other hand, French persecution of the Huguenots was greatly resented by the Protestant cantons, and after 1685 many French refugees came to Zürich, Schaffhausen, St. Gallen, Berne, and Geneva, where they were welcomed and protected in spite of protests from Paris. Some further resentment, too, was apparent in these more industrial areas when the adverse effects of the mercantilist legislation of Colbert, partly closing French markets previously open to them, began to be felt.

The Neuchâtel affair

Finally, there came a serious threat of more direct intervention. The principality of Neuchâtel (Neuenburg) which enjoyed cocitizenship with Berne, Lucerne, Fribourg, and Solothurn, had been ruled since 1529 by the ducal family of Orléans-Longueville. The male line of this family became extinct in 1691, and its possessions, including Neuchâtel, were claimed by Armand, prince of Conti, and Marie, duchess of Nemours. The Parlement of Paris, applying French law, decided in favour of the prince of Conti, the devoted servant to, and relative of, Louis XIV. Possession of the principality by him would mean a French pistol pointed at the heart of Berne and a manifest threat to the independence of the Vaud and of Geneva. Berne, therefore, hurriedly secured the local recognition of the claims of the duchess of Nemours, provided a garrison for her in the city of Neuchâtel, and organized a union of the neighbouring towns in defence of her rights. This, and an unwillingness to challenge local jurisdiction, induced Louis to hold his hand until the duchess died at Paris in June 1707. Fifteen candidates now put forward their claims, among them Frederick I of Hohenzollern, recently crowned king in Prussia and nephew of William III of England whose somewhat dubious rights were assigned to him. Great Britain, Holland, Austria, and Sweden supported his case before the Neuchâtel 'Tribunal of the Three Estates', before whom the schultheiss of Berne, Friedrich

Willading, appeared to urge in his favour that the Prussian monarch was Protestant, distant, and relatively insignificant. Louis seems to have been rather lukewarm at the critical juncture in his support of the prince of Conti, and the Catholic cantons failed to exercise all the pressure they might; on 3 November 1707 King Frederick I was declared by the tribunal to be their lawful ruler, and of Neuchâtel his descendants remained princes until Frederick William IV abandoned his claims to authority in 1857.

It was in face of such and similar situations that opinion as to the value of, and therefore about the renewal of, the traditional alliance with France, fluctuated. The celebrated visit to Paris in November 1663 accompanied by much pomp and splendour (and some ill feeling) resulted in arrangements being made once again for the employment of up to 16,000 Swiss soldiers and in the continued official and unofficial distribution of French money in the most profitable quarters. Thus French aggression, while disliked, was condoned. Even the threat to the independence of Geneva, added to so much else that was unpalatable to the confederates, was overlooked in the face of cash received or promised and of inability to take effective action to reply to it.

The Trücklibund. Moreover, after the Second Villmergen War and the peace of Aarau (1712)[3] religious feeling ran so high that it directly affected relations with France. Louis XIV in 1714 was 73, the Swiss alliance would lapse eight years after his death, the succession in France was uncertain, and the possibilities of another arrangement, less favourable to the Catholics, could not be overlooked. Louis's representative, Du Luc, found the moment favourable for a departure from the hitherto invariable understanding that any agreement must be made with the whole confederation, and he now entered into negotiations with the Catholic cantons and their allies. On 9 May 1715 a secret document was executed at Solothurn by which the Catholic states separately, together with the Valais, agreed to the exclusive recruitment of their military personnel for France, the French representative to secure from Berne and Zürich certain restitutions of territory that had been alienated at Aarau. The French king was likewise to mediate in disputes and, in general terms, to support the Catholic states in any controversy within the confederation. This deed was deposited in a sealed metal casket and the transaction later became known as the

---

[3] See p. 197 above.

Trücklibund. It was never formally ratified by Louis and was in no way legally binding upon either side nor was it put into effect. But it illustrated the fatal division of the confederation and the power of France. In fact, the earlier French alliance was renewed by all the states in the usual terms in 1723, and this was again affirmed for the last time in May 1777 at one of the very rare diets of the whole confederation. The partition of Poland which naturally caused some alarm helped to bring about a necessary unanimity. The *Trücklibund* is of significance only because it indicated, what was true of the whole of the eighteenth century, that the Swiss confederation hardly existed save in its separate component parts.

Aristocracy and oligarchy. In these, however, there was plenty of life. Conservative orthodoxy in politics, in religion, in manners, in dress, and even in thought was taken for granted. There were antiquated observances, superstitious practices, ancient laws and regulations, censorship, and corruption everywhere, accompanied by many signs of intellectual enlightenment and physical well-being. Berne was ruled by a small hereditary aristocracy. There were about 250 families capable of ruling (*regimentsfähige*) and about 70 of these divided the control of the state between themselves. The Wattenwil, Jenner, Steiger, Tscharner, and Graffenried were the Bedfords, Grenvilles, Rockinghams, Devonshires, and Portlands of the day. They filled the 299 chairs of the great 'council of 200'; they ruled through the small councils and through the cabinet of 16. There were lucrative governorships to share among themselves, and marriages into this select society were carefully arranged and frequently heavily paid for. Proud, arrogant, and self-confident, they nevertheless governed well and were accepted with affectionate respect in the city and in both the French- and the German-speaking territories under their overlordship.

In Zürich and Basle this oligarchic regime was based less on birth than on industrial and commercial success. In Zürich the gilds or city companies provided the succession of rulers. Inheriting from Zwingli and his followers a high sense of civic duty, recruited from commercially enterprising traders and manufacturers, the paternal puritanical regime was accepted with cheerful acquiescence by the majority. The city ruled the country and the gilds ruled the city; criticism alone was feared and freedom of writing and speech were therefore suppressed. Popular education, while encouraged, meant the acquisition of traditional knowledge in the traditional way and the inculcation of habits of obedience. When the Macaulay of Switzerland, Johannes von Müller, issued the first volume of his great history, the title-page bore the imprint of Boston to avoid police prosecution for sedition. Basle was devoted almost entirely to the expansion of local industry and commerce, the government of the state (with the bishop of Basle, an imperial prince, in its borders) being in the hands of the gilds, as in Zürich, but with an element of chance deliberately intro-duced to prevent the ascendancy of age and wealth.

Berne was the state that attracted most attention. A governing class, competent and devoted to duty, a fair balance of trade and agriculture, an assured public income from foreign investments (i.e. external military service), all made for stability and popu-larity. In Berne, as to some degree in contemporary England, the ruling aristocracy considered participation in trade as incom-patible with its public duties and position in society, thus releasing all its energies for government. In general the rule of the patricians of Berne over their state was excellent, subject, however, to one important qualification. In the French-speaking territory of the Vaud, which had been annexed in 1536, the noble landowners were discontented because they had been deprived of their ancient rights and powers, while the common people regarded with indifference and dislike the rather expensive, if not seriously oppressive, rule of German-speaking Bernese bailiffs. There was, in fact, a consistent undercurrent of opposition which gradually developed into a kind of local separatist movement which found a leader in 1723 in Abraham Davel. A man of deep religious convictions and a soldier who had served with distinction in the Second Villmergen War, Davel believed that the neglect and exploitation of his homeland accounted for what he regarded as the wickedness and irreligion of its people, and he further felt con-vinced that only through political independence could spiritual reform be brought about. When his somewhat naïve request for self-government was rejected, he led some 500 followers to Lausanne in March 1723 and urged the city council to act as rulers of the capital of an independent state. They refused, and instead arrested and later condemned Davel, who suffered the death penalty with courage and quiet conviction that his ideals would conquer. The rising was a farce as well as a failure, but the repute of Davel grew with the years and his name later achieved an unjustifiable renown, a kind of symbol of Vaudois independence.

Davel's attempt may be described as the most idealistic of the popular risings. There were others: that led by Lawrence Zellweger in Appenzell Ausserrhoden in 1732; that against French influence in Zug in 1733 (in which Josef Anton Schumacher overthrew for two years the Francophile family of the Zurlauben); that of 1763 in Schwyz, similar in its purpose; the Lucerne trials of 1764 in which the clericals triumphed; the campaign of the followers of Chenaux in 1781 against the traditional rulers of Fribourg. Probably the most significant of all, however, and certainly the best publicized later, was the Henzi rising in Berne.

Samuel Henzi. Samuel Henzi (1701–49) was an able Bernese citizen of good family whose early poverty excluded him from any hope of participation in the administration. Self-educated, he turned with enthusiasm to French literature, opposed the popular local 'German Society' and in 1744, as a recognized malcontent, was forced to leave Berne for Neuchâtel. Increasingly dissatisfied, on his return in 1748 he failed to obtain a librarianship for which he had hoped, retired to Paris and became the chief figure in a conspiracy to overthrow the government and to insist upon a wider franchise (but very far from a popular or democratic one) for the choice of councillors. The plot was betrayed, Henzi and the other ringleaders arrested and executed, so that the only effect was to preserve even more narrowly the privileges of the select families, admission to whose exclusive ranks and monopoly of power became even more difficult until the end of the old confederation.

Geneva. When this came about, one of the first places to suffer was Geneva. In this city, of which Rousseau was so childishly delighted to describe himself as citizen, there were four classes of inhabitants—the citizens proper (*citoyens*), the burghers (*bourgeois*), the residents (*habitants*), and their children (*natifs*). An effort had been made in 1707 by an able advocate, Fatio, to enlarge the numbers of those eligible for election to the city councils, but the only result was that he was shot as a dangerous conspirator. There were further popular demands for more equitable taxation in 1734, which were followed by rioting in 1737, sufficiently serious for French, Bernese, and Zürich troops to be called in to restore order. A mediation regulation was, however, accepted in 1738, improving the city's government and guaranteed by France. Rousseau, who had been obliged to leave his Genevan home for Neuchâtel, produced *Lettres de la Montagne,* which in 1766 caused another riot, a further liberal edict in 1768, and yet another disturbance fourteen years later. This time France, Sardinia, and Berne intervened to maintain and even to intensify the aristocratic regime, but discussion and disagreement continued, so that before the century was out Geneva was not only a home of revolutionary thought but came in 1789 very much under the influence of Paris, and in 1794 enjoyed its own reign of terror until the city and its lands were annexed by France in 1798.

Distinguished visitors. Switzerland, like Great Britain, was the home in the eighteenth century of many visitors who stayed for long periods and in some cases themselves affected, and were in turn affected by, the thought and outlook of their adopted country. Some were political or religious refugees, others foreigners seeking repose, favourable conditions for study, or the curative properties of baths or pure air. Of the names connected with the lake of Geneva in this century that of Voltaire (1694–1778) was probably the best known. He lived at Prangins near Nyon in 1754–5, in Lausanne in 1756–8, and spent much of his later life in Ferney, which although across the frontier, in an age in which frontiers were far less barriers than they have since become, gave the confederation some claim to a share of this renowned figure. Certainly his influence on Swiss thought was considerable.

Voltaire's contemporary, Edward Gibbon (1737–94), so utterly unlike him in outlook save in disrespect for the Christian religion and yet almost equally popular as a writer and certainly far greater as a historian, lived for fifteen years in Switzerland. *The Decline and Fall of the Roman Empire* was completed at Lausanne in June 1787 in a 'country which I have known and loved from my early youth. Under a mild government, amidst a beauteous landscape, in a life of leisure and independence, and among a people of easy and elegant manners.' Not only might it have been difficult for Gibbon to find in England the freedom from distraction necessary to make leisurely work possible, but also the story of the Swiss confederation made a strong appeal to his imagination. He wrote, in French, an *Introduction à l'histoire générale de la république des Suisses,* but he left it incomplete and had no intention of publishing it. It would not, indeed, have been popular in the forest cantons had it appeared, for the sceptical author accepted the then new and unpopular demonstration of the legendary nature of the story of William Tell.

Gibbon might have been even more closely connected with the lake of Geneva. In his *Autobiography* he tells of his love for the young Susanne Curchod, who married instead the celebrated banker and minister of Louis XVI, Necker. Her daughter was the equally renowned Madame de Stäel who, during her long sojourn at Coppet near Geneva, completed *De l'Allemagne*. Benjamin Constant (1767–1830) again, in spite of his Oxford and Edinburgh training, could not bear to be absent for long from his beloved Vaud.

Travellers in considerable numbers and from more than one country had been writing accounts of Switzerland for home consumption all through the century. One of the best appeared from a London press: *An account of Switzerland written in the year 1714* by Abraham Stanyan, whose acute and accurate knowledge has been praised by many modern writers. The best known of the *Travels in Switzerland* was that published in 1789 by William Coxe[4] which, like other of the learned archdeacon's books, deservedly had a wide circulation and was much drawn upon by later writers. Slowly, too, travel conditions made it possible for a growing number of tourists to appreciate Swiss scenery, relatively accurate cartography was now possible, and maps, reliefs, and panoramas multiplied. About the middle of the eighteenth century modern alpinism may be said to have started. There had, indeed, been sporadic and personal attempts upon peaks at least since the days when Petrarch made his famous ascent of Mont Ventoux in 1336, but it was not until Mont Blanc had been conquered in 1786 that mountaineering became that combination of sport, pleasure, and personal adventure which made a special appeal to Englishmen. The story of the attraction to the mountains and the compensation thus provided to Switzerland for the loss of mercenary service by the development of hotel-industry suited to the 'playground of Europe' belongs to the nineteenth century, but its origins lie in an earlier past.

Rousseau. Interest in mountains was one facet of the new attrac-

---

[4] He had also written *Sketches of the natural, civil, and political state of Swisserland*, London, 1779.

tion to nature which so characterized the age. Of this Rousseau was peculiarly the prophet. His idealism contrasted profoundly with the matter-of-fact smugness of the age of reason; his teachings about popular sovereignty and the general will proved solvents of the custom-hardened class consciousness of the old confederation. In spite of its suppression by the censors, *Émile* brought not only converts but visitors; many came to see the house of the most renowned of the 'philosophers', thus adding to the growing stream of tourists. The *Contrat Social*, published in 1762, intensified popular feeling against the too great privileges of the aristocracy, and, even if discontent was not at once translated into effective action, the moral basis of the existing structure of society had been sapped. A desire for simplicity and retirement began to take the place of elaborate adornment and excessive publicity, and sentimentality displaced scepticism and rationalism. The French Revolution was to a small but real extent an attempt to translate some of Rousseau's theories into practical and institutional terms, and, since the Swiss confederation, like the U.S.A., was republican in an age of monarchy (however repentant) the long residence of Jean Jacques on Swiss soil was not without its results.

Education: Pestalozzi. Rousseau's theories about education could not fail to be read by an intelligent people. The Swiss peasant was not, indeed, usually either literate or interested in things of the mind, and there were many labourers in the larger cities who were equally without formal instruction, but a monopoly of learning for the children of the rich could scarcely be justified in the face of the new thought of the day. There were few schools and fewer competent teachers in eighteenth-century Switzerland; contemporary descriptions of unintelligent learning by rote in overcrowded school-rooms forced on the boys for whom a little painful instruction was provided, explain much. When *Émile* was published in 1761, Heinrich Pestalozzi of Zürich was fifteen years old, but he early imbibed many of its ideas, tried somewhat ineffectively to put them into practice, and then, in 1781, expounded his theories in *Lienhard und Gertrud*. The simplicity and sentimentality of this book had far-reaching effects and helped to enable the author to set up schools based on his methods elsewhere.

Building. Some part of this achievement, which excited much attention in the nineteenth century, was due to the manifest existence of a distinctive Swiss culture. In the Swiss cities imitation rather than originality was at first sight apparent. There were, indeed, some capable architects and builders, such as those who raised the churches of Schwyz, St. Gallen, and Solothurn, or re-built the monasteries at Einsiedeln, Pfäfers, and Engelberg, but Swiss baroque and rococo derived from, and were dependent upon, south German models which were copied with modifications. Per-haps the best achievement was to be seen in the stained glass of the churches and city halls, in the design and construction of beautiful furniture, in the great delicacy of ornamentation in armour and domestic utensils, in pottery, wood-carving, tiles, and designs for the great stoves without which no large house was complete.

Literature. It was in the sphere of religious and political thought that Switzerland had contributed much to the sixteenth and seven-teenth centuries and such speculations continued even when self-satisfied orthodoxy, enlightened scepticism, or a narrow, legalistic pietism seemed to be dominant in Europe. Beat Ludwig von Muralt (1665-1749) of Berne, who also wrote some incisive letters about the English, and J. J. Bodmer (1698–1783) of Zürich com-bined piety with politics. Bodmer covered up the radical nature of his egalitarian ideas by putting them forward in the guise of rather fourth-rate poems and plays. He thus evaded the censor-ship and was able to advocate a united Switzerland with an elected representative assembly. Similar suggestions were put forward by Franz Balthasar (1689–1763) of Lucerne and the Basle philan-thropist, Isaac Iselin (1728–82). Together they demonstrated that Catholics and Protestants could agree about the need for a united country. The foundation of a Helvetic society in 1762 demon-strated their belief in greater national unity if only for purposes of security. Annual conferences were held, Salomon Hirzel of Zürich was chosen as president, patriotic poems were composed and pamphlets issued, all in support of that moderate degree of national co-ordination which was finally to be achieved in 1848. Of more limited objective, but equally in favour of greater centralization and equally inter-denominational, was the Helvetian military society founded in 1779 to urge the need for a national army, and for defence preparations, which should leave less to last-minute improvizations and to the whims of the most recalcitrant of the states.

Lavater. Probably the figure of greatest local intellectual renown in his own age, and one almost entirely overlooked since, was

Johann Caspar Lavater (1741–1801) minister of St. Peter's church at Zürich. He anticipated a coming struggle between science and religion and spent much of his restless, active life trying to reconcile reason and revelation, philosophy and the Bible. Traveller, poet, political theorist, he became more and more convinced that he had received a special revelation from heaven to carry on his mission of reconciliation. Between 1775 and 1778 he published four large quarto volumes on the subject of physiognomy in which he demonstrated how character could be told from the external physical attributes of men and women, particularly the face, features, bearing, height, and posture. They were widely read and translated into several languages. He was in some ways the precursor of the phrenologists of the next century, and almost as self-deceived as they were, but his energy, his powers of conversation, his self-assurance and his fundamental kindliness secured him many friends, including Goethe and Herder.

The Swiss universities and academies of the eighteenth century at Geneva, Lausanne, Basle, and Zürich were too closely controlled by the local authorities, by antiquated statutes, and by property, patronage, and hereditary rights to be able to exercise any strong influence upon Swiss intellectual activity. None the less, in direct or indirect dependence upon them, a considerable succession of learned men reminded Europe of Swiss interest in scholarship. No less than five members of the family of Bernouilli at Basle were distinguished mathematicians and astronomers; Horace de Saussure of Geneva and Johannes Gesner of Zürich were botanists known far from their own land, while Albrecht von Haller of Berne enjoyed a reputation for omniscience in all fields of natural science which was supported by over 100 books and treatises. As an anatomist alone, he has secured a sure place in the history of science. Nor were the Swiss contributions of the century to geography, history, geology, statistics, and philology much less significant, and they were widely appreciated in Germany, France, and even in the states of the New World. Among the artists, Anton Graf of Winterthur (1736–1813) found discriminating patronage at the court of Saxony, and to England came Henry Fuseli (Johann Heinrich Füssli, 1741–1825) of Zürich, whose portrait-painting earned him money and renown, so that for many years he was a familiar figure at the Royal Academy. Sculptors and architects, too, mainly from the Ticino, secured employment at the imperial court of Russia and from the enlightened Frederick IV of Denmark, thus spreading farther the artistic reputation of their country.

The French Revolution. When the Estates General of France met at Versailles in May 1789 there was nothing to indicate that the French monarchy might succumb and little to suggest that anything more than some modification of the burden of taxation, with, of course, political implications, would result. The Swiss states were accustomed to the existence of a strong and wealthy France upon their western frontier: if the financial difficulties of their neighbour could be resolved, there would be the greater assurance that adequate money would be available for the payment of soldiers and pensions. The thought of the 'philosophers' was, indeed, well known in Swiss intellectual circles, but there was little that suggested that it might lead to any violent upheaval. There had been a renewed outbreak of social discontent at Geneva in 1782 from which Mallet du Pan had learnt something, but this hardly affected the confederation. The Swiss peasants governed themselves in the 'democratic' cantons and were well governed in the 'aristocratic' ones. There was no court, no federal government, no civil list, no cabinet, hardly anything that could be called a foreign policy. Some intellectuals might feel that the censorship was oppressive and that the laws of their states were in urgent need of revision, but their opinions were not likely to disturb settled governments which had behind them the experience and accumulated traditions of the past together with power and a firm grasp of the realities of the present.

In none of the cities, Berne, Basle, or Zürich, was there anything that could be thought of as a proletariat or that could play the role of the Paris mob. Nor was the Swiss peasant oppressed. In the Catholic states the church was not unduly wealthy and was, in general, popular; the scandals that disgraced the Gallican church could hardly occur in a country where the Protestants were alert to watch and to proclaim the shortcomings of the other side. There were those who thought of themselves as nobles, particularly in Berne, and who dressed and acted as if they were the counterparts of the French *seigneurs*, but their landed property was not extensive and their feudal rights, if irksome, were not the ludicrous survivals of medieval times that were so oppressive in France and the empire. Above all taxation was light.

The toiler in the fields felt that he was reasonably rewarded for his labours, and if there were local conditions that were unsatisfactory, there was nothing that was unendurable. Some artisans objected to the artificial gild regulations, but again there was no sense of intolerable injustice. Privilege existed everywhere, but even if disliked by a few it was in no danger of abolition.

The weakness of the confederation lay in its divisions. There was no adequate armed force ready to deal with an invader and little feeling that neutrality must be defended at any cost. Not until a canton felt its own border to be in immediate danger did the common people see the necessity for fighting. There was no feeling of political unity and little realization that a Swiss way of life must be preserved. Indifference and resignation were general. Some of the thoughtful and well-read citizens were sympathetic to the new phrases current in France—they wanted wider liberty in city and country, greater equality between the too rigidly differentiated classes, truer fraternity:

> Wer frühe den Tyrannen dräut,
> Dem Laster gleich die Knechtschaft scheut,
> Der, der hat Schweizerredlichkeit.

To achieve this, external pressure was necessary. Switzerland both was, and is, too small to be able to resist indefinitely pressure from an adjacent great power, and the teaching of the 'rights of man' was soon to have this sort of force behind it. Freedom of speech and religious toleration were to come from Paris and there were a few who were always willing to follow Paris wherever its claims might lead or however its demands might vary.

The anxiety of certain Swiss governments to maintain the *status quo* had resulted in the exile to France of a number of political refugees, particularly from the Vaud, who found willing supporters among the left wing of the National Assembly. These formed, in Paris, rather on the model of the Jacobins, a Swiss club, of which Castellaz of Gruyère was a leading member. They sent quantities of propaganda literature in favour of the new revolutionary principles to Switzerland where, in spite of efforts to exclude them, these pamphlets circulated widely. They also tried to undermine the loyalty and repute of the Swiss guards who were responsible for the safety of Louis XVI, and they succeeded in raising once more the old controversial issue of Swiss mercenary service, winning a number of adherents, chief among them Frédéric-César de Laharpe, to the new ideas. Laharpe was invited by Catherine the Great to Russia, and was allowed to give some instruction to her grandson, Alexander, which was to have strange after-effects. The correspondence and writings of Laharpe were directed in considerable measure against the autocracy of Berne, and, aided by the advocacy on the spot of Henri Monod, were remarkably successful in creating a general feeling of unrest and discontent. There was, even in 1791, a feeble attempt at revolt or at least of refusal to pay taxes, but this was easily suppressed by armed forces.

In January 1792 François Barthélemy arrived as ambassador of the new French government, anxious to prevent the confederation from joining the enemies of France who had many supporters among its leading members. His efforts to maintain the divisions in the confederation which favoured inaction and his endeavours to secure friends wherever possible, were on the way to success, but they were negatived by French threats of violence. With the French occupation of the lands of the bishop of Basle, with the massacre of the Swiss guards at the Tuileries, and with the renewed threat to Geneva, the old confederation was confronted with an entirely new situation out of which, after nearly a quarter of a century of threats, occupation, and war, a new Switzerland, itself unmistakably sprung from the old, was to arise.

IX

THE OVERTHROW AND
RECONSTRUCTION OF THE CONFEDERATION

Influence of the French Revolution. When the Revolution broke
out in France, at that time Switzerland's most powerful ally, this
great convulsion could not fail to spread to the confederation. The
country was stirred to its depths, economically, spiritually, and
socially. The Revolution, a turning-point in history all over
Europe, was particularly so in Switzerland. The opponents of
the Revolution were the cantonal governments together with the
townsmen in any kind of privileged position, and the professional
officers in foreign service; all these remained loyal to the old
French monarchy. They opposed the doctrine of the rights of man
then gaining ground in the country, for it struck at the root of
their privileges. The Swiss churches were hostile to the doctrine of
natural law, which had now passed into political action, and, once
the Revolution had taken an anti-Christian turn, they united with
the non-democratic states to form one firm counter-revolutionary
front.

The partisans of the Revolution in the confederation at first
formed only a small minority, mainly recruited from among the
young disciples of the *Aufklärung* in the cantonal capitals and
the country towns. The Age of Enlightenment had been the
formative experiment of their youth which had prepared them
for the great political experience of the Revolution. They expected
from it nothing less than the dawn of a new era for mankind,
while the more moderate and traditionally minded spirits were
content to hope for national regeneration. These abstract ideas of
revolution found particularly favourable ground in the French-
speaking parts of the country, especially in the district of the
Vaud, where geographical proximity, personal relationships, and
a common language all helped. Here, too, opposition arose among
the educated classes of the towns, which were no longer content
to be accounted subjects and for whom Berne was an obstacle to
personal advancement. While unrest was spreading among the

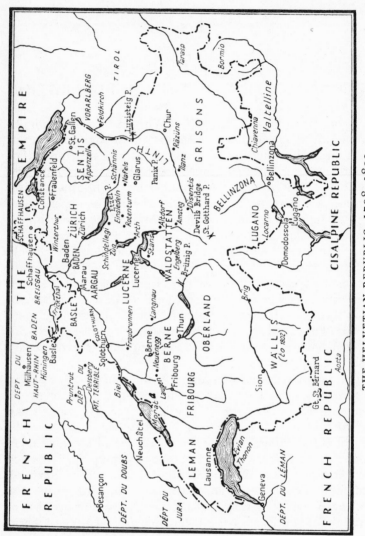

THE HELVETIAN REPUBLIC, 1798–1802

more alert minds in the towns, the country people in the Vaud and elsewhere remained unaffected. They were content enough to be ruled in a patriarchal fashion by their benevolent patrician lords and, in fact, resisted the invader with more spirit than did the enfeebled cantonal governments.

Preservation of neutrality during the Napoleonic Wars. It was the duty of the diet to regulate the relations of the confederation with revolutionary France, since it was the diet which had concluded the alliance with the French monarchy. Uncertain, however, whether the king had been sincere in his approval of the new constitution, it sent no official reply to the French communication on the subject. Further, when the diet ascertained the terms of the oath to this constitution which was to be administered to the Swiss troops in French service, it ordered them not to take it. There were two further points which put difficulties in the way of Franco-Swiss relations at the time; firstly, the revolutionary propaganda which was flooding Switzerland from Paris; secondly, the French *émigrés*. The latter had settled for the most part in the frontier towns of Solothurn, Fribourg, and Neuchâtel, where they awaited the day of their return. To the French government they could not fail to seem a perpetual menace, and the French people were annoyed by the warm welcome extended to these French aristocrats and churchmen by the ruling classes in Switzerland.

In spite of these causes of friction between Switzerland and her oldest ally, however, she proclaimed her traditional neutrality at the outbreak of the war. At that time, the statesmen of Switzerland were more than ever tempted to give way to their anti-revolutionary feelings and convictions, and to join the coalition against France. To a good many of them, Austria and Prussia seemed the defenders of a divinely appointed social and political order, and Switzerland's future depended on their victory. But in spite of these feelings the policy pursued by the statesmen of the confederation remained cool and shrewd. The belief that Austria harboured plans of restoration with respect to Switzerland died hard in the country. The confederation thus could not desire a total defeat of France, since that ally still offered the most powerful support against further encirclement by and dependence upon Austria. For it was further feared that, should the emperor be victorious, he would denounce the treaty of Westphalia and thus threaten Swiss independence. In view of this situation, the diet was unanimous in its resolve to preserve its neutrality.

And there the matter stood, even when Franco-Swiss relations were subjected to one of the severest strains they had ever experienced. On 10 August 1792 the Paris mob stormed the Tuileries and massacred five or six hundred of the king's Swiss bodyguard. The French government also violated the capitulation by dismissing the Swiss mercenaries stationed all over the country and sending them home without pay. This breach of faith and the insult to Swiss military honour it implied aroused passionate feeling in Switzerland. The feelings inflamed by the massacre would have been an excellent means of heading Switzerland into the coalition camp, especially as news of the failure of the revolutionary armies was then pouring in. Yet a sober, realistic spirit still prevailed in the foreign policy of the confederation; its only response to the French provocation was to break off official relations with the French government and recall all troops serving in France.

In her war against the coalition, France likewise respected Swiss neutrality. When the French invaded the prince-bishopric of Basle in 1792, only that part of the country was occupied which unquestionably belonged to the Holy Roman Empire and in which German troops had been stationed. The French did not touch the remaining portion of the bishopric which had for centuries shared citizenship with Berne. Meanwhile, the most important Jura passes and points of entry into Switzerland were in French hands, so that Berne posted troops along the Jura frontiers.

Throughout the Continent, the French Revolution moved victoriously forward. We may ask why, in the first flush of her revolutionary power, France did not also overrun the confederation. The reason was that she stood in great need of Swiss neutrality, particularly in the economic field. Since the spring of 1793, the coalition of Prussia, Austria, and Sardinia had been joined in turn by Great Britain, Holland, Spain, Naples, and the German empire. These powers enclosed France in a blockade which was only open along the Swiss frontier. Since France was not economically self-supporting she sought what she lacked in Switzerland. Above all, she required grain, animals, cloth, arms, copper, and saltpetre. When the Swiss stocks were exhausted, speculators and merchants bought up in Swabia and Austria, Italy and Hungary, whatever goods were in short supply and dispatched them to France through Switzerland. For a number of years, France was thus dependent on Swiss transit traffic for important supplies. It was the realization that France stood to gain so much from Swiss neutrality, and that the long Swiss frontier offered her protection along her flank, that moved Robespierre to make his sensational speech on the friendly relations between his country and Switzerland.

Opposition movements. It was these peaceful relations with France which allowed the malcontents in Switzerland to proceed to action. Fired by French revolutionary ideas and ancient confederate notions of liberty, the country people of Stäfa on the lake of Zürich drafted a general petition to their government demanding a free constitution embracing town and country on equal terms. In particular, they complained of the privileges of the city gilds and of the oppressive burden of taxation. They also petitioned to be made eligible for admission to higher education and to commissions in the army. Before the final text of their memorial had even been drawn up, it was intercepted by the government of Zürich which took extremely harsh action, inflicting heavy fines and even threatening to use the death penalty. Yet for all its severity the government could not extinguish the smouldering fires. Discontent spread underground, appealing to ancient chartered rights, and in the end a request was made to other states of the confederation for support. The Zürich government regarded this as high treason. Troops were sent to Stäfa and the insurgents were punished collectively but with the result that the old, easy-going, patriarchal relationship between Zürich and its subjects became a thing of the past. There were, too, other parts of the confederation in which there was unrest among the subject peoples, particularly among those of the Prince Abbot of St. Gallen and of the Grisons.

It was, however, the loyalty of the Vaud which was most profoundly shaken, and riots took place there as early as 1791 and 1792. Outlawed Vaudois, banished Valaisans, and refugees from Stäfa met in Paris with other Swiss and there formed an extremely enterprising Swiss revolutionary centre. Its moving spirit and intellectual leader was Frédéric-César de Laharpe, a Vaudois of commanding personality, a man of untamable revolutionary fervour and a passionate patriot. Humiliated by the rulers of Berne and resenting the implacability with which they persecuted his family, he had found employment in Russia where he had educated the grandsons of Catherine the Great in the principles of the *Aufklärung*. He had now undertaken to pave the way for the French invasion of Switzerland by a series of publications in Paris. He argued that it was not only the duty but also the privilege of the French to help the Vaudois to regain their ancient liberties. Ultimately his pamphlets culminated in a direct invitation to France to invade Switzerland, even drawing the attention of the French directory, perpetually in need of money, to the well-filled treasure-chests of the cantonal governments of Switzerland.

There were, however, less fanatically minded men in Switzerland who realized that the narrow oligarchic system of government must come to an end, that the relatively loose federation of states must be tightened and liberal institutions introduced into the rigid state system. As Pestalozzi said: 'If only Zürich could make a sacrifice of her own free will! For in the end, she will have to make it, whether she will or no.' And Johannes von Müller, the historian, added: 'I fully realize the bitterness of the pill which the towns will have to swallow in surrendering their privileges to the national good. But there is only one answer to that—there is no other way. Do what must be done, lest others do it for you.' These, however, were voices crying in the wilderness.

Internal dissension. The profound and enduring impression made by political and economic events led to a thorough-going clarification of ideas in Switzerland. The people split into a war party and a neutral party, and their desperate struggles for the leadership of the confederation, which lasted until its overthrow, were marked by internal disunion and vacillation. The hesitations and uncertainties of the time are most clearly reflected in the history of Berne, the leading member of the confederation at that time. The war party was led by its vigorous chief magistrate, Nicolaus Friedrich von Steiger, the only Swiss statesman of the day who was able to think on European lines. From the start he proclaimed his conviction that Switzerland must abandon her traditional neutrality and join the European crusade against the Revolution, not for reasons of self-preservation but as a moral duty. 'You cannot escape the tiger's claws by patting them', as he said. On the other hand, he was perfectly clear in his mind that the confederation would not enter upon a policy of aggression without the support of the counter-revolutionary forces. The patrician classes and Catholic Switzerland, whose religious feelings had been outraged by the excesses of the Revolution, were of one mind with him.

The party of neutrality found its chief support in Zürich and Basle. Under the influence of Zürich, the *Vorort* or chief state of the confederation, the whole of eastern Switzerland joined it. Their aim was to preserve Switzerland's traditional neutrality in all circumstances, even at the cost of further humiliating concessions to the military power of her neighbour. Though they were in entire opposition to the democratics ideas of the French Revolution, and hence, as regards home policy, in full agreement with Steiger, they believed that the obsolete ship of the confederate state could only be piloted through the storms of revolution by going to the utmost lengths to meet France and thus obtaining the most peaceful solution possible. The most cogent argument in favour of this cautious policy was the inner disunion of Switzerland and the inadequacy of her defence forces.

These two political parties in the confederation were evenly balanced. Under the influence of Steiger's party, the allied powers of Sardinia, Spain, and England were actually allowed to recruit mercenary troops in 1793 and 1795. When the British ambassador published a pamphlet appealing directly to the people of Switzerland to break with France, he met with opposition in prominent quarters, but was allowed to carry on his political activities unmolested. Great Britain, after all, was standing out more and more as the chief adversary of the French Revolution. The conservative island power pitted its strength against the revolutionary continental power, and struggled with its ancient rival for command of the seas and for world trade. Pitt used the military powers of Europe against France, subsidizing them to an extent unprecedented in English history. Unable to defeat the French armies in the field, he tried to foment a counter-revolutionary movement in France by supporting the royalists. Switzerland was the best place from which to put such plans into action, for it was there that conspiracies could best be planned and secured by armed force.

In Sir William Wickham, Pitt found a diplomat who was fully

conversant with conditions on the Continent and in Switzerland and whose energy and astuteness fitted him for so onerous a task. Swiss territory, moreover, was an excellent observation post from which a first-rate secret service could be organized all over the Continent. Wickham worked hand in hand with royalist agencies in Paris, bribed royalist generals, introduced counter-revolutionary propaganda into Paris, and accumulated war material along the Jura frontier, the point at which the internal and external counter-revolutionary movements met. There Wickham had a frontier service of his own which allowed his emissaries and spies to pass without hindrance. He himself settled at Lausanne in order to be near Lyons, a centre of revolt, and constantly moved from place to place in Switzerland. In this way, England endeavoured to draw Switzerland into her struggle against the Revolution. As the French armies advanced victoriously through south Germany and north Italy, the Directory became more exacting and finally demanded Wickham's expulsion from Switzerland. To spare that country embarrassment, Wickham left of his own accord.

The French invasion and fall of the old confederation. It was in the south that France treated Switzerland most unceremoniously. After the conquest of northern Italy, Napoleon's violations of the frontiers of the Cisalpine bailiwicks and plans of attack on the integrity of Swiss territory never ceased. To the Swiss representatives at Milan, Napoleon made a non-committal proposal that the confederation should cede the southern part of the Ticino to Lombardy, thus making the frontier run along rivers and lakes. Since, by the treaty of Campo Formio between France and Austria in 1797, the last enemy of France on the Continent had been reduced to silence, she was free to devote her attention to Switzerland. The hazardous position in which the confederation stood is best described in the words of a Bernese statesman: 'Nous nous trouvâmes mieux entre deux nations ennemies qu'entre deux qui sont amies.' Napoleon's decree that the three Grisons provinces, Valtellina, Chiavenna, and Bormio were free to join the Cisalpine Republic was a bitter blow. But the actual severance of these provinces was less startling than the reasons given for it: 'for no people can be subject to another people without a breach of international law.' Those were the trumpets of Jericho which could not fail to bring the old confederation crashing to the ground. The loss of the Valtelline valleys was a considerable strategic injury to Switzerland, for the Swiss frontier was thus deprived of yet another protective bulwark, this time in the south-east.

Behind these repeated French onslaughts, it was not difficult to discern the determination of the Directory to disregard the neutrality of Switzerland should need arise. There were people in the country who sat waiting with folded arms for their fate to befall them, as men will sit waiting for some inevitable natural catastrophe, and a good deal of responsibility must be laid at the door of the men in leading positions. Part of the blame for the destruction of the old confederation by the French Revolution must be borne by Laharpe of Vaud and Peter Ochs of Basle. Both, the one from wounded pride and the other from wounded vanity, egged on the French to military intervention, and even gave them hints as to how that intervention could best be justified on historical grounds.

The case against Ochs is made graver by the fact that, though a member of a neutral state, he conspired with France. He supported Swiss neutrality only so long as it was in the French interests. When it had served France's turn he showed how to destroy it. The separation of Geneva and the prince-bishopric of Basle from the Swiss body politic caused him great satisfaction. Even the violation of the Swiss right of asylum, the hall-mark of Swiss neutrality, was approved by him and he likewise agreed to the demand of the Directory that all *émigrés* should be expelled from Switzerland. When Ochs went to Paris on an official mission in 1796 he had, on his own request, conversations there with the leaders of France on the need for a revolution in Switzerland sooner or later and gave them advice as to how to proceed.

This country now presented a pitiable spectacle of confusion and weakness. The malcontents had already risen in several places. Reform parties were founded in Zürich and Basle, but Basle was the only member state of the confederation to carry out reform independently and of her own free will. All the other cantons shrank from forestalling the revolution by political, military, and social reforms. The ruling classes dug their own grave by their stubborn refusal to surrender their privileges. Nor was even the last diet of the old confederation, which sat at Aarau in 1797–8, capable of taking any vigorous action. It reflected in miniature

the conflicts and hesitations which prevailed through the confederation. In the end, as a last resource, it called for a renewal of
the oath to the confederation, but that historical gesture remained
a mere outward show.

Hardly had this oath been taken when news of the revolution
in the Vaud reached Aarau. On 23 January 1798 representatives
of the towns of the Vaud had proclaimed 'The Republic of Lake
Leman' and constituted themselves as a 'provisional representative body of the Country of Vaud'. Following this example there
were popular risings in the Lower Valais, Fribourg, Solothurn,
Lucerne, and Basle (country), and in some places the bailiff's offices
were set on fire. Now that the deadly work of French propaganda
had worn down Swiss resistance, a continuous series of French
demands, each more outrageous than the last, was made upon
the diet. The breaches of faith and acts of violence which France
committed at that time in preparation for the invasion were so
crass that they were deplored even by so unscrupulous a diplomat
as Talleyrand.

Since Berne was the military mainstay of the old confederation,
the French concentrated their attack on that point and after a
series of sham negotiations invaded Bernese territory. Outnumbered in troops and arms by two to one, shamefully abandoned
to her fate by her fellow confederates, her resistance almost paralysed by internal factions, Berne still had the courage to resist and
thus saved the military honour of the confederation. At Neuenegg
in the west, a Bernese force succeeded in repulsing the invaders.
Yet that act of heroism came too late to save the city. On 5 March,
near Grauholz, an hour's march north of Berne, 900 Bernese
soldiers were killed, including the aged Schultheiss, Steiger, in the
uniform of a private soldier. The French then entered the city,
which had never yet seen an enemy within its walls.

Old Berne fell in the Revolution like some hoary oak, whose
decaying trunk snaps in the whirlwind. She fell, carrying the
whole confederation with her. It was not only the perfidy of the
French and the treason of her own faithless sons which brought
about this resounding fall, it was also the condition of a body
politic grown too old and weary to find fresh life in its own
substance.

Switzerland under French occupation. The ideological slogans
used by the French to adorn their callous proceedings in the

country they had conquered could not conceal the fact that power politics had led them to invade Switzerland.

Both Brune, the French military and political plenipotentiary, and the war commissioners confiscated the wealth of the richer states, one particularly rich booty, the Bernese treasury, falling into their hands with ten millions in cash and eighteen millions of bills, almost entirely English. Part was immediately sent to Lyons to finance the forthcoming Egyptian campaign. When, shortly after, Brune was sent to Italy, his carriage collapsed under the weight of the stolen money. It is impossible to estimate the damage done to public and private property by heavy requisitions, billeting, blackmail, and loot. A political cartoon of the time shows people of Zürich dancing exultant round the tree of liberty while the commissioner of the Grande Nation is carting away the stolen money-bags under the flag of freedom and a strong military guard.

The new territorial and constitutional form of Switzerland was entirely adjusted to the requirements of France. In the south, Valtellina, Bormio, and Chiavenna had already been torn away. The prince-bishopric of Basle and Bienne had been occupied. Neuchâtel was completely cut off from Switzerland and Mülhausen was compelled to join France. The citizens of Geneva were obliged to conclude a union with their great neighbour under the menace of the French guns. For a time the very unity of Switzerland seemed threatened. But, however profoundly the confederation was divided by internal factions, conservatives and revolutionaries at once opposed any further attempts at dismemberment.

The First Helvetic constitution. Switzerland was unable to carry out her constitutional reform alone. This was the work of a victorious France, which, even here, pursued her own political aims under cover of her revolutionary mission. At the beginning of 1798, Peter Ochs of Basle submitted to the directory the draft of a united Helvetic constitution which in all essentials followed the French constitution of 1795. Ochs was neither able nor willing to promote an organic development of the old constitution. He regarded this not very original product as merely provisional in character. The Directory, however, adapted the draft still more closely to its own constitution, and ordered its representative to impose this botched-up travesty, which had already been circulated widely in print, on Switzerland. On 12 April 1798 the representatives of ten cantons proclaimed at Aarau, where French troops were on the spot, the 'One and Indivisible Helvetic Republic' dictated by France. Nobody thought of consulting the people.

The republic was divided into twenty-three cantons. Ten new cantons, formed of the old associated districts and common bailiwicks, were added to the thirteen states of the old confederation. All inequality before the law and hereditary distinctions of rank were abolished. Every male inhabitant of a commune acquired Swiss citizenship on attaining his twentieth year.

The constitutional form of the republic was a representative democracy. A hundred citizens first met in a constituent assembly. Their powers were slight and were confined to voting on any amendments to the constitution submitted to them, and to the annual election of delegates to elect the representatives. That was the individual citizen's sole share in the government of the state. The legislative power rested entirely with the two chambers; the Great Council proposed legislation which the senate could adopt or reject, but not alter. In major constitutional questions, on the other hand, the initiative lay with the senate, while the Great Council could only approve or reject. In this unfortunate division of labour, the dispatch of business, already hampered by friction, became still more difficult. The executive consisted of a directory of five members elected by the legislature by a very complicated procedure. This was responsible for the internal and external security of the state, commanded the armed forces, executed the law, negotiated with other countries, and concluded treaties. It also made all appointments to higher government posts and thus controlled the entire machinery of state. The unlimited powers of the directory in the administration of the whole country largely arose from the introduction of a system of prefects, rigidly centralized as in France. Local autonomy was thus abolished and the whole power of state was concentrated in the hands of the directory.

The citizen was compensated for the paucity of political rights remaining to him by a wealth of individual liberties which all derived from the ideology of the French Revolution and were based on the fundamental doctrines of natural law. Freedom of the press, of association, and petition were particularly welcome to the militant Helvetic republic, while less value was attached to freedom of conscience. Ultimately, those liberties proved longest-lived which were most intimately bound up with the economic interests of the people, such as freedom of settlement and the prospect of releasing agricultural land from feudal impositions. New fiscal principles also arose from the general change of outlook.

The rationalistic characteristics of the constitution were balanced by others of a more emotional kind. Strict instructions were given for the solemn oath and the patriotic festivals, organized by the government, which were to mark the political coming of age of the young citizen and his entrance into the army. Their purpose was to awaken in the Helvetic republic, as in France, that mystic faith in the free united nation which had intoxicated revolutionary France.

The Helvetic republic was an artificial, theoretical construction, based on the ideas of the French Revolution. Its principal innovations were the unified state, the ideal of democracy, and the introduction of civil liberties. The variety of political outlook and local autonomy were suddenly replaced by a uniform administrative machinery. The ultimate result was a completely unified bureaucracy under republican colours, whose institutions showed little faith in the newly liberated people. A number of innovations never really came into force during the Helvetic period, while others vanished without leaving a trace within a few years. This was particularly due to the fact that the new legal theories had been forced on the country by foreign bayonets. This artificial *Rechtsstaat,* moreover, ignored a history of five centuries' growth and, being a foreign body, had no roots in the past to nourish it. A country varying so widely in natural conditions, religion, customs, and language could not, in the long run, endure an imposed bureaucratic uniformity.

Resistance in the Alpine cantons. This rigid bureaucracy, and the curtailment of political rights it brought with it, could not but outrage the natural independence and deep-rooted democratic feelings of the *Landsgemeinde* cantons. The proclamation of freedom of conscience and the introduction of the new calendar were interpreted as the beginning of heresy and unbelief. For even inner Switzerland knew of the secularization of France. The popular risings of 1798 showed how seriously Catholic and democratic old Switzerland took this threat to its peculiar form of life and religion. But in spite of their heroic resistance, the Swiss of the inner cantons were defeated in the decisive engagements at the beginning of May; they capitulated to the superior power of France and submitted to the Helvetic constitution.

When the Helvetic councils decided that all citizens, without exception, even the 'ministers of religion', were to take the oath of citizenship provided for in the constitution, the rebellion in Nidwalden flamed up again. The men of Nidwalden, deaf to argument, heard only the inward voice which called upon them to take up arms for the things they valued most, religion and independence. On 9 September 1798 General Schauenbourg broke the fierce resistance of the tiny state by a concentrated attack. Infuriated by the heroic courage of these men of the Alps, the French soldiery overran the country in a blind lust of destruction. Over 500 Nidwaldeners were killed and whole villages were wiped out. Even Schauenbourg was shocked. But there were few who realized at the time how noble and tragic was the fate of the people who, unmoved by the lure of material advantage, gave their lives to defend their beloved and traditional way of living. The martyrs' blood of Nidwalden was not shed in vain. It awoke the numbed spirit of the confederation to fresh life and bore witness to the resolute strength of the Swiss people and their determination to be themselves.

Switzerland as a European theatre of war. At the demand of the French government, Switzerland was forced to conclude a perpetual military alliance with France. Laharpe himself had characterized the dictated treaty as unacceptable, as the grave of freedom; but in vain. Switzerland had to choose between signing the treaty or being annexed to France. The purpose of the alliance was to give the French Directory the legal right to make what use it liked of the Swiss army and Swiss territory, one of the most important strategic bases in Europe. The treaty further obliged the Helvetic republic to keep two roads open to France for military and commercial purposes in peace and war. The whole was tantamount to a surrender of Swiss neutrality. By another clause, Switzerland was deprived of her right of asylum. The worst thing, however, was that France guaranteed the unified constitution, and thus claimed the rights of intervention in the internal affairs of Switzerland.

As a satellite state of France, Switzerland was of necessity involved in the European wars then breaking out. Since the chief opposing forces in the Second Coalition War had taken up their positions in the south of Germany and north of Italy, Switzerland, with the Alpine passes, came to occupy an important key position. In May 1799 the allies entered Swiss territory. Masséna, the general commanding the French and Helvetic forces, retired to Zürich. When the Russian Suvoroff, coming down the valley of the Reuss on his way from Italy in continuous contact with the French, arrived at Altdorf, the French blocked his way into eastern Switzerland. Then Suvoroff began that remarkable retreat into the Vorarlberg which has become a classic in the history of warfare. From the middle of October 1799 the whole of Switzerland, with the exception of the Grisons, was under French rule.

The foreign invaders left behind them a ravaged country and an exhausted people. Never since it came to birth had the confederation suffered so terribly. The year 1799 added to the general misery with a bad harvest and a general rise in prices. Trade and industry languished. Out of a total population of 133,000 the new canton of Säntis had 20,000 unemployed. What the Helvetic Directory lacked to combat this distress was not goodwill, but means. Private charity was called on where possible, and Pestalozzi was sent to superintend the orphanage in Stans, thus gladly devoting his powers to reconstruction.

Cultural policy of the Helvetic republic. France had promised the rural populations of Switzerland that the oppressive feudal dues should be abolished without compensation. It was this prospect which was chiefly instrumental in winning over the Swiss peasant to the side of the revolution. Feudal dues included compulsory labour such as the corvée, and actual taxes such as tithes and ground rents. The new constitution, however, did not merely order the abolition of these basic dues but declared them redeemable. The peasants felt that they had been cheated, and, yielding to their pressure, the legislature abolished some of the dues. As a result of these premature measures, which broke with all tradition, the state found itself without any financial resources whatever and could no longer meet the most urgent necessities. A conflict of unprecedented violence arose over the question whether compensation should or should not be paid for the expropriation of the dues. With characteristic peasant selfishness, the demand was made that there should be no compensation for the abolition of any dues whatever, public or private, and finally a compensation law was passed and had to be repealed. It was these first revolutionary laws which were largely responsible for the financial ruin of the state.

In ecclesiastical policy the dispute between old and new spiritual forces was particularly profound and violent. Here the Christian community stood opposed to secular society, belief in revelation to reliance on reason. While in France the Revolution had caused a complete separation between church and state, the Helvetic republic, after long hesitation, rejected the idea of independent churches. It was force of circumstances rather than any inward conviction which led it to revive the old state churches by endeavouring to insert the church into the new constitution. The constitution proclaimed the freedom of conscience in the same way as France and America, so that the old compulsion in matters of faith was abolished. One of the immediate consequences of that principle was, of course, the recognition of freedom of religious observance and the equality of all religious communities. The state, however, as the higher authority, took over the control of the churches. It promised not to interfere with their internal affairs but to tolerate religious communities only so long as they offered no threat to public order. Ministers of religion of all denominations were excluded from the franchise and public office. Thus the clergy, like the old rulers, were deprived of their privileges.

Since the Helvetic republic had extended the scope of the state's activity, it needed to open up new sources of revenue for the state. The principle of the equality of all men and its corollary that every citizen had to make an equal contribution to the expenditure of the state led to the system of direct taxation. In the eighteenth century such taxation had been practically unknown in the confederation. The first Helvetic fiscal law provided for both direct and indirect taxes and thus furthered the transition from the old natural economy to present-day world economy.

Education. One of the first paragraphs of the Helvetic constitution declared: 'The two pillars of the common weal are security and enlightenment. Enlightenment is better than wealth and splendour.' It was this fundamental principle, proclaiming the education of the people to be one of the essential tasks of the democratic state, that underlay the ambitious efforts of the republic in the direction of educational reform. The aims of the Helvetic republic in public education, some few of which were actually attained, are a fine testimony to its national spirit and directed the educational policy of Switzerland until the present century. Those achievements are almost entirely the work of Philip Albert Stapfer. As a principle, the Helvetic republic placed all education under state control. Stapfer's chief aim was for uniformity. He demanded compulsory education for both sexes, cheap to all and free to the poor, preliminary military training and handicraft work for the boys, domestic-science schools for the girls, medical inspection of schools, pensions for teachers at sixty-five, and a great many other things which only our own day has seriously attempted to put into practice. But in his zeal Stapfer considerably overrated the intelligence of school-children. No law concerning primary education was passed. The executive council, however, was able to give binding force to the principle of general primary education, which was felt as a grave breach of private liberty. According to Stapfer's plan the whole education system was to culminate in the foundation of a national university. What he meant by that was a centralized institute of higher education for the ablest men in the country which he hoped would strengthen the unified state. His message to the executive council showed how much his scheme owed to these motives, and what exaggerated hopes he placed on it: 'This institution will be the focus of the intellectual powers of the country, the means of fusing its still separate elements, and the cultural storehouse of the three nations whose centre is Helvetia. It may be her task to blend German depth with French versatility and Italian taste.' Stapfer's scheme was wrecked by its cost and by the opposition of the existing cantonal universities and academies. They could hardly be expected to sign their own death-warrant for the sole purpose of putting into action the dream of a fanatic. The view gained ground that, in a country so diversified as Switzerland, local characteristics must be respected and when, towards the end of the Helvetic period, the ideal of an absolutely unified state began to lose its force, the administration of public education passed from the central government into the hands of the cantons.

Stapfer also wished to establish training colleges for teachers, a plan which also failed for lack of funds. The republic, on the other hand, gave strong support to Pestalozzi's educational schemes. Convinced of the pedagogic value of his method and the national importance of his work, it gave his institute something like the status of a national school. Without the help of the republic,

Pestalozzi would hardly have been able to mature his teaching methods and exert a European influence.

His international fame as a teacher stands in strange contrast to his personal fate. His life was a series of disappointments. True, under his vigorous guidance, model institutes were founded at Burgdorf and Yverdon and were visited by teachers and educationists from all over Europe, yet every one of Pestalozzi's foundations came to grief. His genius as a teacher lay in the fact that he looked on education as a perpetual challenge which could never be fully met. What he cared about was not educational theory, for he ranked action above speculation; he was happiest, and suffered least from anxiety, when he could relieve actual distress, collect poor orphans round him, and educate them, as at Stans. For in the soul of the child he found the one remnant of innocence which the degenerate world of his time had not cast away. There was still a trace of the image of God in the soul of the child; and his aim was to help the children to grow into pure and good human beings. Hence, in his view, children should not have alien ideas forced upon them; the task of the teacher is rather to awaken the latent powers of the children and help them to unfold naturally in the same way as the gardener tends his plants. He should bring the individual seed which lies in every young human being to flower, and thus foster his personality. Yet Pestalozzi was far removed from the sentimentality of Rousseau, which cast a glow over the merely childish; he called Rousseau's *Émile* a dream book, just as he repudiated the 'charlatan recipes' of the pedagogic theorists of the *Aufklärung*. The process of education he had in mind, he said, should take as its exemplar the formative love of the mother. He looked forward to seeing the never-failing spring of mother-love poured out over a larger circle of educated people, and saw his justification in Christ's saying about children of whom is the kingdom of Heaven. His compassion went out to the country-folk, the poorest and most defenceless in the world.

Blessed with an unusual capacity for love, faith, and self-sacrifice, Pestalozzi devoted his life to education. For him it consisted of three stages; the family, the community, and the state. That was the ideal underlying his popular work *Lienhard und Gertrud*. The central figure of this plain tale is a poor bricklayer's wife; by self-discipline in prayer and work she fulfils, selflessly and naturally, her appointed task of bringing up her children and her example becomes an incentive to the whole village. The renewal of the state and society, according to Pestalozzi, must proceed from the 'sanctuary of the home', that is, from the blessings of a true family life, from greater social justice, and from a purer morality. He saw clearly what was wrong with his time, which he realized was a time of change and crisis. When the forgotten poet and pedagogue was touched with the breath of world revolution, he turned with passionate eagerness to the social, economic, and political questions of his day, even to the problem of an international society, and attained an insight of rare depth. Salvation must come from the poor, and that could only happen on a religious basis. 'There is no salvation for a continent which has sunk to the depths, morally, spiritually, and socially, save in education: training in humanity, the formation of human beings.'

Language and letters. There is no better proof of the strong feeling of community between governors and governed in old Switzerland than the behaviour of the Ticinese and the French Swiss. When both the French and the Cisalpine republics began to propagate the ideal of union in the neighbouring parts of Switzerland, which spoke the same language, the Ticinese and Vaudois, once subject peoples, at once proclaimed their loyalty to the Helvetic republic and were incorporated into it, in spite of the harshness of their former rulers. But the same ideal of the old democratic union of free men was so deep-rooted in the minds of all, the fusion of different races in one state had come to be so much taken for granted in the course of the centuries, that no other way seemed possible. Up to that time only associated or subject peoples had been promoted to full citizenship, but the Helvetic republic now consisted of German, French, and Italian people all equal before the law. This led to a clarification of the idea of Swiss nationality. In its composition the confederation did not correspond to the current idea of a nation and could not take its stand on community of language or race. The Helvetic people, therefore, saw Switzerland's mission in the very diversity of her civilization. The ideal of the confederation was to restore all men to their original equality by obliterating frontiers. Inspired by the true spirit of the age, Laharpe defined the goal of the new Switzerland thus:

The necessity of learning German, French, and Italian should strengthen the manifold relations between the races and enable our country to develop education and culture; in this way, the hidden treasures of those languages would be revealed, and we should see the end of the barbarian prejudices which have made men rivals, enemies, and finally slaves.

Thus the new national ideal was imagined in the form of a *Helvetia mediatrix*, and the end of all conflicts of race or tongue. The Helvetic republic elevated itself into a symbol of Europe or even of mankind.

The official language of the old confederation, the league of the Alemannic members, had been exclusively German. By raising the French and Italian subject districts to the status of cantons with equal rights the Helvetic republic founded a multilingual Switzerland. In this way it checked the growth of a different language for rulers and ruled wherever there were signs of it. The actual practice of trilingualism met with not inconsiderable difficulties. For a number of representatives of the people understood one language only, so that interpreters had to be employed for voting in the chambers. Helvetic laws and resolutions were printed in German and French and in Italian if required. In this way a new application was given to the principle of equality before the law which was to illuminate the future and help to solve the problem of minorities.

The mood of revolution, the disruption of public life, the miseries of war, found no true reflection in poetry. The poems of liberty echo with the thunder of hollow revolutionary rhetoric. They seem to be mere echoes of the violent party conflicts, whether their writers raise their voices in the fierce slogans of revolution or scorn the oppression of Frankish tyranny. It is useless to seek in them either linguistic originality or poetic value. The satiric poems of the time were the most successful.

The inward regeneration of Switzerland found its supreme expression in the work of Pestalozzi. Though by nature a thinker, Pestalozzi devoted himself utterly to the practical service of the community. He was convinced that the moral renewal of the strength of Switzerland could only be achieved from below, that is, through the people. To give him an opportunity of influencing the people directly, the government made him the editor of the *Helvetisches Volksblatt*; but it was another tragic error for Pestalozzi to imagine that he was a journalist. He also published a number of pamphlets and tales intended to enlighten his contemporaries on the social and political questions of the day and to train them in Helvetic citizenship. In the last resort, Pestalozzi regarded the state as a vast educational institute for all the citizens, and his firm faith in the victory of reason, in the good of man, and in the worth of the Swiss people reveals him as the noblest type of educator and patriot.

General characteristics of the Helvetic republic. In their struggles for national regeneration, the people of the Helvetic republic took too little trouble to root their modern democracy firmly in the ground from which the old confederation had sprung. A wealth of new ideas certainly came to enrich public and private life, and legislation began to deal with questions which have only recently found a solution. A great deal was done to develop public spirit in Switzerland. Yet there are dark shadows over the whole picture—foreign tyranny, the miseries of war, party conflicts, and financial distress. What brought the doctrinaire leaders of the republic to grief was that, ignoring history, they imagined that the salvation of Switzerland lay in a unified state created by reason and they put this alien ideal into action by force, quite disregarding the innate Swiss bent to self-determination. They thus imposed on the country the dreary equality of a centralized bureaucratic state which the confederation with its diversity of race, religion, and language could not endure. Where the republic betrayed itself as most fundamentally un-Swiss, however, was in its submission to the French invasions and the final surrender of Swiss independence; these things could not but bring more trouble in their train. Practically all the schemes of the republic came to grief. But though its noblest endeavours to weld the diverse elements of Switzerland into one whole and raise the country to a higher stage of civilization broke against the hard resistance of reality, the ideal did not quite disappear. It lived on in many a Swiss heart as an unrealized dream which came true in the nineteenth century.

Under Napoleonic rule

The Act of Mediation. The very handsome document in which the 'First Consul of the French Republic' proclaimed his mediation in Switzerland enumerated the constitutional principles of the nineteen equal cantons with a chapter for each canton and a twentieth setting forth the actual articles of confederation. All the districts taken from Switzerland during the Revolution, such as the Valais, Geneva, and the prince-bishopric of Basle remained in the hands of the French; Neuchâtel was added to them in 1806. The thirteen old cantons were reinstated almost unchanged. Six new cantons were added: St. Gallen, the Grisons, Aargau, Thurgau, the Ticino, and Vaud. This division of the country has remained unaltered up to the present day.

The Act of Mediation abolished the old subject districts; all privileges of place or birth and intercantonal or foreign alliances were prohibited. Six cantons were appointed director cantons, to hold office for one year in turn. The supreme power of the confederation was represented by the chief magistrate of the canton in office who took the title of *Landammann* of Switzerland. With this innovation, a single individual was for the first time charged with the representation of the country at home and abroad.

The Act of Mediation was not an organic remoulding of the Helvetic constitution but a complete break with its unifying principles. The result was partly federal in character. The cantons regained practically all their old sovereign rights, such as the control over finance and coinage, posts, customs, education, the monasteries, and certain monopolies. None the less the institutions of the old confederation were not completely restored. Napoleon incorporated some of the lasting results of the Revolution in the new order and gave them constitutional force. The constitution proclaimed freedom before the law, recognized a general Swiss citizenship, guaranteed the right of freedom of settlement and occupation, and other things besides.

The originality of these acts can only be fully appreciated if they are regarded as Napoleon's personal creation. They owed less to his magnanimity than to his power of calculation. At the last audience he gave to the consulta, he announced his programme: 'I shall never suffer any influence in Switzerland except my own, even though it should cost me 100,000 men.' The constitution, which was not laid before the people, but imposed by the mediator, was intended to keep Switzerland in a permanent state of weakness and dependence on France. Napoleon wanted the country to be split up into cantons, he wanted a weak diet and a weak army, not because such things met the true needs of the country, but because they served the interests of France. The new office of *Landammann* gave him a tool with which he could at once bring pressure to bear on the whole of Switzerland. The seal was set on Switzerland's subjection when Napoleon took the Act of Mediation under his guarantee and refused to admit any amendment of the national or cantonal constitutions.

Swiss troops in Napoleonic service. In order to keep the Swiss army at his own beck and call, Napoleon forced the diet to conclude a military capitulation for a period of twenty-five years and a military alliance for fifty years. That gave him the right to recruit 16,000 men in Switzerland. If French territory were attacked, Switzerland had to permit a further recruitment of 8,000 volunteers, so that the bulk of the Swiss army was serving Napoleon's policy of conquest. Napoleon also laid down the lines of Swiss foreign policy by allowing her to conclude further capitulations only with powers friendly to himself. Neutrality thus became an empty word, meaning nothing to Napoleon, as he himself said.

Switzerland soon found herself surrounded by Napoleon's empire and satellite states. An independent foreign policy was thus impossible and every annexation and every new state founded by his power caused alarm, for the strategic importance of Switzerland was obvious. During those years, the statesmen of the confederation fought silently and doggedly for the preservation of Swiss independence.

The high price in blood which Switzerland paid Napoleon was a kind of compensation for the fact that her territory had no longer to serve as the theatre of war as it had once done. Up to the summer of 1806 Napoleon made no use of his right to raise mercenaries, but when he was preparing his campaign against Prussia he ruthlessly put the capitulation into action. Even so, his officers did not succeed in recruiting the numbers allowed, for the sturdy young Swiss had no mind to sell their skins in Napoleon's plan of conquest. The capitulation, which spoke of 'voluntary and unforced enlistment', was then arbitrarily interpreted by the emperor to mean that Switzerland was bound to supply him with four regiments of 4,000 men each. To forestall reprisals, Switzerland resorted to despicable means to complete the regiments. Napoleon further required of the diet that it should refuse the right to enlist mercenaries to powers not allied with France. This was a blow aimed at Britain, whose Swiss mercenaries had just reached their full strength. There was nothing for the diet to do but to issue a strict prohibition of any recruitment which was not in the interests of France.

In Napoleon's campaign against Austria in 1809 the diet proclaimed its neutrality and ordered the frontiers to be manned. None the less French troops violated Swiss territory several times and Switzerland was unable to resist. The arbitrary nature of Napoleon's treatment of Switzerland may be seen in the new military capitulation which he forced on the diet in 1812. The right to recruit became an obligation to supply 14,000–15,000 men, and Switzerland bound herself by treaty to follow the French emperor.

In the Russian campaign, the Swiss regiments were soon reduced by hardship and sickness. They showed great courage in covering the French retreat over the Beresina and took their share in saving the main French army from absolute annihilation. In the end, only 700 Swiss, some permanently disabled and crippled, returned home.

Cessions of territory. In 1806 France had adopted a menacing attitude towards Switzerland when Napoleon bartered Neuchâtel for Hanover with the king of Prussia. The little principality which, as an associated district, had for centuries protected the eastern flank of Switzerland against France, was given in fief by Napoleon to his chief of general staff, Marshal Berthier. What the vigilant confederation had prevented at the beginning of the eighteenth century had now come to pass; French troops were able to advance into the neighbourhood of Berne without hindrance. Following up the seizure of the papal states and the North Sea coast, Napoleon now put an end to the fictitious independence of the Valais. The Valais had an importance which was quite out of proportion to its density of population and military power because of its situation as a land of passes. At this time the vital factor was the Simplon road, the link between France and Italy. On the specious grounds that the Valaisan republic was in a state of anarchy, Napoleon, in 1810, proclaimed its union with France. A French prefect now governed the new 'Simplon Department' from Sion. In the same year, by a brutal act of violence, Napoleon had the canton of Ticino occupied by Italian troops. It was mainly economic reasons, the desire to put an end to the smuggling of English goods from Germany through Switzerland to Italy that caused this action, but at the same time ideas of annexation by Milan played their part. The proposed permanent 'correction of the frontiers' in the lower Ticino was, however, frustrated by the overwhelming determination of the people to remain Swiss.

Under the continental blockade. Napoleon had two aims in his blockade of Britain: first, by bringing the whole Continent into his system he wished to destroy English trade and thus deal his enemy a fatal blow. Secondly, he aimed at the economic domination of Europe by France. How utterly Switzerland was at the mercy of France owing to the Mediation became clear when, from the start, the increased duty on cotton, aimed against Britain, was applied to her too. Intimidated by mass confiscations, the diet submitted to the blockade of its own accord. The only exception to it was cotton yarn, which was essential to the Swiss textile industry. But even the French decrees of 1810, extending the blockade to all colonial goods, were by Napoleon's order applied to Switzerland as well. When the *Landamman* demurred, he was received with a flood of charges: Switzerland was at the heart of English smuggling in Europe and a complete blockade of Switzerland would be imposed. This must have led, within a short time, to the throttling of the Swiss cotton industry and catastrophic unemployment at the beginning of winter. Napoleon agreed to relax the blockade a little, but in spite of these special privileges Swiss national economy suffered greatly. One ancient firm after another went bankrupt. Hundreds of unemployed emigrated from the east of Switzerland, and the cantonal governments had to organize relief measures to deal with destitution.

Cultural reconstruction. Although Switzerland was under steady and extreme pressure in her foreign policy, the exhausted country managed to find a breathing-space for reconstruction. Economic, as well as intellectual and artistic, life centred in the cantons. The diet was, therefore, unable to bring about the unification of the coinage which would have been so beneficial. In this field, a disastrous confusion prevailed which prevented any reasonable exchange of money. Similarly, every attempt to standardize weights, measures, and the postal system was thwarted by the sovereignty of the cantons. The customs system relapsed into its old localism. Internal customs and tolls became numerous and transit traffic dwindled. Even the rights of freedom of settlement, trade, and industry were constantly endangered by local action.

Like the constitution of the French consulate, the Acts of

Mediation had suppressed the freedom of the press. The *Landammann* recommended to the cantons a careful scrutiny of all printed matter; he may have acted chiefly out of deference to Napoleon, whose distaste for free expression of opinion was notorious, but the cantons were only too willing to follow the instructions of the *Landammann*, so that the old veil of secrecy might be cast over the transactions of the government. The old censorship was re-introduced even in the new cantons, which were otherwise liberal in outlook; newspapers, pamphlets, books, lending libraries, book-shops were all subject to its control. Any discussion of political topics was penalized by heavy fines, and the complete muzzling of the press in the end killed all expression of public opinion on political matters.

Some cantons set about releasing the land from tithes and ground rents, others faced the serious problem of the homeless. An excellent illustration of the spirit of reconstruction which then animated the Swiss republic was the improvement of the river Linth. In former times the silt carried down by the river dammed up the Walensee, often flooding the whole district and carrying disease into the neighbouring villages. The central government, with the support of the cantonal governments and private philan-thropic societies, took up the matter as a patriotic duty. The Linth was diverted into the Walensee and thus the marshes of the low-lands of Glarus could be drained and reclaimed for agriculture.

In education the Mediation had put a number of reform schemes into action. Many cantons made genuine efforts to improve their rural schools. The continuation courses for elementary school-teachers founded by the philanthropist Emanuel von Fellenberg became famous. Where Pestalozzi failed the stronger-willed Bernese patrician succeeded, namely in the organization of a comprehensive educational institute. Fellenberg dealt success-fully with two problems of the day—national education and the improvement of agriculture. In his opinion, work on the land not only improved physique but also developed the mind. Goethe owed to Fellenberg's educational work the basic ideal for his *Pädagogische Provinz*. The whole of European education, indeed, was enriched by the achievements of Pestalozzi, Fellenberg, and Pater Girard of Fribourg: through them Switzerland became a model country for education, even if the cantons devoted more attention to higher than to elementary education, founding grammar schools and academies directly dependent on the state.

Intellectual life. The Mediation stood between the Age of Enlightenment and the Romantic movement, and had affinities with both. This is exemplified by Johannes von Müller, the versatile spirit who became the Swiss Tacitus. Goethe, Herder, and Schiller revered him as the greatest historian who had ever written in German and the Romantics gave unrestrained expression to their feelings for the master historian. Müller possesses the historian's supreme virtue—the capacity for sympathy with the times he portrayed. The aim of his *History of the Swiss Confederation* was to contribute to the political education of the people and, by the example of its heroic age, to inspire a regenerated Switzerland with self-reliance, strength of mind, and love of liberty. Müller also wished his work to have a political influence on his own times and therefore attached himself to anyone who could give him an opportunity for political activity. His many changes of front were due not to opportunism but to the hope of greater influence. It is moving to see this great scholar and writer, over-burdened with public business, wresting his true life-work from himself with the utmost sacrifice. His *History of the Swiss Confederation* is in the form and content, the culminating point, still unsurpassed, of a century-old development of Swiss historiography. With it Müller made one of the most important Swiss contributions to the intellectual life of Germany in the Romantic period. It was as a patriot that Müller wrote his history. It was his patriotism which caused him to idealize the original confederates who, he believed, had always kept faith. He therefore made over-much of the significance of past events, he was uncritical in his use of authorities, accepting, for example, the work of Aegidus Tschudi as correct and impartial. He was more concerned about the literary style of his work than about its scientific accuracy. For him history was a work of art. His vigorous intellect was subjected to his emotions and to his desire to see men and events as a whole. It was thus that he succeeded in recreating the active life of the cities and valleys of old Switzerland, and it was thus that he was able to convey local conditions so successfully. Müller fused poetry with history and was unconcerned about its philosophy.

No German historian had so strong a sense of form as Müller. It meant more to him than criticism. He subjected matter to form.

His style derived from the classics, especially Tacitus, where he found power, dignity, and precision. As a young man he had noted: 'From the barbarian invasions to Erasmus, men stammered; from Erasmus to Leibnitz, they wrote; from Leibnitz to Voltaire, they reasoned; I will speak.' He sought in chronicles and ancient documents long-forgotten truths. Into the whole story he poured his personality, his vigour, and emotion, yet he never lost control of his material and he always remained master of his pen. And thus the whole man lives in his work. He was a master of every means of creating atmosphere. On the other hand, he was only partially successful in his presentation of the social side of history because the art of its presentation had not been invented. Whenever he has to present a picture he is brilliant. Portraits, battle-scenes, the primitive life of the mountain-dwellers—all these are admirable. In his hands, the much-decried middle ages were seen in their true value, and he gave of them a picture drawn with love, if not with accuracy. Chivalry, the church, the city, lived again. It is for this reason that Müller meant so much to the Romantics. Under his eyes, even local history became world history; a peculiar sense of greatness informs the whole.

If his style was too obscure for his work ever to become popular, nevertheless to the educated reading public at home and abroad, he gave much. To their surprise he showed them Switzerland as a nation. His contemporaries delighted in the myth of the Swiss past which he had so splendidly created. When their country collapsed in 1798, the despairing Swiss found consolation and fresh strength in Müller's work. When Europe was turning its back on Switzerland in indifference, it was the heroic struggle of the old cantons and Müller's history which revealed the vitality and uniqueness of the country and led Europe to recognize once more this singularly individual people and state.

In a general way the epoch of the Mediation was permeated by a nostalgia for the ancient strength of Swiss popular life. It comes out in the herdsmen's festivals at Unspunnen, which became famous. After the long presence of the alien in their midst, the Swiss wished to feel themselves Swiss again. Science and literature vied with each other in discovering and renewing popular customs and language. The study of local dialects was renewed. The 'Alpenrosen' became the mouthpiece of patriotic poetry. Johann Rudolf Wyss of Berne wrote the hymn *Rufst Du, mein Vaterland,* which has become the national anthem, Johann Gaudenz von Salis-Seewis of the Grisons sang 'the dear home of his loved ones', the tales of Ulrich Hegner of Winterthur dealt with the most recent political past, and Johann Martin Usteri of Zürich wrote delicate idylls of past times in dialect. The one who touched the emotions most deeply, however, was Gottlieb Jakob Kuhn, whose poem *Ha an em Ort es Blüemli gseh* has become a popular folk-song.

The unsophisticated work of Dean Philippe Bridel of Montreux was inspired by the same nostalgia for Switzerland's past. His *Étrennes Helvétiennes*, which appeared annually for many years, revived the national feeling of French Switzerland and helped to bridge the linguistic gulf which divided the confederation. The spirit of the Muses' court at Coppet was far more cosmopolitan. In her hospitable home, Madame de Staël gathered men of talent about her. She belonged to Switzerland by her birth, her life, and her work. This brilliant circle of wits and intellectuals, nicknamed the States General of European public opinion, was frequented by the Genevese historian Sismondi, for whom liberty was the breath of life, and by Benjamin Constant the advocate of French liberalism.

Side by side with these individual efforts a number of national societies were active in uniting and promoting cultural activities. The Helvetic society was re-founded, and a Swiss art society formed. The general union of forces which the Helvetic republic had attempted in vain to bring about in the political field seemed to be succeeding on a national scale under the Mediation in the intellectual world. A particularly fine instance was the revival of national music, especially in choral singing. The founder of this musical speciality, which means so much to the social life of Switzerland, was Hans Georg Nägeli of Zürich. His aim was to promote the education of the people by singing, and to turn the whole country into a land of song. With his friend Pfeifer, he published a handbook for teachers of singing on Pestalozzi's lines, which soon became famous and which he followed up with other books on the teaching of music.

The versatile and creative Nägeli, however, not only formed choirs and published books on the teaching of singing; he was also a composer and musical critic of international repute and a publisher of classical music, discriminating as well. Mention may also be made of Xavier Schnyder who had studied music with Beethoven in Vienna and was an outstanding composer of operas, oratorios, and cantatas.

The passage of the allies. The course of the struggle between Napoleon and the allies was followed in Switzerland with great anxiety. For Switzerland, victory for the Mediator would have probably meant the loss of the Ticino and a still closer dependence on France. Immediately after the battle of Leipzig (16–19 October 1813), *Landammann* Reinhard convened a diet at Zürich for the purpose of deciding what policy Switzerland was to pursue in the changed international situation. It issued a solemn proclamation of armed neutrality but did not recall the regiments in French service. Confederate troops were posted along the Rhine in the north and also in the Ticino, which meant that that part of the country was recovered. The diet also withdrew from the continental system which had been forced on it.

There was nothing for Napoleon to do but to recognize Swiss neutrality which might serve to cover his rear and flank. The question whether Switzerland would, after all, be involved in the European struggle depended on the decisions of the allies. The Austrian commander, Schwarzenberg, was of the opinion that the main army should enter Franche-Comté by way of the Rhine and Switzerland in order to occupy Burgundy and Champagne. Czar Alexander of Russia declared that he would regard a breach of Swiss neutrality as a declaration of war against himself. Metternich, however, who was the real leader of the allies and was opposed to Alexander, set out to transfer the ancient influence of France in Switzerland to Austria so that he might obtain secure frontiers in the west. But if Switzerland were to become dependent upon Austria, the Napoleonic institutions must be abolished, and this required an allied invasion.

Metternich now put into action the diplomatic machinery he manipulated with such skill. Not a stratagem, not a subterfuge, was left untried. He sent secret agents into Switzerland with orders to get into touch with discontented patricians, to stimulate pro-Austrian feeling, and to induce Switzerland to join the coalition. Yet with all his promises he was unable to shake the majority of Swiss statesmen from their determination to maintain their neutrality. The only men who gave unreserved support to Metternich's schemes were the unconditional champions of a complete restoration. It was they who applied for the help of Austria at the allied headquarters, and Metternich made clever use of this fact to make it appear to the allies that Switzerland herself had asked for intervention.

In December 1813 the Austrians gave notice of the intended invasion by the allies in the form of an ultimatum to the commander of the troops of the confederation stationed at Basle. Any resistance by the small frontier forces to the far superior armies of the allies seemed hopeless. The Swiss statesmen let things take their course, confining themselves to feeble protests against the invasion which they could not prevent. The confederation again succumbed to overpowering pressure from outside and disruptive forces inside the country, to the lack of a spirit of self-sacrifice in a people worn down by long foreign domination, and to the jealousy and incompetence of its political and military leaders.

The allies entered Swiss territory along the line from Basle to Schaffhausen, then marched to Alsace or over the Jura into France. They promised by proclamation that the discipline of the troops in transit should be enforced and full compensation given for their maintenance, a promise which was only partly kept, Switzerland suffering greatly from the passage of foreign soldiers.

Reconstitution of Switzerland. Metternich imagined that he could rule Switzerland best by reinstating the Bernese patriciate in power, restoring their overlordship of Vaud and Aargau and thus making Berne the ruling canton of the country. When Austrian troops entered Berne, the old government returned to power and proclaimed its inflexible determination to restore the old order. Following the example of the most powerful member of the confederation, the patriciates of other cantons reversed the political situation and united in an 'Old Switzerland' under the leadership of ultra-Conservative Berne. They were opposed by the new cantons, and civil war was imminent. These conflicting forces made it difficult for the diet at Zürich to find a new basis for the life of the nation, and it took the threat of an allied intervention to bring the parties to reason and mutual understanding. In September 1815 the draft of the federal pact was solemnly declared to be the fundamental law of Switzerland. Except as regards their frontiers the freedom of action of the nineteen cantons was recognized: reaction carried the day.

The brilliant assembly in Vienna which was to give a new order to Europe after twenty years of war with France was also charged with the settlement of such Swiss questions as had not found a solution. For that reason, representatives of the central government of the confederation, together with those of the cantons, smaller districts, and cities, immediately left for the congress in order to represent before a European forum interests which at times came into serious conflict. The aims of the instructions given to the plenipotentiaries by the diet were the recognition of Switzerland as a neutral, independent country, certain cessions of territory, and a manageable military frontier. In addition, a large number of private envoys attempted to secure other concessions, mainly of a financial and territorial character. A special allied commission was appointed at Vienna to deal with Swiss affairs, with Canning as its adviser.

When this commission recognized the integrity of the nineteen cantons, all cantonal territorial claims were definitely settled. Thus Berne received a territorial expansion which was not entirely welcome, namely, the prince-bishopric of Basle and the city of Bienne. The question of what was to happen to the three former districts of the Grisons—Chiavenna, Bormio, and the Valtellina—was settled against Swiss interests since Austria annexed them all. The fact that the work of the Swiss envoys was hampered by mutual suspicion made it easy for their opponents to obtain the cession of these strategically important frontier districts to Austrian Lombardy. The question of Geneva, however, took a happier turn; its territory was rounded off, and thus Switzerland had security of the west. The Genevese envoy, Pictet-de Rochemont, induced Sardinia to cede ten communes south of the city to the canton of Geneva and open the Simplon road on the south shore of the lake to traffic with Switzerland on condition that the north of Savoy should be neutralized. These arrangements were incorporated in the final act of the Congress of Vienna.

Faced with Napoleon's return from Elba, the congress powers had speeded up the settlement of Swiss affairs. The immediate concern of the diet in the fresh outbreak of war between the allies and the emperor was merely to protect neutral Swiss territory. This time, however, the allies were by no means prepared to respect Swiss neutrality. They forced the diet to conclude the convention which resulted in the passage of allied armies in the neighbourhood of Basle and the participation of 20,000 Swiss troops in the campaign in Upper Burgundy.

Recognition of permanent neutrality. The representative sent by Switzerland to the second congress at Paris was Pictet-de Rochemont, of Geneva. After long and difficult negotiations he obtained from France the cession of a narrow zone along the right shore of lake Geneva, which at last permitted direct contact between Geneva and Vaud, and hence between Geneva and the rest of Switzerland. He also obtained the agreement of the powers to a further extension of the neutrality of Savoy.

His outstanding achievement, however, was that the position of the confederation in international law was established by treaty. In accordance with his excellent draft, which was not substantially amended, the powers, on 20 March 1815, recognized the permanent neutrality of Switzerland and guaranteed the integrity of her territory. Further, in the same document they recognized 'that the neutrality and integrity of Switzerland and her independence from any foreign influence are in the true interests of European policy as a whole'. Pictet had succeeded in securing this statement, which is of supreme importance for the conception of Swiss neutrality, against the will of Metternich. The acceptance of Swiss neutrality as serviceable to general interests of Europe was based on long historical experiment which showed that the violation of Swiss neutrality might turn to the disadvantage of all countries. This realization that the principle of Swiss neutrality was a European necessity gave Switzerland a far greater feeling of security than any solemn guarantee in writing.

Restoration and liberalism

The federal pact and the cantonal constitutions. The spirit of the post-revolutionary period was a product of romanticism in politics and religion, in science and literature. At first there was no fully developed theory of conservatism; it was merely a general attitude. It was only in opposition to liberalism that it set to work to define its principles. The most impressive statement of the theory of the state from the Conservative standpoint came from Carl Ludwig von Haller of Berne. He ceased to take an active part in the politics of his native city on his conversion to Catholicism, but his writings had the more lasting influence on that account both at home and abroad.

Haller gave a European epoch its name and a programme. In his *Restauration der Staatswissenschaft*, he set out, after legitimate government had been restored, to reinstate law on its throne too, and to 'crush the reptile of Jacobinism'. In particular he opposed Rousseau's artificial doctrine of a social contract, and attempted to refute it by demonstrating the natural origin of all government. According to him, government springs from the general law of nature, according to which 'the more powerful rules' and the weaker finds support in the stronger: government and subjection are in accordance with the immutable order of God, but not freedom or equality. Governments, therefore, rule not in virtue of the right entrusted to them by the people, but in virtue of their own right. Unlike other theorists of political romanticism, Haller took his robust fundamental idea not from the middle ages but from his direct observation of the powerful privileged families of Berne. Next to Haller, it was Joseph de Maistre who exercised the greatest influence on Catholic conservatism in Switzerland.

The federal pact born of this spirit was a compromise between the reactionary aims of the Conservatives and the more moderate demands of the Centralists, though in all essentials, the principle of the federative state prevailed. The powers of the central government were still more curtailed than in the Act of Mediation, so that the sovereignty of the twenty-two cantons was restored except in respect of the army. For the practical application of neutrality, provision was made for an army of 32,886 men, and a war fund was founded. The Federal Pact, like the Act of Mediation, recognized no subject districts. The diet was composed of equal representative groups from the twenty-two cantons who voted according to their instructions. By a three-quarters majority it decided questions of peace and war, was the supreme military authority, and concluded treaties with other countries. Zürich, Berne, and Lucerne acted for two years in turn as the *Vorort* or representative canton of the confederation. The cantons reserved the right of mutual alliance in so far as it did not affect the confederation; on the same condition they obtained the right to conclude military capitulations and trade agreements with other countries. Existing customs duties and tolls were left unchanged to give the cantons an opportunity of rehabilitating their finances, while the Bund went empty handed. Swiss citizenship and the freedom of settlement of occupation, of conscience, and of worship were abolished.

On the other hand, at the instigation of the papal nuncio, religious houses and chapters were placed under the guarantee of the Bund. The article by which the exercise of political rights could never become the exclusive privilege of one class of citizens in the canton was powerless to break down the old privileges of place and birth. Intentionally, there was no amendment clause; no further alterations of the constitution could be carried out by legal methods. Thus the federal pact was a mere expedient to hold together conflicting forces which threatened to burst asunder at a touch.

The revision of the cantonal constitution was carried out in many places only after violent public disturbances. In accordance with the trend of the time, the cantons, having become more independent, set about restoring pre-revolutionary conditions. In the Alpine democracies the return of the old order was welcomed with exultation. The *Landsgemeinde* remained the supreme power throughout. Nidwalden deprived old-established 'settlers' of their franchise, but restored the vote to the fourteen-year old sons of old native families. The oligarchic methods of the ancient regime came into force again. The civic cantons of Berne, Lucerne, Solothurn, and Fribourg invested the patriciate with hereditary power and laid strong emphasis on the prerogatives of the town over the country. The people did not vote as citizens but in corporations. Even in the principality of Neuchâtel, which had received a charter from the king of Prussia, the old native aristocracy came back to power. Schaffhausen and Geneva were less extreme in their restoration than the aristocratic cantons, but gave the town much more power than the country. In the cantons of St. Gallen, Aargau, Thurgau, Vaud, and the Ticino, democratic and liberal ideas did not quite disappear. The new constitutions naturally had to pay their tribute to the spirit of the time by restricting the franchise and conferring privileges in education and property on the aristocracy, but the old privileges of place and birth were not retained.

Under the tutelage of the Holy Alliance. Not long after Switzerland had laid down her programme of foreign policy in the Act of Neutrality, she was faced with the momentous decision of whether she would join the Holy Alliance which, in the hands of Metternich, had developed out of the hazy and rhetorical declarations of Czar Alexander into a political instrument of a conservative, anti-revolutionary, and repressive character. All the European states, with the exception of Turkey, were invited to join the Holy Alliance; only the pope refused. It is characteristic that the objections to joining it were most pronounced in Britain and Switzerland. It ran counter to tradition in both countries to enter into a European federation and so to bind foreign policy for an indefinite period. In the end, Switzerland's adhesion was cautious and noncommittal.

The fears that Switzerland, as a member of the Holy Alliance, would be committed to giving military assistance and thus become involved in international conflicts, proved groundless. The explicit assumption, however, that the Holy Alliance might entail foreign intervention in Swiss home affairs proved correct to a degree that had never been anticipated. True, the leaders of Swiss foreign policy had prevented an Austrian protectorate from succeeding to Napoleon's protectorate, but the concert of the great powers was placed in such perfect harmony that it was impossible for Switzerland to strike a note of her own. Resistance to the solid front of the powers was as impossible as it had been to Napoleon's European supremacy. As the great powers assumed more and more a definite political constitution and a definite political mentality, it became more and more difficult for Switzerland to abide by her old and peculiar political outlook and her independent foreign policy. It was not until Great Britain began to depart from the policy of the Holy Alliance and Europe began to split into an eastern and western block that Swiss neutrality could develop freely.

The Swiss soldier had not lost his reputation for reliability, so that it was possible to conclude favourable military capitulations with France and Holland. In the aristocratic cantons an officer's career provided a means by which the sons of ruling families might issue from the cramped provincialism of their homes into a larger world. Yet the friendly military relations with France did not prevent Louis XVIII from joining the other continental powers in the growing political pressure they were bringing to bear on Switzerland. These leaders of the Holy Alliance arrogated to themselves the right of intervention in any country in which legitimate sovereignty seemed threatened. At its congresses, it sat in judgement on the weaker states whose independence faded into an insubstantial shadow.

While Switzerland was very inadequately represented abroad, a number of powers kept permanent embassies in Switzerland as a token of their interest in the restored confederation. That interest, however, turned more and more into an undesirable surveillance which several times led to interference in the sovereignty of Switzerland as established by international law. The persecution of persons denounced as revolutionary by the reactionaries drove large numbers of refugees into the country. For centuries past, the confederation had granted asylum to political refugees by a wise application of its right of asylum. Now, heedless of that tradition, the powers demanded that Switzerland should hand over all suspects. Thus Louis XVIII was able to obtain the expulsion of the 'regicides' from Vaud, though he could not prevent the settlement in Switzerland of Napoleon's relations.

The reactionary interest in Switzerland reached its culmination after the Congress of Verona. In a monitory note, Metternich demanded the expulsion of the 'criminal associations' which were spreading anarchy in the neighbouring countries, otherwise Switzerland would run the risk of forfeiting her right to remain neutral. Fearing an intervention, the diet, in 1823, issued a 'Press and Aliens Conclusum' binding on all cantons. It urgently recommended them to avoid anything which might give rise to justifiable complaints in their treatment of foreign affairs in newspapers and pamphlets, and made the regulations against refugees more severe. It was not until 1829 that the cantons were at last able to shake it off. The fact that no conflict arose between Switzerland and the powers and that the latter, if anything, moderated their language, is due in the main to the quiet pressure of Great Britain under Canning.

Economic strangulation. It certainly seemed as if the most severe economic pressure had been removed from Switzerland when the continental blockade was raised. Yet Restoration France had no mind to change its economic power policy towards Switzerland. Under Napoleon's protection policy French industry had grown excessively and was now defenceless against superior foreign competition. In these circumstances increasingly severe customs tariffs were imposed which ultimately amounted practically to a prohibition of imports and excluded Swiss industrial products from the French market. The harmful effects of this exclusion and the failure of the crops in the famine years 1816–17 caused economic crises and increased the distress of the people. A prospect of breaking through the French tariff wall opened when the Bourbons came to conclude the military capitulations with Switzerland. The industrial cantons at once put forward their demands—no soldiers without better trade relations. But France refused to treat 'muslins and military' in the same agreement and carried through the signature of the capitulations without any guarantee.

When France's lead in tariff reform was followed by Austria, Spain, Holland, and Naples, the only markets open to Switzerland on the continent were Germany and central Italy. In 1832 France extended the prohibitive customs duties to agricultural produce, whereupon the agricultural cantons entered the lists. In reply to this French provocation the diet drafted a decree by which most imports were subjected to import duties. But only thirteen and a half cantons agreed to the 'Reprisals Concordat' involving a pitched battle with the vast trade and industry of France. With this split in the country there was no prospect of successful reprisals against the economic enemy. It was above all the lack of central political leadership which was responsible for this weakness in the Swiss defensive measures. The difficulties of the confederation caused by foreign tariffs had, however, fruitful results. Swiss industry had to seek for an opening in world markets. The sharpening of the competitive struggle meant the birth of Switzerland as a centre of world trade and industry.

Forms of government under the Restoration. At this time, the life of the Swiss state depended even more upon the cantons than under the Act of Mediation. The Conservative governments once again felt the security which comes from the exercise of authority. Although the theories of divine right found a hearing, as a whole the sober-minded Swiss rebelled against any extreme form of conservatism in government. The cantonal governments were above all realistic in their proceedings. Even the patriarchal welfare policy was, within limits, resumed and often at considerable sacrifice the cantons built roads and erected necessary public buildings.

During this Indian summer of patriarchal splendour all matters of government were kept strictly secret, as they had always been. Publicity was feared and freedom of the press no longer existed. The common people scarcely noticed this. Exhausted and bewildered by the storms of the revolution, they were glad of a respite which gave them time to recuperate. It was considered natural that the business of government should continue to be in the hands of experienced old families which were regarded with veneration and trust.

Before long, however, the wealth of the ruling classes, a part of their privileged position, began to decline. In the aristocratic cantons, class feeling prevented them from improving their material position by engaging in industry or trade. In the other urban cantons, some old families turned their privileges to good use in business, and thus provoked criticism of the whole system. The fact that the aristocracy had only been able to resume its authority under foreign protection caused many to regard it with disfavour. The extreme localism of state sovereignty was a further burden on the patriarchate. The belief that the capacity to govern was innate and hereditary in a certain class of society dwindled more and more. Those sections of the population which had been influenced by the Enlightenment began to consider the patriciate not as a ruling caste appointed by God but as a kind of political party which had illegally arrogated to itself exclusive power in the state.

The liberal spirit. The French Revolution of July 1830 aroused intense interest in Switzerland where it seemed to herald a new era. What this new era implied was by no means clear to the Swiss youth even when it became the theme of much excited rhetoric at their students' meetings and shooting matches. Glowing with optimism, men ceased to believe in the sinfulness of human nature and saw only the good in man, the unlimited perfectibility of mankind and human institutions. Freedom was the word which delighted the hearts of many as it had done two generations before when Rousseau laid an awakening age under the same spell. At first the innovators dreamed of some vague liberty which the forefathers of Switzerland may once have had. French liberalism and German idealism clarified their ideas until they issued in a definite demand for personal freedom with all its consequences such as the freedom of the press, religion, and occupation. At the same time the cry for political freedom was heard. If all men are born free and equal why should government be in the hands of a privileged caste? The privileges of birth, it was said, were irrational and even immoral. The watchword of the champions of liberty was 'careers open to ability'. The supreme power of the state was to be wielded no longer by a small privileged class but by the people as a whole. That was the doctrine of the sovereignty of the people. And, quite illogically, the deduction followed—*vox populi, vox Dei*. Thus, another aim of the Liberals was the establishment of the rule of the people, or democracy. Nevertheless, the sovereignty of the people as preached by the Liberals remained moderate and semi-aristocratic. What democracy meant to them was the full development of the individual.

The new liberal theory of the state found its supreme expression in France in the work of Benjamin Constant, a native of Vaud. Rejecting Rousseau's direct democracy he claimed that the sovereign people should exercise its rights by representation. As a declared enemy of the Jacobins he demanded a restriction of the sovereignty of the people in order to render individual liberty secure against mob rule. In opposition to Montesquieu's separation of powers he advocated a concentration of all powers in a representative assembly. Thus in the Swiss regeneration movement the desire for liberal freedom from the state went hand in hand with the desire for the participation of all in the state, and the idea of inalienable liberties was accompanied by the ideal of the rule of the people, the practical result of which was a combination of liberalism and democracy.

The Regeneration movement. This 'Regeneration' movement was in the main political in character. The ultimate aim was a new constitution, and in the struggle the press, the clubs, and public demonstrations took their part. For the most part, the movement resulted in a change of political front, the oligarchic state being replaced by a people's state and the representation of the states by the representation of the people. The leaders of the Liberals, however, had not only political, but cultural and social aims in view too. They wanted to shake the people out of its lethargy by the reform of education from the primary school to the university. But the protagonists of education betrayed their lack of confidence in the political maturity of the lower classes by their tenacious defence of a representative constitution. The leaders of the revolution felt something like doubts of democracy. Among the people, however, political passion was far stronger than the desire for education. What the masses demanded with violence was political and social liberation, not cultural independence.

National forces, the urge towards a unification of the Swiss state, doubtless contributed something to this movement; for the mass of the people, however, the canton was their true home, and not Switzerland. Social motives are clearly apparent. The new feeling of equality in those classes of society which felt their unprivileged position came out in the catchwords of Equality and Justice. Those who proclaimed them belonged to the middle class and to the peasant class in the small country towns. But in these towns, too, there lived the new ruling class—lawyers, schoolmasters, doctors, industrialists, business men, innkeepers, and wealthy farmers. Hence increased attention began to be paid to the country districts.

The outbreak of the Regeneration movement was mainly due to economic forces. With the promise of economic freedom, large sections of the population were won over to the Liberal movement. The promise that the problem of tithes and ground rents would at last find its solution moved the conservative farmers to join the Liberals. By the founding of state banks, personal dependence on the landlords was to be transformed into impersonal dependence on the savings banks. Trade and industry, too, which played a particularly important part in the work of social change, hoped for an adaption of the political system to new conditions. Industry, then in a period of rapid development, found itself hampered at all points by legal barriers and wanted more room. Out of this there grew the demand for a unified state. That class of the population which was economically secure and socially superior, the new middle class, having risen above the care for their daily bread, began to take an interest in affairs in general.

Liberal revolutions. At the national shooting match at Berne in July 1830 there was thunder in the air. A few days later, the news of the Paris Revolution fell like a thunderbolt. The spark of the revolution spread like wildfire especially in the rural districts where there were free fights for the French newspapers. All hoped that the new dawn in France would bring fresh life to the confederation too.

But in the sober Swiss fashion the people only proceeded to take action a few months later. A number of men travelled round the country in secret, collecting support. They encouraged the people to state their demands in writing, and then a summary of them was made and spread in pamphlet form. In this way, the cantonal movements were saved from local dispersion and gained greatly in force. These manifestoes formed the common political creed of the people and the demand for constitutional reform was now presented to the cantonal governments in the form of petitions.

But the governments, unteachable as ever, took only half-measures since they had neither the courage to defend their positions by force of arms nor the energy to reform the constitutions on liberal lines. Then the Liberals began to force the issue of constitutional reform by marches on the capitals and mass meetings. There were demonstrations in a number of cantons. Particularly impressive *Landsgemeinden* were held at Uster (canton of Zürich) and Münsingen (canton of Berne). The governments yielded to the force of the popular will, and a revolution of this significance has seldom taken so bloodless a course. Even though the leaders of the victorious revolution were to be swept away from their positions by the wave of radicalism, the success of the revolution was permanent.

Practically everywhere constitutional commissions were set up to change the old oligarchic state into a modern democracy. Liberalism triumphant was to prove its right to live by its solution of this problem. Although the new constitutions were, in a general way, formed on the lines of the liberalistic French constitution, they had nevertheless to be adapted to Swiss conditions, to be examined and fought for point by point, a process which was responsible for many unusual and thoroughly Swiss details. All started from the same principles, but those principles were differently applied in the various cantons. Most of the constitutions proclaimed the sovereignty of the people as the supreme principle. Yet they conferred the bulk of the constitutional rights of the people on its representative body, the Great Council. Under this system, very extensive powers were given to the Great Council as the embodiment of the will of the people. Its transactions were, like public administration all over the country, public, again the mark of a sovereign people. The periodical re-election of the government derived from the same principle. The franchise did not entirely meet the demand for equality before the law; it was made dependent on property or some certificate of higher education. Large sections of the population remained ineligible for office. Personal liberty was everywhere constitutionally guaranteed. The familiar corollaries of that doctrine, which European liberalism had written on its banners, such as the freedom of conscience, the press, petition, assembly, trade, commerce, and settlement were enumerated separately, and secured to the citizen the sphere of private freedom for which he had struggled. It was, after all, these liberties which had given the name of Liberal to the whole movement. Finally, the constitutions also contained provisions for their own amendment.

The apprenticeship of democracy. It is not the fact of a written constitution but the spirit in which it is applied which determines the fate of the people who live by it. The Liberals, inexperienced in government, were guilty of many blunders in the early days, but they prepared to make full use of their power. A noisy period of rhetoric, reckless action, passionate party struggles, dangerous conspiracies, and personal persecution set in. The new epoch was illuminated, not by the dawn of modern ideals but by the vivid lightning-flashes of a fierce political thunder-storm. Representative democracy had to fight for the form in which it was to endure. Many a man bled to death in the struggle, and officials and government changed with unprecedented rapidity.

Grave charges were soon brought against the young democracy. Most of them voiced the great disappointment caused by the inability of victorious liberalism to introduce at once the material improvements it had promised. The Liberals proved a failure in the solution of great economic problems. Their abiding creation was in the domain of public education, and it was their educational idealism that found expression. They reformed the primary schools from top to bottom, founded training colleges, and crowned their work in Zürich and Berne by founding universities. For one of the ideals of the Liberals was to open the way to higher education to all citizens, irrespective of birth. Further, the young state required properly trained civil servants and teachers capable of absorbing the new spirit and spreading it among the people. It was essential for it to be supported by an executive which was of one mind with it. Native teachers united with those from other countries in creating an organism which, at bottom, remained Swiss throughout. Thus the university teachers became the political educators of the nation. They trained the men who were later to develop and transform the state.

Split in Switzerland and failure of reform of the confederation. The liberal and democratic ideas of revolutionary France found their way into the frontier canton of Neuchâtel where they poured fresh vigour into the Republican party. In the alert industrial

population of the mountain districts they found a steadily growing following, while the old-established aristocratic families were
louder than ever in their assertion of loyalty to the crown of
Prussia. This led to a passage of arms between the Republicans
and the Monarchists which was suppressed by the federal diet. In
Schwyz, too, the new spirit caused serious disturbances, which
threatened to split the canton. In Basle, the movement brought
about a fierce local conflict and led to the separation of the city
from its rural hinterland. From the outset, the clash was more
bitter in Basle than elsewhere and was exacerbated by economic
motives. The rural districts demanded representation according
to the number of inhabitants, which would have given them a
large numerical preponderance in the Great Council, while the
city, which bore the chief burden of taxation and was the centre
of education, considered its duty done when the rural districts
were given a simple majority. Unfortunately, action on both sides
embittered the conflict and finally destroyed a community of interests which had lasted for centuries. In 1832 the rural communes
united to form a separate half-state, Basle Land, and adopted a
decidedly democratic constitution.

These disturbances aroused passionate partisanship in the other
parts of Switzerland. The old order exulted over the Liberal setback while the new order was promising help to their fellow
Liberals in the three cantons. In 1832, seven Liberal cantons concluded a concordat to safeguard their new constitutions; five cantons concluded an opposition pact. These disputes provided no
favourable ground for federal reform. The leaders of the Reform
movement had long since realized that reform in the cantons must
be followed by the reform of the confederation including the unification and strengthening of the Bund. A special commission of
the diet prepared in draft a 'Federal Pact of the Swiss Confederation', which was kept within the bounds of the attainable and was
a kind of golden mean between the centralistic and federalistic
tendencies. But this outline of a federal state met with vigorous
opposition from the extremists on both sides. On the one hand,
the Centralists wanted more centralization while the Federalists
feared for the independence of the cantons. Conservatives in some
other countries opposed the unification of Switzerland. Austria
declared that she could only recognize the neutrality of Switzerland as guaranteed by the congress powers so long as there was no

attempt at a unilateral amendment of the federal pact of 1815. Yet the diet ventured to put the draft pact up for discussion. A second draft constitution was prepared which took more account of the growing strength of the Federalistic feeling and curtailed the powers of the Bund. If at least this revised draft had been put into action peacefully it might have averted the troubles of the following period. But it was not.

Conservative reaction. A number of interventions in Switzerland on the part of Austria and France led to no settlement of internal differences. Many Swiss who had acclaimed the new ideal with rejoicing turned back to moderate conservatism, sickened by the Liberal conflicts. This Conservative counter-trend first made political headway in the canton of Zürich. Large sections of the population were merely bewildered by the flood of legislation with which the Liberals attempted to make the country happy. The inevitable rise in taxes also contributed to a general sobering down of feeling. Highly explosive social material was created by the Liberals' lack of insight into the distress of the weavers. It was, however, the reform of the primary schools which estranged most people. When a Liberal theologian was appointed in the university, the country-folk rose and advanced on the town, singing hymns. In 1839 a new administration was formed composed of conservatives with religious sympathies. In Lucerne political opinion also veered round to a combination of the absolute sovereignty of the people with the Catholic church (1841) and the new government there communicated its constitution to the pope.

Political writing. Poets in the reform period turned to the political activity of the moment and entered the party struggle. Their short-lived verse was inspired by the joys of liberty on the one hand, the glorification of the old order on the other. What seems now mere rhetoric was then born of genuine enthusiasm and actual experience. What today looks like stubborn defence of obsolete forms against the irresistible march of time, arose from an intense conviction that liberalism was undermining religion and the common weal, and breaking down the strength of the Swiss people. Often this ephemeral poetry descended to violent polemic and abuse of the opposite party, facts which may also be explained by earlier repression.

The Liberal beliefs in progress found its most skilful interpreter in Heinrich Zschokke, an immigrant from Prussia, and a faithful adherent of German idealism. A most fertile and industrious writer, he helped to educate the people in liberal ideas without engaging himself fruitlessly in merely ephemeral questions. His work for popular education had very great influence. In comparison with this nimble-penned journalist, Jakob Stutz, the popular poet of Zürich, showed a profounder understanding of the real needs of the working classes; there is more originality in his writing. The Conservative outlook found a stout defender in Abraham Emanuel Fröhlich, a deeply religious pastor who resisted the advance of liberalism with indefatigable zeal and passionate hatred. His songs, fables, and rhymes are inspired by true public spirit and the joy of battle against Liberal aims and personalities. Other party poets included Thomas Bornhauser, Josef Anton Henne, and Johann Jacob Reithardt, whose work was a faithful reflection of the thought and feelings of their fellow citizens.

X

THE FOUNDATION OF THE FEDERAL STATE

Radicalism. Since the fall of the old confederation and the creation of the Helvetic republic, two political views had been in opposition —the ancient historical conception of the state, and the modern idea of a *Rechtsstaat*. The conflict between them led to a number of amendments to the constitution, but in spite of temporary settlements no lasting compromise was achieved. In the federation of states which was restored in 1815 the Liberals soon ceased to feel at home. To their mind, the federal pact in force was not only detrimental to the common good but incapable of safeguarding the national interests abroad. After several cantons had adopted liberal constitutions in the 1830s, the Liberals considered that the time had come for a regeneration of the whole confederation on their lines. The reform of the federal constitution, however, undertaken with high hopes, with profound insight into the true nature of the confederation and with real political vigour, was a lamentable failure. A first attempt in 1832, highly praised in an official report by Pellegrino Rossi, a recently naturalized Genevese, was defeated in the diet. A second modified scheme the following year was voted on by a few cantons, but as there seemed no prospect of success it was silently dropped. The successful resistance of the supporters of the traditional federal form of government relied mainly upon the Conservatives and the smaller states, but even the larger states with wider and more liberal views were not prepared to vote the considerable revenues that a new Bund would require unless they secured a proportionate increase in their own political influence. Political reform and economic reform, in fact, must go hand in hand.

It was the younger Radicals who felt called upon to solve this national problem; indeed, they looked upon it as their historic mission. Their chief inspiration was the idea of the Swiss nation. That idea had gained great strength under repeated humiliations from abroad, and had become one of the powerful forces of the day. Indeed, national feeling may be said to have been the most effective weapon of the reformers. Their aim was to overcome the separation of national life by a unified state on Liberal lines, and to arouse the nation to vigilance and action. They foresaw a self-reliant federal state, strengthened by internal union, possessing a financial system and an army of its own, which should safeguard the national security and meet threatening powers on an equal footing.

The democratic ideas of the Radicals came out in their demand for equal suffrage, the abolition of the last remaining privileges, proportional representation, and the publicity for government proceedings. The Radicals also put forward a number of Liberal demands, such as the freedom of worship, of the press, and of association, to be imposed by the Bund upon unwilling cantons. The Radicals, however, were less anxious for freedom from state intervention than for the continuous co-operation of the people in the national life. They conceived of a powerful state and desired its sphere to be as extensive as possible in comparison with the sphere of individual rights. To them the will of the people was sacred; it was the supreme court of appeal. Should it come into conflict with the constitution in force it was the latter which must yield.

By reason of their keener social conscience and greater sense of social responsibility, the Radicals were also protagonists of social reform. They did not, however, contemplate a thorough-going reorganization of existing property rights; property was, in their eyes, inviolable. Nor did they aim at a fundamental change in the structure of society; they were not social revolutionaries. In their opinion the fact that the lower classes had acquired political rights opened up to them the way to a higher social status.

Economic questions gave the Radicals their most powerful incentive. They demanded the abolition of the local customs barriers and of all bridge and highway tolls, the unification of the postal system, of coinage, and weights and measures. The existing chaos in the national economy should make way for order and freedom of commercial intercourse. Not until that was done could international traffic, the exchange of goods between the south and north of Europe, again pass through Switzerland as it had done once, since Switzerland was the natural country of transit. The Radicals wished to make of Switzerland a single economic organism as her neighbours were. Measures of nationalization were to pour fresh life into the body politic and strengthen it for the part it had to play in international economic competition. They pointed out that Switzerland, owing to internal disunion, had, to her shame, succumbed to the pressure of foreign powers. The leaders of the Radical party indulged in the wildest visions of present and future: 'All over the earth, wherever the courage and endurance of the Briton has found a footing, you will find the free Swiss as his faithful companion, seeking a market for the arts and industries of his own country.'

It was above all the behaviour of the Radicals which aroused bitter opposition. Whenever it seemed necessary they broke the law to win their victories. Self-styled political revolutionaries, they saw more merit and heroism in enforcing the will of the people than in bowing before the old order. In their eyes an unlawful act ceased to be unlawful if it was committed for the sake of a moral idea. A number of Radical leaders won their positions by breaches of the constitution and acts of violence and then legitimized them by an appeal to the will of the people.

The shooting matches of these years were displays of Radicalism, Radical *Landsgemeinden*, at which the leaders disseminated the new ideas and gathered their followers. The astonishing increase in the number of such festivals at the time may be explained by the predominantly political character of the meetings; the people flocked to see itself; they were modes of expression of national self-consciousness.

The dissolution of the Aargau monasteries, the Jesuit question, and the secession campaigns. The Radicals won their first great victory in the canton of Aargau where the Catholic minority rose in indignation and stormed the cantonal capital with an armed force which was repulsed by government troops. The victors were persuaded that the riot had originated in and been supported by the monasteries, which were centres of resolute resistance to the new ideas. At the demand of the Radicals, Aargau at once dissolved its monasteries and this not without harshness. A number of cantons protested against this step and charged the canton with a breach of the constitution, since article XII of the federal pact expressly guaranteed the existence of the monasteries and their property. The Aargau decision to secularize them roused the Catholic world far beyond the Swiss frontiers, and the question of the monasteries, at first a legal dispute, became a political issue. More and more it became a cancer in the body of the confederation.

In the midst of its triumphal progress, radicalism encountered the opposition of the extreme form of catholicism, namely, the militant order of the Jesuits. There now set in between these forces a struggle in which the whole of Switzerland and all classes of the people took a feverish part; rarely had civil war in Switzerland been preceded by years of such profound disturbance. It was not really a religious conflict, for the original parties to it were not Protestants and Catholics but disbelievers and Ultramontanes. Practising Protestants did not at first consider themselves involved.

In Lucerne, Josef Leu von Ebersol, a man much beloved by the people, was working for the admission of the Society of Jesus to the canton. He fervently hoped that their activity would lead to a firmer popular acceptance of the new Christian democracy. His closest political associates still hoped to avert the threatening danger. As a result of Radical provocation and the dissolution of the Aargau monasteries, however, they moved into the Jesuit camp. After stormy sessions, the Great Council of Lucerne in 1844 adopted an agreement with the Jesuits by which theological teaching, the seminary, and worship in one part of the town were placed in their hands.

The transference of higher teaching to the order was certainly no breach of the federal pact; the Jesuits were already acting as teachers and preachers in Fribourg, Valais, and Schwyz. Besides, Lucerne was its own master in all questions of education and could appoint whom it pleased to the direction of its higher educational institutions. Thus by the federal law then in force no objection was possible. Yet the step taken by Lucerne proved to be a grave political mistake. The provocative invitation given to the Jesuits by the leading canton of the confederation at that time of tension turned a purely local dispute into a national one. The Swiss Radicals, to a man, took the decision of Lucerne as a declaration of war. For them the Jesuits were the avowed enemies of progress, the systematic oppressors of a free world order, the representatives of suspicion and ignorance, the creators of civil dissension. The Radicals now had the watchword with which they could rally waverers to their cause, and they proceeded to declare the Jesuits a national peril.

On both sides feeling rose to fever-pitch. Anti-Jesuit societies were formed. The passions of the people were shamelessly played on until they burst into flame. When the Radicals of Lucerne realized that the call to the Jesuits could not be legally withdrawn they recklessly resolved to take the law into their own hands and in December 1844 organized a riot in the town which was put down without difficulty by the government and punished with unnecessary severity.

The anti-Jesuit movement thereupon gained strength among the Radicals in other cantons. Huge popular demonstrations demanded active support of the Aargau decision from the cantonal governments. In the mind of the common man, if the text of the federal constitution stood in the way of the expulsion of the order, a new federal law must be enacted for the purpose. The Radicals of Lucerne boldly proceeded to prepare a new armed expedition with their fellow Radicals. The general anarchy reached such a point that the governments of the Radical cantons, completely neglecting their duty, left the insurgent Radicals an almost free hand and did not even intervene when the *Freischärler,* as the Radical volunteers were called, helped themselves to arms and ammunition from the city arsenals. Certain cantonal authorities played a double game by closing their eyes to the lawless goings on, and later posing before the confederation and the outside world as deluded defenders of the law. Universal lawlessness seemed the order of the day not only among the people but in the governments too.

At the end of March 1845 the *Freischärler,* a motley troop of 3,600 men under the command of Ulrich Ochsenbein, a Bernese captain, advanced from the canton of Aargau over the Lucerne frontier, and on the evening of the following day had reached the outskirts of the city. The startled government was already thinking of abdicating. Ochsenbein, however, partly from reasons of humanity, refrained from bombarding the city, whereupon his exhausted troops fled in disorder. Half of them were taken prisoners, 500 were killed. It was, perhaps, well, for a victory of the *Freischärler* would not have provided a proper solution of the great problem. A passage of arms was, of course, hardly to be avoided, but to be of enduring value it would have had to be fought out by the whole nation and not merely by a chance collection of lawless adventurers.

The formation of the Sonderbund. Feeling themselves endangered by these onslaughts the Catholic cantons of Lucerne, Uri, Schwyz, Unterwalden, Zug, Fribourg, and Valais concluded a defensive pact among themselves. Its aims, though not set down in writing, were later admitted to have been chiefly directed against the impending reform of the confederation and against the introduction of a unified government at the expense of cantonal sovereignty. The league declared itself defensive in character, formed for protection against a repetition of the attacks; its sole purpose was stated to be the security of the territory of the seven cantons and their independence against further invasion. As soon as any of the cantons received reliable information of any actual or impending attack it was forthwith to regard itself as committed to raising the troops adequate to the situation without awaiting official notification from the canton in question. The union was placed under the leadership of a committee with almost plenipotentiary powers, consisting of one deputy from each of the treaty cantons; it bore the ominous name of the war council.

The founders of this Sonderbund, as it was soon aptly named, had taken the greatest care to avoid any violation of the letter of the federal pact: article VI provided that no canton should enter upon alliances which might be prejudicial to the confederation or to the rights of other cantons. The question was merely whether the whole of Switzerland was prepared to believe in the defensive character of this political and military league and whether it was not at variance with the spirit of the federal pact.

When the diet came to deal with the question of the Sonderbund, a few cantons, Vaud, Zürich, Berne, Solothurn, and Geneva, which had hesitated till then, elected Radical governments. The whole country, tense with excitement, watched St. Gallen enter the Radical camp. With that, the twelfth cantonal vote was attained and an absolute majority in the diet secured. *Douze voix font loi* proclaimed the Radicals of French Switzerland.

Preparations for war. Ochsenbein, the former *Freischärler*, now president of the Bernese government and in that capacity president of the confederation, opened the diet in Berne with dignity. The fateful meeting was being watched from abroad, for its decisions might have consequence outside Swiss territory. Ochsenbein began his lengthy but skilful presidential address with a reference to the general importance of the session, and then, with candour and firmness, went on to discuss the character and aims of the Radicals. An open conflict between stability and progress could not be avoided; it was now Switzerland's sacred duty to set up a new Bund for the whole nation. It was thereupon resolved by a narrow majority that the Sonderbund should be dissolved as incompatible with the federal pact, and there is no doubt that the twelve cantons and two half-cantons represented the majority of the Swiss nation. Yet it was a revolutionary measure for the Radicals to settle a constitutional question by a mere majority vote. The same majority, together with the canton of Basle Stadt, elected a committee for the revision of the federal pact. As regards the Jesuits, an appeal for the expulsion of the order was sent to Lucerne, Schwyz, Fribourg, and Valais, along with a formal prohibition by the confederation of the admission of the Society of Jesus.

The Radicals now pressed for vigorous action on the decisions of the diet. They raised troops and elected Colonel William Henry Dufour, a Conservative Genevese, then sixty years of age, as their commander. The army of the diet was thus commanded by a man whose personality was to mean much for the conduct and issue of the war. The choice shows with what political intelligence and high sense of responsibility towards the nation as a whole the Radicals were able to act at really decisive moments; it further testifies to the earnest endeavour towards moderation made by the leading moderate Radicals. By accepting the command, Dufour, in the eyes of Switzerland and the world at large, legalized the war preparations of the diet. Conservative officers of high standing followed his lead and joined the confederate army. His character and personality were in every way attractive: benevolent, unselfish, moderate, he had the qualities of the good citizen as well as of the soldier, simplicity and loyalty. It was the combination of these characteristics that made him the uniquely great man that he was; a sincere Christian and a student of the classics, his personality was a source of strength to all. In the commander-in-chief, the plain soldier saw the prototype of all that was best in Switzerland.

The Sonderbund was equally convinced of the justice and necessity of the war. A community of religion and the sense of danger gave a solidarity to their determination to resist which, worked upon by their political and religious leaders, rose at times to fanaticism. Preparations for war were made with tremendous energy. The war council ordered earthworks to be constructed, the reserves called out, and arms purchased. By an unlucky chance a consignment of rifles which Fribourg had bought in France was delayed at Neuchâtel. Munitions from Austria were also intercepted in the Ticino, whereupon the diet prohibited the import of arms by the Sonderbund. In the *Landsgemeinden* and in the churches, popular feeling for a holy war for the old confederation and the old faith found fervent expression. The Sonderbund, however, lacked unity of command.

No clear line had been drawn between the civil and military authority. The war council and the army command stood side by side in an unhappy equality. Again and again the particular interests of individual cantons interfered in the general plan and frustrated any comprehensive unity of plan or action. Constantin Siegwart of Lucerne, who possessed the necessary strength of will and energy in action, realized that he lacked military experience. In vain he applied to Austria for a superior commander. Then the war council elected Johann Ulrich von Salis-Soglio, a native of the Grisons, as commander-in-chief. He was by training and profession an officer, but he lacked the capacity for independent strategy and for vigorous action. None doubted his personal bravery, but that could not make up for his lack of professional skill and of the intuition necessary to a commander. Nor had he the perseverance to overcome all set-backs. He was not the man to remain calm in the midst of the storm.

Civil war. After a further meeting of the diet a final conference between the parties led to no agreement. The majority of the cantons, with Neuchâtel and Appenzell Ausserrhoden, now resolved to break up the Sonderbund by force of arms. Its fate was sealed very soon. The total forces of the Sonderbund side numbered 79,000 men as against the 99,000 men of the diet. In addition the Sonderbund side was much weaker in trained soldiers. It has indeed caused some surprise that, in view of this numerical and material superiority on the side of the diet, the Sonderbund should have still imagined victory possible. The Sonderbund, however, recalled that in the past history of Switzerland, great victories had been won against superior numbers, while many hoped that if they held out intervention would come from abroad. And, too, a miracle might happen.

The courage of the Sonderbund militia was of little avail against General Dufour's superior strategy. He first ordered a concentric advance on Fribourg; on 14 November it capitulated to superior numbers without serious resistance. The canton was obliged to dismiss its troops, withdraw from the Sonderbund, and admit a confederate occupation. A new provisional government was set up which expelled the Jesuits.

Some scattered Sonderbund successes in the Ticino and Aargau were powerless to overcome the disastrous impression made by the fall of Fribourg. Dufour immediately ordered a concentric march on Lucerne. In face of this threatening advance, Zug left the Sonderbund and surrendered without a struggle. The main engagements took place in very cold weather on 23 November at Gisikon and Meyerskappel. The Sonderbund had occupied fortified positions there and defended themselves bravely, making good use of the terrain. On the confederate side it took the courageous personal intervention of the commander-in-chief before his frightened troops could be led to the attack and to victory. At nightfall, the Sonderbund leaders fled with the Jesuits across the lake to Fluelen. On the evening of the following day, Lucerne, besieged on all sides, surrendered, and part of the victorious confederate army entered the town. A few days previously, Siegwart had implored Metternich to arrange for a military occupation of the Ticino: he now sent repeated formal appeals in the name of the war council for armed intervention by Austria. But no foreign help arrived, and Siegwart, with a few friends, escaped across the alps to Milan, where like many others he remained in exile and poverty. Valais was the last canton to lay down its arms; the members of the Sonderbund were obliged to pay the costs of the war and to set up new administrations.

The civil war had lasted twenty-five days. Dufour had manœuvred rather than fought and thus spared many lives. On the side of the confederates were 78 dead and 260 wounded, on the Sonderbund side, 50 dead and 175 wounded. Dufour won the hearts of the defeated by his repeated appeals to his troops to spare the civil population of the enemy. It does the General the highest honour that he inflicted no fresh wounds on the body of the confederate state with the weapon it had placed in his hands, but healed those which already existed.

The attitude of the powers. While the powers were still considering how they would intervene in Switzerland, the Sonderbund had ceased to exist. Although certain governments regarded it with the greatest sympathy as the guardian of the Conservative principle, there were many obstacles in the way of intervention. Metternich had long advocated intervention and was endeavouring to bring about an understanding among the five powers in order to prevent the rise of a powerful Radical republic in Switzerland, but the British cabinet held severely aloof. Palmerston steadily upheld the principle of non-intervention and repeatedly offered his services for peaceful negotiation. He early branded the Sonderbund as illegal and congratulated Ochsenbein on his 'well-known firmness of character'. He openly declared himself opposed to any interference and exerted his great diplomatic powers to frustrate it.

Palmerston's policy was supported by public opinion in England. True, both cabinet and public were at first on the side of the moderate Conservatives in Switzerland because they suspected the Radicals as enemies of Christianity and political extremists. *The Times*, for instance, at first refused to print the diet's proclamation to the Swiss people, but later sent a special correspondent to Dufour. The *Seven Letters concerning Politics in Switzerland* published by the historian George Grote in the *Spectator* did a great deal to bring about a change in public opinion in England. He sympathized with and understood the confederates and did all he could to win the educated public over to their side.

Siegwart's appeals to the powers for help had grown ever more urgent. Metternich sent money and arms and threatened the frontier cantons with reprisals, while the French Minister promised to bring pressure to bear by means of military demonstrations, but at the critical moment he was disowned by his government. Finally, after long negotiations among the powers, an identical note was sent by them to the Swiss government. By the time this reached Switzerland the war was over and the Sonderbund dissolved; the notes were delivered, but to the great indignation of the other states, without British support. Instead, Palmerston sent Stratford Canning, whose term of office at Berne won him universal respect, with instructions to do all he could in the cause of peace. When he arrived in Berne on 7 December 1847, Stratford Canning found the war over. He could now advise a course of extreme moderation upon the Radicals so that hostile powers should be given no pretext for reprisals or blockade.

The government of the confederation was now able to inform the powers that an offer of mediation presupposed a state of war which no longer existed; further, this attempt at mediation was at variance with the position of Switzerland in Europe as recognized by treaty and also with the constitution of the confederation. For the last time the eastern powers attempted to frustrate the reform of the confederation, this time by presenting a collective note. The answer of the diet, drawn up in firm but tactful terms by Jonas Furrer, burgomaster of Zürich, claimed for Switzerland the right to amend her constitution as she thought fit. There was a new tone of self-reliance in the document. Finally, as regards foreign policy, the Sonderbund War meant Switzerland's final release from tutelage and complete national independence.

Shortly after this exchange of notes the European crisis of 1848 broke out. Following the February Revolution in Paris, the Republican party in Neuchâtel rose and overthrew the Royalist government by armed force, set up a republic, and thus cut the bond between Neuchâtel and the king of Prussia. The powers were too busy with the troubles of their own countries to pursue their plans of intervention in Switzerland and the confederation was left undisturbed to establish a firm confederate state in the midst of a distracted Europe.

The federal constitution. The credit for having moderated the excesses of radicalism in the constitution must go to a handful of far-sighted members of the progressive party. Deeply stirred by the events of the day they laid aside all party feeling and set to work in the service of their country. Politicians and party leaders from the lower classes of society, many of them ardent advocates of the political and social ideals of those classes, became prudent statesmen in positions of responsibility. But they had little understanding for what was of permanent value in the existing order, and thus could not bring about a fusion of old and new. They realized that the parts of the confederation, disunited yet seeking union, could only be brought together again, that the revolutionary forces could only be held in check and order restored if, by moderation and compromise, an acceptable agreement could be reached. They had plenty of common sense and experience of government acquired in administrative work for their cantons and communes. It was a good thing for Switzerland that the men who played the leading part in the Reform commission were all of this constructive, statesmanlike turn of mind—Ulrich Ochsenbein, Joseph Munzinger, J. Conrad Kern, Henri Druey, and Jonas Furrer.

Furrer, in particular, rising to the full heights of his statesmanship in the wider framework of the confederation, steered this
middle course with wisdom and unerring insight. A native of
Winterthur, which was an early centre of the new ideas, he had
studied law in Germany and later practised as a lawyer in his
native canton. Unlike many of his Liberal and Radical contemporaries, he was self-controlled and indulged little in flights of
rhetoric. He tried to convince his hearers by the plain force of his
reasoning, going straight to the essential point and the real issue.
Taking his stand as a lawyer, his aim was to bring about reform as
far as possible by legal means, so that Switzerland might freely
adopt the form of government which she desired. He combined
intense political convictions with great practical circumspection.
Calm and unmoved amid all the attacks, no matter how base,
launched against him by the extremists of his own party, he followed his course with single-minded devotion. Unwillingly, and
moved only by a sense of duty, he gave up his profession to accept
the burgomastership of Zürich and a seat on the Revision commission. It was only gradually, moved by his strong sense of
responsibility to the common weal, that the level-headed Furrer
allowed the private citizen in him to be submerged by the statesman. Of all his contemporaries he was the only born leader. How
exemplary his attitude was, can be seen in Gottfried Keller's note
in his diary confessing the debt of gratitude he owed to Furrer
and his political friends. It was self-discipline, says Keller, which
turned the vague revolutionary into a self-reliant and far-sighted
statesman.

The Revision commission performed the astounding feat of producing a complete draft of a federal constitution in less than two
months. When the commission met at the beginning of 1848 it
soon came to the conclusion that canton sovereignty must make
some sacrifices to the central authority and that cantonal interests
must be subordinated to national interests. It was not the first time
that the ideal of a bicameral system had arisen in debates on a
constitution for the confederation. Greeted at first with grave misgivings, it found a surprising degree of support even in the Conservative *Landsgemeinde* cantons. When it was realized that the
political formula of the bicameral system would permit a smooth
fusion of old and new, an agreement was soon reached on the
supreme representative bodies of the nation and the cantons.

A legislature was created consisting of a Council of States, while the executive was handed over to the Federal Council. The cantons were given two months only in which to accept or reject the project. Except in Fribourg it was put to the popular vote in all cantons. When the diet reassembled the results of the voting were summarized as follows: $15\frac{1}{2}$ cantons with 1,897,887 votes had voted in favour; $6\frac{1}{2}$ cantons with 293,371 votes had voted against. On 12 September the diet adopted the new constitution by 16 and 2 half-state votes.

The federal constitution transformed the confederation into a body politic which stood midway between a federation of states and a unified state. It was a compromise between the demand for a centralized state which still persisted from the time of the Helvetic republic and the existence of sovereign cantons. The compromise was most clearly to be seen in the legislature. It consisted of the National Council which represented the nation as a whole, and the Council of States, which represented the cantons. In the period which followed, the more the movement of population and hence the mixture of population increased inside Switzerland, the more the National Council came to represent the Swiss people as a whole. The Council of States, on the other hand, although by the constitution it had to contribute to the formation of the will of the state, remained at all times the true guardian of cantonal traditions. The decisive factor, however, was now the people and not the states. For it was not the cantons which had founded the new federal state; it was a national act which had the people behind it.

For the first time since the Helvetic republic, a permanent executive was created in the form of a Federal Council of seven members. It ensured greater independence at home and abroad than the old system of government by the three representative cantons in turn, subject as they were to local influences. Another innovation was the creation of a special body for federal jurisdiction, namely, the Supreme Federal Court. Since the election of the federal judges is carried out by the Federal Assembly, the legislature, political influence can be brought to bear, without, however, necessarily affecting the independence of the judiciary.

While the sole purpose of the old pact had been to maintain national independence abroad and peace and order at home, the new constitution included other national provisions; the protection of the rights and liberties of the citizens of the state came first and then followed the promotion of the national welfare. A good deal of the business of state was to be concerned with the internal life of the nation, and the Bund was provided with the means, formal and material, to that end. Since this was now made financially independent, it was thus able to fulfil most expectations, making extensive use of its rights to erect public buildings and promoting a good deal of cultural activity.

The centralizing aims of the Radicals achieved their first success in the sphere of foreign policy. The far-reaching loss of the independence of the cantons in foreign policy naturally had a sobering effect on cantonal feelings. The prohibition of cantonal military capitulations also restricted contact with other countries. This article of the constitution had been preceded by heated debates, since it affected not only deeply rooted opinions, but material interests too. It was more particularly in the poorer, predominantly agricultural, districts that military service abroad was regarded as an economic necessity. This had also given the cantons the opportunity of ridding themselves of undesirable citizens, and, still more important, had relieved the cantons to a large extent of the burden of military training. In patrician circles, where foreign service had been the rule for centuries, the new regulation was felt as a financial and social loss. But it could not be denied that the exodus to foreign service was harmful to home industry.

The constitution clarified and reinforced the competence of the Bund in respect of the maintenance of law and order within the country. Violent action, such as that of the *Freischaren,* was prohibited. The Bund also prohibited secessionist movements and the conclusion of political treaties between the cantons. That involved supervision not only of foreign policy, but also of the home policy of the cantons. More and more their public life lost its former violence and became both peaceful and legal. This development was furthered by the fact that the cantonal constitutions were subject to approval by the Bund, which examined them for their compatibility with the federal constitution. In this way the Bund was influential in standardizing the various cantonal constitutions and thus further promoted the unification of Switzerland.

This tendency to unification was particularly marked in the regulation of what was known as 'material matters'. The customs,

which had up to that time been under the sovereignty of the cantons, were now declared to be the affair of the Bund, and this
cleared away the ancient obstacles to free traffic, recognized only
federal customs at the frontiers, and thus gave fresh life to trade
and traffic. The abolition of internal customs came extremely late
in Switzerland, for customs unions had long since been formed
elsewhere, as in the German Zollverein. Any further delay in the
unification of the Swiss economic system might have led to serious
inconvenience, for the country would have run the risk of being
cut off from international traffic and losing her old position as the
country of transit between the north and the south of Europe.
A federal postal system prevented local disputes; and currency,
weights, and measures were now unified.

These regulations of 'material matters' led to a new settlement
of the financial relationship between the Bund and the cantons.
The Bund now had revenues of its own, and the old relationship
was reversed. While the Bund, up to that time, had lived on the
generosity of the cantons, it now had its own federal sources of
income. To cover their expenses, however, the cantons remained
in possession of the salt monopoly, the stamp tax, the tax on wine,
and some degree of local direct taxation.

As regards the army there was a division of powers between the
Bund and the cantons which opposed centralization with peculiar
obstinacy, seeing in this field their last line of defence of cantonal
sovereignty. The Bund was made responsible for advanced military
training; infantry training and instruction, including promotion
of lower ranks, were left to the cantons. Universal compulsory
military service was accepted as of ancient tradition, but no canton
could maintain a force of more than 300 men without federal
permission.

The Radicals attempted to centralize education by founding a
federal university and federal training colleges for teachers. These
institutions were to be centres of national unity. The various parts
of the nation were to find a common meeting-ground in an intellectual centre from which a new Helvetic spirit might spread amongst
the people. But these ambitious schemes were wrecked by the
popular preference for leaving education in the hands of the cantons, so that the only plan actually carried out was the founding
of a federal institute of technology.

The 'rights of the people and the citizen' which had already been established in the cantons, were now guaranteed by the Bund. This higher power protected both individuals and larger associations against arbitrary actions on the part of the cantons. Every Swiss citizen possessed in the Bund direct guarantees of his legal freedom; from that time on, minorities were free from any infringements of their rights. The Bund secured freedom before the law, freedom of settlement, of worship, of the press, of association, and of trade and industry. This time it was not, as under the Helvetic republic, a catalogue of abstract principles, but of real liberties which had been won by hard struggles. Even if these principles were not put into practice in their entirety from the start, it was these which first made political freedom possible.

By their self-denial the victorious Radicals showed unusual comprehension of the constitutional possibilities of their age. The solution arrived at was so elastic that the constitution could, in the future, be expanded and adjusted to the necessities arising from national and international developments. Thus the body politic could be reformed by constitutional methods and revolutionary violence could be avoided.

In the light of the outstanding political and military success of the Radicals, which would have permitted them to exploit their victory by establishing a unified constitution, what had been created was a model of self-denial. The Radical architects of the federal constitution aimed, not at a provisional, but at a permanent foundation for the new Switzerland, and for that reason took full account of ancient historical forces. The federal constitution, elaborated with so much statesmanship, so profound a sense of political justice, and with so much common sense, contributed greatly to the pacification and reconciliation of the opposing forces in the country. It was so successful that, no later than the following year, citizens of the defeated cantons and the oppressed social classes declared that they would offer their services to the Bund and fight in its army at the slightest sign of a threat to Switzerland from the outside.

The battle for the new order in Switzerland was over. 'When I look round me on this great day', said Jonas Furrer, the first president of the confederation, 'I feel like a man awaking out of a nightmare to a peaceful life.' Many Swiss felt with exultation that the Swiss people had, in a spirit of liberty and progress, opened the way to a higher life. But, like every milestone on a nation's road, the creation of the federal state was the starting-point for fresh development. As the retiring diet believed, Switzerland would continue to fulfil, as determinedly as ever, the tasks which Providence had appointed her in the European system of states; she would abide by the principles of humanitarianism and justice and would, in the future as in the past, be in a position to repudiate any demands made upon her which conflicted with the honour of the ancient confederation and the dignity of a free and independent people.

More than ever, Switzerland, transformed by her own will and patriotic action, came to feel herself a nation. Her nationhood was not based on language, race, or culture, but on common historical experience and general consent to the Democratic–Republican order. The people had reached maturity.

The federal constitution is the finest monument which the Switzerland of 1848 raised to herself. Its foundations still stand firm today although in the course of over a 100 years there have been many changes.

Foreign Relations: the new Switzerland in revolutionary Europe

The federal constitution of 1848 did much to clarify and strengthen the position of Switzerland in foreign affairs. From that time on, only one body in the country was competent in matters of foreign policy; the Bund alone had the right, not only to declare war and make peace, as hitherto, but also to conclude alliances and treaties with other countries. Thus the cantons were deprived of the power of carrying on their own foreign policy. They merely retained the right to conclude agreements with foreign powers in exceptional cases, such as economic matters, frontier traffic, and the police, though even such agreements had to be compatible with the law of the Bund. On the other hand, the cantons were empowered to enter into relations with the subordinate authorities of foreign states.

The unification of the country was soon to offer a better guarantee of national independence. For while in earlier times, owing to the alternation of the *Vororte*, the foreign policy of the confederation had been subject to some variations, a central authority with full powers in questions of foreign policy now ensured unity of decision and consistency of action. By the constitutional restriction of cantonal freedom in foreign policy, it became more difficult for other countries to interfere in the internal affairs of Switzerland with the help of individual cantons and parties. This meant that the period of foreign tutelage was at an end. As the creators of the new federal state had wished, the Swiss people now stood united in face of the outer world, as a people with a fully developed national feeling.

An expression of this endeavour to detach Switzerland from all foreign commitments was the prohibition of foreign military capitulations, it being implicitly assumed that mercenary agreements still in force would remain so till their expiry. It was also decided that the members of the federal authorities and the military officers and civil servants of the Bund should be prohibited from accepting pensions, salaries, gifts, titles or orders of merit from foreign governments. Independence even in such details was a matter which the founders of the federal state took most seriously.

While Switzerland was still engaged in centralizing authority in foreign affairs, she was faced with the necessity of giving a fully responsible definition of her relationship to other countries. To the powers, the diet passionately asserted its right to adopt what constitution it pleased and, on historical and legal grounds, repudiated any claim to intervention. The determination to remain free of all foreign influence found clear expression in a note to the powers drafted by Jonas Furrer which sounded a note of pride not heard before. The confederation was beginning to feel itself a nation and to meet other countries with self-confidence.

Soon after, the diet defined its position on the old fundamental principle of Swiss foreign policy, namely, neutrality. The king of Sardinia, about to make war on Austria, offered to conclude with Switzerland an offensive and defensive alliance. The *Vorort* had just written to the cantons:

Just as Switzerland regards the organisation and settlement of her internal affairs as matters upon which she alone can decide, she will, on the other hand, endeavour to maintain her neutrality in the conflicts of foreign states without flinching and in this respect too, will conscientiously fulfil her existing treaties.

There now followed in the diet a heated debate on the meaning and practice of neutrality. The extreme Radicals, partisans of an idea of the solidarity of the nations, wished to come to the help of all peoples struggling for their freedom, for there, too, the vital principle of Switzerland was at stake. In their opinion Switzerland should abandon her old passive neutrality in favour of an active policy and thus fulfil her mission as a liberator. The majority of the diet, however, refused to countenance any surrender of neutrality, and stood fast to the traditional policy of non-intervention in foreign disputes; it also took up this attitude with respect to a proposal by Geneva to occupy Savoy when the time should come.

In the storms of revolution which again broke over Europe about the middle of the century, Switzerland resisted all temptations to act the part of champion of republicanism. The Federal Council therefore refused every appeal for help from the revolutionaries on the grounds of neutrality as a principle of international law in spite of all references to republican and revolutionary solidarity. The European revolutionaries became more and more frank in their design of using Switzerland as the fountain-head of the general unrest. In particular, the Italian arch-conspirator Mazzini branded the aloofness of the neutrals as immoral and, with the help of his secret associations, 'Young Europe', and 'Young Switzerland', attempted to draw the confederation into the European whirlpool. The national government, itself a product of groups with similar ideas, but now capable of statesmanship, fought on two fronts against foreign agitators and against the extreme Radicals in Switzerland itself. One of the most difficult tasks the Federal Council had to face was to restrain its own people from active partisanship in contemporary disputes, and to bring them to acknowledge the principle of non-intervention, which Switzerland had not so long before claimed from Europe in her own interests. The strict observance of the principle of neutrality encountered much difficulty on both the northern and southern frontiers of the country. The Ticinese grew so enthusiastic for the cause of their brothers in Lombardy that they even allowed certain breaches of neutrality. To punish them Austria expelled all the Ticinese from Lombardy and broke off trade and postal relations with Switzerland which did great harm to the Ticino. The risings in the south of Germany made similar breaches of neutrality only too likely, and troops were sent to the northern frontier. The frontier districts of Switzerland were swarming with refugees, the country town of Liestal having been for long past an asylum for left-wing German intellectuals, a fact which was prejudicial to the relations between Switzerland and the German states. A serious danger threatened the country when a large Prussian force, which had just put down the risings in Baden, concentrated on the frontier and seemed to be on the point of marching into Switzerland to restore the Royalist regime which had been overthrown in Neuchâtel. It was only the action of the powers, Great Britain above all, which prevented Prussia from carrying out this plan.

The refugees. Merely because of its difference, the Liberal and Republican confederation could not fail to be a thorn in the flesh of the Conservative and Royalist powers. But the principal charge brought against Switzerland was her admission of refugees. True, the Federal Council had removed them to the interior of the country and expelled those who protested against their internment. The refugees imagined that they could claim asylum in Switzerland as a kind of internationally guaranteed right, while Switzerland declared the right of asylum to be entirely voluntary. Although the confederation fulfilled all its commitments under international law, it was branded by the foreign press as the refuge of the enemies of law and order and a nest of European revolutionaries. A conference of the powers met to consider the final solution of the refugee problem and contemplated intervention, while the Federal Council was also exposed to sharp attack from the Radicals. It was charged with having betrayed the cause of the people by having entrenched itself behind a selfish policy of neutrality instead of raising the flag of revolution, while to make matters worse members of certain cantonal governments were making common cause with the foreign immigrants. Mazzini, for example, was able to elude the long search for him in Switzerland by going from hiding-place to hiding-place.

At first, the majority of the Swiss population gave a warm welcome to the refugees, who were regarded as martyrs in the cause of liberty. Committees were formed to distribute gifts, to arrange public meetings, and to find work for them. In this way Switzerland gained much that was to be of value for the future. Gradually, however, the confederation came to feel that this host of unemployed, who, to make matters worse, prejudiced foreign relations by their conspiracies, was becoming a public nuisance. The arrogance of certain refugees, who protested publicly against their internment, also contributed to the growing coolness. The Federal Council ordered their expulsion only when they could not fall into the hands of their persecutors and when a new asylum could be found for them in Britain or North America. In several cases the Federal Council was content to turn a blind eye or was duped by the cantonal police. It strained every nerve to induce the foreign governments to grant their subjects an amnesty and take them back again. Austria was the first state to pardon and readmit the Lombard internees, upon which nearly all the Italians left Switzerland. Towards the end of 1849 the German governments also showed themselves more accommodating so that Switzerland was gradually cleared of these difficult visitors.

Several of those who remained settled down in Switzerland and made their home in the country. They found work in the grammar schools and universities and were a great asset to higher education in Switzerland. As scholars, writers, and artists, they enriched the intellectual life of Switzerland; this is obvious from such names as Karl Vogt, Gottfried Semper, Ferdinand Freiligrath, Richard Wagner. Even so the refugee question continued to involve Switzerland in grave embarrassment in its foreign policy.

The Neuchâtel conflict. This may be seen best in the greatest crisis of foreign policy which the young federal state had to face— the Neuchâtel conflict. In 1848, the connexion between Neuchâtel and Prussia had been broken by republican revolution as a result of which Neuchâtel adopted a Republican constitution and was recognized by the federal state as a Swiss canton. But King Frederick William IV of Prussia, taking his stand on history, had never fully recognized this *fait accompli*, and had made no secret of the fact either to his loyal subjects in Neuchâtel or to the Swiss federal authorities. When a dispute on the railway question arose among the Republicans in Neuchâtel, the Royalists renewed their relations with Berlin, where they were encouraged by the court, and began a counter-revolution. During the night of 2–3 September 1856 they gained control of Le Locle and of the castle of Neuchâtel. Next day, in spite of mediation by the confederation, troops of the Republican militia stormed the castle and captured the ringleaders with 600 of their followers, leaving a number of dead and wounded.

Prussia now protested and called on the powers to intervene.

But Europe as a whole had no intention of allowing war to break out in the heart of the Continent on account of a rising in Neuchâtel, and sought a peaceful solution of the dispute. The emperor Napoleon III, who did not wish to see a Prussian army on the south-east flank of France, undertook to act as mediator. Towards Switzerland he took up the attitude of a European judge, and required her to settle the dispute, abandon the prosecution of the rioters, and release the prisoners, promising in return that he would use his influence to bring the king of Prussia to abandon his claims on Neuchâtel. Switzerland, for her part, was not prepared to release these valuable hostages until the king had formally abandoned his claim. The situation was made more critical by the obstinacy of both parties. Prussia then attempted to rouse the whole of Germany and, though this was unsuccessful, the king ordered a mobilization for the beginning of 1857 and prepared for a campaign against Switzerland.

Tremendous excitement spread through the country, affecting even the former Sonderbund cantons. With one accord, all classes of the people rallied round the Federal Council, upon which the Federal Assembly conferred absolute plenipotentiary powers to arrive at a peaceful settlement, and, if necessary, to prepare for war. Even before Prussia had mobilized, there were 30,000 men under Dufour's command on the northern frontier. It was naturally feared in Europe that an attack on Switzerland might lead to a rising of oppressed minorities all over the Continent. Federal Councillor Stämpfli, for instance, used these invisible allies of Switzerland as a threat, even though he wished the struggle to preserve its national character.

In this strained situation, the British cabinet under Palmerston once again intervened. Of the signatories to the Vienna treaties, Britain alone had repeatedly and emphatically reminded the king of Prussia of the guarantee of Swiss neutrality. The attitude of Britain had been from the first benevolent to Switzerland. The British government was not prepared to support the Prussian reactionaries for the material reason, among others, that the economy of England required peace on the Continent; a continental war might easily spread and entail serious economic disadvantages. Further, Britain was anxious to prevent a *rapprochement* between France and Prussia to which the Neuchâtel conflict might lead. Above all Britain desired peace. The Swiss and British systems of government were not fundamentally dissimilar and, in general, their material interests coincided.

The young Swiss federal state saw in Britain its most reliable friend, one which alone was believed to be free from self-seeking. A close understanding arose between the representative of Great Britain and the head of the Swiss political department, while some English ministers actually sought the acquaintance of Swiss party leaders in order to learn at first hand the views of the most influential confederate politicians. The British government recommended moderation to Switzerland, but advised her to settle the Neuchâtel dispute once and for all. British diplomacy consistently maintained an attitude of benevolent moderation; on the one hand, it endeavoured to strengthen the spirit of resistance of the Federal Council, on the other hand, it sought to avoid any decisive strengthening of Stämpfli's hands lest, having grown too self-assured, he might cause war by 'republican' provocations; yet it was careful never to promise material assistance for, as the British minister said in Berlin, England could hardly hasten to Switzerland's help with her navy.

About the turn of the years 1856–7, war was regarded as imminent. Since Britain regarded Frederick William IV as the aggressor, she brought strong diplomatic pressure to bear on the Prussian government, emphasizing, in a series of notes, the guarantee by the Vienna treaties of Swiss neutrality, independence, and integrity:

> The hostile proceedings contemplated by the King would therefore not only be a subject of deep and painful regret to the community of European Nations, but would also be at variance with positive engagements taken by Prussia towards all the other powers who were contracting parties to those engagements. . . . Her Majesty's Government would earnestly request His Prussian Majesty to consider how painful and distressing must be the spectacle presented by the military force of one of the great monarchies of Europe marching to attack a small but free State, in order to enforce rights which have been left in abeyance for eight years.

Meanwhile, those parts of the confederation which did not regard the possibilities of a peaceful solution as yet exhausted (for the most part the industrial classes of eastern Switzerland) had also been able to make themselves heard. It was agreed in the course of further negotiations with Napoleon to release the prisoners without trial, while expelling them from the country until the Neuchâtel question was finally settled. In that way, it was thought, the king would be morally bound to abandon Neuchâtel in order to make it possible for his loyal subjects to return home. After a dramatic conference in Paris, during which Great Britain supported Switzerland unwaveringly, the king, who lost his nerve after stubborn resistance, abandoned his sovereign rights over Neuchâtel for all time, while Switzerland admitted the canton of Neuchâtel to full rights as a member of the confederation. The confederation had to bear the costs, promise not to impose extraordinary taxes on the loyalists, and issue a general amnesty.

The grave danger which had threatened the young federal state contributed in a large measure to overcome the internal factions which had filled the first half of the nineteenth century. The confederation was first really moulded into a nation under pressure from abroad. Switzerland now knew that her new central organ was able to cope with a foreign crisis and had successfully defended her independence.

The abolition of mercenary service. In the war for the unification of Italy the Federal Council safeguarded Swiss interests with the same determination. Switzerland was involved in the Italian struggle against Austrian suzerainty in so far as enthusiasm in the Ticino for the Italian cause was again difficult to hold in check, and troops had to be sent to the Grisons and the Ticino to prevent violations of the frontier. When dispersed Austrian troops filed over the frontier, the Federal Council ordered them to be interned in the interior of the country in accordance with detailed arrangements which were approved by the powers and represented an expansion of international law. It may be regarded as a recognition of Switzerland's neutrality in the war that representatives of the belligerent powers assembled in Zürich for the final peace negotiations.

The Italian war led to a further detachment from foreign commitments and a clarification of the ideal of Swiss neutrality. For a long time past the bulk of the people had felt mercenary service to be incompatible with the dignity of the new Switzerland; thus in the federal constitution the conclusion of military capitulations had been forbidden. The existing Neapolitan agreement was still in force, but was felt to be particularly offensive because the mercenaries were used to protect the reigning power against popular movements. A mutiny, which broke out among the so-called Swiss regiments, led to violent debates in the confederate councils and in public, after which the confederation issued a resolution imposing severe penalties not only on the recruitment of mercenary troops but also on enlistment in foreign armies; the only thing permitted, on certain conditions, was service in the national armies of foreign countries. With that, the ancient system of foreign service, once an economic necessity in the overpopulated confederation, came legally and finally to an end. It deprived the Swiss of one form of livelihood which was in any case diminishing in the epoch of national armies, and expanding industry at home was able to absorb those who had formerly left the country.

The end of the states of the church also meant the disbandment of the battalions in the service of the pope. Only the Swiss guard continued to exist. During the American Civil War and the First World War, thousands of Swiss fought in the regular armies of other countries as they had the right to do by the regulation of 1859. Since 1927, however, any enlistment in foreign service without permission of the Federal Council has been prohibited by a new military criminal law.

The Geneva Red Cross Convention. During the Italian war, Henri Dunant, a member of an old Calvinist family of Geneva, had realized the inadequacy of the military medical services. In his pamphlet *Un Souvenir de Solferino* which was widely read, he put forward a plea for the foundation of voluntary associations for the improvement of the care of wounded in war. On the initiative of the Public Assistance Society of Geneva, a meeting of experts was held in 1863, with Dufour in the chair, which founded the International Red Cross. In the following year the Federal Council called a diplomatic conference at Geneva at which a convention was concluded. It bound the signatory states to recognize the Red Cross as an auxiliary service of the army, to care for all wounded irrespective of nationality, and to neutralize the medical services. It decided to use as a symbol of recognition the red cross on a white ground, these being the federal colours reversed, and by 1868 all European nations had signed the convention.

Thus through the devotion of Dunant and the indefatigable self-sacrifice of his collaborators in Geneva, a humaner law of war was created and the ideal of humanity spread from this organization in Switzerland into European international law and soon conquered the whole civilized world. The work of the Red Cross in the two world wars of the twentieth century is well known.

The dispute over Savoy. As a sequel to the Italian independence movement the Savoy question again arose. The treaties of 1815 had neutralized north Savoy and given Switzerland the right to occupy the country in the event of a war between neighbouring powers, though the Federal Council made no use of this right in 1859. When it was learned after the war that King Victor Emmanuel of Sardinia was about to recompense Napoleon III for his help by the cession of Savoy, the Federal Council, very reasonably, tried to prevent any infringement of Swiss rights. The press and the radical associations then started a violent attack on the French emperor as a traitor to his early ideals of liberty. The Federal Council, carried away by the reckless spirit of Stämpfli, was even moved to make demands on France which had little legal justification. It explained to Napoleon how both the balance of power in Europe and the security of Switzerland would be jeopardized by a union of Savoy with France, in view of the historical connexión of the neutralized districts of the north of Savoy with the confederation. Napoleon, although favourably disposed to a settlement of the kind, could scarcely agree to part with what he did not yet possess. Irritated by the growing agitation in Switzerland, and moved to caution by national trends in his own country, he cleverly played off the unity of Savoy against its dismemberment and in 1860, without first informing Switzerland, signed the annexation of the whole province by France.

Then the storm broke loose in Switzerland. The extreme Radical party aimed at a military occupation of neutralized Savoy, which would have led to war with France. A ridiculous expedition to Thonon, undertaken by a handful of irresponsible Genevese, came to grief, but was a revelation of the dangerous height to which the political temperature had risen. The Federal Council, isolated in Europe, was in a difficult position. Switzerland now had to pay for her inadequate representation abroad—she had agents only in Paris and Vienna and was therefore inadequately informed about affairs. Great Britain, upon whom the new Switzerland had relied in foreign difficulties, now failed her; she was not prepared to satisfy the Swiss desire for annexation at the cost of her friendship with Napoleon. It also became evident now that many people in Switzerland objected to the Federal Council's reckless and inconsistent criticisms of Napoleon. There was no such popular rising as in the Neuchâtel conflict. France made adroit use of the internal dispute between the war and peace parties in Switzerland to organize a plebiscite on the union in Savoy. By a majority, Savoy voted for union with France while retaining the free zones with Geneva. Events passed Switzerland by and France's promise to come to an agreement with Switzerland on the Savoy question with the assistance of the powers was never fulfilled. The settlement with regard to the Vallée des Dappes, which had long been promised to Switzerland, was more successful. This strategically important district lying in the western slopes of the Jura was divided between France and Switzerland, so from that time on both countries had their own road through the district.

Effects of national wars. The European movement which throughout the Continent aimed at the foundation of national states, meant a serious threat to the existence of the Swiss federal state. In the nationalist revolution of the mid-century the call of blood, ignoring historical frontiers, had been heard. The feeling of nationalism, which up to then had been mainly confined to the cantons, had not so far become part of the Swiss consciousness, so that sympathies with foreigners speaking the same language—the Alemanic Swiss with the German, the French Swiss with the French, the Ticinese with Italy—were still unrestrained. The principle of nationality, proclaimed as a gospel in other countries, loomed dark and menacing over the future of Switzerland, since, carried to its logical conclusion, it could not but lead to a partition of Switzerland among her neighbours.

True, the national wars of the sixties did not affect policy, but, in spite of the strictest national neutrality, feeling was unusually strong. In the American Civil War the Swiss government, supported by public opinion, made no secret, as the war went on, of its sympathy for the northern states. In its Annual Report for 1864, the Federal Council emphasized the similarity between the public institutions of the two republics, and when Abraham Lincoln was murdered after the defeat of the south, the Federal Council cast reserve to the winds. In its official message on the death of the president, a tone of sincere joy at the outcome of the great struggle was clearly to be heard: 'Free Switzerland will never cease to bestow all her friendship on free America and its endeavours towards truth and humanity.' The Federal Council was relieved at this turn in the fortunes of war, regarding it as an improvement of Switzerland's position in foreign affairs. It believed that it would find in that great like-minded sister republic a support against Napoleonic France. Switzerland was almost the only European state to have sympathized entirely with the Union and acclaimed its cause as the cause of justice. Thus it was an official appreciation of this attitude by the Union when its minister wrote to the Federal Council. 'If other Governments have sympathised with a rebellion against popular institutions and in favour of despotism, the government and people of the Helvetic Republic have never wavered in their friendship towards a greater sister-republic and in fidelity to their own ancient tradition.' To strengthen its bonds with the 'mightiest free state in the world' the Federal Council proposed that a Swiss legation should be established in Washington; a suggestion, however, which was not carried out till 1881.

The friendship between the republics was less evident in these official contacts than in public opinion as expressed in newspapers, pamphlets, and popular assemblies. The leading Radicals in particular had by no means regarded it as their duty to hide their sympathies, and in their own words admitted no *neutralité de sentiment*. They had even demanded an alliance with the northern states which, like themselves, were struggling for liberty and unity. The victory of the northern states, they declared, was the judgement of God on the monarchical powers and was of decisive importance for the future of liberty throughout the world. Only a few conservative Federalists supported publicly the cause of the southern states which recalled their own fight for traditional, local, and rural democracy.

At the end of the Civil War the feeling prevalent among the people found expression in a peculiar and very Swiss action, the so-called 'address' movement. It began with Lincoln's assassination, which the friends of the Union proclaimed as the martyrdom of the apostle of liberty. Some 300 addresses of sympathy were spontaneously drawn up by governments, communes, associations, and individuals, and soon numbered over 20,000 signatures. These addresses were collected and handed over to the American legation which forwarded them to the state department as 'the aggregate and congregate voice of all Switzerland, whose hearts, voice and prayers have been with our government in all the long and bloody struggle'. The state department expressed its thanks for this demonstration of solidarity and remarked that the step taken by Switzerland stood in notable contrast to the usual forms of intercourse among the nations. In actual fact the Swiss people here entered into direct spiritual contact with its sister-republic America in a way which had never been done before and which ignored the barriers of neutrality. It was a huge demonstration and its public character was emphasized by the fact that a large number of members of the government had signed the address. The popularity of this action is proved, among other things, by an event in Glarus 'where the whole free community of the people, in one of those solemn ceremonies which are peculiar to it, bared their heads in solemn silence as an expression of their respect and sympathy for the self-liberation of the noble American people'.

In the midst of the excitement among the Swiss people caused by the American civil war, the Polish revolt of 1863 provoked a further spontaneous manifestation of popular sympathy. The feeling for Poland reached such heights at times that Russia made serious objections which were countered by the Federal Council with a statement of the right to the free expression of opinion in Switzerland. An endeavour was made to solve the difficult refugee problem by granting Polish refugees Swiss citizenship, and 600 were naturalized in a single year. In the war between Prussia and Austria (1866), public opinion in Switzerland turned against the aggressor just as it had taken the side of Denmark in the Danish-German War. Since the main theatre of war was far away troops were only sent to the south-east frontier where the Italians faced the Austrians. One of the consequences of the war was the establishment of a Swiss legation in Berlin and the improvement of armaments by the introduction of the small calibre repeating rifle.

The Franco-German War, which concluded the nationalist movement in central Europe, was a much graver menace to Switzerland. The unambiguous repudiation of foreign ideologies made it easier for the Federal Council to carry out its policy of absolute neutrality. General Herzog was sent to secure the north-west frontier, a point of danger; and, at the end of the war, one of Switzerland's chief problems was the internment of the French army of the east under Bourbaki which numbered over 90,000 men. Another was the position of northern Savoy about which no action was taken. With the union of Germany a new and powerful military state had advanced to the Swiss frontier. Two neighbours and related national civilizations had adopted centralizing constitutional forms. If Switzerland was to resist this pressure from outside, an internal strengthening of the confederation was indispensable, and this was carried out by Switzerland in the following years by the revision of the federal constitution.

Development and internal policy of the federal state

The Federal Council. One of the most important constitutional questions was the composition of the Federal Council. Organized party government had not yet made its appearance. The seven elected members of the executive all belonged to the Liberal form of radicalism and represented its various shades of opinion; their common adhesion to the nationalist party of progress gave the federal government an unusual unity and vigour in action. In it both the two national religions and the three languages were represented, and any predominance of the large cantons had been avoided by electing capable men from small cantons.

All the federal councillors came from districts and social classes which had been instrumental in carrying out the regeneration. The majority of them had been champions of the revolutionary changes in their home cantons and had for a time acted the part of cantonal dictators, then sat on the commission of the diet against the Sonderbund and subsequently collaborated in the revision of the federal constitution. Thus in addition to their personal energy they brought to their new office political and administrative experience. All were champions of the new ideas and knew what government was. As federal magistrates they laid aside their quarrels and abandoned party politics. That is true even of the impetuous and original Druey, who had at one time been in touch with the Socialists but had been driven to the Centre by the extremists in his own Radical party. Above all, the first President, Furrer, who had only been persuaded to accept his election by a kind of 'moral torture', now came fully into his own as a calm, vigorous, and moderate governor, setting aside his own advantage and sacrificing much of his personal happiness to the welfare of the state.

The choice of the capital still awaited its settlement. There was violent rivalry between Berne and Zürich, and Berne won by a large majority. It was favoured by its geographical situation on the boundaries of German and French Switzerland. The choice may have been partly determined by the recognition of Berne's great historical achievement and in particular by its vigorous advocacy of the revision of the constitution.

Parliament. The centre of gravity of political power, however, was not the executive but the legislature. The Federal Assembly elected the Federal Council which remained dependent upon it and was its right hand. Thus the constitutional life of young Switzerland presented all the characteristics of parliamentary government. An arbitrary distribution of electoral districts secured the majority to the victors of 1847 for a long time to come. That majority stood for Liberal radicalism in politics and economics. Since the defeated Sonderbund cantons counted only a very few members, and they were treated like culprits, the power of the Liberal–Radicals was absolute. At first the parliamentary struggle went on only between the more moderate and the more extreme groups in the Liberal–Radical party. The leadership fell to the large deputation from Zürich, Berne, and Vaud. In spite of personal changes and various cantonal party movements the parliament retained its original character unaltered for some twenty years. The political tendencies which had laid the foundations of the federal state now worked themselves out. It was a definite advantage for the prosperity of the new Switzerland that both home and foreign policy was determined by a unified majority in parliament and the Federal Council. Though its behaviour was somewhat crude and ruthless, it was at all times powerful and active. Historically, it must be credited with having consolidated the federal state at home and abroad.

On the basis of the federal constitution, there soon formed a small group of remarkable men who had all the power in public affairs in their hands. The leader of these 'federal magnates', as their nickname was, was Alfred Escher, probably the most versatile and vigorous man in Switzerland. Descended from a rich and aristocratic Zürich family, the young lawyer and politician had had a meteoric career. At the age of 29 he was already burgomaster of his home canton and completely dominated it. His wide knowledge of public affairs, his immense energy, and his impressive appearance soon won him respect in federal politics. Escher's opening and closing speeches as president of the National Council, his 'speeches from the throne' as they were called, proclaimed, with fine restraint, the dignity of Switzerland to an attentive

Europe. He opposed any participation in the revolutionary struggles of neighbouring countries, but did not abandon his belief in the mission of Switzerland which was, by her mere existence as a citadel of European liberty, to point the way to a better future. Thoroughly versed in all economic questions, he was one of the first to realize the importance of the railway in the development of Switzerland, and became the herald of the new means of transport. He was the most powerful supporter of the principles of *laissez-faire* in economics and politics.

The only man who could hold his own beside the influential Zürich financier was his contemporary, Jacob Stämpfli, a Bernese man of the people. Son of a poor peasant, educated at the new Law School of Berne, upright and unyielding, Stämpfli was branded by his enemies, to whom he showed little mercy, as a Socialist. The people felt that this plain and outspoken man understood their wishes and needs; his sympathy with the common people, combined with great ability and indefatigable energy, made him a popular favourite and ensured him power. He entered the Federal Council at the age of 34; he was president three times in nine years and inspired it with fresh spirit. In the Federal Council he was what Escher was in the National Council. The two men, so widely different in descent and character, were long united in a political friendship and between them controlled the parliamentary life of Switzerland. Behind Escher there stood Zürich and the whole of eastern Switzerland, while the great power of Berne, Aargau, and Solothurn followed in Stämpfli's train. The federal state was evolved under the propitious star of this union. The one held economic, the other political sway. In foreign politics and the railway question, however, their personal contrast became opposition. There were violent clashes which ruined Stämpfli's career; he died a beaten and disappointed man.

Among the few deputies from the former Sonderbund cantons, Philipp Segesser of Lucerne was eminent in political sense and personal culture. He was the born leader of an opposition. His vigilant eye, which no weakness of his opponent escaped, and his sarcastic wit won him the hatred of the majority, and he was often held up as an enemy of his country. But Segesser was sufficiently sure of himself to uphold his convictions against the prevailing tendencies. He was a man of principles—Conservative and old confederate—which he did not abandon after the revolution. As an adherent of the historical school of law, he rejected all unhistorical, untraditional, and artificial constitutional innovations. He turned against liberalism and radicalism because they had not grown organically out of the people and the cantons but were the creation of theory and cosmopolitanism. His ideal was the independent growth of the individual canton, the inviolable independence and separate life of each state of the confederation. He feared from an authoritarian and liberal confederation the destruction of supreme political values; in his view the local life of the cantons could only be secured by a far-reaching federalism. He therefore protested vigorously against the states-rights bias of the federal state, to which he was opposed on principle.

Unification of customs, post, currency, and army. With a view to the unification of the economic life of the confederation, the federal constitution had provided for a number of central institutions which were now established by the legislature. The cumbersome internal customs barriers were abolished and freedom of traffic within the country secured. To save expense the merchants of St. Gallen had at one time dispatched their famous linen to Marseilles, not through the Swiss midlands, but by a 42-hour route via Strassburg. The endless nuisance of continual unloading, reloading, weighing, and yet more customs, involving an enormous waste of time and increased transport costs both for the home and foreign market, now at last came to an end. The establishment of the new unified federal customs tariff provoked a dispute between the advocates of protective tariffs and the free traders. Against the protective tariff there were above all practical reasons, such as the requirements of the factories, which needed cheap raw materials. But a pure free-trade policy was bound to be defeated because the confederation lived on the customs revenues. Finally, an agreement was reached on a moderate tariff system which left the basic freedom of traffic intact. The new customs regulations furthered the economic development of the country and provided the confederation with revenues sufficient to cover the costs of the federal administration. Later, the customs revenues became sufficient to allow the confederation to hand over part of them to the cantons and to develop its welfare policy yet further.

The confederation had also to compensate the cantons for their loss of post-office revenues when the postal system was transferred to the confederation. Up to that time, the cantons had either administered the postal system themselves, leased it to other cantons or private concerns, or even left it to free competition. Thus there were on Swiss territory eighteen postal administrations directed on purely fiscal and commercial grounds. It cost more to send a letter from Geneva to Zürich than from Geneva to Algiers. People had not yet realized that the aim of a state institution should be not profit but the economic prosperity of the country. With the rapid development of new means of transport and the entry of Switzerland into world traffic, the wild confusion of the Swiss postal service could no longer exist. The federal law of 1849 brought a sound organization of postal traffic and introduced a reasonable system of postal rates, while in 1851 the confederation took over the construction and working of the telegraph.

As to currency, a state of chaos prevailed in Switzerland which was most detrimental to the national economy. Certain cantons used their sovereignty in money matters to mint their own coinage, but debased it while retaining the old denominations, devalued their exchanges, and did all they could to exploit this source of revenue by other selfish devices. Mercenary service and foreign trade brought foreign money into Switzerland, so that in time every kind of coinage found a home in the country. Every attempt at reform was thwarted by the sovereignty of the cantons which protected the old easy-going ways. Here, too, the federal constitution created a much-desired unity by handing over the monopoly of the mint to the confederation. This difficult question again provoked a split. Berne, Basle, the whole of French Switzerland and the Ticino were in favour of the introduction of the French franc system, while the east of Switzerland, led by St. Gallen, were in favour of the south German gulden. The French franc and the French monetary standard won the day. The chaos of the coinages vanished. The reform of the coinage was felt at the time to be one of the most beneficial acts of the new confederation, and it led to an affiliation of Swiss industry and banking to France, then the largest capital market in Europe. A further consequence of this reform was the entry of Switzerland into the world coinage system of the Latin coinage union of 1865.

It took more time to carry out the unification of weights and measures aimed at by the confederation. True, the confusion in this field was great. But the old systems did less public harm and were more deeply rooted in tradition. The federal law concerning the new weights and measures still retained the foot and the pound and it was not until 1875 that the pure decimal system was made compulsory.

The unification of the army also made progress, without, however, achieving complete centralization. The main law of military organization of 1850 restricted military service to the age of 20–34, and in some cases 40, prescribed annual drills, inspections, and standardized arms. Almost unlimited powers were conferred on the General. The strength of the regular army was now 77,000 and of the reserve 48,000, so that the federal army numbered in all 125,000 men. The world outside began to recognize the military efficiency of the Swiss militia as a power to be reckoned with in case of war.

The universities. The success of centralization in higher education was very restricted. The federal constitution had conferred on the young state the right to found a university and a school of technology. Radical idealism looked to a federal university which should reconcile religious differences, diminish racial differences between Germans and Latins, and promote the sense of community among Swiss of different races. The same faith was expressed in the assumption that the state might prove an incentive to intellectual life so that a common Swiss sense of freedom and mutual tolerance might be implanted in all classes of the people. A further contributing factor was also the desire of the young federal state to focus the native power of the Swiss mind in a single place and there display it to the world. Nor must the Radical conviction of a Swiss mission in Europe be underrated. Escher called the plan the finest task which Swiss culture had to achieve. His own city of Zürich was to be the seat of the federal university. But the scheme of a federal university met with unsurmountable objections. The French Swiss dreaded Germanization, the Catholics feared for their religion, the Federalists for the local interests of the cantons. Basle, Zürich, and Berne already had universities; Geneva, Lausanne, and Neuchâtel academies. They did not wish their institutions to atrophy by reason of the great federal university. The training of their pastors, judges, and teachers was not a matter of indifference to them since the humanities must always have a general foundation in philosophy, and the approach to them and the manner of thought about them are in part formed by education. The linguistic and cultural minority joined forces with the religious minority in opposition to the majority. They did not want a great light in the centre with darkness on the fringe. In view of these criticisms, the Council of States threw out the bill. It was realized that the attempt to fuse the three national cultures in one was no desirable goal; each should rather develop along its own lines. Spiritual unity was desirable in the political, but not in the cultural field, and the idea of a Swiss university has steadily lost ground since.

While the federal councillors were rejecting the university, they resolved on the foundation of a school of technology. The rapid development of industry required the provision of higher technological training, so that a central institute for technical and scientific studies met a real need. Freedom in teaching was guaranteed to the teaching staff. All three national languages were to be represented in teaching. The first academic year began in Zürich in 1855, and ten years later the building, planned by Gottfried Semper, was finished. The federal school of technology was a visible summary of the technical achievements of Switzerland, and equipped the country for European competition in industry, architecture, engineering, trade, transport, forestry, agriculture, and the sciences.

Railways. While the solution of most economic questions was little noticed by the very politically minded Swiss people and was really taken seriously by the upper class only, the railway question actively interested the common people. In railway building Switzerland had at first been behindhand. What was feared from the new means of transport, in Switzerland as everywhere else, was excessive immigration, general restlessness, and the impoverishment of innkeepers and carriers. Further, it was considered that the railway had not developed sufficiently from the technical point of view to cope with a mountainous country. For ingrained Federalists the railway was a detested instrument of centralization. The farmers foresaw quite rightly that it would result in a fall of prices; as later development has shown, corn and vine-growing have actually declined under the influence of the increase in world traffic. But the main obstacle was certainly the economic and political dismemberment of the country. It was natural that the industrial north and east should be more interested in the new means of transport than the agricultural west, for industry could not but be anxious for raw materials to enter the country as quickly and cheaply as possible, so that the sale of its products might be accelerated. Zürich and Basle, as the biggest centres of Swiss industry, stood opposed with railway schemes of their own. The only result of the confusion in railway policy was that, in the midst of the preparations for the civil war of 1847, it was possible to open the first Swiss railway from Zürich to Baden.

The railway question was soon the subject of debate in the Federal Assembly. In 1850 the councillors enacted an expropriation law which gave the Bund the right to dispose of land freely in the interests of a national railway system. The Federal Council appointed two English engineers as experts with instructions to prepare a report on the laying out of railway lines in Switzerland. These experts, in their report, emphatically advocated the sacrifice of local to general interests. As main lines they recommended the so-called railway cross, a line running between the lakes of Geneva and Constance through the Swiss midlands, with a second line from Basle to Lucerne via Olten which should advance as far as possible on the Gotthard route. They considered an Alpine railway as impracticable on technical and financial grounds, and, in the light of the experiences of France and Belgium, they advised against a purely private concern.

This raised the vital question of private enterprise or state control. The Federal Council drafted a bill which was based on the English scheme as far as the technical side went, but for the rest urgently recommended state construction by the Bund and the cantons. In that way the confederation would remain master in its own house. The majority of the commission of the National Council, under Stämpfli, were still more determined in its support of the state. In their view, means of transport in free, democratic countries such as Switzerland, were there to serve the common welfare; they should not be left to the greed of speculators but should be made a national matter, and hence be placed under the federal legislature. The railway system, the link between all states and cities, should be the monument of living democracy.

In opposition to this view, the minority, through its spokesman Escher, absolutely opposed the state railway; the private companies should not be interfered with; they worked better and more cheaply than the state, and would provide the necessary capital more quickly. Further, the whole country rebelled against a national debt of a hundred million francs. In actual fact, the councillors decided by a large majority for private railways and the exclusion of the Bund from participation. In the railway law of 1852, control by the Bund was almost entirely eliminated. The right to grant concessions was given to the financially stronger cantons. The confederation could object only on military grounds, but not on grounds of traffic policy. As the sequel showed, this law resulted in a kind of union of state and private construction, for a number of lines had to be assisted by the canton concerned from the start. The idea of a federal railway system had been frustrated by the combination of various forces—distrust of an omnipotent Bund, misgivings on the question of the national debt, local stubbornness, and a vigorous economic liberalism, which joined forces with federalism.

Private enterprise now flourished extremely, assisted by foreign capital and home politicians. A realization of the future importance of the new means of transport united with the spirit of adventure in the private companies to make them a great power. Railway questions soon cast party life into the shade. Switzerland was a prey to a genuine fever of speculation with all its unpleasant concomitants such as ruthless competition, fraudulent dealings, dispersal of strength. The gleaming rails, contrary to prophecy, were, for the time being, powerless to make brothers of the Swiss. Fierce railway quarrels were fought out in council halls and newspapers, some of them coming to an end only with the bankruptcy of the railway companies. At the beginning of the sixties there was a decline of zeal for railway building.

In this way an extremely dense railway system soon came to cover the Swiss plateau. Up to 1860, 663 miles had been laid by private enterprise. But owing to the lack of a forceful central policy there was no planned system. It grew piecemeal, responding to needs as they arose. Only a few of the main lines showed any profit; no interest at all could be paid on more than half the total share capital. With the merging of a number of smaller lines the railway policy of Switzerland passed into the hands of four big companies.

The jealousy between two leaders of the country broke out into open hostility on the question of how the main line between east and west was to run. It galled Stämpfli's strong feelings as a statesman to see the Bund powerless in face of the high-handed companies. Sad experience with the canton of Berne confirmed him in his conviction that institutions of such importance to the state as railways should not be at the mercy of private enterprise, and he took up the struggle against the second power in the state, the 'Barons of the Bund'. In 1862, as president of the confederation, Stämpfli published an appeal to the public in a pamphlet which set forth a plan for re-purchase of all the railways by the Bund. But all his attempts were thwarted by local and private interests.

After twenty years of railway construction in Switzerland, all the bigger towns were linked up among themselves and with other countries. Increased traffic did much to tone down the differences between the various parts of the country and the various classes of the population. It paved the way for the democratic and centralizing turn Swiss politics were to take later.

The problem of carrying the railway over the Alps was still unsolved. When the Austrian Brenner line and the French Mont Cenis line were opened in 1867 it looked as if Switzerland was to be completely cut off from international transit traffic. It was high time for a settlement of the hotly disputed question of an Alpine railway if world trade was not to by-pass Switzerland entirely. A number of schemes existed of which the Gotthard seemed the most practicable. A rivalry arose among the partisans of the various schemes and noisy disputes filled Switzerland. New Sonderbunds of an economic kind were formed. The prospects of the Gotthard line improved greatly when Escher's north-east line reached it. In this way the Gotthard gained the ablest personality and the financially most powerful man in the country. In 1866 Italy came out on the side of the Gotthard, followed by the north German confederation, then by Baden and Württemberg, and later by the new German empire. The matter had been settled by the economic requirements of the now national states to north and south. The Federal Council at once convened an international conference of the interested states at Berne, which resulted in the Gotthard agreements, that of 1869 with Italy, and that of 1871 with the German empire. The costs were estimated at 185 million francs, Italy being responsible for 45 million, the united Gotthard cantons and Germany for 10 million each. As a kind of compensation, the contributing countries were granted minimum rates and a most-favoured clause for their mutual transit traffic. In accordance with its constitutional position, the Bund took no financial part in the enterprise. It showed the greatest interest in the scheme, however, and offered its services. It concluded the agreements and reserved itself the right of controlling the building and working of the line.

The financing, building, and superintendence were transferred to the Gotthard railway company, Escher being elected first chairman of the management. Louis Favre, of Geneva, was put in charge of the construction of the tunnel. Work had been going on for some years when it was realized that the estimate had been too low. When the public learned of this gross error, the old opposition flared up again at home and abroad. It took the united resolution of all the Gotthard party to weather the storm. Escher saved his work by sacrificing his position. He resigned from the management of the Gotthard line which he had created and to which he had devoted his best powers. The very men who had once wished, in the days of his success, to confer on him the title of Escher von Gotthard, lampooned his fall. It was as if democracy had borne this outstanding personality too long, and must needs take its revenge on the man who set it at nought. By a law of 1878 the Bund became responsible for part of the excess costs. Once the necessary credit was secured, the line was rapidly completed, and in 1882 the Gotthard line was opened with what was then the longest tunnel in the world.

The experiences of the Gotthard affair made an amendment of the old and obstructive railway law a necessity. While the influence of the Bund on the railways had formerly been restricted to the utmost, the new law placed the control of the railways in its hands.

Church and state. Conflict between church and state caused as much agitation as the railway question. The dispute with the church was begun by the encyclical of Pope Pius IX which enumerated all the heretical doctrines of modern times (1864) and foreshadowed the declaration of papal infallibility (1870). This attack on the spirit of the times was an offence to the Radical trust in modern civilization; they wished to adapt Christianity to the civilization of the time and were prepared to follow the teachings of Christianity only in so far as they promoted their belief in progress. In their faith in the omnipotence of conscious knowledge, the Radicals had lost their direct relationship to the unseen world. What they cared about was the maintenance of the world they knew, and so their Christianity took on that optimistic and utilitarian bias which is diametrically opposed to the original Christian doctrine. Further, the Radicals acknowledged only one supreme legislative power in the state, namely, the secular power, and were prepared to enforce ruthlessly the supremacy of the state over the church.

When the bishop of Basle gave orders for the infallibility of the pope to be proclaimed in his· diocese, a powerful ecclesiastical opposition set in. Under the influence of similar events in Germany it led to the foundation of Old Catholic communities which did not acknowledge the new dogma and which claimed to return to the old one and indivisible church. They also carried out a number of reforms including preaching in the vernacular, the abolition of compulsory auricular confession, of fasting, of the worship of the saints, and of compulsory celibacy for priests.

Faced with the decision as to what attitude it should adopt towards these trends in church affairs, the state promised the Old Catholics protection. They seemed to stand for a nationalization of catholicism in constitution and culture and it suited the state very well to weaken the dependence of the Catholic clergy on Rome and transfer that dependence to itself. After the proclamation of the dogma of infallibility, the cantons of the diocese of Basle informed Bishop Lachat that they would not recognize the validity of the resolution of the Vatican Council and forbade further proclamations. Since Lachat ignored this prohibition he was removed from office while the property of the diocese was secularized.

In the canton of Berne the conflict was particularly dramatic. The state carried on the struggle against the church with the prejudice which regards ultramontanism as an enemy of the Gospel and of national independence. Yet it was just in Berne that the state was made to realize the limitations of its power. In 1873 the government called on the entire clergy to break off all ecclesiastical intercourse with Bishop Lachat. But the clergy put its ecclesiastical duty before its political duty. Ninety-two priests from the Jura protested against the deposition of Lachat and declared that they would continue to promulgate the communications of their rightful bishop. The government sentenced them to fines and imprisonment, and in cases of continued resistance threatened them with expulsion from the country. By a special enactment Berne subjected the clergy to state approval, popular election, and, on the Prussian model, to a state examination. This violent law, however, did not do the state much good, for the Catholic populace stood by its bishop and its reprimanded priests even when the government sent troops to the disturbed districts.

Meanwhile the dispute between church and state had broken out in full force in Geneva. When Pope Pius IX appointed Mermillod to be priest-in-charge of the city, both the Genevese and the federal authorities refused to recognize the papal order and expelled him from the territory of the confederation. A law of 1873 prohibited all the activities of the religious associations in schools and hospitals, prescribed popular election of the clergy, compelled them to take the oath to the government, and forbade the institution of an independent bishopric of Geneva. In reply to a papal encyclical couched in insulting terms the Federal Council handed the papal agent his passports. That act abolished the standing nunciate which had been founded after the Reformation. During its three centuries of existence, the nuncio had often exercised a determining influence in the ecclesiastical and political life of the confederation. Catholic Switzerland greeted the sudden abolition of the venerable institution with indignation, though that could not change the *fait accompli*.

But the more ruthless the action taken by the state against the Roman Catholic clergy, the more stubborn grew their resistance and the popular support of it. It was yet another proof of an old truth, namely, that the spiritual life cannot be suppressed by state regulation but can only be conquered by superior spiritual weapons. What the secularist movement lacked was true humanity and the power to give life valid aims. Unaware of the imponderabilia of spiritual life, the state attempted to force the church into its logical system. The Radicals, who had originally taken up the struggle on behalf of the unconditional spiritual freedom, did not flinch from the grossest spiritual authoritarianism. The result was that instead of founding a strong national church it paved the way for anti-clericalism. Its permanent legacy was the so-called 'Kulturkampf' articles in the revised constitution of 1874. It was a misfortune for Switzerland that the conflict reopened the half-healed religious wound and thus prevented the quiet fusion of opposing factions, the slow internal growth of both sides into a Swiss nation.

Towards the end of the seventies feeling became less intense.

The state realized the inadequacy of its methods and the change of personalities facilitated an agreement between the rival camps. In 1907 Geneva resolved on the separation of church and state, thus paving the way to a peaceful relationship between the state and church authorities which was a boon to the whole community. In 1921 Berne rejoined the bishopric of Basle. It was high time for church and state to stop wasting their powers in the fruitless struggle, for social questions claimed their energies more worthily and urgently.

In the end, the necessary foundations for a practical agreement were found, the state abandoning its claim to absolute sovereignty, while the church ceased to enforce all the requirements of the Syllabus. To the credit of the state there stood the preservation of the liberty of individual conscience. As to the church, which had learned much in the struggle, its firmness prevented the creation of a harsh and one-sided ecclesiastical law.

The democratic movement. Since the Liberal movement of the thirties had established representative democracy throughout Switzerland, the ultimate power lay with the Great Council. This body elected the executive and kept the civil servants in a state of permanent dependence. The rights of the people were restricted to voting on the constitution, and the election of representatives to the legislature. The people were not consulted in questions of legislation or other matters. Thus from 1830 the parliamentary system prevailed in the cantons and the confederation till it was superseded in the sixties in the cantons by pure popular sovereignty. Here, too, the confederation followed the example of the cantons.

In general the wealthier classes in the rural districts and the upper middle classes in the towns were the ruling classes. Protected by the freedom of trade and industry, they strengthened their positions as leaders of commerce and industry and promoted the growth of capitalism and individualism. It was these classes which formed the shareholders into great limited companies for the railways and on the stock exchange. Members of the same classes sat in the cantonal and great councils. In this way economic and political liberalism entered on a close alliance. Administration and legislation came increasingly under the influence of these leaders of the national economy. Policy was in the hands of the few, and only a fifth of the electorate continued to vote.

Among the masses of the non-privileged there arose a fierce opposition to the old rulers of the moneyed aristocracy. The promoters of this popular movement formed a left-wing party which took the name of Democratic. It was composed of humble people, industrial workers, and inferior officials, and was joined by some self-styled intellectuals. Here new classes rose, a new political will was formed which strove to get the power of state into its hands with the help of adult suffrage, which had by now been introduced throughout the country.

The means by which pure democracy could become a reality were discovered in the native Swiss institutions of the referendum and the popular initiative. They were the successors of ancient Swiss institutions. For centuries past, full citizens in the *Landsgemeinde* cantons could take a direct part in legislation by deciding on legislative proposals and resolutions in the public vote in the Ring or by making such proposals themselves. The federal constitution had imposed on the cantons an obligatory referendum for constitutional questions. The Democratic movement now introduced the compulsory legislative referendum into the separate cantonal constitutions too, that is to say, the right of the people to give the final decision on the legislative proposals of the legislature. In this way, the once omnipotent great councils dwindled into mere preparatory chambers, representative democracy became pure democracy, and the people became the real legislator.

Another popular right of the time was the initiative, that is, the right of the people to propose laws or amendments of the constitution. While the referendum only entitled the people to express their opinion on a law already enacted, the initiative conferred on it the power of making new laws. While the main point of the referendum is in rejection, the initiative calls on the people to co-operate in the business of state, to do constructive work on constitutional and legislative matters. This institution is based on the belief that the people has as much common sense as the legislature. Thus it became possible for the people to take policy into its own hands over the heads of the legislative bodies and thus dethrone parliament.

In addition to this new legislation by the people the Democrats were aiming at the popular election of the cantonal councils, in order to liberate them from dependence on the legislature and to bring them directly under the popular will. The demand for the popular election of the cantonal governments betrayed the grave distrust of the old official apparatus and of a bureaucracy which was out of reach of the popular will, and the desire for a shortening of the term of office arose from the same dislike of the power of officials who were felt to be harnessed to politico-economic powers.

In Zürich the constitutional conflict became extremely important, for the victory of the Democrats in the chief Liberal canton affected the whole of Switzerland. In addition to the extension of the people's rights, the Zürich Democrats demanded a juster distribution of public costs by a more stringent sliding-scale in taxation, the abolition of school fees and the promotion of primary education, free military equipment, the payment of salaries to councillors, greater freedom of the press, and other things besides. That meant a crushing defeat of the earlier Liberal parliamentarism. Alfred Escher's outstanding position in the canton collapsed. In the same year Berne, Lucerne, and Solothurn also revised their constitutional laws on democratic lines. Gradually the new people's rights—in various forms and in varying degrees —were adopted by all the cantons, the last to do so being Fribourg in 1921.

With these two instruments of the referendum and the initiative, and in certain cantons with the discharge of councillors by the people, the rule of parliament was superseded by direct democracy. The referendum had at first been feared as a revolutionary institution. But experience was to show that it exercised a moderating influence, especially on radical legislatures. As a necessary concomitant to the referendum, the initiative enables the people to dispense with the leadership of the councils and itself to direct the legislature. It is, and remains, a condition, however, that an initiative has the majority of the people behind it, for that is the only sanction of popular legislation. Any citizen who can gain the majority is constitutionally enabled to enforce any measure he will. Thus with the introduction of democratic institutions the right to revolution, which had so often been used in Switzerland in the nineteenth century, became void. People soon became familiar with the new rights; in the course of time these came to be a means of political education of the people, and by abolishing purely party government they helped a great deal to stabilize public life.

XI

THE REVISED FEDERAL CONSTITUTION

The birth of the new federal constitution. Internal peace, economic prosperity, and success in foreign affairs made the federal constitution seem perfect and as if divinely inspired. The impulse to change came from outside. France offered a free-trade commercial treaty which looked promising for Swiss industry, on condition that the French Jews, like all other French citizens, should enjoy the right of free settlement and the free practice of a trade. This was granted by the federal authorities. But the federal constitution did not extend freedom of settlement to the Jews—for commercial, not religious, reasons—so that the Swiss Jews were now less favoured than their foreign co-religionists. In order to do away with an inequality which had no justification, the Federal Council, with the legislative, proceeded to a revision of the constitution, taking the opportunity of revising other articles at the same time. There were no revolutionary provisions among them; it was rather a question of removing a few blemishes from the constitution. But the people could not be moved to take an interest in such questions. Thus in 1866 the only article to be adopted was that relating to the Jews, and Switzerland was the last country in central and western Europe to place the Jews on an equal footing with the rest of the population.

It lay in the nature of Swiss public life, however, that new political ideas about the increased co-operation of the people in government should spread from the cantons to the confederation. The demand for greater centralization, put forward unsuccessfully by the Radicals in 1848, continued to make itself heard. In many fields of public life this need for centralization was more than ever apparent. The powers constitutionally conferred on the state were inadequate and the political movement to increase them was gathering strength. This movement now aimed at expanding and strengthening the power of the state even at the expense of individual freedom.

The constitutional movement was set going by historical events in the outer world, including the formation of great national states in the immediate vicinity of Switzerland, the Franco-German War, and the conflicts between church and state. It appeared necessary, if greater resistance were to be offered to the centripetal tendencies of the great national cultures and the pressure from the neighbouring great military powers, that the intellectual and material forces in the country should be more closely united. The shift in the magnetic field of Europe led to a deterioration of the political and strategic situation of Switzerland. In addition, the fluctuations of imperialist world politics bred unrest and increased the feeling of insecurity which seldom left the confederation during the nineteenth century.

Switzerland learned a lesson from Prussia's victory over Austria and France. In order to adapt their own armaments as far as possible to those of other countries, the federal authorities submitted a draft revision of the constitution which completely unified the military system. The civil law was to be common to the whole confederation and criminal law and procedure were placed under federal control. The Radicals, supported by the Socialists, strongly advocated the centralization of education, and demanded that elementary schools should be compulsory, free, and secular. In the revision programme of the Radicals, the confederation was to have authority in many other fields and, although popular participation in federal legislation would limit the authority of the Bund, its powers would still be far reaching.

Thus came about the first violent clash between Centralists and Federalists since the creation of the federal state. The political minority of the Catholic Conservatives was joined by the linguistic minority of the Radical–Democratic French cantons which had been roused by the dread of Germanization. They were not ready to sacrifice their cantonal autonomy for any consideration whatever. This caused a significant change in the party structure of the confederation. Up to that time the Swiss had joined and parted forces among themselves without any racial considerations being involved; the idea of nationality now appeared as the new rallying cry and its attractiveness steadily increased. A rift became gradually visible, running right through the country, splitting it into two halves with different racial bases and different cultural achievements.

The two opposing tendencies were incorporated in two outstanding statesmen. As a Vaudois, Louis Ruchonnet, later federal

THE LINGUISTIC DIVISIONS OF MODERN SWITZERLAND

German
French
Italian
Romansch

Schaffhausen

St. Gallen
Herisau
Appenzell
Frauenfeld
Winterthur
Zürich
Glarus
Schwyz
Altdorf
Zug
Bellinzona
Lugano

Basel
Liestal
Aarau
Olten
Solothurn
Biel
Lucerne
Sarnen
Stans
Thun
Interlaken
Sion

Porrentruy
Fribourg
Montreux
la Chaux de Fonds
Neuchâtel
Lausanne
Geneva

St. Moritz
Chur

councillor, defended the sovereignty of the cantons with shrewd-
ness yet with comprehension for the needs of the country as a
whole. His aim was to have the indispensable federal regulations
carried out as far as possible by local powers, so that limits might
be set to the growth of the detested bureaucratic state; his skilful
compromises were not a proof of weakness but of the instincts of
a statesman. This plain man of the people stood uncompromis-
ingly by his principles, never wavering in his support of the
popular referendum.

Federal Councillor Emil Weltli, on the other hand, opposed the
referendum. A representative of German Swiss liberalism, he
disliked popular appeals. Relying on intellect alone, he set to work
heroically on the whole complex of revision questions, and determined to enforce his will even against the wish of the people. A
commanding personality, who had never ceased to enrich his mind
with the study of the classics, he was an impressive speaker who
combined prudence with the impulsiveness of genius. It was
genuine concern for the future of his country which moved him
to stand for the unification of the army and the railways. His followers entered the electoral struggle with the battle-cry 'One law,
one army', while their French Swiss opponents countered with
their pregnant *Ne centralisons pas, unifions*. His draft constitution was rejected by a narrow majority.

The result of the vote put fresh heart into the partisans of revision. The elections to the National Council gave a large majority
to the revisionists, for although the people had rejected its representatives' work, it nevertheless returned them to Berne. 'Revision
is dead, long live revision', the deputies proclaimed, and immediately elaborated a second draft. In order to spare the feelings of
the French Swiss, the centralistic provisions were considerably
modified. What was desirable was replaced by what was attainable;
the army to be composed of cantonal contingents with some of the
officers appointed by the cantonal authorities; the provision of
uniform and equipment was to be undertaken by the cantons; the
unification of law was to be confined to a code of obligations, including trade and exchange law; primary education was to be free
and secular; the initiative was to be abolished but the optional
referendum retained; the Federal Court was to be established as
a permanent institution.

The dispute between church and state after 1870 helped the

cause of the revisionists, and the so-called *Kulturkampf* articles were inserted into the new revision draft. Their object was to protect the state against ultramontane aggression, to extend the expulsion of the Jesuits to other orders, and to prohibit the building of new and the repair of old religious houses. In 1874 the people adopted the new constitution by 340,000 votes to 198,000 and by $14\frac{1}{2}$ to $7\frac{1}{2}$ cantons, and it has remained the foundation of the Swiss state, although a number of modifications have been found necessary. It was necessary to secure a constitution of enduring vitality adaptable to new forces and capable of organic development.

Results of the revised federal constitution. The adoption of the revised federal constitution was followed by a period of active legislation, for the new principles had now to be given statutory form. The initiative in this came from the Federal Council, the chambers and the parties alike.

The new organization of the army, which was soon given the status of law, gave the army a more uniform structure and hence made possible a closer collaboration between the various armed forces of the confederation. Further, the Federal Council centralized education and prolonged the period of training for recruits. This rapid development of the army caused a sharp rise in the budget, as in other European countries, from $3\frac{1}{2}$ million francs in 1874 to 13 million in 1875. In order to cover the deficit of 3 million in the federal accounts, Switzerland followed the example of other countries by issuing loans. While in 1860 the individual citizen paid only 1·69 francs in taxation, this figure had been multiplied sevenfold by 1880, with corresponding discontent among the people.

The Federal Council provided for compulsory free education under state supervision and with religious freedom, but no adequate system of federal inspection was possible. The schools themselves came entirely within the competence of the cantons. When the federal authorities decided to make an order for the execution of the education articles drafted by a member of the board of education, the cantons protested stubbornly against any such regimentation from above. With their effective war-cry 'No school bailiffs', they defeated the federal bill in the popular vote of 1882. Thereupon the confederation confined itself to issuing general instructions for the execution of the education articles.

The development of education spread in breadth; it came to cover technical training in trade, industry, agriculture, commerce, and domestic economy. Girls were included and schools were found in the most remote mountain villages. The people cheerfully approved the steadily growing expenditure for primary education, believing this to be the most effective way of promoting general progress. In 1871 the expenditure for primary schools amounted to 8·7 million francs, in 1894 18·9 million. In order to enable the cantons to fulfil their duties more efficiently, the Bund has, since 1903, granted them considerable annual subventions.

This intensive development of public education up to the grammar-school stage, led to a flight from manual work and to the draining of workers from agriculture and industry; a large number turned to 'black coat' occupations. The result was an extensive social levelling. The rise in average education met the needs of democracy. At the same time the Swiss were more adequately equipped for the international competition then setting in.

By the creation of the permanent Federal Court, the political federal authorities were excluded from constitutional conflicts between the individual citizen and the cantons, and the Federal Court was not given power to decide whether a law is constitutional, as is the case with the Supreme Federal Court in the United States. The Federal Court, however, could take action against cantonal laws. Since 1874 the Federal Court has also been empowered to regulate the laws applying to trade and traffic on a uniform basis. Thus in 1881, the Swiss code of obligations was declared to be in force; it standardized the law of trade and exchange, a step which immensely facilitated business transactions within the confederation.

The federal law on the granting of Swiss citizenship ignored cantonal sovereignty. It laid down that the applicant should have been for two years regularly domiciled in Switzerland and made the grant dependent on the Federal Council. Swiss citizenship necessarily included citizenship of canton and commune and freedom of settlement.

The working classes had played a great part in the democratic movement of the seventies, and they relied on state support against the demands of industry. The revised federal constitution therefore contained provisions for security and welfare in factory work. It was only to be expected that the present-day protection of the worker should take its rise in those districts where the industrial situation involved problems of this kind. In factory inspection, Glarus, with its highly developed cotton-printing industry, led the way, going even farther than Great Britain. As far back as 1848, it enacted a law which introduced the shift-system for continuous factory work and restricted men's work to thirteen day and eleven night hours. Glarus then endeavoured to bring about an intercantonal agreement on the work in spinning factories, but did not succeed. Glarus was the first European state to give the twelve-hour day for factory work the status of law. A number of welfare enterprises on a humanitarian basis bore testimony to the anxiety for the alleviation of the evils brought about by industry. Even in the fifties, institutions such as soup-kitchens, factory savings-groups, building societies for workers' houses at a low price or rent, were founded for the benefit of craftsmen and labourers by social associations and workers' unions.

The democratic movement having worked for the protection of the workers in individual cantons, next sought to carry out its schemes on a uniform basis throughout Switzerland with the help of the Bund. The federal factory law of 1877 enforced the eleven-hour day, which was unusual at that time, restricted night work to a minimum, and made the free Sunday the rule. Children under 14 were not admitted to factory work, and night work by young workers was only allowed as an exception. Further provisions dealt with the protection of women and the building and working of factories. In execution of the law a federal inspectorate of factories was established; its application has caused no appreciable loss to Swiss industry.

Troubles in the Ticino. The political storms which had gradually subsided in the other cantons were still raging unchecked in the Ticino. Even after the Conservatives had obtained a majority in the Great Council election of 1875, the Radicals did not abandon their claim to power. It was a misfortune for the canton that the two parties were practically of equal strength. Further, the religious conflict rendered existing differences more acute. Complaints of breaches of the constitution, dishonest electoral practices, and other arbitrary actions by the canton accumulated at Berne, but these complaints were not taken too seriously, so that the crisis continued. Demonstrations and counter-demonstrations led to riots and bloodshed, and a federal commissioner had to be sent to restore order and prevent the outbreak of civil war.

The democratic innovations which had been introduced, however, did not satisfy the Radicals. Like the Carbonari in their day, they began to undermine the government. In 1889, Ticinese living abroad streamed home to the elections in loyalty to their homeland. The parties even chartered ships on which hundreds of Ticinese were brought back to Europe from America. Although the elections resulted in a draw, the Conservatives, by the use of the majority system, were able to secure two thirds of the seats in the Great Council. A Radical initiative for the abolition of such abuses was dealt with very casually by the Great Council. Then the Radicals took the law into their own hands, and in 1890 there were risings in Bellinzona and Lugano. The rebels seized the public buildings, imprisoned the Municipal Council, and set up a provisional government.

The Federal Council at once resolved on military intervention, and sent a commissioner with two battalions into the insurgent district. Through the intermediary of the federal authorities, a joint government was formed. The introduction of proportional representation did a great deal to soothe political passion in the canton. It secured to the parties a representation corresponding to their strength and eliminated the need for the abuses which had been practised up to that time. In 1892 the people of the Ticino adopted a constitution which extended the people's rights, and the Radicals again came into power.

Conflict with Bismarck. The period of internal disturbances and external shocks was followed by one of political calm. It was as if the country was seeking a respite from past troubles in a great effort for economic recovery. No part was taken in the imperial or colonial policies of the great powers. Switzerland affected to believe that 'Power is in itself evil' and the Swiss, neutral citizens of a small state, applied their best powers to its internal development. Endeavours were made to put cosmopolitan ideals into practice; a number of international organizations set up their headquarters in the country. Diplomatic representation abroad was established, but unwillingly and on a meagre scale. It was during this period of internal calm that international law assiduously sought a formula for the theory of neutrality. The average Swiss began to regard his neutrality as a protective bulwark behind which he could go about his lawful occasions unmolested.

Since internal peace had been restored to the confederation, its neighbours had ceased to regard it as a focus of infection and a carrier of the germs of social revolution. The general settlement and the economic rise of Switzerland created a mood of confidence, and caused the rest of the world to overlook the exceptional constitutional situation of the small republic. Nobody thought of abolishing it; it merely aroused curiosity and interest. Switzerland still remained a favourite asylum for political refugees, yet her attitude towards them was radically changed. While in earlier times the democratic refugees had been welcomed by the federal authorities as persecuted brothers in the faith, the anarchists and communists were now looked upon as mere enemies of their own country, with whom the confederation had as little in common as their own governments. A large number of Russian nihilists, inspired by a fanatical faith in the miraculous powers of science, were working at Swiss universities, especially Zürich and Berne. The loose life and continuous plotting of these semi-Asiatic intellectual immigrants gave rise to repeated complaints. The refugees from the eastern states owed their toleration to the right of asylum to which Switzerland clung as implicit in her sovereignty, allowing no foreign power to curtail it. After the defeat of the Commune in Paris, a large number of refugees from France sought shelter in Switzerland, causing disputes with the Thiers government, but relations with the French republic remained cordial. The publication of anarchist newspapers in Switzerland was carefully watched.

The sudden quarrel with Bismarck showed that the external security of Switzerland was an illusion. At first, official relations with the German empire were entirely correct and friendly. Though Swiss public opinion had little affection for the chancellor, more particularly since the religious conflict and the issue of the edicts against the Social Democrats, official relations remained for the time unaffected. Far-sighted minds in Switzerland certainly feared trouble from the concentration of power in the north, which might seriously restrict Swiss neutrality. Bismarck was particularly irritated because the German Socialists who had sought refuge in Switzerland from his edicts were stirring up agitation against his government there. But when a Prussian inspector of police, who was attempting to secure a spy on Swiss territory, was arrested by one of the cantonal governments and expelled from the country by the Federal Council, Bismarck tried to make use of the incident to strike a blow at the refugee German Socialists. He demanded from Switzerland the immediate withdrawal of the order of expulsion with an apology, failing which he would cease to respect Swiss neutrality. Germany, he said, would be obliged to set up a police force of her own in Switzerland, the Swiss police being inadequate. The Federal Council, led by Numa Droz, firmly repudiated this interpretation of Swiss neutrality: as a neutral state, the confederation claimed, like every other sovereign state, the right to police its own territory itself. Bismarck, it would appear, took war with Switzerland into serious consideration. In the end, he himself called off the conflict, which had been exaggerated into a dispute in international law. All Swiss judgements of Bismarck agreed in their repudiation of the idea of power he stood for. It was a characteristically Swiss attitude, for the very vulnerable neutrality of the little confederation surrounded by great powers can only live if the rule of law is binding on all. The distrust with which Switzerland has at all times regarded any disturber of the balance of power in Europe was instinctively turned against Bismarck.

Importance of neutrality in the Age of Imperialism. As long as the European balance of power remained stable, the small state of Switzerland had every prospect of preserving its independence and neutrality in spite of being surrounded by great powers 'as if by a wall of iron'. By this time, the confederation had become a mere pawn in the policy of the powers, but pawn of great importance, especially in view of its situation in military strategy. Since the Gotthard tunnel had been opened in 1882, the most important route between the north and south of Europe ran through Swiss territory. One of the most important east–west routes also lay in Swiss territory and had often served as a convenient transit road in the past. All this gave the small country a kind of controlling key-position in the central Alpine region and placed it in the centre of international politics. It can therefore be no matter for surprise if the general staffs of the powers repeatedly included Switzerland in their plans. Neutral Switzerland offered all her neighbours welcome cover on their flanks. A violation of her neutrality by an enemy might be a blow on a sensitive spot. The high command of every foreign army had to give serious consideration to the question of whether there was more to be gained by respecting or by violating Swiss neutrality. Ultimately, all these calculations issued in the question of whether Swiss neutrality was to be really trusted, that is, whether Switzerland was willing and strong enough to protect her neutrality against threatened violations.

In the staff conversations of the Triple Alliance, the problem of Swiss neutrality loomed the larger as it became clearer that the allies were aiming at turning the political alliance to military ends. It was in the first place military circles in Italy which conceived the idea of using the Gotthard route to send troops to their northern ally in case of war with France. As soon as Bismarck came to know of these schemes he categorically opposed them. The chancellor, a realist in politics, adopted this attitude, not on legal grounds, but out of pure opportunism. What he had to reckon with were the possible consequences of a breach of international law and the strength of the Swiss army. Similarly, the German Chief of Staff, Field Marshal von Moltke, was prepared to respect Swiss neutrality in a war with France. It is also probable that France, Switzerland's western neighbour, had no designs on Swiss neutrality either.

Suspicions of the reliability of Swiss neutrality were particularly strong in diplomatic and military quarters in Great Britain. Since England had arranged an Entente Cordiale with France, she had been keeping a vigilant watch on the central powers, her probable enemies in case of war. From 1909 to 1911, the British military attaché in Rome, who was also attached to the British legation at Berne, sent home alarming memoranda on the attitude of Switzerland. Ultimately, he actually assumed the truth of a rumour that a secret military agreement had been concluded between Switzerland and the central powers, especially Austria. At first, the Foreign Office showed little confidence in these sensational reports, but later, Sir Edward Grey, the British Foreign Secretary, seemed disposed to believe them, until the Foreign Minister at Berne categorically denied a secret alliance between Switzerland and Austria.

It was, however, not only foreign general staffs, but foreign diplomatic circles also which began to take Swiss neutrality more seriously. Several times in the settlement of international disputes, Swiss arbitrators were called in, since, as citizens of a permanently neutral state, they seemed to offer the best guarantee of impartiality. Thus after the conference of the powers in Algeciras, the organization of the Moroccan police was entrusted to a Swiss. In reply to those who advised against the acceptance of international positions of the kind, the Federal Council gave it clearly to be understood that Switzerland had no mind to abstain entirely from world politics but was ready to do all that lay in her power wherever her services were required.

At the beginning of the twentieth century the neutral territory of Switzerland came to be used more and more as the seat of international offices, for instance, the Postal, Telegraph, and Railway Freight Unions. More and more, too, Switzerland was chosen as the meeting-place of international conferences. The impartial atmosphere of the country seemed to offer the most convenient place for discussion. This provoked some banter about the diplomatic tourist traffic, but there is no doubt that Switzerland's international standing was improved by the fact that she lent her neutral territory for negotiations or for the settlement of European differences, not to speak of the duty incumbent on a neutral state like Switzerland to do everything in its power to 'contribute to the settlement of international crises', as the Federal Council put it. Thus in 1912, the peace negotiations after the Italo-Turkish war about Tripoli took place at Ouchy-Lausanne. In 1913, forty-one members of the German Reichstag met 164 French deputies and twenty-one senators at Berne at a conference of mutual understanding, the result of which conference was the founding of the Interparliamentary committee, which met at Basle just before the war.

It seems a matter of course that Switzerland should also take part in the Peace conferences at the Hague. She signed all the agreements at the first conference in 1899 with the exception of that relating to land warfare since it denied military privileges to a people rising against an enemy invasion. The confederation also adopted the resolutions of the second Hague conference in 1907, at which the position of neutral states was discussed.

It was, however, the steady growth of Switzerland's defensive strength which did most to inspire respect for Swiss neutrality both at home and abroad. In 1907, a law was enacted providing for extensive improvements in the army, which much increased its mobility and striking force. By this reform the strength of the Swiss army was fixed at 281,000 men, with 200,000 auxiliary troops. A large number of observations by superior officers of many countries testify to the increase of respect for the Swiss army. The Federal Council's consistent policy of armed defence of neutrality was crowned in 1912 by a proclamation to the army commanders on the application of neutrality, the first injunction being strictest impartiality. The attitude of neutral Switzerland in the event of war was thereby clearly and resolutely defined.

Social and economic policy

Agriculture and agrarian policy. The development of modern means of transport placed Switzerland in direct dependence on the economy of the world market. Switzerland was no more able than other countries to protect her agriculture from the universal agricultural crisis. As late as the middle of the nineteenth century she was chiefly engaged on the production of cereals and was able to produce enough for her own requirements for 300 days. The development of the means of transport and the active exchange of goods did away with the high prices and the famine which had in earlier times accompanied any local failure of crops. But the same achievements of modern times was responsible for the import of cheap grain from Russia which led to a fall in prices and hence a reduction in the value of home crops. For that reason the Swiss farmer began to abandon the growing of corn, and the area of land under grain began to shrink. As early as 1887, home-produced grain sufficed for less than six months, by the end of the century only for seventy days, and since then, only for the farmers' own use.

On the other hand, the produce from pasture, stock-raising and dairy-farming rose in proportion. The Swiss soil and climate were specially suited to those branches of agriculture. The Swiss farmers carried out this reversion to the more native forms of agriculture, stock-raising, and fodder-growing, with energy and foresight. The number of livestock doubled in the second half of the nineteenth century. While at one time the chief export of live-stock from Switzerland had been horses, it was the export of cattle which now flourished. The animal food industry, the produce of dairy-farming and milk processing now worked for the export market. The greatest development was in the manufacture of cheese. The export of cheese increased forty times in the course of the century, and amounted to 36 per cent of the total value of agricultural exports. New products came into being such as condensed milk and chocolate. Before the First World War the value of these two exports amounted in all to some 100 million francs.

In the course of time agriculture and its export produce began to suffer from the competition from other countries and their customs tariffs. The wine industry was affected by the import of wine from France. At first there was no question of protective tariffs for agricultural produce. The principle of free trade was still held in high esteem by all classes. Instead of protective tariffs, assistance was given to agriculture in the form of subsidies. The confederation gave grants to agricultural training-schools in order to rationalize agriculture and increase its yield by the introduction of modern methods. Cattle-breeding associations, too, were supported by public funds.

But in the long run the agricultural crisis could not be overcome by subsidies alone. To defend the interests of the farmers an increasing number of agricultural associations were founded which united in 1897 to form the Swiss Farmers' Association. This was followed by the establishment of a Swiss Farmers' Secretariat. In 1891 the farmers succeeded for the first time in enforcing protective tariffs for agricultural produce.

Farmers and citizens. The romantic travesty in the literature and art of the eighteenth century of the Swiss countryman and dairyman soon made way for a greater realism. Jeremias Gotthelf's novels of peasant life and Juste Olivier's descriptions of the life of the people in the Vaud had some share in the change. The farmer, that characteristic figure of Switzerland, was again seen as he was; a man bound by tradition and the soil, of few words, reserved and circumspect, tenacious in the pursuit of his aims, clear-sighted and realistic in his grasp of the world about him, harshly averse to any kind of romanticism or mere intellectualism, racy and concrete in speech, intent on the preservation of his heritage.

The upshot of the struggle between townsman and peasant, which had lasted for centuries, was that the Swiss national character bore the imprint of the peasant. In the nineteenth century, he had gradually gained complete political equality and dominated the state by his large voting power. At the same time he had gained economic independence by shaking off the great burden of taxation on persons and property. The farmers' emancipation movement had been supported by the Liberal and Radical parties.

The farmer not only left his mark on Swiss culture as a whole; he actually created Swiss democracy with that peculiarly conservative tinge which probably exists elsewhere only in Britain. This centre of gravity in the farming class has up to now protected the country from revolutionary change. At the beginning of the century, only 6–7 per cent. of the total population lived in the towns. The rise of industry barely affected this proportion at first, for it was mainly carried on in the form of cottage industries, so that the worker was not obliged to abandon his way of living. The large number of small and medium-sized towns long retained their rural atmosphere. But even when masses of workers left the country for the towns, the farmers remained the predominant factor in Swiss politics and culture, even though only a minority of the population was engaged in agriculture.

The numbers of tradesmen and craftsmen in the cities have at all times been recruited from the country-side. Several causes contributed to the move to the towns which at times looked like a flight; an excess of agricultural labour due to the introduction of machinery, the falling-off in cottage industries, the traditional over-population. In characteristic fashion, however, the workers and tradesmen who had left the country to settle in the towns by no means lost touch with their country home. This slow penetration of the town by the country led to the social levelling and the mixed urban and rural population which are so typical of Switzerland. This social process also established a community between town and country. It explains so many characteristics of the Swiss townsman—his bluntness, which at times turns to rudeness, his reasonableness, his dislike of the merely clever, his wholesome antipathy to mere outward polish, smooth forms and hollow phrases, but also his occasional lack of imagination, of intellectual charm, and of the gifts which adorn life.

The urban population which had come from the country brought with them the firm resolve to get on in the world. They worked for their economic and social rise with intense energy and attained political power with the help of democratic popular rights. The old families in the towns which had been deprived of their privileges by the Liberal and Radical revolutions were now overshadowed economically by these sturdy immigrants. The young wealth of industry also undermined the traditional social structure. Even so, the worse aspects of the age of big business took on less ugly forms than in neighbouring countries. It was the lower and middle classes which reduced the essential problems of life to freedom and equality; set the tone in public life, in the schools, in parliament, in the press; dictated taste, and created a new form of Swiss life and Swiss intellectual outlook. The political and economic leaders of the second half of the century were mainly drawn from this class.

Industry. An Englishman who came to Switzerland on an official mission in the 1830s stated in his report that Switzerland possessed the soundest and most efficient industry on the Continent. The difference between the now partly industrialized confederation and its still predominantly agricultural neighbours had already struck earlier foreign observers; for one thing the policy of neutrality had averted war from Swiss territory so that there had never been a total interruption of economic development. Since the policy of neutrality did not extend to trade and industry, Swiss trade suffered no great losses in European wars. Further, mercenary service, pensions, and foreign exports had brought in considerable foreign capital which went to the benefit of home industry or was directly invested in it. The Swiss right of asylum also brought refugees to Switzerland for 200 years, mainly Protestants from France, Savoy, Great Britain, and Holland; they enriched home industry by creating new branches or modernizing existing ones. And, finally, the central situation of the country and the wealth of its watercourses, favoured an unusual development of industry, for most of the Swiss industries required mechanical power. It was for that reason that, up to the introduction of steam engines, practically all the factories were built on medium-sized and small rivers.

From the start the state had left industry a free hand to recruit labour. With its measures of unification of the customs, weights and measures, and the coinage, and with the enactment of the statutory freedom of settlement and occupation, the federal state had provided industry with the elbow-room it had so long desired. It was like a tacit alliance between the state and industry. When Swiss industry was linked up with the railway system it was brought into direct touch with world markets and given immense impetus. It was fortunate for Switzerland that the principle of free trade was widely accepted all over Europe, for the growing industry of the country found foreign markets more easily. The confederation concluded favourable trade agreements with most of the civilized countries in the world. The free trade period saw the hey-day of Switzerland's export industry which lasted till late in the seventies. Then, the tariff reform movement, which made itself felt, involving a progressive increase of customs duties, threatened to restrict the market for Swiss goods to a dangerous extent.

Various factors contributed to operate the shift of the centre of gravity within the various branches of industry. The most important were: the landlocked situation of the country, the poverty of the soil and lack of raw materials, the steady rise in wages, and the amount of available capital. These factors obliged Swiss industry to produce for quality, for in that way it could best hold its own against foreign competition. On the other hand, the fact that industry was founded on quality and export only made it more dependent on the fluctuations of international purchasing power and exposed it to crises which threatened its very existence.

The textile industry has always been the most important branch of Swiss industry as a whole. It has had the longest history and at one time rivalled that of Great Britain. When machinery was introduced into the spinning factories they rapidly developed and a boom set in. They were at a disadvantage as compared with Great Britain because coal and raw materials were dear, since they had to be transported by land. Cotton-weaving also prospered enormously with the introduction of the machine loom, but suffered so much from foreign competition that after the First World War it could no longer meet the demand of the home market, the canton of Glarus being most severely affected.

The one branch of industry which was unaffected by the general decline was embroidery. Indeed, owing in the main to the development of machine embroidery, it was able to increase its exports considerably. There was a great demand for it in North and South America, so that the new industry prospered very rapidly. In 1920 the export figure reached the unprecedented sum of 411 million francs. This rise was followed by a disastrous fall in the slump which began in the same year. Its cause was partly the saturation of the North American market which had at one time taken up half of the Swiss embroidery exports. What gave the embroidery industry its peculiar character from the point of view of production technique was the large employment of home workers, who numbered at least half of all those employed. That had some important results; it not only prevented the complete detachment of the industrial worker from the soil, but also checked congestion in industrial towns and hence the formation of an urban proletariat.

In keen competition with the rest of the world, the silk industry also developed great energy, which may be illustrated by the export figures. England headed the list of customers. At the beginning of the twentieth century Switzerland was the second most important silk-exporting country. While the chief centre of silk-weaving was at Zürich, silk ribbons were concentrated at Basle. In spite of early mechanization it was possible to employ home workers. Silk ribbons are of course greatly affected by fashion, yet exports rose until after the First World War. Then the silk-ribbon industry experienced its great collapse.

In connexion with the dyeing of ribbons at Basle, the dyeing and chemical industries grew up there. Although the youngest child of Swiss industry, it rapidly rose to world importance and took its place among the leading Swiss export industries. In 1920 it was already exporting to the value of 309 million francs. Even in the post-war periods of the two world wars this branch of Swiss industry, at any rate, remained vigorous. In close touch with the medical profession and the universities, enterprise and chemical science have created concerns which account for one-eighth of the total production of the world and provide thousands of Swiss with an excellent livelihood.

The watch and clock-making industry, on the other hand, was, with embroidery, most hardly hit by the crisis which followed the First World War, and large districts fell victim to unemployment. Clock-making had long been carried on as a home industry, and created the characteristically Swiss combination of handicraft and agriculture. But the keen competition from abroad finally compelled the watch-makers to abandon their beloved tradition and to introduce factory work. In this way, the cheap mass-produced but well-made 'utility' watch could be put on the market. Geneva, the oldest centre of clock-making in Switzerland, specialized rather in the making of instruments of precision and luxury watches decorated by goldsmiths. The industry works almost entirely for export. It serves the whole world; until a short time ago 87 per cent. of the total world production came from Switzerland.

As a result of the mechanization of the textile industry the machine industry arose at the beginning of the nineteenth century. At first Switzerland had done no more than improve the spinning machines imported from England, but she soon set about manufacturing them herself with growing success. The machine industry became independent; it manufactured not only mechanical looms and embroidery and knitting machines, but later proceeded to power plant. Even in the eighties, the works at Winterthur and Oerlikon were doing outstanding work in the construction of locomotives. Finally, water-power was applied to the production of electricity. Once high tension currents had been conveyed over long distances, a big electro-technical industry grew up. The huge development of the machine industry may be seen very clearly in the rapid rise of the numbers employed; from 3,300 about the middle of the century, these rose to 61,000 in 1924. Unlike the products of the watch-making industry, a quarter of the total production remained in the country. The export list was headed by power plants and locomotives; then came textile and grinding machinery, the leading purchasers being Italy, Great Britain, and Germany.

Swiss economic development has thus been one-sided. Imports of coal and foodstuffs meant a deficit in the Swiss balance of trade which amounted to 550 million francs in the first quarter of the twentieth century, balanced by the profits of the tourist traffic and by interest on foreign investments.

Private capital and the life of the community. The great achievements of Swiss industry, which created an admittedly high standard of living in a small, landlocked country poor in raw materials, arose mainly from private initiative. The embodiment of the modern economic process was the factory owner, the adventurous and creative industrialist who, given the freedom of movement inherent in the capitalistic order, provided thousands of human beings with a livelihood at a time when the country was threatened with unemployment on account of the prohibition of foreign military service. Owing to the rapid development of industry, the population of Switzerland doubled within a century, from 2 million in 1850 to 4 million in 1930. The general standard of living also rose considerably.

The leaders of industry came for the most part from the Protestant parts of the country, and industry spread much more vigorously in the Protestant districts, the Catholic cantons of

central Switzerland retaining their small holdings and handi-
crafts. This is fresh evidence of the influence of religious forces
on economic development. Once more, the Calvinist conception
of duty proved a powerful incentive to energy. At the same time,
the Calvinistic doctrine provided an ethical sanction for capitalism
and compelled the individual to serve the community. Any man
working for selfish and unconscientious aims against the interests
of the common welfare was transgressing a commandment of God
—a fact that did not prevent the occasional ruthless exploitation
of the unpropertied classes. In Switzerland, large-scale industry
began to create welfare institutions at a very early date. These took
their rise, in many cases, in a selfish calculation on the part of the
capitalists as well as to the sense of social responsibility felt by the
industrialists towards the workers.

Socialism. With the rise of capitalism, the distress of the industrial proletariat grew too. The wounds inflicted on the body of the
people by the unrestricted freedom of competition became steadily
more apparent. But since the Radicals did not realize the essential
nature of the shortcomings of the economic system, they could
not combat them effectively. For that reason the workers gradually
lost their faith in the healing and compensatory effects of pure
democracy, and conceived the idea of taking the law into their
own hands. They resolutely abandoned radicalism and aimed at
a thorough reform of the foundations of the whole social and
economic system. Instead of seeking their salvation, as hitherto,
in the bridging of class differences, they took up the notion of the
class war. This development in the direction of a radical socialism was determined by the revolutionary change in economic
and social conditions. In a short time Switzerland was changed
from a mainly agricultural country into a mainly industrial one.
Industrial prosperity not only attracted a large number of foreign
immigrants, it also led to considerable movements of the population within the country, and hence to the destruction of the traditional settled form of life. At the middle of the nineteenth century,
68 per cent. of the population still lived in their home communes:
by its end, only 43 per cent. were doing so. The working classes
produced no characteristically Swiss social doctrine; the socialism
propagated in the country was mainly derived from abroad: the
spirit of the class war first entered the Swiss movement when the
Second International was founded in London in 1864. Only then

did the various workers' associations begin to develop some initiative and a certain unity. The federal authorities were not at all severe in their proceedings against the disciples of communism, and government measures only affected foreigners, some of whom were expelled from the country. Nevertheless, the use of strikes was soon adopted and from 1860 to 1894 there were 520 strikes in Switzerland most of which resulted in a rise of wages. The meagre powers of the central government and the still undeveloped bureaucracy of the Bund made the trade unions more independent, the trade union movement developed rapidly and at the end of the century there were 344 co-operative societies with 117,000 members.

The collapse of the Second International, which followed so soon on its foundation, awakened the need of closer co-operation among the Swiss workers. What was most desired was an organization which should deal with Swiss questions only. In consequence, the Swiss Social Democratic party was founded in Zürich in 1870. The first Swiss national party programme bound the workers to take part in the political development of the country in order to create for the proletariat the situation it wished to achieve. For the present, direct legislation was to be carried out by the people. The programme further demanded an increase of federal centralization, the separation of church and state, and a sliding scale of taxation. This programme represented the first effort to provide the Swiss workers' movement as a whole with a socialist foundation and Swiss leadership, stress being laid on the practical side of the whole question. A new party programme drawn up in 1904 united the various workers' unions on a clarified basis and remained in force till 1917.

Up to this time large sections of the working classes had always regarded socialism with distrust as a foreign product. The Marxist trend towards the centralization and industrialization of the country, and hence, in the last resort, towards the dictator state, encountered natural forces of resistance in Switzerland. The feeling of the workers was still too democratic to admit the split of the people into two hostile classes. Swiss socialism, it is true, recognized the idea of the class war, but clung to democracy, too, and shrank from revolutionary action by the proletariat. The replacement of the prevailing economic system by a Socialist society which should secure the total proceeds of production to the worker seemed to the Swiss Socialists merely justice. Yet there was no absolute declaration of war against the state, no unbridgeable gulf between the Social Democrats and the state. Swiss Social Democracy remained a national movement.

Purchase of the railways by the Bund. The second half of the nineteenth century re-echoed with the battles waged on the question of state or private railway ownership. Private construction having won the day in 1852, it succumbed in its turn to the principle of state ownership fifty years later. This can be explained to a large extent by the fact that the private railways had not stood the test. The companies pursued their own interests without considering the general welfare, and the lack of union had disastrous effects: arbitrary rates, continual changes of locomotives, suspicious financial manœuvring, foreign influence, financial difficulties, ruthless competition among themselves, and hence perpetual disputes. Either the railway companies quarrelled among themselves or got into difficulties between neighbouring communes and cantons, or else the cantons carried on a railway war against each other. The settling of railway disputes was soon the chief business of the Bund; special sessions had even to be called for the purpose. For the most part, however, the Bund could not do much because it lacked the necessary powers. It was for that reason that the right of legislation in railway questions was conferred upon it by the revised federal constitution of 1874. Relying on its own powers, the Bund intervened to settle and regulate matters, but was powerless to eradicate entirely the basic evils of the system.

The chief sufferer in these circumstances was the public. And it was in the public mind that the idea of a state railway gained ground. It had never quite vanished from public discussion. When the concessions came up for renewal in 1883, the councils rejected re-purchase, though only by a small majority. The Federal Council proceeded only to practical experiments in nationalization by partial purchases. In 1891 an agreement for total purchase was arrived at with the most important Swiss railway company, the Central. The referendum, however, was put into action against the agreement and it was rejected by popular vote.

The adherents of the state railway system were so little convinced by the negative result of the vote that only a few years later the Federal Council was able to submit to the people a bill for re-purchase. This bill was violently attacked both at home and abroad. The railway magnates called nationalization an illegal appropriation of other people's property. The voting campaign revealed the conflict between state and private economy, between industry and the peasantry, between state and private finance. The partisans of nationalization expected from it a unification in management, economies, a reduction of rates, higher wages for railwaymen, the extension of the railway system, and finally the amortization of the invested capital within sixty years. The national argument was also used. The slogan: 'The Swiss railways for the Swiss people' proved most effective. Nobody today can blame the opponents of re-purchase if they viewed the optimistic calculations of the Federal Council with some misgivings, and replied with the slogan: 'The Swiss debt for the Swiss people.' The advantages of nationalization were, in fact, much overrated at the time. But who could foretell the coming competition from motor traffic and two world wars?

There was great excitement when the question was put to the popular vote in 1898. The result was 380,000 votes for and 180,000 against. The voting percentage had never before been so high. The outcome had been determined by the Radicals, the Democrats, and the workers. The decisive victory for nationalization came as a general surprise. It was a clear rejection of the liberal principle of inviolable freedom in economic life. When the Bund took over the transport system, a considerable part of the national economy was nationalized and the principle of state ownership had been greatly advanced in Switzerland.

The nationalization of the Gotthard line and the approval of the Gotthard agreement by the Federal Council had serious political consequences. Excitement reached such heights in French Switzerland that an initiative was set on foot for a restriction of the powers of parliament in foreign affairs. All international treaties which were to last over fifteen years were to be submitted to the referendum. The object of this movement was to prevent the conclusion of conventions which might be offensive to national feeling and prejudicial to the national welfare. This new popular right first became effective in 1921 when a treaty with France concerning the free zones in Savoy, which had been recommended by the Federal Council, was rejected by the people.

Changes in party life. The Liberal–Radicals, who had created the new Switzerland, remained the majority party with an absolute majority in a number of cantons and in the confederation for nearly fifty years. Their historical achievements, such as the enforcement of popular rights and the establishment of the federal state, now lay far behind them. It was the Liberal–Democratic party, at all times in favour of centralization, which now took up the cause of nationalization with increasing energy. Though this included various classes of the population it was possible to unite them all with one common party programme. That situation was changed about the turn of the century by the increasing inroads of economics into politics. Up to that time the two great historical parties, Liberal and Conservative, differing only on details, had embraced the whole of the people. They were now forced into an economic policy by the impact of turbulent new forces, and the disintegration of the parties began. The various social classes began to form themselves into economic groups. From the left wing of the Radicals and Conservatives the workers moved into Social Democracy, where they fought for the socialization of all means of production. With this increase in membership the Social–Democratic party, insignificant up to that time, gained in strength and its numbers increased, particularly during the two world wars.

The agricultural classes had already united in the Farmers' Union. Their organization was firm, their secretariat energetic and progressive. Since they found too little support from the old historical parties during the agricultural crisis, they also united to form a political party. This young Agrarian party at once gained a decisive influence on the political life of Switzerland. Their power may be seen in the tariff reform provisions in favour of agriculture. Although that entailed a rise in food prices, the consumers, consisting of members of all other parties—that is, the great majority of the population of Switzerland—did not unite to protect their interests.

The Liberal party had no longer an absolute majority. Coalitions were formed in the parliaments of the cantons and confederation, and this caused some unsteadiness in Swiss political life, till then so uniform. On the other hand, these changes poured fresh blood into it.

The system of proportional representation introduced after 1891 in a large number of cantons and in 1918 into the confederation, did much to break up the uniformity of the federal government. Every minority now had a number of representatives in parliament exactly corresponding to its membership, and, united with other minorities, was able to make its voice heard. At the time when the growing influence of economic factors was splitting up the parties, and the proportional system favoured further secessions, parties based on religion were formed. Government by a single party became impossible. The civil service, local and national, was recruited from all parties, and this made for stability. The tendency to the formation of new groupings, such as the extreme Young Conservatives, balanced by the Communists, has continued, but at the same time there are many who adhere to no party and whose votes often decide an election.

Life and letters. Liberals, Radicals, and Socialists alike were affected by the prevailing belief in progress which had taken on extremely materialistic forms. Hard work, increased production, and money-making became the ideal. The development of technology, the rationalization of methods, the increase of production, were to benefit the masses. It was a feature of the general trend towards democracy that there was a desire to increase the common welfare in order to raise the standard of living of large classes of the population. Material interests came to dominate the thoughts and actions of men more and more. Those branches of study which could be immediately pressed into the service of technology and industry were specially cultivated. Popularized views of science spread among the people and created a large class of half-educated citizens. The acquisition of unco-ordinated learning took the place of education on a sound moral basis. The general levelling affected intellectual life and threatened to depress personal abilities into a uniform average. In a general way, it looked as if democracy had become merely static and was no longer capable of enriching political life.

The periods following the First and Second World Wars showed that this was not the whole story, that the people was not degenerate, but was full of life and strength and ready to enter vigorously into the democratic life of the state. The great development of literature, too, showed that in the clamour of political and economic life, Swiss art and literature had not relapsed into lethargy. The representatives of Swiss intellectual life were all, at heart, formed by their relationship to the Swiss state. All Swiss literature springs from the peculiar character of the Swiss people and state. This is above all true of the Bernese pastor Jeremias Gotthelf, the great novelist of Bernese peasant life. His work was done in the first half of the nineteenth century when there was a shift of historical forces and the Swiss state was exposed to repeated political, social, and religious crises. In that struggle, Gotthelf was the unwavering champion of tradition and of the organic life of home. Originally a leader of the new liberal ideals, he became increasingly estranged from Radical policy and finally turned against it with great violence. His most splendid battle with the Radicals finds its reflection in *Zeitgeist und Bernergeist*. He realized that radicalism was not merely aiming at political and social change, but that the fundamental principles of humanity were at stake. Since the Radicals preached that the goal of human activity, happiness, was attainable here on earth, Gotthelf, with prophetic zeal, proclaimed the eternal life from which alone salvation can come. For him freedom meant Christian freedom. Of the Radicals he wrote: 'Their watchword is progress, their battle-cry freedom. . . . Has there ever been freedom in a sect? Is the denial of a higher world, is the life of the flesh . . . progress?' Radical politics, he insisted, pervaded life in every class of society, devastated the sanctuary of the family, and undermined all Christian teaching. 'Wherever we enter a home, we meet this serpent, this pest of Europe.' Since the new Bernese constitution of 1846 derived from this Radical spirit, he branded it as a 'national disaster'.

Gotthelf's first books, such as *Der Bauernspiegel* and *Freuden und Leiden eines Schulmeisters*, were based on the educational and social problems of the day; they were sociological novels. There is a good deal that is tendentious even in his later masterpieces, such as *Uli, der Knecht*, but it has found creative form. The same mastery can be seen in his short stories, in *Elsi, die seltsame Magd*, where he gave a visionary picture of the fall of old Berne, or in *Die schwarze Spinne*, where he turned a popular legend into mythological form. In his later works, such as *Jakobs Wanderungen*, he attacks the Socialist–Communist propaganda carried on in Switzerland by foreigners. Gotthelf's works were not pure peasant novels, for he turned his Emmental peasants into symbols of humanity. For him the transitory is the parable of the eternal, and all men the image of God. There is something Homeric in all his work.

Zürich's writer, Gottfried Keller, was of one mind with Gotthelf in taking a vigorous part in the political struggles of his time. Keller spoke with contempt of the 'great army of the indifferent and the silent'. He confessed that the present had crushed him in its iron arms, and that it was the challenge of the day which had made a writer of him. In his political poems, he fought, as a Radical, 'on the lusty left of man, on the mighty side of Spring'. That was what made him the poet of Swiss liberalism. As a young man he had sallied forth with the *Freischärler* for the establishment of a national federal state. In his songs and stories he glorified the morality of the democratic community. His *O mein Heimatland* has become one of the finest national anthems Switzerland possesses. In later life he championed the cause of moderation with increasing vigour. When the popular Democratic movement had lost some of its original force, when its inward fire began to fade and it took to concealing its shallowness with patriotic phrases and noisy festivals, Keller came to doubt whether his people were politically mature. In his messages as city recorder to the people on the national day of fasting and prayer, he expressed his growing anxiety at the turn the political life of the country was taking. He complained that the old liberal spirit had vanished. 'It has been replaced by social discomfort, the railway muddle and ceaseless hurry.' With increasing bitterness, the ageing poet attacked the enemies of public life—the love of pleasure, greed, forgetfulness of duty. With his criticisms of the excesses of democracy, which were particularly violent in *Martin Salander*, he almost vied with Gotthelf in gloom. What separated him from the pessimistic pastor was his faith in the inalienable virtues of modern Swiss democracy. Bitter experience did not make the aged Keller repudiate the ideals of his youth. He remained a lover of freedom and progress in every sphere, and imagined that every reasonable human being must think as he did.

At the age of 20, with a 'bungled education' behind him, Keller left his native Zürich to study art at Munich. After long uncertainty he realized that his true medium was not art, but writing. He began with poetry, struggled for years with drama, and in the end found his true vocation in the novel. Under the influence of the German philosopher Feuerbach, he renounced the religious faith of his fathers, and took to a belief in the divinity of all nature. 'The world has become more profound and beautiful to me, life more valuable and intenser, death graver, more disturbing.' His innate indolence nearly ruined his life. From that fate his native city rescued him by conferring on him one of its highest offices, that of city recorder. That was an example of what had already happened more than once in the city states of Switzerland—the same pen did both the administrative and the intellectual work of the community. When Keller had served his native city for fifteen years as a conscientious official, he returned to the freedom of the writer and completed his incomparable work.

In his own life, Keller solved the conflict between the artist and the citizen, between the individual and the community, which had caused him so much suffering. That same conflict pervades many of his books. In his novel *Der grüne Heinrich*, a poetic autobiography, the repentant individualist at last finds his place in the community. Again and again, Keller describes, with his own inimitable humour, strange characters who with pain and toil learn to be useful members of their communities. In the *Züricher Novellen*, an uncle cures a nephew who is afflicted with leanings towards eccentricity by telling him stories of famous eccentrics. *Frau Regel Amrain* is the story of a widow who brings up her son to be a truly democratic Swiss citizen. In them all Keller unwaveringly champions truth, justice, and simplicity.

In Keller's poetic realism, Swiss citizenship found its apotheosis. Seldom has a writer succeeded in representing his country in all its variety with so much truth and significance. And Keller's fellow townsman Meyer pictured him as the guardian angel of his homeland, chiding, exhorting and praising the people as need arose. The people honours in Keller a poetic embodiment of Switzerland.

Conrad Ferdinand Meyer utterly lacked any such close bond with the democracy of his time but not the bond with history. This highly strung, retiring descendant of an old patrician house felt out of place in radical Zürich. He was not much interested in social problems and economic questions, nor had he any great feeling for the people. A conservative aristocrat, though no party man, he repudiated the Democratic movement in his native city. Like most of the figures he created, he faced the history of his times, not actively but passively, as one whose mind was turned inward. He felt paralysed by current events, like his own *Pescara* by the spear of a *landsknecht*. Yet, given to brooding as he was, he took refuge in history not in order to escape the present, but in order to get to grips with it and so overcome it. The words in which he praised the French Swiss historian Vuillemin described his own standpoint: 'To be a son of his time and yet to understand and honour the past, to which we owe so much.' Meyer transferred contemporary problems into the moral and spiritual world of the past, and thus deprived them of their force. His historical background was the Protestant humanism of the sixteenth and seventeenth centuries both in Germanic and Romance Europe, the Swiss form of which was a fusion of both. His *Jürg Jenatsch*, the story of the liberator of the Grisons, where both the people and the individual characters are shown in a rich baroque setting, became the most widely read historical novel in Switzerland.

It is extremely moving to see how this intensely sensitive writer, threatened with the approach of insanity, spent his time in ceaseless work so that he might reap his harvest before the storm should break. After bitter struggles, he had preserved his Calvinistic Christianity and found consolation in his faith in the inscrutable wisdom of God. In a tormentingly slow progress towards maturity, with an effort of will which amounted to genius, he polished his work until it had received its final form. Possessed by the ideal of perfection, he wrote poetry which can stand beside the highest and best in Europe. Its outstanding quality is less its melody than the closeness of its imagery. The mere arrangement of the poems is itself a work of art. His deep sense of religion, his care for form and his expression of sentiment, reflect an artistic humanism which had not previously been at home in Switzerland.

Of all poets, it is Carl Spitteler, the poet of the superman and the supernatural world, whom we should least suspect of any deep attachment to his country. He hated the platitudinous bourgeois democracy of his time, governed as it was by the greed of gain, deafened by the hollow rhetoric of public festivals, and rampant with mediocrity. In contrast to the crass utilitarianism of the world about him, he created a metacosmic world of gods and titans. But the places where they live are Swiss landscapes, and there are echoes of Switzerland in their speech; the gestures of defiance, the inflexible will, are of the pure Swiss heritage. Spitteler, a native of Baselland, was glad to return home after some years abroad. He finally settled at Lucerne where he made a famous speech on neutrality at the beginning of the First World War.

Spitteler's chief works are the monumental epics, *Prometheus* and *Epimetheus*. They move in a world of aesthetic idealism and profound pessimism. Man, the bearer of the spirit and all that is good, fights a desperate battle against the brutal power of reality, against senseless compulsions. The crude and cruel world is a machine which moves by its own laws of merciless necessity. Power, the absolute evil, is victorious, and there is but a slight gleam of hope that the world will be ultimately redeemed by man's unconquerable mind. This scaffolding of ideas is clothed with mythical visions of primitive glory and noble splendour, peopled by a motley host of imagined figures. The allegory is not always clear, it often remains somewhat artificial and intellectual, and the symbolism does not always carry the power to convince. But we are amazed, again and again, by the boldness of its artistic power, the beauty of its imagery and its deep compassion with the misery of the world.

With Gotthelf, Keller, Meyer, and Spitteler, the most widely read writers in German of their time, Switzerland again took the leading position in German poetry which she had had in the eighteenth century. While the same cannot be said of the literature of French and Italian Switzerland, both had a respected place in the literature of those languages. The literature of French Switzerland never admitted the claim, recognized elsewhere, that art must be its own object. Even the writers who strove most to create beauty for its own sake were always preoccupied with moral questions, proclaimed high ideas, declared war on error and endeavoured to exert an educational influence; thus they had a social function. That is true of all the many branches of literature —history, religious and scientific thought, the novel, and poetry itself.

The most delightful reflection of Genevese life is to be found in the work of the artist and writer Rodolphe Toepffer (1799–1846). His figures, drawn from every class of society and every kind of occupation, sketched lightly and humorously with profound psychological insight, enchanted Goethe and have remained fresh in their overbrimming vitality even in our day. Probably the *Voyages en Zigzag* is the most characteristic example of his unique form of art. Toepffer also wrote books on literary, artistic, and moral subjects. In Alexandre Vinet (1797–1847), the canton of Vaud produced a man of extraordinarily profound religious feeling, and one of the most versatile minds of his age. As a young man, he was already lecturing on French language and literature at the university of Basle, and his work there provided him with the basis for his admirable *Chrestomathie française*. Through his work as the literary and religious critic of a Protestant periodical in Paris, he became one of the foremost representatives of French protestantism. As a citizen, he defended the rights of Basle Stadt against Basle Land; as professor of theology at Lausanne, he championed the freedom of conscience and religious worship against government persecution. He acknowledged no right on the part of the state to determine principles of morality and to regiment intellectual and religious life. For that reason he advocated the separation of church and state. The government's sole function was to be the protector of freedom in all its forms. The pedestal of Vinet's statue bears his superb definition of Christian liberalism: 'Christianity is the immortal seed of freedom in the world.' The writer who gave the finest picture of the Vaudois people was Juste Olivier. After a short period as lecturer at Neuchâtel, he was obliged to spend most of his life in Paris, devoured by home-sickness for his ungrateful country. In his *Chansons lointaines* he gave touching and original expression to the spirit of his homeland. The solitary Genevan professor of philosophy, Henri-Frédéric Amiel, was another writer who achieved only posthumous fame from his *Journal Intime*. It is an extremely subtle piece of self-analysis which reveals Amiel as an original thinker. All the conflicting currents of nineteenth century thought and feeling can be seen in this diary. Amiel analyses his age, discusses the rights of democracy, describes landscapes and the seasons, or sinks into cosmic reverie. He recognizes life as a growth of the soul, as the development of a form which is far above reality —all in a wonderful prose style. He felt deeply as a citizen of Geneva, French and Swiss, and took an active part in public life. His *Roulez, tambours* is one of the most popular national songs of French Switzerland. He even believed that it was possible and right for French Switzerland to produce a native literature. In the twentieth century, Charles Ramuz of Vaud drew the most impressive pictures of the beauty of the French Swiss country-side and of the variety of its inhabitants—but he was a European, not merely a regional, writer. His widely translated novels express his individual outlook and personality.

The fine arts. In the second half of the nineteenth century, the artistic monuments of the past, especially of the middle ages, were treated with gross indifference. City walls with picturesque turrets and gates were demolished as obstacles to traffic, frescoes and cloisters disappeared, the treasures of churches and religious orders left the country for the money they would bring. It was a long time before an indifferent government and public realized the value of preserving the country's artistic heritage, and when that happened, many a work of art of a past age had been sacrificed and was irretrievably lost. A Swiss Association for the Preservation of Historical Works of Art was at last founded and its work was crowned by the formation of the Swiss National Museum at Zürich, the purpose of which was to exhibit the artistic products of the Swiss past in a proper setting.

A plain and strict classicism had prevailed for centuries. It determined the forms of building and furniture, and in some places even found its way into popular art. In some way the simplicity and dignity of the Biedermeier and late classical styles must have been congenial to the nature of the Swiss bourgeoisie, for that style had far greater influence in Switzerland than the rococo or baroque. Later, it was invaded by late Renaissance elements, in Gottfried Semper's monumental buildings, for instance. German neo-classicism also left its mark on Switzerland. An attempt was made in the twentieth century to introduce characteristically modern styles into Switzerland in public buildings, such as the Congress House at Zürich and the university building at Fribourg. But again the native rustic style gained the day as a reaction of public feeling against exaggerated rationalism.

There are few Swiss sculptors whose work rises above the average. The Ticinese Vincenzo Vela became popular by the powerful naturalism of his work and by his 'Spartacus', while Richard Kissling of Solothurn made his name by the statue of Tell at Altdorf. Switzerland's greatest achievement in the fine arts is in painting. The finest expression of classicism is to be found in the noble portraits and mythological pictures of the Vaudois Charles Gleyre, and of romanticism in the Italian genre scenes of Léopold Robert of Neuchâtel. Alexandre Calame of Geneva was an outsider. Heedless of the trends of the time, he concentrated on his pictures of the Alpine world.

Arnold Böcklin, a native of Basle and a powerful influence in art, also belonged to no school, but he created one. At first, he devoted himself to landscape. After having discovered his artistic home in Italy, he peopled his landscapes, to deepen their appeal, with the divinities of antiquity. More and more, the human figure came to occupy the foreground of his work, which became steadily more dramatic. With extreme self-assurance, he opened up new paths in painting, while the spiritual quality of his work deepened. At the height of his career, he settled in Zürich, where he became a friend of Gottfried Keller. At that time he was the most famous artist of his day, but he remained extremely simple in character— a typical Swiss whose genius profoundly influenced European artistic feeling.

The artist who came closest to him in his conception of art was Hans Sandreuter of Basle. Böcklin's friend, Rudolf Koller of Zürich, painted superb animal pieces. His 'Gotthard Post' has remained his most famous picture; it conjures up a moment of Swiss life of long ago. Frank Buchser, of Solothurn, painted spirited portraits of the prominent personalities of the American Civil War, and vivid scenes of African native life. Alfred Anker, painter of incidents from Bernese peasant life, Karl Stauffer, the outstanding portrait painter, and Albert Welti, whose chief bequest to the Swiss nation is the mural painting of a *Landsgemeinde* in the hall of the Federal Council of States at Berne, all deserve mention.

National pictures of greater visionary power, greater energy of composition and greater force of execution came from Ferdinand Hodler. His character was a happy and original blend of Alemannic and Romance traits. This son of a Bernese artisan underwent a severe training by a French Swiss artist and settled for life in Geneva. He controlled his elemental power by his sense of form and spiritualized his turbulent massivity by masterly composition. He was obsessed by the passion for ideas and strove for a kind of metaphysical art, without, however, abandoning the richness of his observation. He made the idea, the symbol, visible in the external, sensuous image. In this way he founded a European school of painting and won recognition and admiration far and wide. Both intellectually and artistically, there are typically Swiss traits in his character, so that through him the problem of a Swiss national art again became acute. He was Swiss in a differentiated, enhanced, and general sense. He gave artistically living form to Switzerland's past in many pictures which are faintly reminiscent of the illustrations to the old Swiss chronicles. His frescoes are moving in their greatness, in the tautness of their outlines, the energy of their movement, the clarity of their ideas. The most overwhelming today are the 'Retreat from Marignano', a symbol of the Swiss determination in self-defence, and the monumental 'William Tell', an embodiment of the Swiss passion for freedom.

Scholarship. On the intellectual side, it was history which passed through the most interesting development. Given the heritage of the eighteenth century, the chief aim of historians was at first the continuation of the incomparable work of Johannes von Müller. The most important documents and chronicles were still unpublished and lay unread in libraries and elsewhere. The academic possibilities of proper training were as yet scanty; most historians had studied theology, which gave them their scientific equipment. The historian had not yet won his freedom; whereas in earlier times he had had to bow to the dictates of his governors, he now had to bow to public opinion. In the revolutionary first half of the century, history slipped only too readily into journalism. In short, the position of historical science had not yet been clarified.

The first to undertake the continuation of Johannes von Müller's History of the Confederation was Robert Glutz-Blotzheim of Solothurn. He dealt with the period from 1489 to 1516 with great historical acuteness, but refrained from bathing it in romantic glory, as his predecessor had done. Glutz was succeeded by Johann Jakob Hottinger of Zürich. He wrote on the Reformation with great learning and fair-mindedness, and attempted to emulate Müller in his style. The further history of the sixteenth century was written by Louis Vuillemin with taste and charm, though he remained somewhat entangled in externals and did not grasp the essential problems. The conclusion of Müller's history was written by Charles Monnard, of Vaud, a gifted historian who dealt vividly with the period from 1715 to 1815. He was more interested in the state than any of his predecessors had been, but he showed the characteristic Swiss dislike of theoretical considerations, an aversion to the abandonment of the concrete in favour of the abstract. While the Swiss historians, up to this time, had paid attention rather to the meaning of history and the quality of form, a new trend of methodical and exact criticism now began to take the field. The leader of this critical school was Eutych Kopp of Lucerne. The baseless legend of the origin of the Confederation meant as little to him as the imaginative reconstructions of Tschudi and Müller. Free from all personal bias, he undertook a fresh interpretation of the sources; what was not to be found there he eliminated from history. Kopp's method opened up a fresh path to Swiss historical science, along which many followed him, among others, Frédéric de Gingins-la Sarraz, Pierre Vaucher, Georg von Wyss, Hermann Wartmann. The representatives of the various schools of historical thought united in 1841 to form the National Historical Association of Switzerland, which issued a number of periodicals, and did especially valuable work by publishing reliable editions of original documents.

In more recent times, Swiss history again took to narrative, but this time on the basis of a more highly developed criticism. The majority of historians took their stand on the optimism of the century which had given birth to the new confederation. They supported the new state, advocated centralization in the cantons and confederation, and believed in the uninterrupted progress of mankind. Karl Dändliker set out to serve science and the people, combining mastery of detail with the wider view. He put his whole soul into his *History of Switzerland*, but was not able to base it on one great conception. Johannes Dierauer regarded Switzerland as a nation-state, wrote its political history (of which he was a master), and confined himself to the visible, avoiding everything which lay beneath the threshold of consciousness. Wilhelm Oechsli had more taste than Dierauer for cultural history, for intellectual and economic life, and had a more personal standpoint, which is expressed in his highly individual style. Together with Dierauer, whose truly Swiss sense of reality he shared, he created the historical picture of modern Switzerland.

The great Basle historian, Jacob Burckhardt, stood aloof from all historical schools and from the political conflicts of his day. He was probably the profoundest critic of the culture of his time. On progress, he wrote that it would be a mistake to assume that intellectual progress went hand in hand with material enrichment. The modern spirit of gain merely provoked his dislike and set him in open conflict with the feeling of his time. He had nothing but contempt for the ephemeral optimism which expected an earthly paradise from economic and technological improvements. He detested the railways as the modern means of transport, not only on aesthetic grounds (because embankments, cuttings, and viaducts destroyed the landscape, and the constant whistling of the engines added to present-day noise), but because these 'mixers of mankind' led to centralization in all domains, undermined local character by giving Switzerland a place in the economic system of the world, and thus gave fresh impetus to the greed of gain. The rise of big business, the mechanized division of labour, and, still more, state socialism, were hateful to Burckhardt. He therefore denounced the social policy then setting in, with its protection of the workers and the unjustified interference in society by the state. In his eyes, it all led to the destruction of the independent human being, of free personality, the greatest of all values. Political and economic organizations were ousting the old sense of community. 'Liberal and Radical money-makers' were regimenting the time, proud of their 'unconditional and comfortable gains and the salving of their consciences by philanthropy'. Burckhardt contrasted the insatiable desire for pleasure of the masses with the independence which accompanies a simpler way of living, the restlessness of modern competition and advertisement with the quiet life and spiritual peace. A change could only come from men with an ascetic bent who, aloof from big business and luxury, would 'again help the national spirit and the true soul of the people to find expression'.

Burckhardt was first and foremost a citizen of Basle, and as such a representative of the European tradition and spirit. What he wished to communicate to his fellow citizens was the heritage of western civilization. In his *Age of Constantine the Great*, he dealt with the early Christian and late Roman epoch, his *Civilization of the Renaissance in Italy* was the first profoundly imaginative vision of that age, his *Cicerone* was a guide to the enjoyment of Italian art and monuments. These works made him the greatest historian of civilization writing in German. Burckhardt himself attached less importance to his publications than to his university lectures, to which the people of Basle flocked year after year. With these lectures, and with his other academic work, he served his native community, to which he was bound by deep loyalty. In one of his posthumously published lectures, which was given the title of

Reflections on History, Burckhardt gave a moving definition of the small state:

> The small State exists so that there may be one spot on earth where the largest possible proportion of the inhabitants are citizens in the fullest sense of the word. . . . The small State possesses nothing but real freedom, an ideal possession which fully balances the huge advantages of the big State.

Another famous citizen of Basle was Johann Jakob Bachofen, though he was not in touch with Burckhardt, either personally or intellectually. After having held the chair of Roman law for some time, he devoted himself entirely to his researches into law and the history of religion. Some of these he published, among others his *Mutterrecht*. He shows how, in the origins of human society and civilization, the prevailing form of the community had been matriarchy. He regarded the myth as a key to certain historical knowledge and built up a system of historical philosophy which had considerable effect. A third citizen of Basle, Andreas Heusler, did outstanding work in the history of German and Swiss law, while the principal achievement of the lawyer Eugen Huber was the creation of the Swiss code of civil law. Carl Hilty, a constitutional and international lawyer of Berne, became known to his contemporaries as *Praeceptor Helvetiae*.

It was almost a matter of course that the Swiss should turn to natural science, since the widest climatic variations, and hence the greatest variety in all domains of nature, exist side by side in one small country. Indeed, Switzerland not only followed the development of international natural science receptively, but on occasions took the lead. The country itself offered especially fruitful fields of study. For instance, Switzerland did outstanding work in glacier research in connexion with the ice age, in the question of lake-formation and the lake-dwellings, and it is not by chance that, in medicine, research into goitre took its rise in Switzerland.

In the Age of Enlightenment, the achievements of Swiss scientists and mathematicians had raised the country to the status of something like an intellectual great power. On ground so well-prepared, Swiss science in the nineteenth century was able to make further progress. Its development took place chiefly within the Swiss Natural Science Association which was finally founded, after a number of false starts, in 1815. The work of the association embraced every field of natural science. It was soon subdivided into commissions and sub-commissions, each occupied with some special field of research. Its valuable publications testified to the work of the scientists. The Geological commission began the systematic geological investigation of Switzerland by first clarifying ideas of rock-formation, the situation of earth strata, and the meaning of the organic remains found in them. It then created a model geological map of Switzerland. Generations of scientists took part in this work, among others Peter Merian of Basle, whose *Geologie der Schweiz* marked a milestone in the research into his native country.

In the same way, meteorological research, the Central European measurement of latitude and longitude, and anthropological research were actively promoted. The question which peoples and races first settled on Swiss territory aroused special interest. The discovery of the lake-dwellings by Ferdinand Keller cast fresh light on prehistoric Switzerland and the early history of man in general. Together with other scientists, Keller methodically investigated the sites, and arrived at the conclusion that these were the remains of a race which had built its huts on stakes rising above the surfaces of the lakes; since metal was then unknown, they had made their weapons and tools of stone, bone, and horn. These assumptions were greatly clarified by the work of the real founder of historical palaeontology, Karl Ludwig Rütimeyer. The discovery of the cave-dwellings and the systematic archaeological investigation of the soil brought new knowledge of the prehistory of Switzerland.

The exact sciences, mathematics and physics, were not neglected, stimulated as they were by the teaching at the federal institute of technology and at the universities. Chemistry developed in unprecedented fashion. Eminent scientists worked in laboratories equipped by the governments, and won international recognition. Stimulated by this science, a chemical industry with manifold ramifications grew up and holds an increasingly important place in the world market.

With the world famous Theodor Kocher, medicine, and more especially surgery, reached unprecedented heights at the turn of the century. Kocher lived an uneventful life undeviatingly devoted to his work. He was born at Berne, where he occupied the senior chair while yet a young man, and remained faithful to his native city through fifty years of work, heedless of calls from some of the most eminent of foreign universities. A most creative combination of a strictly logical mind with the ability to apply knowledge once gained, together with an enormous power of work, made him the great classic surgeon. At the university, he trained generations of doctors, implanting in them his own professional ideal. In research, he opened up vast virgin territory and pointed the way in many fields. A great operating surgeon, his handbook on surgery, translated into many languages, had a greater influence in its own domain than any other contemporary work on the subject. The most impressive results of his work for non-surgeons are his research into the pathology of the thyroid and the improvement of the operation for goitre which resulted from it. A host of scientific honours poured in upon this quiet, deeply religious Christian, and culminated in the award of the Nobel Prize for medicine. When at last, in 1917, death overtook its greatest adversary, there was a kind of national mourning.

Alpinism. Interest in the Alps had awakened very early in Switzerland and found expression in a number of scientific works, such as those of Aegidius Tschudi of Glarus, and Konrad Gessner and Johann Jakob Scheuchzer of Zürich. It was not, however, until the eighteenth century, under the influence of Albrecht von Haller's didatic poem, *Die Alpen,* and Rousseau's *Nouvelle Héloïse,* that travelling in the Alps really became popular. Moral enthusiasm for the simplicity and beauty of life in the mountains, artistic delight in the beauty of the Alpine world, and scientific curiosity about the high mountains were the chief factors in this movement. It increased in the nineteenth century with the recognition of the healing properties of mountain air and, still more important, with the development of Alpine sports. All these factors combined to attract an ever-growing number of foreigners to the Alps. The tourist industry became increasingly important in the national economy of Switzerland as an offset to the deficit in the balance of payments due to the lack of raw materials in the country, although it changed the habits of many rural communities.

Travelling in the Alps was also facilitated by the printed maps which had steadily improved since the sixteenth century (such as the *Helvetische Topographie,* by Mathäus Merian), and which gave Switzerland the leading position in European cartography. The development reached its height in the middle of the nineteenth century with Dufour's map of Switzerland on a scale of 1 : 100,000 and the Siegfried Atlas on 1 : 50,000, recognized abroad as the best maps in the world.

The taste for Alpine travelling was also promoted by Swiss Alpine painting, which responded to the appeal of Alpine scenery, and began to reflect it in endless variation. Many travellers wished to take home with them views of the districts they had visited, and this demand was met by the labour-saving process invented by the brothers Aberli; the landscapes were etched in outline on a plate, and a staff of craftsmen coloured the sheets. Aberli had skilful followers in the Lorys, father and son, in Freudenberger and König. These engravings show Alpine landscapes, etched with delicate precision and tinted in soft tones, either as romantic idylls or in classical idealization. The Alpine paintings of Alexandre Calame, Giovanni Segantini, and Ferdinand Hodler of Berne were also extremely popular.

Alpine Switzerland, however, was not only the country of origin of modern cartography and landscape painting. The scientific study of the Alpine world in all its branches also rose here— meteorology, geology, botany, zoology, and their auxiliary sciences. The glacier explorations of the palaeontologist Louis Agassiz became specially famous. The fossil plants of the Alps were investigated in exemplary fashion by Oswald Heer of Glarus, whose bust is in the British Museum, while Friedrich von Tschudi, inspired by the spirit of Humboldt, published a magnificent book on Alpine fauna.

The peaks had to be climbed, however, before the world of the Alps could be scientifically investigated and described. Mountain-climbing had begun as early as the sixteenth century, but with the nineteenth century the heroic age of first ascents began, with Englishmen in the van. About the middle of the century the topmost summits of the Bernina and Monte Rosa were climbed, then came the first ascents of the Wetterhorn and the Matterhorn. While these feats of science and climbing were the achievement of individual mountaineers and Alpine naturalists, Alpine enterprise was taken over and systematically organized by associations. In 1857, the Alpine Club was founded in London, its aims being 'to seek adventure and make scientific observation in the high Alps'. Ten years later, the Swiss Alpine Club was founded with a wider scope. In 1900, it already had 6,000 members and 44 sections; it organized annual excursions to the mountains, supported enterprises for the exploration of Alpine territory, built huts and meteorological stations, laid out mountain paths, helped to improve the guide system; it also published literary works, especially in its own *Annual*.

XII

THE FIRST WORLD WAR AND AFTER

Armament and neutrality. The First World War broke out in
the midst of the National Exhibition at Berne which had opened
with high hopes. It did not, however, find Switzerland unprepared.
When an armed conflict between the great powers seemed inevitable, the Federal Council, with a fine sense of its responsibility
to the country, ordered the mobilization of the whole Swiss army
and took the first military and economic steps for the protection of
the country. It hoped to avert an enemy invasion by a display of
its armed power. Further, the Federal Council convened an extraordinary session of the Federal Assembly. Its demand for plenary
powers for the maintenance of national security met with no
resistance from Parliament. But the choice of the Commander-
in-Chief was to cause great difficulties. The Federal Council was
unanimous in its election of Commander Ulrich Wille, while
Parliament, by a large majority preferred Colonel Theophil
Sprecher von Bernegg. Criticism was soon reduced to silence by
the nation's choice, General Wille. After the General had taken
the oath, Sprecher was appointed Chief of the General Staff. The
two army commanders, so different in appearance and character,
who had already differed on military questions, now spent four
and a half years side by side in perfect understanding, and set the
nation an inspiring example of co-operation.

The war came rapidly, the general mobilization was carried
through with remarkable calm and precision. Whether a sudden
attack by an enemy in the early days of August could be warded
off by an incompletely mobilized army was the anxious question
which oppressed the minds of all. Meanwhile, the Federal Council
had announced to the signatory powers of the Neutrality Act of
1815, and to other states, the firm determination of Switzerland,
'faithful to her century-old tradition, not to depart in any way
from the principles of neutrality'. This attitude, dictated both by
history and by the actual situation, seemed so obvious that it surprised no one, either at home or abroad.

Popular feeling. In Switzerland, the outbreak of the World

War was felt as a kind of natural catastrophe which had descended on mankind with irresistible force. When the first stunned feeling had worn off, people began to inquire into the causes of the disaster, although dispassionate, unbiased reflection was hardly possible and yielded at times to feelings of sympathy and antipathy, or even of hatred.

The German attack on Belgium startled large sections of the population and, especially in French Switzerland, set the tone of feeling. More and more central powers seemed to embody the naked concept of power and the absolutist, anti-democratic principle, which was deeply at variance with the liberal conception of Switzerland. The gravest threat to law and democracy in Europe came from Germany. Just in the few preceding years, Switzerland had been through a profoundly national movement; it was felt that there should be more care for the national way of thinking, the spirit of Switzerland should be awakened, more should be done for education. A general rise in the spiritual and moral tone of the country was desired. This general strengthening of the national feeling had made men more sensitive to foreign influences. The number of foreigners in Switzerland had assumed alarming proportions: 220,000 Germans were living in Switzerland, 100,000 of whom lived in Basle and Zürich alone. In the economic field, especially in certain industries, the preponderance of Germans was causing uneasiness. In the intellectual field, German influence was no less strong. The fact that the German outlook was gaining ground was felt by the French Swiss minority as a threat to their national life.

The violation of the neutrality of Belgium seemed to confirm these fears. French Switzerland passionately upheld the national ideals of independence and democracy. It was a sincere and logical expression of that mood that Germany's action was unanimously condemned and Belgium assured of their moral solidarity. The old fear of Germany and the fate of Belgium won French Switzerland over to the allied cause. When the allies included in their war aims the protection not only of small nations, but of democracy, all hearts went out to them. French Switzerland was entirely in sympathy with France and Great Britain.

For years past, German-speaking Switzerland had followed with admiration the rise of Germany in technology, industry, and commerce. With the south of Germany in particular it felt a kinship of race and culture. In the security of their own Alemannic way of life, which found expression in the very language they spoke, the German Swiss imagined they could think and feel with the Germans without losing their peculiar national character or surrendering their own cultural ideal. Many deplored the act of violence against Belgium, but that did not prevent them from continuing to believe in Germany. This general attitude of French and German Switzerland to the belligerents, however, was not without its reservations. In any case, with a population so diverse in language as that of the confederation, the two camps could not be precisely delimited either by geography or race. Thus, convinced democrats in German Switzerland took the side of the western powers, while a great deal of sincere sympathy was also felt in many quarters for France, which had to suffer the war in its own territory. Following their linguistic ties, the Ticinese sympathized with Italy.

The leading organs of the Swiss press endeavoured to supply an impartial record of events, yet could not but reflect the fundamental attitude of individual groups. A few minor papers allowed themselves to be used as the mouth-piece of foreign views, and thus contributed to the exacerbation of feeling in Switzerland. A deep gulf was opened between the two parts of the country, and understanding across it was at times difficult. At first, the principles of the liberal state prevented the Federal Council from introducing a preventive censorship such as that in force in the belligerent countries. Its control was restricted to the publication of military news. The Federal Council first issued an appeal to the people of Switzerland, exhorting them to impose the greatest possible restraint on the expression of their sympathies, since everything must be subjected to the welfare of their own country. Then prominent intellectuals began to speak, warning their neighbours to take thought, and help to bridge the gulf. With true spiritual independence, without presumption, and with dignity, Carl Spitteler defined the ideal of Swiss neutrality and expressed his sympathy with all the belligerents. 'Come! Looking upon this immeasurable sum of human suffering, let our hearts be filled with silent sympathy and our souls with prayer. Above all, let us bare our heads. Then we shall stand in the true, neutral Swiss attitude.'

Eminent men in western Switzerland rose in vigorous opposition to a conception which set up neutrality as a spiritual ideal, a value and purpose in itself. They recognized neutrality only as a principle of foreign policy, a means of preserving the independence of the country. In their view the only result of neutrality as a fundamental spiritual attitude could be indifference to good and evil, right and wrong. In the intellectual sphere, it must produce unwholesome compromises, and the sad consequences in the political field must be the vanishing of true courage. Regarded in this way, they agreed neutrality must inevitably lead to intellectual and political quietism.

Incidents connected with neutrality. While the federal government and private persons were doing all they could to prevent demonstrations of sympathy for either side, an anti-neutral incident took place in the army command. Two colonels who had regularly supplied the Austrian and German military attachés with the army staff bulletin, which contained a summary of the military operations of the belligerents, were suspended from their civil and military duties. That seemed to clear the air. Then a fresh thunderbolt fell from the political sky. A Swiss Social Democrat national councillor had gone to Petrograd in May, 1917, after the Russian Revolution, and, through the Swiss legation, sent a telegram to the Political department in which he requested information as to the war aims of the central powers, since the conclusion of peace was rapidly becoming an absolute necessity. Over the signature 'Foreign Department', Councillor Hoffmann replied, among other things, that Germany would undertake no offensive as long as a peaceful settlement with Russia seemed possible. This telegram was intercepted by the Russian government, who published it and expelled the Swiss national councillor from the country. In that way, the Kerensky government hoped to avert the Entente suspicion that it was aiming at a separate peace with Germany. In order to spare his country a political crisis at home and abroad, Hoffmann handed in his resignation the day after the publication of the telegram. The Federal Council was unanimous in condemning the high-handed action of its member, and thus restored calm to parliament, the people and the outside world, where the press was already treating the case as a sensation.

The defence of the frontiers. The strategic situation of Switzerland exposed the country to a great risk of enemy transit movement at the outbreak of war. Both sides could threaten the flank and rear of their enemies through Swiss territory. But if Switzerland guaranteed an adequate defence of her frontiers, the belligerents could rest their lines against the Swiss frontier and thus save troops. The realization of this state of affairs had been enough to make the confederation keep up the strength of its militia for the defence of its frontier districts, and the feeling of a people for which military service is a right and not a duty did the rest.

The immediate defence of the frontiers was universally recognized to be the supreme duty at the outbreak of war. The entire army numbered 250,000 men. Since the north-west corner of the country was rightly regarded as most vulnerable, three divisions occupied the line of the Jura from Basle to Les Rangiers. A reserve consisting of three more divisions was placed behind the actual front. This disposal of the troops protected the frontier against both France and Germany; it remained practically unchanged throughout the war.

This long standing-by, the interminable waiting for something to happen, inseparable from a condition which was neither peace nor war, made great demands on the endurance and morale of the troops. As the First World War showed, disaffection appears more readily among troops who are not under fire. When fighting ceased in the immediate neighbourhood, many, in unjustifiable optimism, regarded the danger as past. They looked on frontier service not only as extremely monotonous, but as unnecessary, and could not understand why they were not allowed to return to civil life where so many urgent duties awaited them. Ripe crops were to be harvested, daily work resumed. These moods and wishes were the natural reaction of a militia accustomed only to short periods of military service.

In order to keep abreast of the rapid development of foreign armaments, considerable numbers of machine guns were imported. Hand grenades were introduced as a new weapon of defence. Aviation in particular made a fine start. The construction of aircraft was begun and the first military airfield established at Dübendorf, near Zürich. The new clothing of the army in field-grey was finished by the end of the war, and the troops were also equipped with steel helmets. In contrast to former European wars, there were no serious breaches of neutrality. Such as there were consisted for the most part of flights over projecting tongues of land. Bombs fell, but no lives were lost.

The good side of military service was seldom recognized. People had eyes only for the immediate contribution of the army to public welfare; the construction of roads and bridges, the clearing of the passes, labour aid to the rural population, and so on. Less obvious, though much more important effects of the war were to be seen in the training of the people—the improvement in the physique of all able-bodied men, the toughening of the will, the respect for work for its own sake. The daily intercourse with fellow soldiers of other social classes led to greater social understanding and a desire for better social development. More than once, the desire for a truly moral democracy, for a new political order, found expression during frontier service. Further, the contact with Swiss of a different language, race, and culture, the time spent in unknown parts of the country, all acted as an education of the nation. For the experience of history strengthens patriotism no less than the immediate experience of the concrete, palpable soil of home and its people. Thus frontier service became a training ground for the Swiss spirit.

War economy. Switzerland was threatened by dangers other than military. She ran serious risk of being cut off from her food supplies, and it was doubtful whether this small country in the heart of a Europe bristling with armaments would not soon fall victim to famine. Its agricultural produce was insufficient to feed the people, and its industry was largely dependent on foreign raw materials. The stoppage of imports was a matter of life and death to the confederation. Switzerland was importing 40 per cent. of her total consumption of food, mainly in the form of grain, flour, and wheat. Since she obtained most of her grain from Russia and overseas countries, and had no direct access to the sea, she was dependent on the good will of her neighbours for the maintenance of her communications with her foreign food sources.

For a time it was possible to maintain the most vital connexions with other countries. But when the economic war became more acute, when the belligerents completely blockaded each other and Italy entered the war, Switzerland was threatened with complete isolation. The supply of food and raw materials became the most important and difficult business of the government. To its painful surprise, the Federal Council learned from the outset that it could not rely on international trade agreements. In their life and death struggle the belligerents had little time to spare for the protests of

Switzerland. Their only aim was to injure the enemy, to reduce him to starvation by an economic stranglehold. They therefore refused to allow the neutrals to re-export imported goods to the countries of their enemies. In order to save the national food-supply, the Federal Council was obliged to submit to a control of imports, especially foodstuffs and raw materials from overseas, which meant a considerable inroad into Swiss independence. The Netherlands had already had to submit to similar conditions.

The first agreement with the central powers was concluded by the Federal Council in 1915. It resulted in the establishment at Zürich of a central office for the import of German and Austrian goods into Switzerland, in particular, coal, iron, and sugar. A few months later, an agreement had to be come to with the Allies. Unlike the central powers, they did not confine themselves to controlling the use of their own products, but extended their control to goods entering Switzerland from neutral countries, especially America, through Entente territory. Since about 80 per cent. of all food and large quantities of raw materials had to pass that way, or even originated in those countries, the negotiations with the western powers turned out much more difficult, and their economic pressure was felt more keenly. The new office soon grew into a large organization. Switzerland had never had to submit to anything like such stringent restrictions of her imports and ex-ports since the time of Napoleon's European blockade.

If she was not allowed to starve, the reasons were not entirely philanthropic; they were utilitarian too. The maintenance of Swiss neutrality seemed advisable not only on military grounds in order to shorten the line of battle and permit the internment of prisoners of war, but also because both sides used this neutral country as a source of war material and of goods for civilian consumption. Their factories were unable to cope with the unprecedented demand for munitions and materials of war. The extensive in-dustrialization of Switzerland enabled her to meet the belligerents' requirements almost entirely. If the powers wished to retain this source of supply, it was not enough to supply Switzerland with raw materials; she had to be fed too. In this way, the country was able to obtain the raw material for the replenishment of her own arma-ments. When Germany declared total submarine war in 1917, Switzerland had no redress against this worst threat of all to her food supply but to protest in the name of international law. Then

Germany opened the port of Cette in the south of France for over-seas imports into Switzerland. An agreement was reached with the United States which more or less safeguarded the bread supply.

To check the growing unrest at home, parliament extended the plenipotentiary powers of the Federal Council to economic questions too, conferring on it in particular the competence to take any legislative steps which might appear necessary to avert difficulties of supply. The council made extensive use of these powers. Anxiety to keep the economic life of the nation in order caused it to violate almost daily the principle of the freedom of trade and industry enshrined in the constitution. For reasons of self-preservation, the Bund had to take into its own hands the organization of the production and distribution of goods. It assisted the production of vital materials and curtailed that of less necessary ones, issued rationing orders, and by all these emergency measures, restricted free competition. Till almost the end of the war, nearly all foodstuffs and industrial war materials were under government control.

The mobilization, and the lengthening watch on the frontiers imposed extraordinary expenditure on the Bund. In order to avoid considerable increases in taxation, loans had to be raised. They were repeated at intervals of about six months; on the home capital market they were, as a rule, heavily over-subscribed. Two loans in America met with the same success. By 1920, the national debt per head of the population amounted to about 500 francs, not counting cantonal and communal debts. The Bund was now faced with the problem of paying interest on, and repaying, the capital it had taken up and thus decided to penalize war profiteers by means of taxation. This step obtained a considerable measure of public support. While many Swiss were practically ruined by the war, others profited by it. Certain branches of the machine, clock-making, and textile industries did well, and the chocolate manufacturers also grew rich on army contracts from other countries. Agriculture also flourished in the absence of foreign competition. Quite apart from the moral effect, the tax on war profits meant a considerable improvement in the financial situation of the Bund.

The return to a peace economy was slow in coming, for the economic war did not cease with the Armistice. It was only gradually and with great caution that the Bund set about relaxing its war emergency measures. When it finally surrendered its emergency powers, the excessive intervention of the state in economic life diminished, and the way was reopened to the vital initiative of the individual.

The general strike. The economic pressure of the war years bore most heavily on the working classes. Prices rose steeply and rapidly, leaving wages far behind; in some cases these were even reduced. Here and there working hours were lengthened and staff reduced. Business men and farmers took advantage of their favourable position, so that the person most heavily struck by the difficulties in the food supply was the manual worker. The hatred of the proletariat for the so-called exploiting classes grew deeper than ever. The worker felt that he had to suffer, not to pay his share of the general debt, but so that others might enjoy themselves. He had to stand by, powerless, while all endeavours to create more bearable conditions came to grief. It is difficult to say who was responsible for this state of affairs, but since the government, in virtue of its emergency powers, decided everything that was to be done, the whole responsibility was laid at its door.

The bitterness of the workers was also fanned by the large number of foreigners who had flooded the country since the outbreak of war. There were, on the one hand, profiteers and money-makers of all kinds for whom there was nothing in the world that was not there for money's sake, and whose sole aim was quick returns. On the other hand, there were the conscientious objectors and deserters. These men began to get into touch with the Swiss Social Democrats and to encourage them in their anti-militarism. Since the Socialist congress at the Bernese villages of Zimmerwald and Kiental in 1915–16, where the foundation stone of the revolutionary International had been laid, an extremely left-wing Socialist group with a Communist bias had been steadily taking shape. The Swiss Social Democratic party, which had once stood for reform by legal methods, was being transformed into a revolutionary organization. To confuse the notion of patriotism, refuse military service, arm the workers in the struggle against the bourgeoisie, and set up the dictatorship of the proletariat were the main tenets of their faith. The arrogance of some of those enjoying asylum in Switzerland went so far that they actually plotted against the Swiss army, to which they owed their safety.

The tone of public discussion betrayed the growing awareness of class differences. The results of the elections showed that the workers' movement was growing, particularly in the big towns.

With that growth, their feeling of power and self-reliance grew too. More and more the Social Democrats lost hope of arresting the impoverishment of the people by parliamentary discussion. Then the idea of bringing the whole matter to a head by means of a general strike began to take shape. It was intended to put labour in power by means of a revolution for the attainment of Socialist aims. The victory of Bolshevism in Russia delighted and inspired the Swiss proletariat; indeed, international events had always played their part in shaping political conditions in the confederation. Lenin had stayed some time at Berne and Zürich, but in 1917 had been allowed by the Germans to travel to Russia with a few companions through Germany in a sealed railway train. His rapid rise to power caused jubilation and raised great hopes among his friends in Switzerland. True, the centre of Swiss Social Democracy was not of his following, but he had devoted adherents in the radical wing, especially among the younger groups. Their watchword was the end of the war and the dictatorship of the proletariat.

These machinations against the state obviously found vigorous support in the Diplomatic Mission of the Soviet republic which had settled at Berne in 1918. It was well provided with money, which it used to promote the world revolution. Under the protection of its position in international law, it carried on an active intercourse with the Swiss Socialists. It was forced to realize, however, that the Swiss peasant, unlike the Russian, could not be won over to revolution for the simple reason that he owned the land he farmed. The agitation in the army was equally unsuccessful. Attempts were made to demoralize the troops by all kinds of underground tactics. But although the men had led a hard life on the frontiers, they paid no attention to the prompting of the Red agents.

When it became known that the Social Democratic party was planning to celebrate the anniversary of the Russian Revolution by a great demonstration in Zürich, the Bund ordered a military occupation of the city. The Social Democratic executive called on the Federal Council to withdraw the troops without delay; the council refused. A general strike was therefore announced for 11 November 1918, to last until the minimum of the workers' demands had been granted. Among other things, they demanded an immediate re-election of the National Council on the proportional system, the introduction of labour conscription, the 48-hour week, and the paying off of the national debt by a capital levy. The staff of the public services also joined the strike. The towns, however, continued to be served with water, gas, and electricity, but the railways practically ceased to run.

In Berne, the Soviet legation, the focus of discontent, had been expelled and conducted with all its staff to the frontier under military escort. At the same time the influenza epidemic made matters worse. On 12 November an extraordinary session of the Federal Assembly was held at which the representatives stood solidly behind the Federal Council. They declared their readiness to introduce political and social reforms, but only by constitutional action. The following day the Federal Council required the Social Democratic party to call off the strike by evening and the party executive surrendered unconditionally.

The most serious constitutional crisis of the war had been overcome. Work was resumed immediately almost everywhere. Proceedings against the strike leaders led to sentences of imprisonment varying from four weeks to six months. But reforms were carried out which the Socialist minority had demanded in vain both before and during the war; the election of the National Council by a new system of proportional representation was introduced and the 48-hour week established by law. A law regulating work in public transport was also passed, and consideration given to old age and disability insurance.

Philanthropic work. In one of its reports to the Federal Assembly, the Federal Council wrote: 'It is one of the privileges of a neutral country to raise the voice of humanity among the warring nations and to help to alleviate the sufferings of war.' Divided in sympathy as it was, the confederation stood together as one man in its will to help. The work done is one of the finest pages in the history of the country.

Immediately on the outbreak of war the Federal Council was charged by a number of countries with the protection of their nationals in enemy countries. Since these duties grew steadily heavier, the Political department was soon obliged to establish a special office for the representation of foreign interests. The repatriation of foreign civilians was a difficult matter for the confederation. From 1914–15, over 20,000 French, German, Austrian, and Hungarian nationals detained by the enemy, and in the summer of 1915, over 67,000 evacuees from the territories occupied by Germany, returned home by way of Switzerland.

The efforts made by the Federal Council for the exchange of the seriously wounded and sick were equally beneficial. An agreement on the subject was signed by Germany, France, Great Britain, Russia, and Belgium which concerned only members of the armed forces who could serve neither in the army nor in instruction or staff work. The Federal Council entrusted their repatriation to the Swiss Red Cross. From 1914 on, the long hospital trains rolled through Switzerland with their load of inhumanly mutilated figures, a dreadful witness to the agony of a world.

The care of the Swiss government was also extended to the fate of the prisoners of war. Many of them were suffering mentally and physically from their isolation behind barbed wire, from scanty and insufficient care. An agreement was concluded between Switzerland, her neighbours, and Belgium, by which sick prisoners of war were enabled to convalesce in Switzerland. From 1916 till the end of the war, she received some 68,000 internees, 37,000 of whom were French. In the various health resorts, they were allowed great freedom of movement. The students among them, who were soon taken charge of by a special aid association, were given the opportunity of attending universities.

A tremendous task was accomplished by the International Red Cross at Geneva. True to its tradition of philanthropy, that city became the centre of a wide-spread international aid organization. The committee of the Red Cross employed an army of voluntary workers. Among other things, it created the office for the missing and wounded, where lists of the dead and prisoners were drawn up, the missing sought for, and the next of kin informed as quickly as possible of their whereabouts and state of health. The agency at Geneva also extended its activities by arranging correspondence between prisoners of war and their families.

The general helpfulness of the Swiss was by no means exhausted by such work. They regarded it as their noblest privilege to alleviate suffering, and devoted themselves to that end with true fervour. Countless charities were founded, each with its own aim and giving help wherever help was needed.

Peace efforts and the peace treaty. Even in the first months of the war, the Federal Council was appealed to from several quarters, as the government of a permanently neutral state, to pave the way for peace negotiations. In view of the rising bitterness between the belligerents, and the stubbornness of their will to destroy their enemies, the Federal Council regarded any such step as entirely useless. Not until Woodrow Wilson, the President of the United States, had invited the belligerents to issue a public statement of their aims in his peace note of December 1916, did the Council feel that the time had come to step forward and participate in his action. In warmhearted words, arising from a truly neutral and humane spirit, it appealed to the belligerents a few days before Christmas. This demonstration was kindly received by public opinion in the belligerent countries, but had no effect whatever on their determination to prolong and win the war.

The news of the Armistice between the Allies and Germany arrived during the agitated days of the general strike. Not until that storm had passed did the country feel it could yield itself up to the joys of peace. The treaty of Versailles, hailed in many places by the ringing of the bells, settled a number of questions which directly affected the confederation. For one thing, the treaty replaced the Rhine shipping acts then in force, which guaranteed the freedom of shipping from Basle to the North Sea, by a new agreement which secured certain rights to France. Further, Germany had to undertake to recognize the termination of the international agreement respecting the Gotthard line within ten years on application by Switzerland. And, finally, the treaty powers, in article 435, recognized an agreement between France and Switzerland according to which the provisions concerning the neutralized zone of Savoy were abolished, the confederation thereby surrendering its right to occupy Upper Savoy. The modern French state had always felt this right as an irritating restriction of its own sovereignty and took the first opportunity of doing away with it. In Switzerland, a new generation in a changed world regarded the obligation to neutralize Savoy, to which their forefathers had clung, as a valueless vestige of bygone times, both from the military and the political points of view. This view was the more obvious in that Switzerland, by renouncing a right that was incontestably hers, was able to obtain a privileged position in the newly founded organization of the family of nations.

The Vorarlberg question. If Switzerland made no effort to preserve ancient neutrality rights on her western frontier, she was equally uninterested in acquiring new ones in the east. The century-old policy of neutrality had completely blotted out any desire for territorial expansion. This was clearly shown by the way in which Switzerland treated the question of a possible admission of the Vorarlberg to the confederation. After the defeat and collapse of the Austrian monarchy, the Vorarlberg proclaimed its right to self-determination and adopted a democratic constitution. A powerful and spontaneous movement then broke out among the people, pressing for union with Switzerland.

From the geographical standpoint, this small territory forms the natural rounding-off of Switzerland to the east. Its population, like that of the confederation, is mixed, including a number of mountain people from the Valais who had settled there in the middle ages. Racially and linguistically, there is a close kinship with Switzerland, which comes out in their customs and national character. In their exhaustion after the war, the people of the Vorarlberg saw the confederation as the land of peace. Carried away by their longing for peace and the fraternal feelings of the time, they imagined that they could achieve their ideals best in the neighbouring country. There was strict order there, and there too, in the federal state, they would have the best chance of maintaining their old local independence. In the confederation, the form of state they most desired had been a matter of course from time immemorial.

In Switzerland, where there was no desire for territorial expansion, there were grave misgivings about the inclusion of the little Vorarlberg country, impoverished and Catholic as it was. Yet the appeal of the Vorarlberg did not fall on entirely deaf ears. The history and democratic convictions of the people suggested union. Arguments of military and cultural security were also put forward. But the Federal Council maintained an attitude of aloofness. In 1919, the people of the Vorarlberg voted by a majority of four-fifths (45,566 to 11,209) for union with Switzerland; all the communes, with two exceptions, had voted for the union by an overwhelming majority. Yet more and more obstacles were put in the way of the Vorarlbergers who tried to make a direct appeal to the Peace conference. The Austrian government sought to prevent the Supreme Allied Council from yielding to the appeal. In Vienna, the secession of the little country was painted as the beginning of the disintegration of Austria and its union with Germany, an argument which was not without its effect on the allies. The very Assembly of the Allied Council which had proclaimed the right to self-determination as one of its supreme principles, now ignored its solemn declaration and, at the peace of St. Germain, maintained unchanged the old western frontier of Austria (10 September 1919).

The League of Nations and the Second World War

Entry into the League of Nations. When, towards the end of the war the ancient idea of a league embracing all nations on equal terms took firmer shape, it awakened an eager response in Switzerland. The confederation itself was a union of various races and cultures in freedom and self-determination. It had been for centuries a kind of League of Nations. A League of Nations alone could put an end to the existing state of destructive warfare, and solve the great social problems of the future. If there were in international relations a truly supra-national court of arbitration, the smaller states, and Switzerland in particular, could feel more secure in their independence than hitherto.

Meanwhile, the Allied Peace conference had appointed a commission to draft the Covenant of the League of Nations under the chairmanship of President Wilson. The neutrals were invited to express their opinion on the finished draft. The Federal Council had already appointed a commission to study the future constitution of the League of Nations. Their plan gave the individual states more independence and provided for a less powerful central authority. They naturally attached special importance to the question of Swiss neutrality. Even as a member of the League, the confederation was resolved to remain neutral. The Swiss plan, however, had practically no effect on the final form of the Covenant of the League of Nations; indeed, the conference with the neutral states came too late to make any change in the main lines of the Paris draft. After some hesitation, Geneva was chosen as the seat of the League.

The extreme historical importance of these events was fully appreciated in the confederation, and they were followed with warm sympathy. But the final wording of the Covenant of the League of Nations was a general disappointment. Could this be the legal organization, so much desired and so much belauded, which had seemed to herald the beginning of a new stage in the development of mankind? It did not abolish war; it merely rendered wars of aggression more difficult. It lacked democratic organization and compulsory arbitration. Though these objections to the League were serious, Switzerland was prepared to collaborate in the establishment of world peace. But before her entry into the League could be contemplated, the question of permanent neutrality had to be cleared up. Nobody wished to surrender the principle of foreign policy which had been maintained for four hundred years, and had become the vital principle of the confederation. After exhaustive negotiations with the allied powers, Switzerland had abandoned her right to the neutralization of the north of Savoy, whereupon article 435 was adopted in the treaty of Versailles; the latter recognized Swiss neutrality as an international obligation for the preservation of peace. Thus the Federal Council had achieved the confirmation of its point of view. But beyond that, it wished to have an official pronouncement defining more precisely the rights and nature of Swiss neutrality within the framework of the League. This was done in 1920, in the Declaration of London, by the Council of the League of Nations, which recognized that, by reason of an ancient tradition, Switzerland occupied a peculiar position. It therefore recognized that the permanent neutrality and the guarantee of her territorial integrity, which had entered into international law by the treaties of 1815, were justified in the interests of general peace and therefore consistent with the principles of the League of Nations. The confederation would not be called on to take part in military operations or to permit the transit of foreign troops or even the preparation of military operations on its territory. It was, however, bound to take part in the economic sanctions taken by the League against covenant-breaking states, and was itself prepared to make every sacrifice in the defence of its own territory.

It was only when this exceptional position had been achieved that the Federal Council felt able to recommend to the people that Switzerland should join the League. Originally, it had wished to make the whole question depend on the entry of the United States, but ultimately it abandoned that proviso. By messages to the Councils, worded with great legal skill, by speeches and mass demonstrations and articles in the press, the Federal Council did all that lay in its power to make the question clear and move the people to join the League, in spite of the opposition of the military commanders. The public fully realized the unusual gravity of the decision; there were new and exhaustive discussions of the issues involved, and the question was again clearly presented to the people. Opinion was not divided on party lines except in the Social Democratic party. Since some opposed the League as a creation and tool of capitalism, they told the bourgeoisie, already intimidated by the general strike, that the choice lay between Wilson and Stalin.

Switzerland's entry into the League meant for the average Swiss citizen a break with his most familiar ideas. For over a century the confederation had entered into no alliance with any foreign country, and that reserve had served it well. International agreements were feared as implying breaches of Swiss sovereignty and liberty; the Swiss citizen objected to anything which threatened those supreme political values. And now he was to abandon the traditional foreign policy which had stood the test in the past and was consecrated by tradition. There was in his mind a genuine struggle for clarity in his decision on this vital principle of state. Would it not be better for him to trust his innate sense of reality which, like an inward voice, warned him not to leave the old way, or should he listen to the optimistic appeals of the national government? The people of Switzerland had never been called upon to decide by their vote so vitally important a question of neutrality, a question which might mean life or death to the confederation.

The Federal Council's bill proposing the entry of Switzerland into the League of Nations was passed by the National Council by 115 votes to 50, by the Council of States by 30 to 6. Till the last moment, the result of the popular vote was uncertain. A good many voters decided to accept the bill with the resigned feeling that it was the lesser of two evils. In May 1920 the people voted for entry by 414,830 votes to 322,937. It was chiefly the solid vote of French Switzerland which had brought about this result, while there was a majority against the bill in eastern Switzerland. In the States, the majority was narrow—$11\frac{1}{2}$ to $10\frac{1}{2}$ votes. With that, the confederation had decided a most important question of her foreign policy.

Co-operation in the League. Whatever subsequent opinion may be held as to the entry of Switzerland into the League of Nations, one thing seems certain: after the long dangers of the war years, participation in the international peace organization gave the small state of Switzerland the feeling of security which it so much desired and which it had so painfully lacked in its self-imposed isolation. Swiss foreign policy, whatever new and tempting possibilities might open before it, remained fundamentally faithful to its old principle of neutrality. In its cosmopolitan surroundings, it strictly observed its old impartiality, and remained faithful to the maxim of Niklaus von der Flue, the guardian angel of the confederation: 'Keep out of foreign disputes.' It was Giuseppe Motta who now steered the little Swiss ship of state through the stormy seas of international politics, heedless of the attacks which came first from the right, then from the left. The fact that, while preserving and enforcing Swiss interests, Switzerland was able to make valuable contributions to the international policy of solidarity, is due to the nature of the Swiss federal state.

From the start Switzerland clearly defined her position in the League of Nations Assembly. She repudiated on principle any responsibility for actions on the part of the League of Nations Council in which she had no share; she further refused, in accordance with her tradition, to assume any of the territorial guarantees stipulated by the League of Nations. Switzerland, however, found herself in a somewhat delicate position when it came to the provisions of the treaty of Versailles whose execution had to be supervised by the League. On the one hand, she had not signed the treaty of Versailles and could therefore legitimately feel that she had no obligations on that score. On the other, she was bound to co-operation by her membership of the League. In this ambiguous situation, which could not but result in compromises, Switzerland constantly endeavoured to give clear expression to her neutral attitude and to recall her peculiar position to the members of the League.

Switzerland regarded it as one of her main tasks to advocate the universality of the League. The absence of the United States was less disturbing than that of her powerful neighbour, Germany. The Swiss delegation lost no opportunity of reminding the Assembly of this unsolved problem, and constantly urged that her greatest neighbour should be a member of the international peace organization to which she herself belonged.

It was also consonant with Swiss neutrality that Switzerland should be mainly occupied with those aims of the League which were concerned with the development of international relations under international law, while remaining aloof from anything connected with the system of sanctions against covenant-breaking states. For the settlement of disputes, the League of Nations had instituted a complicated process of arbitration which, however, had no binding force. Arbitration in international conflicts was not even compulsory for members of the Permanent International Court. The Swiss delegation never ceased to advocate the compulsory settlement of international disputes by a firmly established arbitration procedure. That system had long been familiar to the confederation, which had often, in the past, established by treaty the settlement of disputes between the states by arbitration, and had put it into practice. What Switzerland was primarily aiming at was bi-lateral agreements with other states on arbitration procedure. In Swiss eyes, the only guarantee of world peace was a community of nations whose relations would be regulated by legal agreement, and would at all times be subjected to the judgements of a Supreme Court of Justice. And Switzerland was the first member of the League, with Poland and Belgium, to sign the compulsory arbitration clause in 1920. The famous Locarno Pact of 1925 was also concluded on Swiss territory.

The attitude of Switzerland within the League can be seen very clearly in the incident known as the Vilna dispute. In 1920, Polish irregulars had occupied the town of Vilna in violation of the armistice with Lithuania. Since Poland and Lithuania had acquired their independence, Vilna had been in dispute between them. In order to put an end to the quarrel the League of Nations decided to organize a plebiscite in Vilna under the protection of an international force. The Belgian, British, and Spanish contingents were to be sent through Switzerland, Austria, and Czechoslovakia. The Federal Council, however, taking its stand on the Declaration of London, categorically refused free passage to the troops even though they were not engaged on military operations but on purely peaceful business. By refusing the transit of troops in so positive a fashion, Switzerland avoided what might have been a very dangerous precedent, and made it quite clear that no military act on the part of the League should be carried out on Swiss territory unless the confederation gave its explicit authorization.

On the other hand, Switzerland laid aside her reserve in foreign policy when it came to giving financial aid to her neighbour Austria, then faced with financial collapse. Yet even here, she managed to avoid any international commitments. The traditional reserve of Switzerland prevented her from signing the protocols of the League respecting the financial restoration of Austria, but she took an active part in the financial action. From public funds the confederation lent Austria 20 million gold kronen without guarantee, while the Swiss banks subscribed 25 million Swiss francs to the international Austrian loan, not to speak of other financial aids. Switzerland was doubtless moved to support Austria by philanthropic feeling, but political considerations played their part too. It could not be a matter of indifference to her if Austria collapsed, and so reduced the number of her neighbour states to three.

Nor was Switzerland infringing her policy of neutrality when she accepted the international agreement prohibiting war as an instrument of international policy known as the Kellogg Pact. The principles of that declaration of peace were identical with those represented by Switzerland. It also goes without saying that Switzerland could co-operate without reserve and without a breach of her neutrality in the philanthropic and non-political work of the League, for instance, the Commissions on Health, Intellectual Co-operation, the Drug Traffic, the White Slave Trade, the I.L.O., and all kinds of economic matters, as well as in the International Court of Justice at the Hague. Switzerland also supplied the League with many notable experts, who worked entirely in a private capacity, for the solution of difficult questions.

Later, when the feeling against the uncongenial totalitarian constitutions of Switzerland's neighbours to north and south became manifest all over the country, and animosity against the aggressive spirit of those countries broke out, the statesmen of Switzerland did all they could to prevent the steady course of the Swiss policy of neutrality from being altered. Motta drew a clear line of demarcation between the ideals of home and foreign policy by declaring that it was impossible to base international relations on a community of constitutions and a similarity of political ideas. Switzerland was indeed less troubled by the ideology of totalitarianism than by the German theories of race. Although she was not directly affected when Hitler's Germany left the Disarmament Conference and the League in 1933, there were obvious possible dangers. These she sought to minimize by strengthening her defences. Official relations with Germany continued to be friendly, but in the following year they were disturbed by a press dispute, as a result of which the government of the Reich refused to allow the leading Swiss newspapers to enter Germany. Switzerland protested passionately in the name of the freedom of the press, the country recognizing as a principle that only the state is neutral, while its citizens could not be directly bound by international obligations, so that no breaches of neutrality could be committed by private persons. The constitutional principle of the freedom of opinion was in no way weakened.

The Swiss Federal Government also did all it could to maintain friendly relations with Fascist Italy. At the end of 1924, an arbitration treaty was concluded between the two countries. Italo-Swiss relations were put to a severe test in the Abyssinian war. The question was whether Switzerland was to take part in the sanctions applied by the League in 1935. On the one hand, as a member of the League, the confederation was bound by treaty to participate in those sanctions; on the other, it was opposed, not only for reasons of state, but out of a legitimate neutral feeling deeply rooted in tradition, to any unneutral action against a friendly neighbour. Swiss foreign policy was here faced with one of its most thorny problems. The solution was that Switzerland joined the embargo on the export of arms, but, in old Swiss fashion, applied it equally to both parties to the conflict, that is, to Abyssinia as well, thus causing a veritable storm of indignation in Geneva. Switzerland also took part in the refusal of credit and the embargo on the export of war material, but refused to join the boycott of Italian goods and the interruption of trade relations.

As regards relations with Russia, Switzerland had, since the establishment of the Soviet republic, consistently refused to resume relations with it, while intimating on various occasions from the middle of the thirties on that it would be desirable for this state of things to come to an end. The same and similar reasons which moved the Federal Council to adopt so intransigent an attitude made Switzerland one of the few members of the League to vote against the admission of Russia in 1934.

The Spanish Civil War opened the eyes of many people in Switzerland to the implications of neutrality, for it showed that the principle which prevented the neutral confederation from adopting an official attitude to conflicts in other countries was not yet understood by large sections of the population. A large number of Swiss demanded that the Federal Council should maintain

relations with the Spanish republic as the only legitimate government of the country. Such demands were an echo of a good deal of
the nineteenth-century ideology of the solidarity of the nations.
But those who directed Swiss foreign policy at the time were not
diverted from their strictly neutral course by any such currents
in home politics.

Return from differential to integral neutrality. In the thirties
the signs of disintegration in the League were growing more and
more manifest. Its impotence in the Sino-Japanese War and the
failure of the Disarmament conference were portents of the coming catastrophe. The more that process of disintegration advanced,
the less could the small state of Switzerland hope for protection
from the international organization. Switzerland was therefore
obliged, more and more, to keep out of international entangle-
ments and to rely above all on her own strength. This naturally led
to the abandonment of differential in favour of integral neutrality.
As soon as public opinion in Switzerland appreciated this trend in
foreign policy, a similar battle flamed up as had been waged round
the entry of Switzerland into the League. But now the strongest
supporters of the League were the Socialists and the left wing because they imagined that their social ideals could best be realized
by an international peace organization, while on the other hand,
a large number of former supporters of the League, especially in
French Switzerland, recognized the grave dangers entailed for the
confederation by the new situation.

In 1937, after the abrogation of the sanctions against Italy, the
conviction slowly gained ground in Switzerland that the collective
security of the League could no longer give adequate protection to
the small state of Switzerland. This view was confirmed by statements made by foreign statesmen. For example, the British Prime
Minister, Neville Chamberlain, said in the House of Commons in
1938: 'We must have no illusions, still less must we mislead small
nations by inducing them to believe that the League of Nations
can protect them from attack, while we know perfectly well that
they can expect no help from Geneva.' The confederation had now
regretfully to make it quite clear that its neutrality could no longer
be differential in character. In accordance with its ancient traditions, with its geographical situation, and the history of the
country, that neutrality must be absolute. The union of Austria
with Greater Germany in 1938 could not but precipitate Switzer-

land's return to her integral neutrality. On 14 May the League of Nations Council passed a motion in the following terms: 'In consideration of the peculiar situation of Switzerland due to her perpetual neutrality, the League of Nations takes cognizance of the intention of Switzerland not to participate henceforth in any way in the application of sanctions provided for by the Covenant and declares that she shall no longer be called upon to do so.' In the same document, the Council noted that the Swiss government had declared its readiness to retain its position as a member of the League unaltered in all other relationships.

Thus after eighteen years of collective security, Switzerland had withdrawn to her old position of absolute neutrality, where, relying only upon her own strength, she awaited the gathering storm.

Preparation for emergency. When her neighbours to north and south transformed themselves into gigantic military camps and clearly threatened aggression, the Swiss citizen was forced to admit the hard truth that an improvement of the national defences was one of the most vital matters of state. The Bund bought arms and munitions, lengthened the training period for recruits, asked for and obtained, with general approval, large credits for further purchases of material, and in 1938 thoroughly reorganized the army. Only two years before, the Swiss people had subscribed an army loan of 322,000,000 francs, a public demonstration of its determination to resist. Such things involved great sacrifices in view of the small size of the country, and of the economic difficulties. These votes were regarded everywhere as the expression of a complete national preparedness, in which even the Social Democrats joined.

Economic and military preparation went hand in hand. Having learned from their experience in the First World War, the people realized that a country poor in raw materials, cut off from the sea and encircled by belligerent countries would suffer greatly from its position. Government granaries and private store-rooms were filled. It is to such measures that Switzerland owed her power to endure throughout the war. It was the head of the Department of Supply who, in a tone of sturdy independence, remarked after Germany's invasion of Austria: 'All nations must know that whoever respects us and leaves us in peace is our friend; but whoever should attack our independence and our political integrity must expect war.'

In the light of the increasingly aggressive theories of German National Socialism, people began to reflect on their own national constitution, which they had taken for granted too long, and to examine its fundamental principles. Men turned back to the past to see what bound yesterday to today, and where energy and initiative were required for the future. The peculiarly Swiss form of democracy was recognized as a combination of the liberties of the old League of the Confederates with the modern conception of freedom, and a distinction was drawn between the organic popular democracy of Switzerland and other continental democracies. Federalism, which unites member states of different culture and size with equal rights, and thus provides the perfect solution of the problem of minorities, was seen to be the necessary constitutional form of the Swiss nation—the many in the one. When it became known that, in official German training regulations, Switzerland was regarded as part of the Reich, and that Switzerland had been incorporated into the Reich on official German maps, the confederation redoubled its resistance to such outrageous assumptions. In that struggle, statesmen, historians, and journalists united to mobilize the moral resistance of the people. The German Swiss became more interested in his dialect and native literature. In 1939, Romansh, which Italian philologists were claiming as an Italian dialect, was made one of the four national languages by popular ballot. The most striking manifestation of this defence of the national spirit was the great National Exhibition at Zürich in 1939. There the common man could muse over pictures of Switzerland's past, grasp the significance of the Christian, Federal, and Red Crosses, enjoy the achievements of Swiss labour and take fresh heart before the statue of the Swiss soldier. It was a testimony to the living tradition of the country.

Armed neutrality. When war broke out, the General was unanimously elected by the Federal Assembly. When Henri Guisan of Vaud was elected commander-in-chief of the Swiss forces by 204 votes out of a total of 229, it looked like a withdrawal from the German bias in military organization. Throughout the period of mobilization, General Guisan kept the affections of all parts of the country and all classes of the population. His forthright and chivalrous personality seemed to incorporate the nation's determination to resist. The Federal Assembly proclaimed the united will of the confederation 'to preserve its neutrality in all circumstances and against all powers'. On 31 August 1939 the Federal Council issued a declaration of neutrality to the powers and gave the order to mobilize, which was followed two days later by an order for general labour conscription. Switzerland was determined not to be involved in any European war.

When war broke out 400,000 men were with the colours. That number was increased, in the course of time, by the members of the auxiliary services and by the home guard to 850,000. There were never less than 100,000 men on active service, an impressive number in proportion to a total population of only four million. The world realized that Switzerland would oppose any power which attacked her with all the strength she had. At the beginning of the war, the situation was similar to that of 1914. The country was encircled by belligerents of both camps, and by countries not yet involved in the struggle. To meet this situation, strong guards were placed along the northern and western frontiers, while weaker defences were placed to the south and east. The whole situation changed completely with the fall of France—which brought a wave of 50,000 French and Polish troops into the country, who had to be interned—and the entry of Italy into the war. Switzerland was now entirely surrounded by Axis powers. The anxious question now was whether the confederation could resist the gigantic armies of tanks, the unprecedented fleets of aircraft, the paratroops and infantry. The civilian population was already beginning to leave the more exposed parts of the country for the interior, though there was neither disorder nor panic. It had been a matter of common knowledge that, should one belligerent commit a breach of neutrality, the other could be regarded as an ally and the defence of the country attached to a European front. But now that way out was cut off too.

The réduit. Within a very short time, General Guisan, abandoning obsolete ideas of national defence in favour of fresh and vigorous plans, had carried out a complete revolution in the Swiss defences. He concentrated the core of the army in the interior of the country, so that, sacrificing for the time being the bulwarks of the frontiers and the midlands, he could carry on the defence of Swiss independence in and along the Alps. The so-called réduit comes from the theory of fortification, and means a fort set up inside of another so that the defence of the main fort can be prolonged long enough for the enemy to be driven away. To admit that part of the country must be temporarily sacrificed to save the whole in the struggle with an enemy of superior military strength showed a great spirit of realism. The idea of the réduit—it was never put to the final test—put fresh heart to all in the darkest days. The people looked upon its Alpine fortress in the heart of the country with pride and confidence, and had faith in its invincibility. Not until the German armies were defeated and driven back into their own country, not until the last savage struggle began, did the Swiss army leave the mountains and again man the frontiers against possible invaders.

Switzerland had more than once been in serious danger of attack from German armies concentrated on the frontier for the purpose. There is no question that the German High Command had long had in mind to insert the Swiss 'hedgehog', both militarily and economically, into the Nazi plan for world conquest. Why in the end, the German army commanders did not invade Switzerland cannot be said with certainty. Possibly the Führer considered that the number of troops required for the conquest of a small country without raw materials was not worth while; he may have been unwilling to have considerable forces fully engaged for a long period. Moreover, the Gotthard line, by which coal could be carried to his Axis partner, was so serviceable to him that he may have regarded the destruction of the tunnel—which was mined by the Swiss and would unquestionably have been blown up if the country had been invaded—as too serious a loss. After the landing of the British and American forces in France and North Africa, Germany had her hands full with her own defence, and could not take on a new enemy, however small. Thus Swiss independence was preserved throughout the war. Swiss air neutrality was violated several times, at first by German, later by American aircraft. Some bombardments caused considerable damage, the most serious case being that of Schaffhausen which cost forty lives.

The economic war. As in the First World War, Switzerland again had a hard struggle to maintain a minimum standard of living. Harnessing all her strength to the task, she endeavoured to avoid entanglement in the blockade and counter-blockade of the belligerents and keep free of their economic supervision. Threatened with the stranglehold of the Axis powers, she was obliged to deliver to them food, manufactured goods, and war material. Yet she never abandoned the neutral principle of impartiality, of the formally equal treatment of the belligerents, and in spite of the increasing shortage of means of transport, was able to export goods of military importance to the Allies through German-occupied territory. It was only by rendering these services to both sides that she was able to obtain the raw materials necessary to keep her industry going at all. Exchange traffic with other countries was regulated by trade negotiations of increasing difficulty, though no political concessions or forced export of human labour was required from her. That the attitude of Switzerland, approved by both sides and in full accordance with the provisions of international law, benefited not only herself but Europe as a whole was to be realized at the end of the war. When peace was concluded, Switzerland was able to apply her economic potential intact and without delay to European reconstruction. In order to preserve the life of the nation, fresh sources of food had to be discovered inside the country. Agricultural production had to be completely transformed. Production for export had to be switched over to corn-growing and dairy farming for home requirements. Under the supervision of the Department of Agriculture, pastures were ploughed up, woods were cleared, meadows drained and their productivity increased. The Swiss, it was said, must kneel in the furrow if they did not want to kneel before foreign masters. Men not absolutely required for the army were diverted to the land. By means of concentrating exclusively upon home consumption, agriculture succeeded in feeding the industrial population. As in the belligerent countries, food was strictly rationed, and soon economic life, in all its details, was under government control, federal and cantonal. An overwhelming majority of the people approved of that control. The government organization of the economic life of the country, which yet left private initiative some free play, not only preserved Switzerland from serious distress, but also averted unemployment and thus helped to prevent social upheavals such as the general strike of 1918. The Wages Compensation Fund, which was inaugurated in good time for the soldiers on active service and their families, also contributed to the preservation of social peace. While certain sections of the industrial population suffered most from the rise in prices, there was no sharp contrast between town and country such as had more than once threatened the peace of the confederation, and no estrangement between these basic elements of the Swiss population.

Opposition to National Socialism. While in the First World War there had been a deep rift between the German- and French-speaking parts of the country, they were now one in their determined resistance to foreign propaganda, whatever its source. With their faith in the individual destiny of every part of the people within the people as a whole, with their profound insight into the significance of the federal organization of law, the Swiss clung to their federalism. The variety of their ways of living was for the Swiss the guarantee of the supreme values of personality. The confederation had no mind to standardize its multifarious forces; its aim was to unite them creatively in their awareness of the confederation as a whole. The intellectual and cultural bonds between Alemannic Switzerland and Germany now began to break; the Ticino, passionately democratic, cooled in its friendship for Italy, and after the establishment of the Vichy régime, French Switzerland began to withdraw from France. This must not be taken to mean that cultural self-sufficiency was set up as a permanent ideal, for in their heart of hearts, the people knew that the smallness of the country required a compensation in the breadth of its supranational culture, and that it is un-Swiss to be merely Swiss. Feeling an inward repulsion to their immediate neighbours, people began to forge fresh links with the English-speaking world, whose constitutions were felt to be akin to that of Switzerland.

National Socialism was relentless in its efforts to impress its ideas on Switzerland, so as to make the country ripe for union. Secret associations clandestinely distributed prohibited propaganda, disguised officials of the German consulates kept records of the political opinions of Swiss citizens, spies possessed themselves of military and economic secrets. But, faced with the sturdy Swiss power of resistance, the Nazis recruited very few followers. Only a few Swiss descended to serving the enemy and preparing acts of sabotage for the event of war. Seventeen traitors were shot after trial by court martial and the death penalty was pronounced on fourteen absentees. But Switzerland never knew the dangerous fifth column which existed in all the countries overrun by Hitler, and assisted him in his invasions. All parties proclaimed their horror of the foreign doctrines and their faith in the ideals of the one motherland. Its liberties seemed the strongest safeguard against all despotism, whatever its form or origin. Political peace found its expression in the entry of the Social Democratic party into the Swiss executive and the bourgeoisie began to take social reform more seriously.

To prevent any doubt arising as to the feelings of the government and the army commanders, however, the following statement was published in 1940: 'Should any news be spread by radio, leaflets or any other means, casting doubt on the will to resist of the Federal Council and the army command, such news is to be regarded as the fabrication of enemy propaganda. Our country will defend itself to the utmost, and with every means of defence in its power, against attack.' In spite of this official strengthening of the spiritual forces of resistance in the people, not a few Swiss, a short time later, succumbed to the shock of Hitler's invasion of western Europe. The world situation, in the summer of 1940, seemed desperate. France laid down her arms. Holland, Belgium, Luxemburg, and Denmark were overrun. Italy entered the war at the side of her Axis partner, and Russia was allied with Germany. Great Britain alone carried on the struggle, but withdrew to her island, remote and inaccessible to Switzerland. Influential voices could already be heard, proclaiming in public the doctrine of defeat, advising economic and political adjustment and pressing for the dismissal of anti-German newspaper editors. Evil rumours flooded the country from time to time, embittering the war of nerves and disheartening the people. The sound and firm popular feeling of Switzerland found a support in the unwavering attitude of its General. At the end of July, he convened a meeting of the superior officers on the Rütli, 'so that we may hear the mysterious call from the past which comes from that place'. His order of the day hammered an inflexible determination to resist into the minds of his hearers. In an appeal to the people, he said: 'We can only respect those who are determined to resist and know how to do it. . . . If it is true that all signs of weakness on our part are being used against us, it is equally true that all signs of strength proclaim our unflinching determination to stand firm.' The General's words seemed like an answer to the demands of the conquerors. Defeatism, as a general feeling, practically disappeared. It was realized in Switzerland that a policy of fear was the worst of policies, and that she could only count on her integrity if she appeared before the world fully conscious of her value, with uprightness and courage. In 1942, the Federal Council, in a special resolution, explicitly imposed penalties on any propaganda 'aiming at the abandonment of the neutrality of the country'.

It was very much against the grain, and only under the impression made by the huge armies of Germany, that the Swiss submitted to a number of restrictions of their liberties. While it is a matter of course that a democracy, in time of crisis, should surrender some of its liberties to a small group capable of speedy action, it is nevertheless dangerous to surrender certain of those liberties for any length of time. How two-edged such a weapon of defence can be was shown by the censorship of the press. Its aim was to prevent the provocation of the German power-politicians by heedless expressions of opinion. That, however, involved a weakening of the vigilant spirit of resistance in Switzerland by a suppression of the news of the German advance. And indeed, both the fact of those restrictions and the measures taken by the censorship were again and again the subject of heated discussion. In spite of the censorship, the press, in all shades of political opinion, provided the public with the essential news. For it was generally realized that in a democracy like Switzerland, foreign politics could not be withheld from public discussion, and the right was claimed that even a neutral country should have an opinion of its own on what was going on in the world. The Swiss were equally determined to give public expression to their repudiation of any disparagement of the Swiss principle of foreign policy, of falsifications of Swiss history and the casting of doubt on the Swiss right to live.

The prohibition of the Communist party, issued before the outbreak of war, and the subsequent prohibition of the Nazi front, were almost unanimously approved. Political parties which counted on any kind of foreign help in order to obtain power were dissolved. Even the democratic and neutral state was obliged to resort to force in the protection of its liberties.

Active neutrality. About the granting of asylum, on the other hand, people were not all of one mind. The influx of refugees, already considerable in 1933, now swelled to unforeseen proportions. What the Swiss people would have preferred was to throw the frontiers wide open and admit all the thousands who wished to save their mere lives, if nothing else, from the atrocities of their pursuers. But the government was already warning the country of the dangers of overcrowding, and reminding it of the bounds set by necessity to the admission of refugees. Nevertheless, in spite of the threats of the German rulers, Switzerland housed over 100,000 refugees in the darkest days of the war.

In a general way, the confederation regarded it as its privilege and duty as a neutral country to alleviate the sufferings of war so far as lay in its power and was consistent with the general provisions of international law. In addition to a large number of unofficial charities, such as the Red Cross and the Children's Aid, mention must be made of the work done by the government in the service of the belligerents, that is, the safeguarding of numerous foreign interests in enemy territory. In this field, Switzerland was entrusted with very onerous duties. Her work of charity was crowned by the inauguration of the National Fund for War Sufferers. In a message to the Federal Assembly the Federal Council said:

> After the long years in which we had little time to think of anything but the threat of war and the efforts it demanded, not only the Federal Council, but the whole people of Switzerland, feel a deep desire to resume their contacts with the countries visited by war, and to do so by means of a work which bears witness to true brotherly feeling.

In response to this message, the Swiss authorities unanimously voted, in 1944, a first contribution to the National Fund of 100 million francs, which was raised to 250 million by 1948. True to the old principle of impartiality, help was given to the sufferers in all countries which had taken part in the war: France, Italy, Great Britain, Austria, Germany, Belgium, Holland, Luxemburg, Norway, Finland, Poland, Czechoslovakia, Hungary, Yugoslavia, Albania, Greece, Roumania. Food, clothing, shoes, medicines, tools, building materials, agricultural implements and seeds were distributed, huts put up for emergency dwellings and workshops of all kinds, veterinary, surgical, orthopaedical, and technical missions were organized, and tens of thousands of children threatened with tuberculosis were housed, while tuberculous adults were placed in Swiss sanatoria.

When at last the noise of arms died down in the world in 1945, it was as if the country heaved a sigh of relief. Switzerland could say that she had fulfilled to the full the pledge of neutrality given in 1939. The end of the war came like the awakening from a nightmare which had stifled her for years. From her enforced isolation, she was gradually able to resume that intercourse with the free countries which is natural to her. The resumption of relations with

Russia, which had been broken off in 1921, was consistent with the neutral principle of impartiality in relations with all countries, and also took account of the change in the balance of power in Europe. Switzerland was prepared to co-operate sincerely in the new community of nations which was to arise from a stricken world, for it was hoped that the new world would not consist of a few great powers parcelling out the earth among themselves, with the small states forfeiting their self-determination and separate existence. The realization of the high function of neutrality as the ultimate foundation on which the confederation rests, however, made the people one with the government in their refusal to surrender the maxim of foreign policy which had stood the test for centuries, and resolve to enter the new security organization of the United Nations only on condition that permanent neutrality was preserved. The mere fact that the principle of neutrality in foreign affairs had rescued the confederation and its independence amid all the various European complications and conflagrations, had imprinted the traditional maxim of foreign policy deep in the national consciousness.

As a general rule, it is insufficiently realized that Switzerland cannot lay aside or alter her inherited principle of foreign policy without profoundly affecting the structure of the federal state. Neutrality is a slow product of all that went to make it, is a factor in all the institutions which are usually summarized under the one notion of Swiss liberties. Switzerland's neutrality is not only the local consequence of her geographical situation and small size. There are also close links between neutrality and federation. The multiplicity of races and languages is also closely connected with Swiss neutrality, as are the aims and practice of the right of asylum. From time immemorial, she has been in the fortunate position of being able to subordinate her foreign to her home policy, while the great powers have had to adapt their home to the requirements of their foreign policy. A surrender of absolute neutrality would also jeopardize this position.

Swiss neutrality is not for the occasion, but for ever. It affords other states an element of certainty in a shifting international scene, as the experience of centuries shows. Precisely because Switzerland has declared her neutrality perpetual, and because therefore her attitude to other countries does not alter amid the flux of international relations, she cannot be accused of trimming her sails to the wind for her own profit. Switzerland carries the heavy burden of armed neutrality without trying to gain power from a favourable political juncture—unlike neutrals for the nonce, or mere 'non-belligerents'. Because Swiss neutrality springs neither from opportunism nor indifference, it is fitted to make a serious contribution to the preservation of peace in Europe. It is based upon unconditional observance of treaties and excludes war as an instrument of policy. It is thanks to this that Switzerland has become the seat of international organizations that serve the social and economic welfare of the world and diminish the evils of war.

Because Swiss perpetual neutrality is rooted in these principles, it is perfectly compatible with the machinery of international law and peace. In a world based on law and justice she can perform important functions and take her share in the working of inter-state organizations. The work of the International Red Cross, for example, is specially well performed against a backcloth of neu-trality—and in fact grew out of the perpetual neutrality of Switzerland. The efforts of the confederation to preserve peace will be the more effective the farther she can keep herself from being involved in war. Not in spite of her neutrality, but *because* of it, Switzerland can render invaluable services to an organiza-tion for international peace. In face of an international order established by treaty, of a European system of states, the principle of Swiss foreign policy will always be: Neutrality and Solidarity.

BIBLIOGRAPHY

THE fact that there is a very large historical literature about the Swiss, written for the most part in German (often translated into French), is in itself a factor in Swiss history. Only a small selection of this considerable material can be given in this *Short History*. A complete bibliography of recent material is contained in the *Repertorium* edited by J. L. Brandstetter (Basle, 1892), continued by H. Barth (Basle, 1906), and as *Bibliographie der Schweizergeschichte* (Basle, 1914–15). This is kept up to date by periodical contributions published annually or at intervals in the *Schweizerische Zeitschrift für Geschichte* (Zürich), the leading historical journal.

General works.

J. DIERAUER, *Geschichte der Schweizerischen Eidgenossenschaft*, 5 vols., Gotha, 1920–4, vol. 6 by Hans Schneider, Zürich, 1931.

K. DÄNDLIKER, *Geschichte der Schweiz*, 3 vols., Zürich, 1934–7.

H. NABHOLZ, L. V. MURALT, R. FELLER, and E. BONJOUR, *Geschichte der Schweiz*, 2 vols., Zürich, 1932–8 (useful bibliographies).

GOTTFRIED GUGGENBÜHL, *Geschichte der Schweizerischen Eidgenossenschaft*, 2 vols., Zürich, 1947.

Geographisches Lexikon der Schweiz, 6 vols., Neuchâtel, 1902–10.

Historisch-Biographisches Lexikon der Schweiz, 7 vols., supplement, Neuchâtel, 1921–34 and the series *Schweizer Kriegsgeschichte*, 12 parts, Berne, 1915–35 (all translated into French) are valuable.

H. AMMANN and K. SCHIB, *Historischer Atlas der Schweiz*, Aarau, 1951.

Chapters I–V :

J. J. FRÜH, *Geographie der Schweiz*, 3 vols., Aarau, 1930–8.

F. STÄHELIN, *Die Schweiz in römischer Zeit*, Basle, 1948.

E. MEYER, *Die Schweiz im Altertum*, Berne, 1946.

A. GASSER, *Entstehung und Ausbildung der Landeshoheit im Gebiet der Schweizerischen Eidgenossenschaft*, Aarau, 1930 (a little controversial).

E. HEYCK, *Geschichte der Herzöge von Zähringen*, Freiburg i. B., 1891.

O. REDLICH, *Rudolf von Habsburg*, Innsbruck, 1903 (indispensable for growth of Habsburg power).

The conclusions of W. OECHSLI, *Die Anfänge der Schweizerischen Eidgenossenschaft*, Zürich, 1891, have been modified during the last half-century, especially by K. MEYER in (e.g.) *Die Gründung der Eidgenossenschaft im Lichte der Urkunden und der Chroniken*, Zürich, 1939 (cf. H. G. WIRZ, *Quellenwerk zur Entstehung der Schweizerischen Eidgenossenschaft*, Abteilung III, *Chroniken*, Bd. I, Aarau, 1948).

P. E. MARTIN, 'The Swiss Confederation in the Middle Ages' in *The Cambridge Medieval History*, vol. vii, Cambridge, 1932 (bibliography).

A. LARGIARDÉR, *Geschichte von Stadt und Landschaft Zürich*, 2 vols., Zürich, 1945.

BIBLIOGRAPHY

R. Feller, *Geschichte Berns*, vol. i, Berne, 1946.

R. Wackernagel, *Geschichte der Stadt Basel*, 3 vols., Basle, 1907–24.

Chapters VI–VIII:

W. Oechsli, *History of Switzerland*, Cambridge, 1922, with bibliography, remains a valuable introduction in English.

The same writer's 'Orte und Zugewandte' (*Jahrbuch für Schweizerische Geschichte*, vol. xiii), Zürich, 1888, contains indispensable constitutional matter.

E. Toutey, *Charles le téméraire et la ligue de Constance*, Paris, 1902; A. Büchi, *Kardinal Matthäus Schiner als Staatsmann und Kirchenfürst*, 2 vols., Zürich, 1923, 1937, deal with politics.

The Swiss Reformation has an enormous literature, some of which is summarized in E. Egli, *Schweizerische Reformationsgeschichte*, Zürich, 1910.

The critical edition of Zwingli's writings, *Huldreich Zwinglis sämtliche Werke*, Berlin, Leipzig, 1905 ff., by Egli, Finsler, Köhler, Farner, Blanke, and Muralt is not complete, but a useful selection was made in *Ulrich Zwingli: eine Auswahl aus seinen Schriften*, by Finsler, Köhler, and Rüegg, Zürich, 1918.

W. Köhler, *Huldrych Zwingli*, Leipzig, 1943.

G. von Schulthess-Rechberg, *Heinrich Bullinger*, Halle, 1904.

R. Feller, *Der Staat Bern in der Reformation*, Berne, 1929; vol. ii, 1954.

É. Doumergue, *Jean Calvin*, 7 vols., Paris, 1899–1927.

P. C. Planta, *Geschichte von Graubünden*, Berne, 1913.

F. Pieth, *Bündnergeschichte*, Chur, 1945.

E. Rott, *Histoire de la représentation diplomatique de la France auprès des cantons suisses*, 10 vols., Paris, 1900–35.

R. Feller, *Ritter Melchior Lussy*, 2 vols., Stans, 1906–10.

Chapters IX–XII:

E. Bonjour, *Die Gründung des Schweizerischen Bundesstaates*, Basel, 1948.

W. Oechsli, *Geschichte der Schweiz im 19. Jahrhundert*, 2 vols., Leipzig, 1903–13.

Maxime Reymond, *Histoire de la Suisse*, 4 vols., Lausanne, 1931–43.

La Suisse au dix-neuvième siècle (ed. by Paul Seippel), 3 vols., Lausanne, 1899–1901.

E. Bonjour, *Histoire de la neutralité suisse*, Neuchâtel, 1949.

E. Ermatinger, *Dichtung und Geistesleben der deutschen Schweiz*, Munich, 1933.

E. His, *Geschichte des neuern Schweizerischen Staatsrechts*, 3 vols., Basle, 1920–38.

W. E. Rappard, *L'Individu et l'état dans l'évolution constitutionnelle de la Suisse*, Zürich, 1936.

INDEX

The names of the cantons are not indexed.

INDEX

Grossmann, 150.
Grossmünster, the, Zürich, 148.
Grote, George, 266.
Gruet, Jacques, 170.
Gruyère, 192.
— (Greyerz), Counts of, 174, 371.
Gueffier, 181.
Guisan, Henri, 366.
Gümmenen, 62, 66.
Guntramm, 56.
Gustavus Adolphus, king of Sweden, 183.

Habsburg, castle, 66.
— dukes, *et passim*, 2.
Hadlaub, Johannes, 53.
Hagenbach, Peter von, 125, 126.
— Stephen, 127.
Hague Conference, second, 313.
— International Court at the, 362.
Haller, Albrecht von, 207, 340.
— Berchtold, 156.
— Carl Ludwig von, 243.
Hallwill, Türing von, 116, 122.
Haner, 152.
Hanover, 234.
Hard, 139.
Hartmann von Aue, 52.
— IV (Kiburg), 65.
— V (Kiburg), 65, 66.
Haslital, the, 34, 40, 65, 66, 95.
Hassfurter, 133.
Hauenstein, the, 10, 11, 63, 74.
Hedio, 159.
Heer, Oswald, 341.
Hegner, Ulrich, 239.
Heidelberg, 154.
Helvetic republic, the, 222 f.
— society, the, 206.
Helvetii, the, 23, 24, 25, 27, 28, 29, 30, 31, 36, 37.
Helvetisches Volksblatt, 230.
Henne, Josef Anton, 256.
Henry III of France, 172.
— IV of France (Navarre), 177, 179, 180, 181.
— bishop of Basle, 68.
— of Luxembourg, king of the Romans, 83, 84, 87.
— III of England, 65.
— IV, emperor, 48.
— V, emperor, 48.
— VI, emperor, 48.

Henzi, Samuel, 202.
Herder, 207, 237.
Hérens, Val d', 16.
Héricourt, 128.
Hertenstein, 133.
Herzog, general, 285.
Herzogenbuchsee, 194.
Hesse, Philip of, 158.
Heudorf, Bilgeri von, 122.
Heusler, Andreas, 338.
Hilty, Carl, 338.
Hirzel, Hans Kaspar, 187.
— Salomon, 206.
Historical Association of Switzerland, 336.
Hitler, Adolf, 362, 368, 370, 371.
Hodler, Ferdinand, 334, 341.
Hoffmann, councillor, 346.
Hohle Gasse, the, 79.
Hottinger, Johann Jakob, 335.
— Klaus, 151.
Huber, Eugen, 338.
Huguenots, the, 19.
Hugues, Besançon, 164.
Humboldt, 341.
Hüningen, 197.
Hussgen, John, of Weinsberg, 154.
Hutten, Ulrich von, 151.

Igis, 153.
Index of forbidden books, 173.
Initiative, 300 f.
Interlaken, monastery of, 95.
International, the second, 321.
Interregnum, the Great, 48.
Irgenhausen, 36.
Iselin, Isaac, 210.
Ittingen monastery, 152.

James V, king of Scotland, 120.
Jenatsch, Georg, 182, 183.
Jenner family, 200.
Jerome, St., 158.
Jesuits, the, 260 f., 306.
Jews in Switzerland, 302.
Joanna of Aragon, 141.
John XXIII, pope, 112.
Jonas, Justus, 159.
Jougne, Col de, 10, 129.
Jud, Leo, 150.
Julian, emperor, 37.
Julius II, pope, 144.

Kaiser, Jacob, 158.
Kaiseraugst, 36.

382

INDEX

Simmental, 16.
Simplon pass, 2, 11, 12, 234.
Sino-Japanese war, 364.
Sion, 8, 50, 109, 112, 113, 148, 173, 234.
— bishop of, 165.
Sismondi, 239.
Social Democratic Party, 351, 359.
Society, the Helvetic, 206.
Sonderbund, the, 261 ff.
Sotto Cenere, 192.
Spain, Civil War in, 363.
Speicher, 110.
Speyer, diet of, 159.
Spitteler, Carl, 330, 345.
Splügen pass, 2, 11.
Sprecher von Bernegg, Theophil, 343.
Stäel, Madame de, 204, 239.
Stäfa, 215.
Stalin, 359.
Stammheim, 151.
Stämpfli, Councillor Jakob, 278. 279, 282, 288, 293, 294, 295.
Stans, 134, 176, 225.
— agreement of, 134, 193.
Stanyan, Abraham, 204.
Stapfer, Philip Albert, 227.
Stauffacher, the, 104.
Stauffer, Karl, 334.
Steiger family, 200.
— Nicolaus Friedrich von, 216, 217, 220.
Stein am Rhein, 36, 37, 119.
Stilicho, 37.   [161, 168, 174, 197.
Strassburg, 37, 43, 126, 156 159, 160,
Stüdenberg, 32.
Sturm, 159.
Stüssi, Rudolf, 114, 115.
Stutz, Jakob, 256.
Styria, 70, 98.
Sundli, 154.
Supreme Allied Council, 356.
Sursee, 63.
Suvaroff, 12, 14, 225.
Swabia, duchy of, 49, 60, 97, 99.
— league of, 139.

Tacitus, 30.
Tell, William, 21, 79, 80, 204.
Ten Jurisdictions, league of, 153.
Ternier, 166.
Testament, New, 148.
Tetrapolitana, 160.
Teutoburger Wald, 27.
Teutoni, the, 24.

Textile industries, 188 ff., 318.
Thann, 122.
Theatines, the, 173.
Theiling, Frischhaus, 136.
Theodoric the Ostrogoth, 38, 42.
Thiers, 310.
Thonon, 166, 282.
Thorberg, armistice of, 93.
Thun, 32, 62, 65, 98.
Tiberius, emperor, 26.
Ticino, Val, 13.
Tigurini, the, 24, 25.
Tirano, 182.
Toepffer, Rodolphe, 331.
Toggenburg, 115, 118, 158, 192, 196.
Trent, Council of, 173.
Tribolet, Samuel, 193.
Triesen, 139.
Trücklibund, the, 199.
Tscharner family, 200.
Tschudi, Aegidius, 79, 175, 176, 237, 336, 340.
— Friedrich von, 341.
Tuileries, massacre of, 1792, 214.
Tutilo, monk of St. Gallen, 52.
Tyrol, 78, 97, 98, 138.

Ulrich of Wurtemberg, 160.
Union, the Lower, 126, 130.
Unspunnen, 238.
Urseren, 23, 35.
— valley of, 9.
Uster, 252.
Usteri, Johann Martin, 239.
Uznach, 113, 114, 158, 192, 200.

Vadian, 153.
Vaduz, 139.
Val de Conches, 9.
— de Travers, 1.
— di Bedretto, 9.
Val Formazza, 5.
— Maggia, 195.
— Mesocco, 5, 11.
— Poschiavo, 5.
Valentinian I, emperor, 37.
Valtelline, the, 13, 144, 146, 160, 180, 181, 182, 218, 221, 242.
Varus, 27.
Vaucher, Pierre, 336.
Vela Vincenzo, 333.
Veneti, the, 17, 23.
Venice, 145, 153, 180.
Verdun, treaty of, 45.